# On the Law of War and Peace

*De jure belli ac pacis*

HUGO GROTIUS

*On the Law of War and Peace, H. Grotius*
*Jazzybee Verlag Jürgen Beck*
*86450 Altenmünster, Loschberg 9*
*Deutschland*

*ISBN: 9783988686497*

*Translated by Rev. Archibald Colin Campbell (1774 – 1842)*

*www.jazzybee-verlag.de*
*admin@jazzybee-verlag.de*

*Printed by Libri Plureos GmbH, Friedensallee 273, 22763 Hamburg*

# CONTENTS:

# HUGO GROTIUS: FATHER OF INTERNATIONAL LAW (1583–1645)

Hugo Grotius, born Huig van Groot in Delft, Netherlands, on April 10, 1583, stands as one of history's most remarkable intellectual prodigies and the founding father of modern international law. His family, originally French nobles named de Cornets, had settled in the Low Countries over a century earlier, adopting the Dutch name "Groot" through marriage.

## A Child Prodigy

Grotius displayed extraordinary intellectual gifts from an early age. By nine, he was composing sophisticated Latin poetry. At twelve, he was ready for university studies, and by fifteen, he had edited the complex encyclopedic work of the ancient scholar Martianus Capella. His talents caught the attention of the renowned classical scholar J.J. Scaliger at Leiden University, who made it his practice to mentor promising young scholars in editing classical texts.

At just fifteen, Grotius joined a diplomatic mission to France, accompanying Count Justin of Nassau and Grand Pensionary Johan van Oldenbarnevelt. This early exposure to international affairs would prove formative. After a year in France mastering the language and networking with leading intellectuals, he returned to complete his law doctorate and begin practicing as an advocate.

## Literary and Academic Achievements

Despite his legal success, Grotius remained drawn to literature and scholarship. In 1600, he edited the astronomical poetry of Aratus alongside translations by Cicero, Germanicus, and Avienus. Scaliger praised his work on Germanicus as unsurpassable, though he may have contributed to the revision himself.

Grotius also wrote Latin poetry and three Latin dramas: *Christus patiens*, *Sophomphaneas* (based on the story of Joseph), and *Adamus exul* (Adam in Exile), which reportedly influenced Milton's *Paradise Lost*. These works were translated into Dutch and English, spreading his literary reputation across Europe.

## The Path to Legal Philosophy

In 1603, at just twenty years old, Grotius was appointed official historiographer of the United Provinces to document their struggle for independence from Spain. Around the same time, there were rumors of him being offered the position of royal librarian in Paris, though this appears to have been a political maneuver by Jesuits trying to deflect criticism of their opposition to appointing the Protestant scholar Isaac Casaubon.

Grotius's advancement continued with his appointment as advocate-general for Holland and Zeeland, followed by his marriage in 1608 to Marie Reigersberg, a woman of noble family and remarkable character who would later play a crucial role in his dramatic escape from prison.

## The Genesis of International Law

The foundations of Grotius's revolutionary legal thinking began in 1604 when he wrote *De jure praedae* (On the Law of Prize), though this work remained unpublished until 1868. The immediate catalyst was his work as advocate for the Dutch East India Company, defending Captain Heemskirk's capture of a Portuguese galleon in the Straits of Malacca.

This case forced Grotius to grapple with fundamental questions: What gives a private company the right to seize enemy vessels? More broadly, what makes war lawful? His investigation of these practical questions led him to develop the theoretical framework that would later culminate in his masterwork, *De jure belli et pacis* (On the Law of War and Peace).

From this larger work, he extracted and published (reportedly without his permission) a chapter as *Mare Liberum* (The Free Sea) in 1609, arguing that the oceans belong to all nations—a principle that directly challenged Portuguese claims to exclusive control over Eastern waters. This doctrine later became central to maritime law disputes between England and Holland.

### Political Crisis and Imprisonment

As Grotius rose professionally, becoming pensionary of Rotterdam at just thirty, religious tensions in the Netherlands reached a breaking point. The country was divided between Remonstrants (Arminians) and Counter-Remonstrants (strict Calvinists) over predestination and other theological issues.

Grotius attempted to find middle ground, drafting an edict promoting mutual tolerance and prohibiting ministers from preaching on disputed doctrines. However, the orthodox Calvinists, backed by popular support, found the very word "toleration" offensive. Stadtholder Maurice of Nassau, seeing political opportunity and genuinely inclined toward orthodoxy, sided against the moderate party led by Oldenbarnevelt.

In 1618, Maurice launched what was essentially a military coup, disbanding civic guards and occupying cities with his own troops. Grotius, sent as part of a commission to strengthen the Remonstrant position in Utrecht, found himself outmaneuvered. After a failed attempt to resist Maurice's takeover, Grotius and his colleagues were forced to flee.

Their reprieve was brief. Oldenbarnevelt, Grotius, and other Remonstrant leaders were arrested and tried. Oldenbarnevelt was executed, while Grotius received a sentence of life imprisonment and property confiscation. In June 1619, he was confined to Loevestein Castle near Gorinchem.

### The Great Escape

Prison conditions were harsh, but eventually Grotius's wife Marie was permitted to join him, with the condition that if she left, she could never return. Facing the prospect of lifelong captivity at thirty-six, Grotius threw himself into classical studies, producing translations from Greek tragedians and other authors. As he wrote to his friend Voss, "The Muses were now his consolation."

Marie Grotius devised an ingenious escape plan. Books and laundry were regularly sent to and from the prison in a large chest. Over time, the guards grew careless about inspecting it. On the fateful day, Grotius concealed himself inside the chest. When the two soldiers carrying it complained about its unusual weight, joking that "there must be an Arminian in it," Marie calmly replied, "There are indeed Arminian books in it."

Once outside the prison, Grotius was released from the chest, disguised as a mason with proper tools, and spirited across the border. He first reached Antwerp, then made his way to Paris, arriving in April 1621. His wife joined him in October.

### Exile and Masterwork

In Paris, King Louis XIII granted Grotius a pension of 3,000 livres—a generous gesture that proved largely meaningless since French pensions were notoriously unpaid. Reduced to near-poverty, Grotius desperately sought employment, considering positions in Denmark or practicing law in German courts.

Some relief came through Chancellor Étienne d'Aligre, who helped Grotius collect part of his pension. In 1623, President Henri de Mesmes lent him his château at Balagny near Senlis, where Grotius spent a productive spring and summer. Jacques-Auguste de Thou provided access to his magnificent library.

Under these circumstances, Grotius composed his masterpiece, *De jure belli et pacis* (The Law of War and Peace). The speed with which he completed this work of immense scholarship—largely consisting of quotations from classical and historical sources—amazed his contemporaries. The achievement was possible because he had his 1604 draft as a foundation, plus extensive notes his brother William had compiled while reading classical texts for passages related to law.

The work was printed in March 1625 and distributed at the Frankfurt book fair. Grotius received 200 copies as payment, most of which he gave away to the king, courtiers, and the papal nuncio. The remaining copies, sold at one crown each, didn't even cover his expenses. However, while the book brought no immediate profit, it brought lasting fame that no other legal treatise has ever matched.

### Later Career and Death

Grotius hoped his literary success would soften his enemies and lead to his recall to Dutch service. However, religious animosity proved stronger than admiration for his scholarship. After unsuccessful attempts to return to Holland, he accepted appointment as Swedish ambassador to France.

His diplomatic career proved disappointing. Cardinal Richelieu disliked him personally, hampering negotiations on behalf of Protestant interests in Germany. Grotius never enjoyed the full confidence of the French court and wasted energy on disputes over diplomatic precedence. In 1645, he requested and received recall to Stockholm.

The Swedish court's climate and atmosphere didn't suit him, and he requested permission to leave. During his journey, his ship was driven by storms to the coast near Danzig. He managed to reach Rostock but fell seriously ill. Despite his Scottish physician's optimistic assessment, Grotius declined rapidly and died on August 29, 1645.

### Intellectual Legacy

Grotius was truly a Renaissance polymath, contributing significantly to history, theology, jurisprudence, politics, classical scholarship, and poetry. His biblical commentaries pioneered the grammatical approach to scriptural interpretation without dogmatic assumptions, following principles established by Scaliger.

Like Erasmus before him, Grotius sought reconciliation between Protestant and Catholic Christianity. His *De veritate religionis Christianae* (On the Truth of the Christian Religion, 1627) presented Christian evidences in a way that transcended sectarian differences. This work became wildly popular, serving as the standard apologetics manual in Protestant colleges and being translated into Arabic, Persian, Chinese, and other languages for missionary purposes.

His *Via et votum ad pacem ecclesiasticam* (The Way and Wish for Ecclesiastical Peace, 1642) proposed detailed schemes for Christian reconciliation. This moderate position earned him attacks from both sides—an Amsterdam minister published "Grotius the Papist" (1642), while rumors constantly circulated in Paris that he had converted to Catholicism.

## Founding Modern International Law

Grotius's greatest achievement was *De jure belli et pacis*, which, despite its title, dealt with far more than the laws of war. While he acknowledged debts to earlier writers like Alberico Gentili and Balthazar Ayala on military law, his broader contribution was revolutionary.

Grotius became the first scholar to establish principles of law and morality independent of religious authority. He argued that natural law is unchangeable—even God cannot alter it, any more than mathematical axioms. This law derives from human nature as social beings and would remain valid even if God didn't exist or didn't govern the world.

While Grotius's religious temperament prevented him from fully embracing these radical implications, even their partial application in his work established him as the founder of modern natural law theory and international legal science.

The work had limited immediate impact on military practice, but its publication marked an epoch in legal science. Critics like Thomas De Quincey dismissed it as "empty truisms and time-serving Dutch falsehoods," while defenders like Sir James Mackintosh praised it as "perhaps the most complete work the world has yet owed, at so early a stage in the progress of any science, to the genius and learning of one man."

## Conclusion

Hugo Grotius lived during one of history's most turbulent periods, witnessing religious wars, the birth of modern nation-states, and the expansion of global trade. His unique combination of practical legal experience, classical learning, and philosophical insight enabled him to create the intellectual framework that still governs international relations today.

From a precocious child writing Latin verses to a imprisoned political exile crafting the foundations of international law, Grotius's life embodied the best aspirations of humanistic scholarship: the belief that reason, learning, and good faith could create a more civilized world. His vision of law based on human nature rather than divine command, and of international relations governed by universal principles rather than mere force, remains as relevant today as it was four centuries ago.

# BOOK I

## CHAPTER 1: ON WAR AND RIGHT

*Of War — Definition of War — Right, of Governors and of the governed, and of equals — Right as a Quality divided into Faculty and Fitness — Faculty denoting Power, Property, and Credit — Divided into Private and Superior — Right as a Rule, natural and voluntary — Law of Nature divided — Proofs of the Law of Nature — Division of Rights into human and divine — Human explained — Divine stated — Mosaic Law not binding upon Christians.*

**I**. THE disputes arising among those who are held together by no common bond of civil laws to decide their dissensions, like the ancient Patriarchs, who formed no national community, or the numerous, unconnected communities, whether under the direction of individuals, or kings, or persons invested with Sovereign power, as the leading men in an aristocracy, and the body of the people in a republican government; the disputes, arising among any of these, all bear a relation to the circumstances of war or peace. But because war is undertaken for the sake of peace, and there is no dispute, which may not give rise to war, it will be proper to treat all such quarrels, as commonly happen, between nations, as an article in the rights of war: and then war itself will lead us to peace, as to its proper end.

**II**. In treating of the rights of war, the first point, that we have to consider, is, what is war, which is the subject of our inquiry, and what is the right, which we seek to establish. Cicero styled war a contention by force. But the practice has prevailed to indicate by that name, not an immediate action, but a state of affairs; so that war is the state of contending parties, considered as such. This definition, by its general extent, comprises those wars of every description, that will form the subject of the present treatise. Nor are single combats excluded from this definition. For, as they are in reality more ancient than public wars, and undoubtedly, of the same nature, they may therefore properly be comprehended under one and the same name. This agrees very well with the true derivation of the word. For the Latin word, *Bellum*, WAR, comes from the old word, *Duellum*, a DUEL, as *Bonus* from *Duonus*, and *Bis* from *Duis*. Now *Duellum* was derived from *Duo*; and thereby implied a difference between two persons, in the same sense as we term peace, UNITY, from *Unitas*, for a contrary reason. The ancient Greeks likewise called it a DISUNION of minds; just as they meant the DISSOLUTION of the parts of the body. Nor does the use of the word, WAR, contradict this larger acceptation of it. For though some times it is only applied to the quarrels of states, yet that is no objection, as it is evident that a general name is often applied to some particular object, entitled to peculiar distinction. Justice is not included in the definition of war, because the very point to be decided is, whether any war be just, and what war may be so called. Therefore we must make a distinction between war itself, and the justice of it.

**III**. As the Rights of War is the title, by which this treatise is distinguished, the first inquiry, as it has been already observed, is, whether any war be just, and, in the next place, what constitutes the justice of that war. For, in this place, right signifies nothing more than what is just, and that, more in a negative than a positive sense; so that RIGHT is that, which is not unjust. Now any thing is unjust, which is repugnant to the nature of society, established among rational creatures. Thus for instance, to deprive another of what belongs to him, merely for one's own advantage, is repugnant to the law of nature, as Cicero observes in the fifth Chapter of his third book of offices; and, by way of proof, he says that, if the practice were general, all society and intercourse among men must be overturned. Florentinus, the Lawyer, maintains that is impious for one man to form designs against another, as nature has established a degree of kindred amongst us. On this subject, Seneca remarks that, as all the members of the human body agree among themselves, because the preservation of each conduces to the welfare of the whole, so men should forbear from mutual injuries, as they were born for society, which cannot subsist unless all the parts of it are defended by mutual forbearance and good will. But as there is one kind of social tie founded upon an equality, for instance, among brothers, citizens, friends, allies, and another on pre-eminence, as Aristotle styles it, subsisting between parents and children, masters and servants, sovereigns and subjects, God and men. So justice takes place either amongst equals, or between the governing and the governed parties, notwithstanding their difference of rank. The former of these, if I am not mistaken, may be called the right of equality, and the latter the right of superiority.

**IV**. There is another signification of the word RIGHT, different from this, but yet arising from it, which relates directly to the person. In which sense, RIGHT is a moral quality annexed to the person, justly entitling him to possess some particular privilege, or to perform some particular act. This right is annexed to the person, although it sometimes follows the things, as the services of lands, which are called REAL RIGHTS, in opposition to those merely PERSONAL. Not because these rights are not annexed to persons, but the distinction is made, because they belong to the persons only who possess some particular things. This moral quality, when perfect is called a FACULTY; when imperfect, an APTITUDE. The former answers to the ACT, and the latter to the POWER, when we speak of natural things.

**V**. Civilians call a faculty that Right, which every man has to his own; but we shall hereafter, taking it in its strict and proper sense, call it a right. This right comprehends the power, that we have over ourselves, which is called liberty, and the power, that we have over others, as that of a father over his children, and of a master over his slaves. It likewise comprehends property, which is either complete or imperfect; of the latter kind is the use or possession of any thing without the property, or power of alienating it, or pledges detained by the creditors till payment be made. There is a third signification which implies the power of demanding what is due, to which the obligation upon the party indebted, to discharge what is owing, corresponds.

**VI**. Right, strictly taken, is again twofold, the one PRIVATE, established for the advantage of each individual, the other, SUPERIOR, as involving the claims, which the state has upon individuals, and their property, for the public good. Thus the Regal authority is above that of a father and a master, and the Sovereign has a greater right over the property of his subjects, where the public good is concerned, than the owners themselves have. And when the exigencies of the state require a supply, every man is more obliged to contribute towards it, than to satisfy his creditors.

**VII**. Aristotle distinguishes aptitude or capacity, by the name of worth or merit, and Michael of Ephesus, gives the epithet of SUITABLE or BECOMING to the equality established by this rule of merit.

**VII. [Translator's note:** The eighth Section is omitted, the greater part of it consisting of verbal criticism upon Aristotle's notions of geometrical and arithmetical justice; a discussion no way conducive to that clearness and simplicity, so necessary to every didactic treatise.]

**IX**. There is also a third signification of the word Right, which has the same meaning as Law, taken in its most extensive sense, to denote a rule of moral action, obliging us to do what is proper. We say OBLIGING us. For the best counsels or precepts, if they lay us under no obligation to obey them, cannot come under the denomination of law or right. Now as to permission, it is no act of the law, but only the silence of the law it however prohibits any one from impeding another in doing what the law permits. But we have said, the law obliges us to do what is proper, not simply what is just; because, under this notion, right belongs to the substance not only of justice, as we have explained it, but of all other virtues. Yet from giving the name of a RIGHT to that, which is PROPER, a more general acceptation of the word justice has been derived. The best division of right, in this general meaning, is to be found in Aristotle, who, defining one kind to be natural, and the other voluntary, calls it a LAWFUL

RIGHT in the strictest sense of the word law; and some times an instituted right. The same difference is found among the Hebrews, who, by way of distinction, in speaking, call that natural right, PRECEPTS, and the voluntary right, STATUTES.

**X**. Natural right is the dictate of right reason, shewing the moral turpitude, or moral necessity, of any act from its agreement or disagreement with a rational nature, and consequently that such an act is either forbidden or commanded by God, the author of nature. The actions, upon which such a dictate is given, are either binding or unlawful in themselves, and therefore necessarily understood to be commanded or forbidden by God. This mark distinguishes natural right, not only from human law, but from the law, which God himself has been pleased to reveal, called, by some, the voluntary divine right, which does not command or forbid things in themselves either binding or unlawful, but makes them unlawful by its prohibition, and binding by its command. But, to understand natural right, we must observe that some things are said to belong to that right, not properly, but, as the schoolmen say, by way of accommodation. These are not repugnant to natural right, as we have already observed that those things are called JUST, in which there is no injustice. Some times also, by a wrong use of the word, those things which reason shews to be proper, or better than things of an opposite kind, although not binding, are said to belong to natural right.

We must farther remark, that natural right relates not only to those things that exist independent of the human will, but to many things, which necessarily follow the exercise of that will. Thus property, as now in use, was at first a creature of the human will. But, after it was established, one man was prohibited by the law of nature from seizing the property of another against his will. Wherefore, Paulus the Lawyer said, that theft is expressly forbidden by the law of nature. Ulpian condemns it as infamous in its own nature; to whose authority that of Euripides may be added, as may be seen in the verse of Helena:

"For God himself hates violence, and will not have us to grow rich by rapine, but by lawful gains. That abundance, which is the fruit of unrighteousness, is an abomination. The air is common to men, the earth also where every man, in the ample enjoyment of his possession, must refrain from doing violence or injury to that of another."

Now the Law of Nature is so unalterable, that it cannot be changed even by God himself. For although the power of God is infinite, yet there are some things, to which it does not extend. Because the things so expressed would have no true meaning, but imply a contradiction. Thus two and two must make four, nor is it possible to be otherwise; nor, again, can what is really evil not be evil. And this is Aristotle's meaning, when he says, that some things are no sooner named, than we discover their evil nature. For as the substance of things in their nature and existence depends upon nothing but themselves; so there are qualities inseparably connected with their being and essence. Of this kind is the evil of certain actions, compared with the nature of a reasonable being. Therefore God himself suffers his actions to be judged by this rule, as may be seen in the xviiith chap. of Gen. 25. Isa. v. 3. Ezek. xviii. 25. Jer. ii. 9. Mich. vi. 2. From. ii. 6., iii. 6. Yet it sometimes happens that, in those cases, which are decided by the law of nature, the undiscerning are imposed upon by an appearance of change. Whereas in reality there is no change in the unalterable law of nature, but only in the things appointed by it, and which are liable to variation. For example, if a creditor forgive me the debt, which I owe him, I am no longer bound to pay it, not because the law of nature has ceased to command the payment of a just debt, but because my debt, by a release, has ceased to be a debt. On this topic, Arrian in Epictetus argues rightly, that the borrowing of money is not the only requisite to make a debt, but there must be the additional circumstance of the loan remaining undischarged. Thus if God should command the life, or property of any one to be taken away, the act would not authorise murder or robbery, words which always include a crime. But that cannot be murder or robbery, which is done by the express command of Him, who is the sovereign Lord of our lives and of all things. There are also some things allowed by the law of nature, not absolutely, but according to a certain state of affairs. Thus, by the law of nature, before property was introduced, every one had a right to the use of whatever he found unoccupied; and, before laws were enacted, to avenge his personal injuries by force.

**XI**. The distinction found in the books of the Roman Law, assigning one unchangeable right to brutes in common with man, which in a more limited sense they call the law of nature, and appropriating another to men, which they frequently call the Law of Nations, is scarcely of any real use. For no beings, except those that can form general maxims, are capable of possessing a right, which Hesiod has placed in a clear point of view, observing "that the supreme Being has appointed laws for men; but permitted wild beasts, fishes, and birds to devour each other for food." For they have nothing like justice, the best gift, bestowed upon men.

Cicero, in his first book of offices, says, we do not talk of the justice of horses or lions. In conformity to which, Plutarch, in the life of Cato the elder, observes, that we are formed by nature to use law and justice towards men only. In addition to the above, Lactantius may be cited, who, in his fifth book, says that in all animals devoid of reason we see a natural bias of self-love. For they hurt others to benefit themselves; because they do not know the evil of doing willful hurt. But it is not so with man, who, possessing the knowledge of good and evil, refrains, even with inconvenience to himself, from doing hurt. Polybius, relating the manner in which men first entered into society, concludes, that the injuries done to parents or benefactors inevitably provoke the indignation of mankind, giving an additional reason, that as understanding and reflection form the great difference between men and other animals, it is evident they cannot transgress the bounds of that difference like other animals, without exciting universal abhorrence of their conduct. But if ever justice is attributed to brutes, it is done improperly, from some shadow and trace of reason they may possess. But it is not material to the nature of right, whether the actions appointed by the law of nature, such as the care of our offspring, are common to us with other animals or not, or, like the worship of God, are peculiar to man.

**XII**. The existence of the Law of Nature is proved by two kinds of argument, *a priori*, and *a posteriori*, the former a more abstruse, and the latter a more popular method of proof. We are said to reason *a priori*, when we show the agreement or disagreement of any thing with a reasonable and social nature; but *a posteriori*, when without absolute proof, but only upon probability, any thing is inferred to accord with the law of nature, because it is received as such among all, or at least the more civilized nations. For a general effect can only arise from a general cause. Now scarce any other cause can be assigned for so general an opinion, but the common sense, as it is called, of mankind. There is a sentence of Hesiod that has been much praised, that opinions which have prevailed amongst many nations, must have some foundation. Heraclitus, establishing common reason as the best criterion of truth, says, those things are certain which generally appear so. Among other authorities, we may quote Aristotle, who says it is a strong proof in our favour, when all appear to agree with what we say, and Cicero maintains that the con. sent of all nations in any case is to be admitted for the law of nature. Seneca is of the same opinion, any thing, says he, appearing the same to all men is a proof of its truth. Quintilian says, we hold those things to be true, in which all men agree. We have called them the more civilized nations, and not without reason. For, as Porphyry well observes, some nations are so strange that no fair judgment of human nature can be formed from them, for it would be erroneous. Andronicus, the Rhodian says, that with men of a right and sound understanding, natural justice is unchangeable. Nor does it alter the case, though men of disordered and perverted minds think otherwise. For he who should deny that honey is sweet, because it appears not so to men of a distempered taste, would be wrong. Plutarch too agrees entirely with what has been said, as appears from a passage in his life of Pompey, affirming that man neither was, nor is, by nature, a wild unsociable creature. But it is the corruption of his nature which makes him so: yet by acquiring new habits, by changing his place, and way of living, he may be reclaimed to his original gentleness. Aristotle, taking a description of man from his peculiar qualities, makes him an animal of a gentle nature, and in another part of his works, he observes, that in considering the nature of man, we are to take our likeness from nature in its pure, and not in its corrupt state.

**XIII**. It has been already remarked, that there is another kind of right, which is the voluntary right, deriving its origin from the will, and is either human or divine.

**XIV**. We will begin with the human as more generally known. Now this is either a civil right, or a right more or less extensive than the civil right. The civil right is that which is derived from the civil power. The civil power is the sovereign power of the state. A state is a perfect body of free men, united together in order to enjoy common rights and advantages. The less extensive right, and not derived from the civil power itself, although subject to it, is various, comprehending the authority of parents over children, masters over servants, and the like. But the law of nations is a more extensive right, deriving its authority from the consent of all, or at least of many nations.

It was proper to add MANY, because scarce any right can be found common to all nations, except the law of nature, which itself too is generally called the law of nations. Nay, frequently in one part of the world, that is held for the law of nations, which is not so in another. Now this law of nations is proved in the same manner as the unwritten civil law, and that is by the continual experience and testimony of the Sages of the Law. For this law, as Dio Chrysostom well observes, is the discoveries made by experience and time. And in this we derive great advantage from the writings of eminent historians.

**XV**. The very meaning of the words divine voluntary right, shows that it springs from the divine will, by which it is distinguished from natural law, which, it has already been observed, is called divine also. This law admits of what Anaxarchus said, as Plutarch relates in the life of Alexander, though without sufficient accuracy, that God does not will a thing, because it is just, but that it is just, or binding, because God wills it. Now this law was given either to mankind in general, or to one particular people. We find three periods, at which it was given by God to the human race, the first of which was immediately after the creation of man, the second upon the restoration of mankind after the flood, and the third upon that more glorious restoration through Jesus Christ. These three laws undoubtedly bind all men, as soon as they come to a sufficient knowledge of them.

**XVI**. Of all nations there is but one, to which God particularly vouchsafed to give laws, and that was the people of Israel, whom Moses thus addresses in the fourth Chap. of Deuteronomy, ver. 7. "What nation is there so great who hath God so nigh unto them, as the Lord our God is in all things that we call upon him for? And what nation is there so great, who have statutes and judgments so righteous, as all this law, which I set before you this day!" And the Psalmist in the cxlvii. Psalm, "God shewed his word unto Jacob, his statutes and ordinances unto Israel. He hath not dealt so with any nation, and as for his judgments they have not known them." Nor can we doubt but that those Jews, with whom we may class Tryphon in his dispute with Justin, are mistaken, who suppose that even strangers, if they wish to be saved, must submit to the yoke of the Mosaic Law. For a law does not bind those, to whom it has not been given. But it speaks personally to those, who are immediately under it. Hear O Israel, and we read everywhere of the covenant made with them, by which they became the peculiar people of God. Maimonides acknowledges and proves the truth of this from the xxxiii. Chapter and fourth verse of Deuteronomy.

But among the Hebrews themselves there were always living some strangers, persons devout and fearing God, such was the Syrophoenician woman, mentioned in the Gospel of St. Matthew, xv. zz. Cornelius the Centurion. Acts. x. the devout Greeks, Acts xviii. 6. Sojourners, or strangers, also are mentioned. Levit. xxv. 47. These, as the Hebrew Rabbis themselves inform us, were obliged to observe the laws given to Adam and Noah, to abstain from idols and blood, and other things, that were prohibited; but not in the same manner to observe the laws peculiar to the people of Israel. Therefore though the Israelites were not allowed to eat the flesh of a beast, that had died a natural death; yet the strangers living among them were permitted. Deut. xiv. 21. Except in some particular laws, where it was expressly said, that strangers no less than the native inhabitants were obliged to observe them. Strangers also, who came from other countries, and were not subject to the Jewish laws, might worship God in the temple of Jerusalem, but standing in a place separate and distinct from the Israelites. I. Kings viii. 41. 2 Mac. iii. 35. John xii 20. Acts viii. 27. Nor did Elisha ever signify to Naaman the Syrian, nor Jonas to the Ninevites, nor Daniel to Nebuchadnezzar, nor the other Prophets to the Tyrians, the Moabites, the Egyptians, to whom they wrote, that it was necessary for them to adopt the Mosaic Law.

What has been said of the whole law of Moses applies to circumcision, which was a kind of introduction to the law. Yet with this difference that the Israelites alone were bound by the Mosaic Law, but the whole posterity of Abraham by the law of circumcision. From hence we are informed by Jewish and Greek Historians, that the Idumaeans, or Edomites were compelled by the Jews to be circumcised. Wherefore there is reason to believe that the numerous nations, who, besides the Israelites, practiced circumcision, and who are mentioned by Herodotus, Strabo, Philo, Justin, Origen, Clemens, Alexandrinus, Epiphanius, and Jerom, were descended from Ishmael, Esau, or the posterity of Keturah. But what St. Paul says, From. ii. 14: holds good of all other nations; that the Gentiles, not having the law, yet doing by nature the things contained in the law, become a law to themselves. Here the word nature may be taken for the primitive source of moral obligation; or, referring it to the preceding parts of the Epistle, it may signify the knowledge, which the Gentiles acquired of themselves without instruction, in opposition to the knowledge derived to the Jews from the law, which was instilled into them from their cradle, and almost from their birth. "So the Gentiles show the work, or the moral precepts of the law, written in their hearts, their consciences also bearing witness, and their thoughts the mean while accusing or else excusing one another." And again in the 26th ver.; "If the uncircumcision keep the righteousness of the law, shall not his uncircumcision be counted for circumcision?" Therefore Ananias, the Jew, as we find in the history of Josephus, very properly taught Tzates, or as Tacitus calls him, Ezates, the Adiabenian, that even without circumcision, God might be rightly worshipped and rendered propitious. For though many strangers were circumcised, among the Jews, and by circumcision bound themselves to observe the law, as St. Paul explains it in Gal. v. 3.; they did it partly to obtain the freedom of the country; for proselytes called by the Hebrews, proselytes of righteousness, enjoyed equal privileges with the Israelites. Num. xv. : and partly to obtain a share in those promises, which were not common to mankind, but peculiar to the Jewish people, although it cannot be denied, that in later ages an erroneous opinion prevailed, that there was no salvation out of the Jewish pale. Hence we may infer, that we are bound by no part of the Levitical law, strictly and properly so called; because any obligation, beyond that arising from the law of nature, must proceed from the express will of the law-giver. Now it cannot be discovered by any proof, that God intended any other people, but the Israelites to be bound by that law. Therefore with respect to ourselves, we have no occasion to prove an abrogation of that law; for it could never be abrogated with respect to those, whom it never bound. But the Israelites were released from the ceremonial part, as soon as the law of the Gospel was proclaimed; a clear revelation of which was made to one of the Apostles, Acts x. 15. And the other parts of the Mosaic law lost their peculiar distinction, when the Jews ceased to be a people by the desolation and destruction of their city without any hopes of restoration. Indeed it was not a release from the law of Moses that we, who were strangers to the Commonwealth of Israel, obtained by the coming of Christ. But as before that time, our hopes in the goodness of God were obscure and uncertain, we gained the assurance of an express covenant, that we should be united in one Church with the seed of Israel, the children of the patriarchs, their law, that was the wall of separation between us, being broken down. Eph. ii. 14.

**XVII**. Since then the law given by Moses imposes no direct obligation upon us, as it has been already shown, let us consider whether it has any other use both in this inquiry into the rights of war, and in other questions of the same kind. In the first place, the Mosaic law shows that what it enjoins is not contrary to the law of nature. For since the law of nature is perpetual and unchangeable, nothing contradictory to it could be commanded by God, who is never unjust. Besides the law of Moses is called in the xix. Psalm an undefiled and right law, and St. Paul, From. vii. 12, describes it to be holy, just, and good. Its precepts are here spoken of, for its permissions require a more distinct discussion. For the bare permission, signifying the removal of an impediment, or prohibition, has no relation to the present subject. A positive, legal permission is either full, granting us power to do some particular act without the least restriction, or less full, only allowing men impunity for certain actions, and a right to do them without molestation from others. From the permission of the former kind no less than from a positive precept, it follows that what the law allows, is not contrary to the law of nature. But with regard to the latter kind of permission, allowing impunity for certain acts, but not expressly authorizing them, we cannot so readily conclude those acts to be conformable to the law of nature. Because where the words of permission are ambiguous in their meaning, it is better for us to interpret according to the established law of nature, what kind of permission it is, than from our conception of its expediency to conclude it conformable to the laws of nature. Connected with this first observation there is another, expressive of the power that obtains among Christian Princes to enact laws of the same import with those given by Moses, except such as related entirely to the time of the expected Messiah, and the Gospel then unrevealed, or where Christ himself has in a general or particular manner established any thing to the contrary. For except in these three cases, no reason can be devised, why any thing established by the law of Moses should be now unlawful. In the third place it may be observed, that whatever the law of Moses enjoined relating to those virtues, which Christ required of his disciples, should be fulfilled by Christians now, in a greater degree, from their superior knowledge, and higher motives. Thus the virtues of humility, patience, and charity are required of Christians in a more perfect manner than of the Jews under the Mosaic dispensation, because the promises of heaven are more clearly laid before us in the Gospel. Hence the old law, when compared with the Gospel, is said to have been neither perfect nor faultless, and Christ is said to be the end of the law, and the law our schoolmaster to bring us to Christ. Thus the old law respecting the Sabbath, and the law respecting tithes, show that Christians are bound to devote not less than a seventh portion of their time to divine worship, nor less than a tenth of their fruits to maintain those who are employed in holy things, or to other pious uses.

## CHAPTER 2: INQUIRY INTO THE LAWFULNESS OF WAR

*Reasons proving the lawfulness of War — Proofs from History — Proofs from general consent — The Law of Nature proved not repugnant to War — War not condemned by the voluntary Divine Law preceding the Gospel — Objections answered — Review of the question whether War be contrary to the Law of the Gospel — Arguments from Scripture for the negative Opinions — Answer to the Arguments taken from Scripture for the affirmative — The opinions of the primitive Christians on the subject examined.*

**I**. AFTER examining the sources of right, the first and most general question that occurs, is whether any war is just, or if it is ever lawful to make war. But this question like many others that follow, must in the first place be compared with the rights of nature. Cicero in the third book of his Bounds of Good and Evil, and in other parts of his works, proves with great erudition from the writings of the Stoics, that there are certain first principles of nature, called by the Greeks the first natural impressions, which are succeeded by other principles of obligation superior even to the first impressions themselves. He calls the care, which every animal, from the moment of its birth, feels for itself and the preservation of its condition, its abhorrence of destruction, and of every thing that threatens death, a principle of nature. Hence, he says, it happens, that if left to his own choice, every man would prefer a sound and perfect to a mutilated and deformed body. So that preserving ourselves in a natural state, and holding to every thing conformable, and averting every thing repugnant to nature is the first duty.

But from the knowledge of these principles, a notion arises of their being agreeable to reason, that part of a man, which is superior to the body. Now that agreement with reason, which is the basis of propriety, should have more weight than the impulse of appetite; because the principles of nature recommend right reason as a rule that ought to be of higher value than bare instinct. As the truth of this is easily assented to by all men of sound judgment without any other demonstration, it follows that in inquiring into the laws of nature the first object of consideration is, what is agreeable to those principles of nature, and then we come to the rules, which, though arising only out of the former, are of higher dignity, and not only to be embraced, when offered, but pursued by all the means in our power.

This last principle, which is called propriety, from its fitness, according to the various things on which it turns, sometimes is limited to a very narrow point, the least departure from which is a deviation into vice; sometimes it allows a wider scope, so that some actions, even laudable in themselves, may be omitted or varied without crime. In this case there is not an immediate distinction between right and wrong; the shades are gradual, and their termination unperceived; not like a direct contrast, where the opposition is immediately seen, and the first step is a transgression of the fixed bounds.

The general object of divine and human laws is to give the authority of obligation to what was only laudable in itself. It has been said above that an investigation of the laws of nature implies an inquiry, whether any particular action may be done without injustice: now by an act of injustice is understood that, which necessarily has in it any thing repugnant to the nature of a reasonable and social being. So far from any thing in the principles of nature being repugnant to war, every part of them indeed rather favours it. For the preservation of our lives and persons, which is the end of war, and the possession or acquirement of things necessary and useful to life is most suitable to those principles of nature, and to use force, if necessary, for those occasions, is no way dissonant to the principles of nature, since all animals are endowed with natural strength, sufficient to assist and defend themselves.

Xenophon says, that every animal knows a certain method of fighting without any other instructor than nature. In a fragment of Ovid's, called the Art of Fishery, it is remarked, that all animals know their enemy and his means of defence, and the strength and measure of their own weapons. Horace has said, "the wolf attacks with its teeth, the bull with its horns, and whence is this knowledge derived but from instinct?" On this subject Lucretius enlarges, observing that "every creature knows its own powers. The calf butts with its forehead, before its horns appear, and strikes with all imaginable fury." On which Galen expresses himself in the following manner, "every animal appears to defend itself with that part of its body, in which it excels others. The calf butts with its head before its horns have grown, and the colt strikes with its heel before its hoofs are hard, as the young dog attempts to bite before his teeth are strong." The same writer in describing the use of different parts of the body, says, "that man is a creature formed for peace and war. His armour forms not an immediate part of his body; but he has hands fit for preparing and handling arms, and we see infants using them spontaneously, without being taught to do so." Aristotle in the 4th book, and tenth chapter of the history of animals, says, "that the hand serves man for a spear, a sword, or any arms whatever, because it can hold and wield them." Now right reason and the nature of society which claims the second, and indeed more important place in this inquiry, prohibit not all force, but only that which is repugnant to society, by depriving another of his right. For the end of society is to form a common and united aid to preserve to every one his own. Which may easily be understood to have obtained, before what is now called property was introduced. For the free use of life and limbs was so much the right of every one, that it could not be infringed or attacked without injustice. So the use of the common productions of nature was the right of the first occupier, and for any one to rob him of that was manifest injustice. This may be more easily understood, since law and custom have established property under its present form. Tully has expressed this in the third book of his Offices in the following words, "if every member could have separate feeling, and imagine it could derive vigour from engrossing the strength of a neighboring part of the body, the whole frame would languish and perish. In the same manner if every one of us, for his own advantage, might rob another of what he pleased, there would be a total overthrow of human society and intercourse. For though it is allowed by nature for every one to give the preference to himself before another in the enjoyment of life and necessaries, yet she does not permit us to increase our means and riches by the spoils of others." It is not therefore contrary to the nature of society to provide and consult for ourselves, if another's right is not injured; the force therefore, which inviolably abstains from touching the rights of others, is not unjust. For as the same Cicero observes some where in his Epistles, that as there are two modes of contending, the one by argument, and the other by force, and as the former is peculiar to man, and the latter common to him with the brute creation, we must have recourse to the latter, when it is impossible to use the former. And again, what can be opposed to force, but force? Ulpian observes that Cassius says, it is lawful to repel force by force, and it is a right apparently provided by nature to repel arms with arms, with whom Ovid agrees, observing that the laws permit us to take up arms against those that bear them.

**II**. The observation that all war is not repugnant to the law of nature, may be more amply proved from sacred history. For when Abraham with his servants and confederates had gained a victory, by force of arms, over the four Kings, who had plundered Sodom, God approved of his act by the mouth of his priest Melchisedech, who said to him, "Blessed be the most high God, who hath delivered thine enemies into thine hand." Gen. xiv. 20. Now Abraham had taken up arms, as appears from the history, without any special command from God. But this man, no less eminent for sanctity than wisdom, felt himself authorized by the law of nature, as it is admitted by the evidence of Berosus, and Orpheus, who were strangers.

There is no occasion to appeal to the history of the seven nations, whom God delivered up into the hands of the Israelites to be destroyed. For there was a special command to execute the judgment of God upon nations guilty of the greatest crimes. From whence these wars are literally styled in scripture, Battles of the Lord, as undertaken, not by human will, but by divine appointment. The xvii. chapter of Exodus supplies a passage more to the purpose, relating the overthrow which the Israelites, conducted by Moses and Joshua, made of the Amalekites. In this act, there was no express commission from God, but only an approval after it was done. But in the xix. chap. of Deut. ver. 10, 15. God has prescribed general and standing laws to his people on the manner of making war, by this circumstance shewing that a war may be just without any; express commandment from him. Because in the same passage, a plain distinction is made between the case of the seven nations and that of others. And as there is no special edict prescribing the just causes for which war may be undertaken, the determination of them is left to the discovery of natural reason. Of this kind is the war of Jephthah against the Ammonites, in defence of their borders. Judd. xi. and the war of David against the same people for having violated the rights of his Ambassadors. 2 Sam. x. To the preceding observations may be added, what the inspired writer of the Epistle to the Hebrews says of Gideon, Barack, Sampson, Jephthah, David, Samuel, and others, who by faith made war upon kingdoms, prevailed in war and put whole armies of their enemies to flight. Heb.

xi. 33, 34. The whole tenor of this passage shews, that the word faith implies a persuasion, that what they did was believed to be agreeable to the will of God. In the same manner, David is said, by a woman distinguished for her wisdom, I Sam. xxv. 28. to fight the battles of the Lord, that is to make lawful and just wars.

**III**. Proofs of what has been advanced, may be drawn also from the consent of all, especially, of the wisest nations. There is a celebrated passage in Cicero's speech for Milo, in which, justifying recourse to force in defence of life, he bears ample testimony to the feelings of nature, who has given us this law, which is not written, but innate, which we have not received by instruction, hearing or reading, but the elements of it have been engraven in our hearts and minds with her own hand : a law which is not the effect of habit and acquirement, but forms a part in the original complexion of our frame: so that if our lives are threatened with assassination or open violence from the hands of robbers or enemies, any means of defence would be allowed and laudable. He proceeds, reason has taught this to the learned, necessity to the barbarians, custom to nations, and nature herself to wild beasts, to use every possible means of repelling force offered to their bodies, their limbs and their lives. Caius and Lawyer says, natural reason permits us to defend ourselves against dangers. And Florentinus, another legal authority, maintains, that whatever any one does in defence of his person ought to be esteemed right. Josephus observes, that the love of life is a law of nature strongly implanted in all creatures, and therefore we look upon those as enemies, who would openly deprive us of it.

This principle is founded on reasons of equity, so evident, that even in the brute creation, who have no idea of right, we make a distinction between attack and defence. For when Ulpian had said, that an animal without knowledge, that is without the use of reason, could not possibly do wrong, he immediately adds, that when two animals fight, if one kills the other, the distinction of Quintius Mutius must be admitted, that if the aggressor were killed no damages could be recovered; but if the other, which was attacked, an action might be maintained. There is a passage in Pliny, which will serve for an explanation of this, he say s that the fiercest lions do not fight with each other, nor do serpents bite serpents. But if any violence is done to the tamest of them, they are roused, and upon receiving any hurt, will defend themselves with the greatest alacrity and vigour.

**IV**. From the law of nature then which may also be called he law of nations, it is evident that all kinds of war are not to be condemned. In the same manner, all history and the laws of manners of every people sufficiently inform us, that war is not condemned by the voluntary law of nations. Indeed Hermogenianus has said, that wars were introduced by the law of nations, a passage which aught to be explained somewhat differently from the general interpretation given to it. The meaning of it is, that certain formalities, attending war, were introduced by the law of nations, which formalities were necessary to secure the peculiar privileges arising out of the law. From hence a distinction, which there will be occasion to use hereafter, between a war with the usual formalities o£ the law of nations, which is called just or perfect, and an informal war, which does not for that reason cease to be just, or agreeable to right. For some wars, when made upon just grounds, though not exactly conformable, yet are not repugnant to the law, as will be explained more fully hereafter. By the law of the nations, says Livy, provision is made to repel force by arms; and Florentinus declares, that the law of nations allows us to repel violence and injury, in order to protect our persons.

**V**. A greater difficulty occurs respecting the divine voluntary law. Nor is there any force in the objection that as the law of nature is unchangeable, nothing can be appointed even by God himself contrary to it. For this is true only in those things, which the law of nature positively forbids or commands; no 'n those which are tacitly permitted by the same law. For acts of that kind, not falling strictly within the general rule, but being exceptions to the law of nature, may be either forbidden or commanded. The first objection usually made against the lawfulness of war is taken from the law given to Noah and his posterity, Gen. ix. 5, 6, where God thus speaks, "Surely the blood of your lives will I require; at the hand of every beast will

I require it, and at the hand of every man ; at the hand of every man's brother will I require the life of man. Whoever sheds man's blood, by man shall his blood be shed; for in the image of God made he man." Here some take the phrase of requiring blood, in the most general sense, and the other part, that blood shall be shed in its turn, they consider as a bare threat, and not an approbation; neither of which acceptations can be admitted. For the prohibition of shedding blood extends not beyond the law itself, which declares, THOU SHALT NOT KILL; but passes no condemnation upon capital punishments or wars undertaken by public authority.

Neither the law of Moses, nor that given to Noah established any thing new, they were only a declaratory repetition of the law of nature, that had been obliterated by depraved custom. So that the shedding of blood in a criminal and wanton manner is the only act prohibited by those commandments. Thus every act of homicide does not amount to murder, but only that, which is committed with a willful and malicious intention to destroy the life of an innocent person. As to what follows about blood .being shed in return for blood, it seems to imply not a mere act of personal revenge, but the deliberate exercise of a perfect right, which may be thus explained; it is not unjust, according to the principles of nature that any one should suffer in proportion to the evil he has done, conformably to the judicial maxim of Rhadamanthus, that if any one himself suffers what he has done, it is but just and right. The same opinion is thus expressed by Seneca the father; "it is but a just retaliation for any one to suffer in his own person the evil which he intended to inflict upon another." From a sense of this natural justice, Cain knowing himself guilty of his brother's blood said, "whosoever finds me shall kill me."

But as in those early times, when men were few, and aggressions rare, there was less occasion for examples, God restrained by an express commandment the impulse of nature which appeared lawful, he forbad any one to kill the murderer, at the same time prohibiting all intercourse with him, even so far as not to touch him.

Plato has established this in his laws, and the same rule prevailed in Greece, as appears from the following passage in Euripides, "our fathers of old did well in banishing from their intercourse and sight any one that had shed another's blood; imposing banishment by way of atonement, rather than inflicting death." We find Thucydides of the same opinion, "that anciently lighter punishments were inflicted for the greatest crimes; but in process of time, as those penalties came to be despised, legislators were obliged to have recourse to death in certain cases." We may add to the above instances the remark of Lactantius, that as yet it appeared a sin to punish even the most wicked men with death.

The conjecture of the divine will taken from the remarkable instance of Cain, whom no one was permitted to kill passed into a law, so that Lanech, having perpetrated a similar deed, promised himself impunity from this example. Gen. iv. 24.

But as before the deluge, in the time of the Giants, the practice of frequent and wanton murders had prevailed; upon the renewal of the human race, after the deluge, that the same evil custom might not be established, God thought proper to restrain it by severer means. The lenity of former ages was laid aside, and the divine authority gave a sanction to the precepts of natural justice, that whoever killed a murderer should be innocent. After tribunals were erected, the power over life was, for the very best reasons, conferred upon the judges alone. Still some traces of ancient manners remained in the right which was granted, after the introduction o the Mosaic Law, to the nearest in blood to the person killed.

This interpretation is justified by the authority of Abraham, who, with a perfect knowledge of the law given to Noah, took arms against the four Kings, fully persuaded that he was doing nothing in violation of that law. In the same manner Moses ordered the people to fight against Amalekites, who attacked them ; following in this case the dictates of nature, for he appears to have had no special communication with God. Exod. xvii. 9. Besides, we find that capital punishments were inflicted upon other criminals, as well as murderers, not only among the Gentiles, but among those who had been impressed with the most pious rules and opinions, even the Patriarchs themselves. Gen. xxxviii. 24.

Indeed upon comparing the divine will with the light of nature, it was concluded, that it seemed conformable to justice, that other crimes of great enormity should be subject to the same punishment as that of murder. For there are some rights, such as those of reputation, chastity, conjugal fidelity, submission of subjects to their princes, all of which are esteemed of equal value with life itself, because on the preservation of these the peace and comfort of life depend. The violation of any of those rights is little less than murder itself.

Here may be applied the old tradition found among the Jews, that there were many laws, which were not ALL mentioned by Moses, given by God to the sons of Noah as it was sufficient for his purpose, that they should afterwards be comprehended in the peculiar laws of the Hebrews. Thus it appears from xviii. chap. of Leviticus, that there was an ancient law against incestuous marriages, though not mentioned by Moses in its proper place. Now among the commandments given by God to the children of Noah, it is said, that death was expressly declared to be the punishment not only for murder, but for adultery, incest, and robbery, which is confirmed by the words of Job xxxi. II. The law of Moses too, for the sanction of capital punishments, gives reasons which operate no less with other nations, than with the Jewish people. Levit. xviii. 25-30. Psa. ci. 5. Prov. xx. 8. And particularly respecting murder it is said, the land cannot be cleansed unless the blood of the murderer be shed. Numb. xxv. 31-33. Besides, it were absurd to suppose that the Jewish people were indulged with the privilege of maintaining the public safety, and that of individuals by capital punishments, and asserting their rights by war, and that other kings and nations were not allowed the same powers. Nor do we find that those kings or nations were forewarned by the Prophets, that the use of capital punishments, and that all wars, were condemned by God in the same manner as they were admonished of all other sins. On the other hand, can any one doubt, as the law of Moses bore such an express image of the divine will respecting criminal justice, whether other nations would not have acted wisely in adopting it for their example? It is certain that the Greeks, and the Athenians in particular did so. From hence came the close resemblance which the Jewish bore to the old Athenian law, and to that of the twelve tables of Rome. Enough has been said, to shew that the law given to Noah cannot bear the interpretation of those, who derive from it their arguments against the lawfulness of all war.

**VI**. The arguments against the lawfulness of war, drawn from the Gospel, are more specious. In examining which it will not be necessary to assume, as many do, that the Gospel contains nothing more than the law of nature, except the rules of faith and the Sacraments: an assumption, which in its general acceptation is by no means true. It may readily be admitted, that nothing inconsistent with natural justice is enjoined in the gospel, yet it can never be allowed, that the laws of Christ do not impose duties upon us, above those required by the law of nature. And those, who think otherwise, strain their arguments to prove that many practices forbidden by the gospel, as concubinage, divorce, polygamy, were made offences by the law of nature. The light of nature might point out the HONOUR of abstaining from such practices, but the SINFULNESS of them could not have been discovered without a revelation of the will of God. Who for instance would say, that the Christian precept of laying down our lives for others was an obligation of the law of nature? I John iii. 16. It is said by Justin the Martyr, that to live according to the bare law of nature is not the character of a true believer. Neither can we follow those, who, adopting another meaning of no inconsiderable import, construe the precept delivered by Christ in his sermon on the mount, into nothing more than an interpretation of the Mosaic Law. For the words, "you have heard it was said to them of OLD, but I say to you," which are so often repeated, imply something else. Those of old were no other than contemporaries of Moses: for what is there repeated as said to those of OLD are not the words of the teachers of the law, but of Moses, either LITERALLY, or in THEIR meaning. They are cited by our Saviour as his express words, not as interpretations of them: "Thou shalt not kill," Exod. xx. whoever killeth shall be in danger of Judgment, Levit. xxi. az. Numb. xxxv. 16, 17, 30. "Thou shalt not commit adultery," Exod. xx. "whosoever shall put away his wife, let him give her a writing of divorcement." Deut. xxiv. 1. "Thou shalt not forswear thyself, but shalt perform unto the Lord thine oaths." Exod. xx. 7. Numb. xxx 2. "An eye for an eye, and a tooth for a tooth," may be demanded in justice." Levit. xxxiv. 20. Deut. xix. 21. "Thou shalt love thy neighbour," that is, an Israelite. Levit. xix. 18. "and thou shalt hate thine enemy," that is, any one of the seven nations to whom friendship or compassion was forbidden to be shewn. Exod. xxxiv. 11. Deut. vii. 1. To these may be added the Amalekites, with whom the Israelites were commanded to maintain irreconcilable war. Exod. xxvii. 18. Deut. xxv. 19.

But to understand the words of our Saviour, we must observe that the law of Moses is taken in a double sense, either as containing some principles in common with human laws, such as imposing restraint upon human crimes by the dread of exemplary punishments. Heb. ii. 2. And in this manner maintaining civil society among the Jewish people: for which reason it is called, Heb. vii. 16, the law of a carnal commandment, and From. iii. 17. the law of works: or it may be taken in another sense, comprehending the peculiar sanctions of a divine law, requiring purity of mind, and certain actions, which might be omitted without temporal punishments. In this sense it is called a spiritual law, giving life to the soul. The teachers of the law, and the Pharisees considering the first part as sufficient neglected to instruct the people in the second and more important branch, deeming it superfluous. The truth of this may be proved, not only from our own writings, but from Josephus also, and the Jewish Rabbies. Respecting this second part we may observe, that the virtues which are required of Christians, are either recommended or enjoined to the Hebrews, but not enjoined in the same degree and extent as to Christians. Now in both these senses Christ opposes his own precepts to the old law. From whence it is clear, that his words contain more than a bare interpretation of the Mosaic law. These observations apply not only to the question immediately in hand, but to many others; that we may not rest upon the authority of the Mosaic law farther than is right.

**VII**. Omitting therefore the less satisfactory proofs, as a leading point of evidence to shew that the right of war is not taken away by the law of the gospel, that passage in St. Paul's Epistle to Timothy may be referred to, where the Apostle says, "I exhort therefore that, first of all, supplications, prayers, intercessions, and giving of thanks be made for all men; for Kings, and for all that are in authority, that we may lead a quiet and peaceable life, in all godliness and honesty; for this is good and acceptable in the sight of God our Saviour, who would have all men to be saved, and to come to the knowledge of the truth." I Eph. ii. 1, 2, 3. From this passage, the following conclusions may be drawn; in the first place, that Christian piety in kings is acceptable to God, that their profession of Christianity does not abridge their rights of sovereignty. Justin the Martyr has said, "that in our prayers for Kings, we should beg that they may unite a spirit of wisdom with their royal power," and in the book called the Constitutions of Clement, the Church prays for Christian rulers, and that Christian Princes may perform an acceptable service to God, by securing to other Christians the enjoyment of quiet lives. The manner in which the Sovereign secures this important end, is explained in another passage from the same Apostle. From. xiii. 4. "He is the minister of God to thee for good. But if thou do evil, fear, for he beareth not the sword in vain; for he is the minister of God, an avenger to execute wrath upon them, that do evil." By the right of the sword is understood the exercise of every kind of restraint, in the sense adopted by the Lawyers, not only over offenders amongst his own people, but against neighboring nations, who violate his own and his people's rights. To clear up this point, we may refer to the second Psalm, which although it applies literally to David, yet in its more full and perfect sense relates to Christ, which may be seen by consulting other parts of scripture. For instance, Acts iv. 25.

xiii. 33. For that Psalm exhorts all kings to worship the son of God, shewing themselves, as kings, to be his ministers, which may be explained by the words of St. Augustine, who says, "In this, kings, in their royal capacity, serve God according to the divine commandment, if they promote what is good, and prohibit what is evil in their kingdoms, not only relating to human society, but also respecting religion." And in another place the same writer says, "How can kings serve the Lord in fear, unless they can prohibit and punish with due severity offences against the law of God? For the capacities in which they serve God, as individuals, and as kings, are very different. In this respect they serve the Lord, as kings, when they promote his service by means which they could not use without regal power.

The same part of the Apostle's writings supplies us with a second argument, where the higher powers, meaning kings, are said to be from God, and are called the ordinance of God; from whence it is plainly inferred that we are to honour and obey the, from motives of conscience, and that every one who resists him is resisting God. If the word ordinance meant nothing more than a bare permission, that obedience which the Apostle so strenuously enjoins would only have the force of an imperfect obligation. But as the word ordinance, in the original, implies an express commandment and appointment, and as all parts of the revealed will of God are consistent with each other, it follows that the obedience of subjects to sovereigns is a duty of supreme obligation. Nor is the argument at all weakened by its being said, that the Sovereigns at the time when St. Paul wrote, were not Christians. For it is not universally true, as Sergius Paulus, the deputy governor of Cyprus, had long before professed the Christian religion. Acts xiii. 12. There is no occasion to mention the tradition respecting Abgarus the King of Edessa's Epistle to our Saviour; a tradition mingled with falsehood, though, in some measure founded upon truth. For the question did not turn upon the characters of the Princes, whether they were godly or not, but whether THEIR holding the kingly office was repugnant to the law of God. This St. Paul denies, maintaining that the kingly office, even under all circumstances, was appointed by God, therefore it ought to be honoured from motives of conscience, which, properly speaking, are under the controul of God alone. So that Nero, and King Agrippa whom Paul so earnestly entreats to become a Christian, might have embraced Christianity, and still retained, the one his regal, and the other his imperial authority, which could not be exercised without the power of the sword. As the legal sacrifices might formerly be performed by wicked Priests; in the same manner regal power would retain its indelible sanctity, though in the hands of an ungodly man.

A third argument is derived from the words of John the Baptist, who, at a time when many thousands of the Jews served in the Roman armies, as appears from the testimony of Josephus and others, being seriously asked by the soldiers, what they should do to avoid the wrath of God, did not command them to renounce their military calling, which he ought to have done, had it been inconsistent with the law and will of God, but to abstain from violence, extortion, and false accusation, and to be content with their wages. In reply to these words of the Baptist, so plainly giving authority to the military profession, many observed that the injunction of the Baptist is so widely different from the precepts of Christ, that HE seemed to preach one doctrine and our LORD another. Which is by no means admissible, for the following reasons. Both our Saviour and the Baptist made repentance the substance of their doctrine; for the kingdom of heaven was at hand. By the Kingdom of Heaven is meant a new law, as the Hebrews used to give the name of Kingdom to their law. Christ himself says the Kingdom of Heaven began to suffer violence from the days of John the Baptist. Matt. xi. 12. John is said to have preached the baptism of repentance for the remission of sins. Mark i. 4. The Apostles are said to have done the same in the name of Christ. Acts xi. 38. John requires fruits worthy of repentance, and threatens destruction to those, who do not produce them. Matt. iii. 8, 10. He also requires works of charity above the law. Luke iii. 2. The law is said to have continued till John, that is, a more perfect law is said to have commenced form his instruction. He was called greater than the prophets, and declared to be one sent to give the knowledge of salvation to the people by announcing the gospel. He makes no distinction between himself and Jesus on the score of doctrine, only ascribing pre-eminence to Christ as the promised Messiah, the Lord of the Kingdom of Heaven, who would give the power of the holy spirit to those, who believed in him. In short, the dawning rudiments of knowledge, which proceeded from the forerunner, were more distinctly unfolded and cleared up, by Christ himself, the light of the world.

There is a fourth argument, which seems to have no little weight, proceeding upon the supposition, that if the right of inflicting capital punishments were abolished, and princes were deprived for the power of the sword to protect their subjects against the violence of murderers and robbers, wickedness would triumphantly prevail, and the world would be deluged with crimes, which, even under the best established governments, are with so much difficulty prevented or restrained. If then it had been the intention of Christ to introduce such an order of things as had never been heard of, he would undoubtedly by the most express and particular words, have condemned all capital punishments, and all wars, which we never read that he did. For the arguments, brought in favor of such an opinion, are for the most part very indefinite and obscure. Now both justice and common sense require such general expressions to be taken in a limited acceptation, and allow us, in explaining ambiguous words, to depart from their literal meaning, where our strictly adhering to it would lead to manifest inconvenience and detriment.

There is a fifth argument, maintaining that no proof can be adduced that the judicial part of the Mosaic Law, inflicting sentence of death, ever ceased to be in force, till the city of Jerusalem, and the civil polity of the Jews were utterly destroyed, without hopes of restoration. For in the Mosaic dispensation no assignable term is named for the duration of the law; nor do Christ and his Apostles ever speak of its abolition, except in allusion to the overthrow of the Jewish state. Indeed on the contrary, St. Paul says, that the High Priest was appointed to judge according to the law of Moses. Acts xxiv. 3. And Christ himself, in the introduction to his precepts, declares that he came not to destroy the law, but to fulfil it. Matt. v. 17. The application of his meaning to the ritual law is very plain, for it was only the outline and shadow of that perfect body, of which the Gospel formed the substance. But how is it possible that the judicial laws should stand, if Christ, according to the opinion of some, abolished them by his coming? Now if the law remained in force as long as the Jewish state continued, it follows that the Jewish converts to Christianity if called to the magisterial office, could not refuse it on the score of declining to pass sentence of death, and that they could not decide otherwise than the law of Moses had prescribed.

Upon weighing the whole matter, the slightest ground cannot be discovered for supposing that any pious man, who had heard those words from our Saviour himself, would have understood them in a sense different from that which has been here given. It must however be admitted that, before the Gospel dispensation permission or impunity was granted to certain acts and dispositions, which it would neither be necessary nor proper to examine at present, upon which Christ did not allow his followers to act. Of this kind was the permission to put away a wife for every offence, and to seek redress by law for every injury. Now between the positive precepts of Christ and those permissions there is a difference, but not a contradiction. For he that retains his wife, and he that forgoes his right of redress, does nothing CONTRARY to the law, but rather acts agreeably to the SPIRIT of it. It is very different with a judge, who is not merely permitted, but commanded by the law to punish a murderer with death, incurring guilt in the sight of God, if he should act otherwise. If Christ had forbidden him to put a murderer to death, his prohibition would have amounted to a contradiction, and it would have abolished the law.

The example of Cornelius the Centurion supplies a sixth argument in favor of this opinion. In receiving the holy spirit from Christ, he received an indubitable proof of his justification; he was baptized into the name of Christ by Peter, yet we do not find that he either had resigned or was advised by the Apostle to resign his military commission. In reply to which some maintain, that when instructed by Peter in the nature of the Christian religion, he must have been instructed to form the resolution of quitting his military calling. There would be some weight in their answer, if it could be shown that an absolute prohibition of war is to be found among the precepts of Christ. And as it can be found nowhere else, it would have been inserted in its proper place among the precepts of Christ, that after ages might not have been ignorant of the rules of duty. Nor as may be seen in the xix. chap, of the Acts of the Apostles and the 19th ver. is it usual with St. Luke, in cases where the personal character and situation or converts required an extraordinary change of life and disposition, to pass over such a circumstance without notice.

The seventh argument is like the preceding, and is taken from the example of Sergius Paulus, which has been already mentioned. In the history of his conversion there is not the least intimation of "his abdicating the magistracy, or being required to do so. Therefore silence respecting a circumstance, which would naturally and necessarily have been mentioned, may be fairly taken as a proof that it never existed. The conduct of St. Paul supplies us with an eighth argument on this subject. When he understood that the Jews lay in wait for an opportunity to seize and kill him, he immediately gave information of their design to the commander of the Roman garrison, and when the commander gave him a guard of soldiers to protect him on his journey, he made no remonstrance, nor ever hinted either to the commander or the soldiers that it was displeasing to God to repel force by force. Yet this is the same Apostle who, as appears from all his writings, 2 Tim. iv. 2. neither himself neglected nor allowed others to neglect any opportunity of reminding men of their duty. In addition to all that has been said, it may be observed, that the peculiar end of what is lawful and binding, must itself be lawful and binding also. It is lawful to pay tribute, and according to St. Paul's explanation, it is an act binding upon the conscience, From. xiii. 3, 4, 6. For the end of tribute is to supply the state with the means of protecting the good, and restraining the wicked. There is a passage in Tacitus very applicable to the present question. It is in the fourth book of his history, in the speech of Petilius Cerealis, who says, "the peace of nations cannot be preserved without armies, nor can armies be maintained without pay, nor pay supplied without taxation." There is a sentiment similar to this of the historian, in St. Augustin, he says, "for this purpose we pay tribute, that the soldier may be provided with the necessaries of life."

The tenth argument is taken from that part of the xxv. chap. of the Acts of the Apostles, where Paul says, "If I have wronged any man, or done any thing worthy of death, I refuse not to die." From whence the opinion of St. Paul may be gathered, that, even after the publication of the gospel, there were certain crimes which justice not only allowed but required to be punished with death; which opinion St. Peter also maintains. But if it had been the will of God that capital punishments should be abolished, Paul might have cleared himself, but he ought not to have left an impression on the minds of men, that it was at that time equally lawful as before to punish the guilty with death. Now as it has been proved, that the coming of Christ did not take away the right of inflicting capital punishments, it has at the same time been proved, that war may be made upon a multitude of armed offenders, who can only be brought to justice by defeat in battle. The numbers, the strength and boldness of the aggressors, though they may have their weight in restraining our deliberations, cannot in the least diminish our right.

The substance of the eleventh argument rests not only upon our Saviour's having abolished those parts of the Mosaic law, which formed a wall of separation between the Jews and other nations, but upon his allowing the moral parts to remain, as standing rules, approved by the law of nature, and the consent of every civilized people, and containing whatever is good and virtuous.

Now the punishing of crimes, and the taking up arms to avenge or ward off injuries are among those actions, which by the law of nature rank as laudable, and are referred to the virtues of justice and beneficence. And here is the proper place to animadvert slightly upon the mistake of those, who derive the rights of war, possessed by the Israelites, solely from the circumstance of God having given them the land of Canaan and commissioned them to drive out the inhabitants. This may be one just reason, but it is not the sole reason.

For, prior to those times, holy men guided by the light of nature undertook wars, which the Israelites themselves afterwards did for various reasons, and David in particular, to avenge the violated rights of ambassadors. But the rights, which any one derives from the law of nature, are no less his own than if God had given them: nor are those rights abolished by the law of the Gospel.

**VIII.** Let us now consider the arguments, by which the contrary opinion is supported, that the pious reader may judge more easily, to which side the scale inclines.

In the first place, the prophecy of Isaiah is generally alleged, who says the time shall come, "when nations shall beat their swords into plow-shares, and turn their spears into pruning hooks. Nation shall not lift up sword against nation, neither shall they learn war any more." ii. 4. But this prophecy, like many others, is to be taken conditionally, alluding to the state of the world that would take place, if all nations would submit to the law of Christ, and make it the rule of life, to which purpose God would suffer nothing to be wanting on his part. For it is certain, that if all people were Christians, and lived like Christians, there would be no wars, which Arnobius expresses thus, "If all men, knowing that it is not their corporeal form alone which makes them men, but the powers of the understanding, would lend a patient ear to his salutary and pacific instructions, if they would trust to his admonitions rather than to the swelling pride and turbulence of their senses, iron would be employed for instruments of more harmless and useful operations, the world enjoy the softest repose and be united in the bands of inviolable treaties." On this subject Lactantius, reproaching the Pagans with the deification of their conquerors, says, "what would be the consequence, if all men would unite in concord? Which might certainly be brought to pass, if, abandoning ruinous and impious rage, they would live in justice and innocence." Or this passage of the prophecy must be understood literally, and, if taken in that sense, it shews that it is not yet fulfilled, but its accomplishment must be looked for in the general conversion of the Jewish people. But, which ever way you take it, no conclusion can be drawn from it against the justice of war, as long as violent men exist to disturb the quiet of the lovers of peace. [**Translator's note:** The remainder of this section is omitted, Grotius himself stating it to be only a repetition and enlargement of his arguments immediately preceding it.]

IX. In examining the meaning of written evidence, general custom, and the opinions of men celebrated for their wisdom have usually great weight; a practice which it is right to observe in the interpretation of holy scripture. For it is not likely that the churches, which had been founded by the Apostles, would either suddenly or universally have swerved from those opinions, which the Apostles had briefly expressed, in writing, and afterwards more fully and clearly explained to them with their own lips, and reduced to practice. Now certain expressions of the primitive Christians are usually alleged by those who are adverse to all wars, whose opinions may be considered and refuted in three points of view.

In the first place, from these expressions nothing more can be gathered than the private opinions of certain individuals, but no public opinion of the Churches. Besides these expressions for the most part are to be found only in the writings of Origen, Tertullian and some few others, who wished to distinguish themselves by the brilliancy of their thoughts, without regarding consistency in their opinions. For this same Origen says, that Bees were given by God as a pattern for men to follow in conducting just, regular, and necessary wars; and likewise Tertulian, who in some parts seems to disapprove of capital punishments, has said, "No one can deny that it is good the guilty should be punished." He expresses his doubts respecting the military profession, for in his book upon idolatry, he says, it is a fit matter of inquiry, whether believers can take up arms, or whether any of the military profession can be admitted as members of the Christian Church. But in his Book entitled, the SOLDIER'S CROWN, after some objections against the profession of arms, he makes a distinction between those who are engaged in the army before baptism, and those who entered after they had made the baptismal vow. "It evidently, says he alters the case with those who were soldiers before their conversion to Christianity; John admitted them to baptism, in one instance Christ approved, and in another Peter instructed a faithful Centurion : yet with this stipulation, that they must either like many others, relinquish their calling, or be careful to do nothing displeasing to God." He was sensible then that they continued in the military profession after baptism, which they would by no means have done, if they had understood that all war was forbidden by Christ. They would have followed the example of the Soothsayers, the Magi, and other professors of forbidden arts, who ceased to practice them, when they became Christians. In the book quoted above, commanding a soldier, who was at the same time a Christan, he says, "O Soldier glorious in God."

The second observation applies to the case of those, who declined or even refused bearing arms, on account of the circumstances of the times, which would have required them to do many acts inconsistent with their Christian calling. In Dolabella's letter to the Ephesians, which is to be found in Josephus, we see that the Jews requested an exemption from military expeditions, because, in mingling with strangers, they could not conveniently have observed the rites of their own laws and, would have been obliged to bear arms, and to make long marches on the Sabbaths. And we are informed by Josephus that, for the same reasons, the Jews obtained their discharge of L. Lentulus. In another part, he relates that when the Jews had been ordered to leave the city of Rome, some of them inlisted in the army, and that others, who out of respect to the laws of their country, for the reasons before mentioned, refused to bear arms, were punished. In addition to these a third reason may be given, which was that they would have to fight against their own people, against whom it was unlawful to bear arms, especially when they incurred danger and enmity for adhering to the Mosaic law. But the Jews, whenever they could do it, without these inconveniences, served under foreign princes, previously stipulating, as we are informed by Josephus, for liberty to live according to the laws and rules of their own country. Tertullian objects to the military service of his own times on account of dangers, and inconveniences very similar to those, which deterred the Jews. In his book on Idolatry, he says, "it is impossible to reconcile the oath of fidelity to serve under the banners of Christ, with that to serve under the banners of the Devil." Because the soldiers were ordered to swear by Jupiter, Mars, and the other Heathen Gods. And in his book on the Soldier's Crown, he asks, if the soldier be to keep watch before the temples, which he has renounced, to sup where he is forbidden by the Apostle, and to guard in the night the Gods, whom he has abjured in the day ?" And he proceeds with asking, "f there be not many other military duties, which ought to be regarded in the light of sins?"

The third point of view, in which the subject is to be considered, relates to the conduct of those primitive Christians, who, in the ardour of zeal, aimed at the most brilliant attainments, taking the divine counsels for precepts of obligation. The Christians, says Athenagoras, never go to law with those, who rob them.

Salvian says, it was commanded by Christ that we should relinquish the object of dispute, rather than engage in law suits. But this, taken in so general an acceptation, is rather by the way of counsel, in order to attain to a sublimer mode of life, than intended as a positive precept. Thus many of the primitive Fathers condemned all oaths without exception, yet St. Paul, in matters of great importance, made use of these solemn appeals to God. A Christian in Tatian said, "I refuse the office of Praetor," and in the words of Tertullian, "a Christian is not ambitious of the Aedile's office." In the same manner Lactantius maintains that a just man, such as he wishes a Christian to be, ought not to engage in war, nor, as all his wants can be supplied at home, even to go to sea. How many of the primitive fathers dissuade Christians from second marriages? All these counsels are good, recommending excellent attainments, highly acceptable to God, yet they are not required of us, by any absolute law. The observations already made are sufficient to answer the objections derived from the primitive times of christianity.

Now in order to confirm our opinions, we may observe that they have the support of writers, even of greater antiquity, who think that capital punishments may be inflicted, and that wars, which rest upon the same authority, may be lawfully engaged in by Christians. Clemens Alexandrinus says, that "a Christian, if, like Moses, he be called to the exercise of sovereign power, will be a living law to his subjects, rewarding the good, and punishing the wicked." And, in another place, describing the habit of a Christian, he says, "it would become him to go barefoot, unless he were a soldier." In the work usually entitled the CONSTITUTIONS OF CLEMENS ROMANUS, we find that "it is not all killing which is considered unlawful, but only that of the innocent; yet the administration of judicial punishments must be reserved to the supreme power alone." But without resting upon individual authorities, we can appeal to the public authority of the church which ought to have the greatest weight. From hence it is evident that none were ever refused baptism, or excommunicated by the church, merely for bearing arms, which they ought to have been, had the military profession been repugnant to the terms of the new covenant. In the CONSTITUTIONS just quoted, the writer speaking of those who, in the primitive times; were admitted to baptism, or refused that ordinance; says, "let a soldier who desires to be admitted be taught to forbear from violence, and false accusations, and to content with his regular pay. If he promises obedience let him be admitted." Tertullian in his Apology, speaking in the character of Christians, says, "We sail along with you, and we engage in the same wars," having little before observed, "we are but strangers, yet have filled all your cities, your islands, your castles, your municipal towns, your councils, and even your camps. He had related in the same book that rain had been obtained for the Emperor Marcus Aurelius by the prayers of the Christian soldiers. In his book of the crown, he commends a soldier, who had thrown away his garland, for a courage superior to that of his brethren in arms, and informs us that he had many Christian fellow soldiers.

To these proofs may be added the honours of Martyrdom given by the Church to some soldiers, who had been cruelly persecuted, and had even suffered death for the sake of Christ, among whom are recorded three of St. Paul's companions, Cerialis who suffered martyrdom under Decius; Marinus under Valerian; fifty under Aurelian, Victor, Maurus, and Valentinus, a lieutenant general under Maximian. About the same time Marcellus the Centurion, Severian under Licinius. Cyprian, in speaking or Laurentinus, and Ignatius, both Africans, says, "They too served in the armies of earthly princes, yet they were truly spiritual soldiers of God, defeating the wiles of the Devil by a steady confession of the name of Christ, and earning the palms and crowns of the Lord by their sufferings." And from hence it is plain what was the general opinion of the primitive Christians upon war, even before the Emperors became Christians.

It need not be thought surprising, if the Christians of those times were unwilling to appear at trials for life, since, for the most part, the persons to be tried were Christians. In other respects too, besides being unwilling to witness the unmerited sufferings of their persecuted brethren, the Roman laws were more severe than Christian lenity could allow of, as may be seen from the single instance of the Silanian decree of the Senate. Indeed capital punishments were not abolished even after Constantine embraced and began to encourage the Christian religion. He himself among other laws enacted one similar to that of the ancient Romans, for punishing parncides, by sewing them in a sack with certain animals, and throwing them into the sea, or the nearest river. This law is to be found in his code under the "title of the murders of parents or children." Yet in other respects he was so gentle in punishing criminals, that he is blamed by many historians for his excessive lenity. Constantine, we are informed by historians, had at that time many Christians in his army, and he used the name of Christ as the motto upon his standards. From that time too the military oath was changed to the form, which is found in Vegetius, and the soldier swore, "By God, and Christ, and the holy spirit, and the majesty of the Emperor, to whom as next to God, homage and reverence are due from mankind." Nor out of so many Bishops at that time, many of Whom suffered the most cruel treatment for their religion, do we read of a single one, if who dissuaded Constantine, by the terrors of divine wrath from inflicting capital punishments, or prosecuting wars, or who deterred the Christians, for the same reasons, from serving in the armies. Though most of those Bishops were strict observers of discipline, who would by no means dissemble in points relating to the duty of the Emperors or of others. Among this class, in the time of Theodosius, we may rank Ambrose, who in his seventh discourse says, "there is nothing wrong in bearing arms; but to bear arms from motives of rapine is a sin indeed," and in his first book of Offices, he maintains the same opinion, that "the courage which defends one's country against the incursions of barbarians, or protects one's family and home from the attacks of robbers, is complete justice." These arguments so decidedly shew the opinions of the primitive Christians in the support of just and necessary war, that the subject requires no farther proof or elucidation.

Nor is the argument invalidated by a fact pretty generally known, that Bishops and other Christians often interceded in behalf of criminals, to mitigate the punishment of death, and that any, who had taken refuge in churches, were not given up, but upon the promise of their lives being spared. A custom was introduced likewise of releasing all prisoners about the time of Easter. But all these instances, if carefully examined, will be found the voluntary acts of Christian kindness, embracing every opportunity to do good, and not a settled point of public opinion condemning all capital punishments. Therefore those favours were not universal; but limited to times and places, and even the intercessions themselves were modified with certain exceptions.

[**Translator's Note:** As Grotius has so fully established his argument, it is unnecessary to review his answer to further objections.]

## CHAPTER 3: THE DIVISON OF WAR INTO PUBLIC AND PRIVATE AND THE NATURE OF SOVEREIGN POWER.

*The Division of War into public and private — Examples to prove that all private — War is not repugnant to the Law of Nature since the erection of Courts of Justice — The Division of Public War into formal, and informal — Whether the suppression of Tumults by subordinate Magistrates be properly public War — Civil Power, in what it consists — Sovereign Power further considered — The opinion of those, who maintain that the Sovereign Power is always in the people, refuted, and their arguments answered — Mutual subjection refuted — Cautions requisite to understand the nature of Sovereign Power — Distinction of the real differences that exist under similar names — Distinction between the right to Sovereign Power, and the mode of exercising it.*

**I.** THE first and most necessary divisions of war are into one kind called private, another public, and another mixed. Now public war is carried on by the person holding the sovereign power. Private war is that which is carried on by private persons without authority from the state. A mixed war is that which is carried on, on one side by public authority, and on the other by private persons. But private war, from its greater antiquity, is the first subject for inquiry.

The proofs that have been already produced, to shew that to repel violence is not repugnant to natural law, afford a satisfactory reason to justify private war, as far as the law of nature is concerned. But perhaps it may be thought that since public tribunals have been erected, private redress of wrongs is not allowable. An objection which is very just. Yet although public trials and courts of Justice are not institutions of nature, but erected by the invention of men, yet as it is much more conducive to the peace of society for a matter in dispute to be decided by a disinterested person, than by the partiality and prejudice of the party aggrieved, natural justice and reason will dictate the necessity and advantage of every one's submitting to the equitable decisions of public judges. Paulus, the Lawyer, observes that "what can be done by a magistrate with the authority of the state should never be intrusted to individuals; as private redress would give rise to greater disturbance. And "the reason, *says King Theodoric*, why laws were invented, was to prevent any one from using personal violence, for wherein would peace differ from all the confusion of war, if private disputes were terminated by force?" And the law calls it force for any man to seize what he thinks his due, without seeking a legal remedy.

**II**. It is a matter beyond all doubt that the liberty of private redress, which once existed, was greatly abridged after courts of justice were established. Yet there may be cases, in which private redress must be allowed, as for instance, if the way to legal justice were not open. For when the law prohibits any one from redressing his own wrongs, it can only be understood to apply to circumstances where a legal remedy exists. Now the obstruction in the way to legal redress may be either temporary or absolute. Temporary, where it is impossible for the injured party to wait for a legal remedy, without imminent danger and even destruction. As for instance, if a man were attacked in the night, or in a secret place where no assistance could be procured. Absolute, either as the right, or the fact may require. Now there are many situations, where the right must cease from the impossibility of supporting it in a legal way, as in unoccupied places, on the seas, in a wilderness, or desert island, or any other place, where there is no civil government. All legal remedy too ceases by fact, when subjects will not submit to the judge, or if he refuses openly to take cognizance of matters in dispute. The assertion that all private war is not made repugnant to the law of nature by the erection of legal tribunals, may be understood from the law given to the Jews, wherein God thus speaks by the mouth of Moses, Exod. xxii. 2. "If a thief be found breaking up, that is, by night, and be smitten that he dies, there shall no blood be shed for him, but if the sun be risen upon him, there shall be blood shed for him." Now this law, making so accurate a distinction in the merits of the case, seems not only to imply impunity for killing any one, in self-defence, but to explain a natural right, founded not on any special divine command, but on the common principles of justice. From whence other nations have plainly followed the same rule. The passage of the twelve tables is well known, undoubtedly taken from the old Athenian Law, "If a thief commit a robbery in the night, and a man kill him, he is killed lawfully." Thus by the laws of all known and civilized nations, the person is judged innocent, who kills another, forcibly attempting or endangering his life; a conspiring and universal testimony, which proves that in justifiable homicide, there is nothing repugnant to the law of nature.

[**Translator's Note:** As the topics of the third section have been so fully stated in the second chapter, that section has been omitted, and the translation goes on from the second of the original to the fourth.]

**IV**. Public war, according to the law of nations, is either SOLEMN, that is FORMAL, or LESS SOLEMN, that is INFORMAL. The name of lawful war is commonly given to what is here called formal, in the same sense in which a regular will is opposed to a codicil, or a lawful marriage to the cohabitation of slaves. This opposition by no means implies that it is not allowed to any man, if he pleases, to make a codicil, or to slaves to cohabit in matrimony, but only, that, by the civil law, FORMAL WILLS and SOLEMN MARRIAGES, were attended with peculiar privileges and effects. These observations were the more necessary ; because many, from a misconception of the word just or lawful, think that all wars, to which those epithets do not apply, are condemned as unjust and unlawful. Now to give a war the formality required by the law of nations, two things are necessary. In the first place it must be made on both sides, by the sovereign power of the state, and in the next place it must be accompanied with certain formalities. Both of which are so essential that one is insufficient without the other.

Now a public war, LESS SOLEMN, may be made without those formalities, even against private persons, and by any magistrate whatever. And indeed, considering the thing without respect to the civil law, every magistrate, in case of resistance, seems to have a right to take up arms, to maintain his authority in the execution of his offices; as well as to defend the people committed to his protection. But as a whole state is by war involved in danger, it is an established law in almost all nations that no war can be made but by the authority of the sovereign in each state. There is such a law as this in the last book of Plato ON LAWS. And by the Roman law, to make war, or levy troops without a commission from the Prince was high treason. According to the Cornelian law also, enacted by Lucius Cornelius Sylla, to do so without authority from the people amounted to the same crime. In the code of Justinian there is a constitution, made by Valentinian and Valens, that no one should bear arms without their knowledge and authority. Conformably to this rule, St. Augustin says, that as peace is most agreeable to the natural state of man, it is proper that Princes should have the sole authority to devise and execute the operations of war. Yet this general rule, like all others, in its application must always be limited by equity and discretion.

In certain cases this authority may be communicated to others. For it is a point settled beyond all doubt that subordinate magistrates may, by their officers, reduce a few disobedient and tumultuous persons to subjection, provided, that to do it, it requires not a force of such enormous magnitude as might endanger the state. Again, if the danger be so imminent as to allow of no time for an application to the sovereign executive power, here too the necessity is admitted as an exception to the general rule. Lucius Pinarius the Governor of Enna, a Sicilian garrison, presuming upon this right, upon receiving certain information that the inhabitants had formed a conspiracy to revolt to the Carthaginians, put them all to the sword, and by that means saved the place. Franciscus Victoria allows the inhabitants of a town to take up arms, even without such a case of necessity, to redress their own wrongs, which the Prince neglects to avenge, but such an opinion is justly rejected by others.

**V**. Whether the circumstances, under which subordinate magistrates are authorised to use military force, can properly be called public war or not, is a matter of dispute among legal writers, some affirming and others denying it. If indeed we call no other public war, but that which is made by magisterial authority, there is no doubt but that such suppressions of tumult are public wars, and those who in such cases resist the magistrate in the execution of his office, incur the guilt of rebellion against superiors. But if public war is taken in the higher sense of FORMAL war, as it undoubtedly often is; those are not public wars; because to entitle them to the full rights of such, the declaration of the sovereign power and other requisites are wanting. Nor do the loss of property and the military executions, to which the offenders are subject, at all affect the question. For those casualties are not so peculiarly attached to formal war, as to be excluded from all other kinds. For it may happen, as in an extensive empire for instance, that persons in subordinate authority, may, when attacked, or threatened with attack, have powers granted to commence military operations. In which case the war must be supposed to commence by the authority of the sovereign power; as a person is considered to be the author of a measure which by virtue of his authority he empowers another to perform. The more doubtful point is, whether, where there is no such commission, a conjecture of what is the will of the sovereign power be sufficient. This seems not admissible. For it is not sufficient to consider, what we suppose would be the Sovereign's pleasure, if he were consulted; but what would be his actual will, in matters admitting of time for deliberation, even though he were not formally consulted; if a law was to be passed upon those matters. "For though UNDER SOME PARTICULAR CIRCUMSTANCES, it may be necessary to waive consulting the will of the sovereign, yet this would by no means authorise it as a GENERAL PRACTICE." For the safety of the state would be endangered, if subordinate powers should usurp the right of making war at their discretion. It was not without reason, that Cneus Manlius was accused by his Lieutenants of having made war upon the Galatians without authority from the Roman people. For though he Galatians bad supplied Antiochus with troops, yet as peace had been made with him, it rested with the Roman people, and not with Manlius to determine in what manner the Galatians should be punished for assisting an enemy. Cato proposed that Julius Caesar should be delivered up to the Germans for having attacked them in violation of his promise, a proposal proceeding rather from the desire to be rid of a formidable rival, than from any principle of justice.

The case was thus: the Germans had assisted the Gauls, enemies of the Roman people, therefore they had no reason to complain of the injury done to them, if he war against the Gauls, in which they had made themselves a party concerned, was just. But Caesar ought to have contented himself with driving the Germans out of Gaul, the province assigned him, without pursuing hem into their own country, especially as there was no farther danger to be apprehended from them; unless he had first consulted the Roman people. It was plain, then, the Germans had no right to demand the surrender of Caesar's person, though the Romans had a right to punish him for having exceeded his commission. On a similar occasion the Carthaginians answered the Romans; "It is not the subject of inquiry whether Hannibal has besieged Saguntum, by his own private or by public authority, but whether justly or unjustly. For with respect to one of our own subjects it is our business to inquire by what authority he has acted; but the matter of discussion with you is, whether he has broken any treaty." Cicero defends the conduct of Octavius and Decimus Brutus, who had taken up arms against Antony. But though it was evident that Antony deserved to be treated as an enemy, yet they ought to have waited for the determination of the Senate and people of Rome, whether it were for the public interest not to take notice of his conduct or to punish it, to agree to terms of peace with him, or to have recourse to arms. This would have been proper; for no one is obliged to exercise the right of punishing an enemy, if it is attended with probable danger.

But even if it had been judged expedient to declare Antony an enemy, the choice of the persons to conduct the war should have been left to the Senate and people of Rome. Thus when Cassius demanded assistance of the Rhodians, according to treaty, they answered they would send it, if the senate thought proper. This refutation of Cicero's opinion will serve, along with many other instances to be met with; as an admonition not to be carried away by the opinions of the most celebrated writers, particularly the most brilliant orators, who often speak to suit the circumstances of the moment. But all political investigation requires a cool and steady judgment, not to be biased by examples, which may rather be excused than vindicated.

Since then it has already been established that no war can lawfully be made but by the sovereign power of each state, in respect to all the questions connected with war, it will be necessary to examine what that sovereign power is, and who are the persons that hold it.

**VI**. The moral power then of governing a state, which is called by Thucydides the civil power, is described as consisting of three parts which form the necessary substance of every state; and those are the right of making its own laws, executing them in its own manner, and appointing its own magistrates. Aristotle, in the fourth book of his Politics, comprises the sovereignty of a state in the exercise of the deliberative, executive, and judicial powers. To the deliberative branch he assigns the right of deciding upon peace or war, making or annulling treaties, and framing and passing new laws. To these he adds the power of inflicting death, banishment, and forfeiture, and of punishing also for public peculation. In the exercise of judicial power, he includes not only the punishment of crimes and misdemeanors, but the redress of civil injuries. Dionysius of Halicarnassus, points out three distinguishing marks of sovereign power; and those are, the right of appointing magistrates, the right of enacting and repealing laws, and the right of making war and peace. To which, in another part, he adds the administration of justice, the supreme authority in matters of religion, and the right of calling general councils.

A true definition comprehends every possible branch of authority that can grow out of the possession and exercise of sovereign power. For the ruler of every state must exercise his authority either in person, or through the medium of others. His own personal acts must be either general or special. He may be said to do GENERAL acts in passing or repealing laws, respecting either temporal matters, or spiritual concerns, as far as the latter relate to the welfare of the state. The knowledge of these principles is called by Aristotle the masterpiece in the science of government.

The particular acts of the Sovereign are either directly of a public nature, or a private, but even the latter bear reference to his public capacity. Now the acts of the sovereign executive power of a directly public kind are the making of peace and war and treaties, and the imposition of taxes, and other similar exercises of authority over the persons and property of its subjects, which constitute the sovereignty of the state. Aristotle calls the knowledge of this practice political and deliberative science.

The private acts of the sovereign are those, in which by his authority, disputes between individuals are decided, as it is conducive to the peace of society that these should be settled. This is called by Aristotle the judicial power. Thus the acts of the sovereign are done in his name by his magistrates or other officers, among whom ambassadors are reckoned. And in the exercise of all those right sovereign power consists.

**VII**. That power is called sovereign, whose actions are not subject to the controul of any other power, so as to be annulled at the pleasure of any other human will. The term ANY OTHER HUMAN WILL exempts the sovereign him. self from this restriction, who may annul his own acts, as may also his successor, who enjoys the same right, having the same power and no other. We are to consider then what is the subject in which this sovereign power exists. Now the subject is in one respect common, and in another proper, as the body is the common subject of sight, the eye the proper, so the common subject of sovereign power is the state, which has already been said to be a perfect society of men. Now those nations, who are in a state of subjugation to another power, as the Roman provinces were, are excluded from this definition. For those nations are not sovereign states of themselves, in the present acceptation of the word; but are subordinate members of a great state, as slaves are members of a household. Again it happens that many states, forming each an independent body, may have one head. For political are not like natural bodies, to only one of which the same head can belong. Whereas in the former, one person can exercise the function of the head to many distinct bodies. As a certain proof of which, when the reigning house has become extinct, the sovereign power returns to the hands of the nation. So it may happen, that many states may be connected together by the closest federal union, which Strabo, in more places than one calls a system, and yet each retain the condition of a perfect, individual state, which has been observed by Aristotle and others in different parts of their writings. Therefore the common subject of sovereign power is the state, taken in the sense already explained. The proper subject is one or more persons according to the laws and customs of each nation. This is called by Galen in the sixth book DE PLACITIS HIPPOCRAT ET PLATONIS, the first power of the state.

**VIII**. And here is the proper place for refuting the opinion of those, who maintain that, every where and without exception, the sovereign power is vested in the people, so that they have a right to restrain and punish kings for an abuse of their power. However there is no man of sober wisdom, who does not see the incalculable mischiefs, which such opinions have occasioned, and may still occasion; and upon the following grounds they may be refuted.

From the Jewish, as well as the Roman Law, it appears that any one might engage himself in private servitude to whom he pleased. Now if an individual may do so, why may not a whole people, for the benefit of better government and more certain protection, completely transfer their sovereign rights to one or more persons, without reserving any portion to themselves? Neither can it be alleged that such a thing is not to be presumed, for the question is not, what is to be presumed in a doubtful case, but what may lawfully be done. Nor is it any more to the purpose to object to the inconveniences, which may, and actually do arise from a people's thus surrendering their rights. For it is not in the power of man to devise any form of government free from imperfections and dangers. As a dramatic writer says, I you must either take these advantages with those imperfections, or resign your pretensions to both."

Now as there are different ways of, living, some of a worse, and some of a better kind, left to the choice of every individual; so a nation, "under certain circumstances, WHEN for instance, the succession to the throne is extinct, or the throne has by any other means become vacant," may chuse what form of government she pleases. Nor is this right to be measured by the excellence of this or that form of government, on which there may be varieties of opinion, but by the will of the people.

There may be many reasons indeed why a people may entirely relinquish their rights, and surrender them to another: for instance, they may have no other means of securing themselves from the danger of immediate destruction, or under the pressure of famine it may be the only way, through which they can procure support. For if the Campanians, formerly, when reduced by necessity surrendered themselves to the Roman people in the following terms: — "Senators of Rome, we consign to your dominion the people of Campania, and the city of Capua, our lands, our temples, and all things both divine and human," and if another people as Appian relates, offered to submit to the Romans, and were refused, what is there to prevent any nation from submitting in the same manner to one powerful sovereign? It may also happen that a master of a family, having large possessions, will suffer no one to reside upon them on any other terms, or an owner, having many slaves, may give them their liberty upon condition of their doing certain services, and paying certain rents; of which examples may be produced. Thus Tacitus, speaking of the German slaves, says, "Each has his own separate habitation, and his own household to govern. The master considers him as a tenant, bound to pay a certain rent in corn, cattle, and wearing apparel. And this is the utmost extent of his servitude."

Aristotle, in describing the requisites, which fit men for servitude, says, that 'those men, whose powers are chiefly confined to the body, and whose principal excellence consists in affording bodily service, are naturally slaves, because it is their interest to be so." In the same manner some nations are of such a disposition that they are more calculated to obey than to govern, which seems to have been the opinion which the Cappadocians held of themselves, who when the Romans offered them a popular government, refused to accept it, because the nation they said could not exist in safety without a king. Thus Philostratus in the life of Apollonius, says, that it was foolish to offer liberty to the Thracians, the Mysians, and the Getae, which they were not capable of enjoying. The example of nations, who have for many ages lived happily under a kingly government, has induced many to give the preference to that form. Livy says, that the cities under Eumenes would not have changed their condition for that of any free state whatsoever. And sometimes a state is so situated, that it seems impossible it can preserve its peace and existence, without submitting to the absolute government of a single person, which many wise men thought to be the case with the Roman Republic in the time of Augustus Caesar. From these, and causes like these it not only may, but generally does happen, that men, as Cicero observes in the second book of his offices, willingly submit to the supreme authority of another.

Now as property may be acquired by what has been already styled just war, by the same means the rights of sovereignty may be acquired. Nor is the term sovereignty here meant to be applied to monarchy alone, but to government by nobles, from any share in which the people are excluded. For there never was any government so purely popular, as not to require the exclusion of the poor, of strangers, women, and minors from the public councils. Some states have other nations under them, no less dependent upon their will, than subjects upon that of their sovereign princes. From whence arose that question, Are the Collatine people in their own power? And the Campanians, when they submitted to the Romans, are said to have passed under a foreign dominion. In the same manner Acarnania and Amphilochia are said to have been under the dominion of the Aetolians; Peraea and Caunus under that of the Rhodians; and Pydna was ceded by Philip to the Olynthians. And those towns, that had been under the Spartans, when they were delivered from their dominion, received the name of the free Laconians. The city of Cotyora is said by Xenophon to have belonged to the people of Sinope. Nice in Italy, according to Strabo, was adjudged to the people of Marseilles; and the island of Pithecusa to the Neapolitans. We find in Frontinus, that the towns of Calati and Caudium with their territories were adjudged, the one to the colony of Capua, and the other to that of Beneventum. Otho, as Tacitus relates, gave the cities of the Moors to the Province of Baetia. None of these instances, any more than the cessions of other conquered countries could be admitted, if it were a received rule that the rights of sovereigns are under the controul and direction of subjects.

Now it is plain both from sacred and profane history, that there are kings, who are not subject to the controul of the people in their collective body; God addressing the people of Israel, says, if thou shalt say, "I will place a king over me"; and to Samuel "Shew them the manner of the king, who shall reign over them." Hence the King is said to be anointed over the people, over the inheritance of the Lord, over Israel. Solomon is styled King over all Israel. Thus David gives thanks to God, for subduing the people under him. And Christ says, 'the Kings of the nations bear rule over them." There is a well known passage in Horace, "Powerful sovereigns reign over their own subjects, and the supreme being over sovereigns themselves." Seneca thus describes the three forms of government, "Sometimes the supreme leading men of the state, sometimes this power of the people, and dominion over the people themselves is vested in a single person." Of the last description are those, who, as Plutarch says, exercise authority not according to the laws, but over the laws. And in Herodutus, Otanes describes a monarch as one whose acts are not subject to controul. Dion Prusaeensis also and Pausanias define a monarchy in the same terms.

Aristotle says there are some kings, who have the same right, which the nation elsewhere possesses over persons and property. Thus when the Roman Princes began to exercise regal power, the people it was said had transferred all their own personal sovereignty to them, which gave rise to the saying of Marcus Antoninus the Philosopher, that no one but God alone can be judge of the Prince. Dion. L. liii. speaking of such a prince, says, "he is perfectly master of his own actions, to do whatever he pleases, and cannot be obliged to do any thing against his will." Such anciently was the power of the Inachidae established at Argos in Greece. For in the Greek Tragedy of the Suppliants, Aeschylus has introduced the people thus addressing the King: "You are the state, you the people; you the court from which there is no appeal, you preside over the altars, and regulate all affairs by your supreme will." King Theseus himself in Euripides speaks in very different terms of the Athenian Republic; "The city is not governed by one man, but in a popular form, by an annual succession of magistrates." For according to Plutarch's explanation, Theseus was the general in war, and the guardian of the laws; but in other respects nothing more than a citizen. So that they who are limited by popular controul are improperly called kings. Thus after the time of Lycurgus, and more particularly after the institution of the Ephori, the Kings of the Lacedaemonians are said by Polybius, Plutarch, and Cornelius Nepos, to have been Kings more in name than in reality. An example which was followed by the rest of Greece. Thus Pausanias says of the Argives to the Corinthians, "The Argives from their love of equality have reduced their kingly power very low; so that they have left the posterity of Cisus nothing more than the shadow of Kings." Aristotle denies such to be proper forms of government, because they constitute only a part of an Aristocracy or Democracy.

Examples also may be found of nations, who have not been under a perpetual regal form, but only for a time under a government exempt from popular controul. Such was the power of the Amimonians among the Cnidians, and of the Dictators in the early periods of the Roman history, when there was no appeal to the people, from whence Livy says, the will of the Dictator was observed as a law. Indeed they found this submission the only remedy against imminent danger, and in the words of Cicero, the Dictatorship possessed all the strength of royal power.

It will not be difficult to refute the arguments brought in favour of the contrary opinion. For in the first place the assertion that the constituent always retains a controul over the sovereign power, which he has contributed to establish, is only true in those cases where the continuance and existence of that power depends upon the will and pleasure of the constituent: but not in cases where the power, though it might derive its origin from that constituent, becomes a necessary and fundamental part of the established law. Of this nature is that authority to which a woman submits when she gives herself to a husband. Valentinian the Emperor, when the soldiers who had raised him to the throne, made a demand of which he did not approve, replied; "Soldiers, your election of me for your emperor was your own voluntary choice; but since you have elected me, it depends upon my pleasure to grant your request. It becomes you to obey as subjects, and me to consider what is proper to be done."

Nor is the assumption true, that all kings are made by the people, as may be plainly seen from the instances adduced above, of an owner admitting strangers to reside upon his demesnes on condition of their obedience, and of nations submitting by right of conquest. Another argument is derived from a saying of the Philosophers, that all power is conferred for the benefit of the governed and not of the governing party. Hence from the nobleness of the end, it is supposed to follow, that subjects have a superiority over the sovereign. But it is not universally true, that all power is conferred for the benefit of the party governed. For some powers are conferred for the sake of the governor, as the right of a master over a slave, in which the advantage of the latter is only a contingent and adventitious circumstance. In the same manner the gain of a Physician is to reward him for his labour; and not merely to promote the good of his art. There are other kinds of authority established for the benefit of both parties, as for instance, the authority of a husband over his wife. Certain governments also, as those which are gained by right of conquest, may be established for the benefit of the sovereign; and yet convey no idea of tyranny, a word which in its original signification, implied nothing of arbitrary power or injustice, but only the government or authority of a Prince. Again, some governments may be formed for the advantage both of subjects and sovereign, as when a people, unable to defend themselves, put themselves under the protection and dominion of any powerful king. Yet it is not to be denied, but that in most governments the good of the subject is the chief object which is regarded: and that what Cicero has said after Herodotus and Herodotus after Hesiod, is true, that Kings were appointed in order that men might enjoy complete justice.

Now this admission by no means goes to establish the inference that kings are amenable to the people. For though guardianships were invented for the benefit of wards, yet the guardian has a right to authority over the ward. Nor, though a guardian may for mismanagement be removed from his trust, does it follow that a king may for the same reason be deposed. The cases are quite different, the guardian has a superior to judge him; but in governments, as there must be some dernier resort, it must be vested either in an individual, or in some public body, whose misconduct, as there is no superior tribunal before which they can be called, God declares that he himself will judge. He either punishes their offences, should he deem it necessary; or permits them for the chastisement of his people.

This is well expressed by Tacitus: he says, "you should bear with the rapacity or luxury of rulers, as you would bear with drought, or excessive rains, or any other calamities of nature.

For as long as men exist there will be faults and imperfections; but these are not of uninterrupted continuance, and they are often repaired by he succession of better times." And Marcus Aurelius speaking of subordinate magistrates, said, that they were under the controul of the sovereign: but that the sovereign was amenable to God. There is a remarkable passage in Gregory of Tours, where that Bishop thus addresses the King of France, " If any of us, Sir, should transgress the bounds of justice, he may be punished by you. But if you exceed them, who can call you to account? For when we address you, you may hear us if you please; but if you will not, who can judge you, except him, who has declared himself to be righteousness?" Among the maxims of the Essenes, Porphyry cites a passage, that "no one can reign without the special appointment of divine providence." Irenaeus has expressed this well, " Kings are appointed by him at whose command men are created; and their appointment is suited to the condition of those, whom they are called to govern.' There is the same thought in the Constitutions of Clement, 'You shall fear the King, for he is of the Lord's appointment."

Nor is it an objection to what has been said, that some nations have been punished for the offences of their kings; for this does not happen, because they forbear to restrain their kings, but because they seem to give, at least a tacit consent to their vices, or perhaps, without respect to this, God may use that sovereign power which he has over the life and death of every man to inflict a punishment upon the king by depriving him of his subjects.

**IX**. There are some who frame an imaginary kind of mutual subjection, by which the people are bound to obey the king, as long as he governs well; but his government is subject to their inspection and controul. If they were to say that his duty to the sovereign does not oblige any one to do an act manifestly unjust and repugnant to the law of God; they would say nothing but what is true and universally admitted, but this by no means includes a right to any controul over the Prince's conduct in his lawful government. But if any people had the opportunity of dividing the sovereign power with the king, the privileges of the one, and the prerogatives of the other ought to be defined by certain bounds, which might easily be known, according to the difference of places, persons, or circumstances.

Now the supposed good or evil of any act, especially in political matters which admit of great variety of opinions and much discussion, is not a sufficient mark to ascertain these bounds. From whence the greatest confusion must follow, if under pretence of promoting good or averting evil measures, the people might struggle for the Prince's jurisdiction: a turbulent state of affairs, which no sober minded people ever wished to experience.

**X**. After refuting false opinions, it remains to apply some cautions, which may point out the way to ascertain correctly the person to whom sovereign power, in every state, of right belongs. The first caution necessary is to avoid being deceived by ambiguous terms, or appearances foreign to the real subject. For instance, among the Latins, although the terms PRINCIPALITY and KINGDOM are generally opposed to each other, when Caesar says, that the father of Vercingetorix held the principality of Gaul, and was put to death for aiming at sovereign power; and when Piso, in Tacitus calls Germanicus the son of a Roman Prince, not of a Parthian King; and when Suetonius says, that Caligula was on the point of converting the power of a prince into that of a king; and Velleius asserts that Maroboduus not contented with the authority of a prince over voluntary adherents and dependen s, was grasping in his mind at regal power; yet we find these terms though in reality very distinct were often confounded. For the Lacedaemonian chiefs, the descendants of Hercules, though subject to the controul of the Ephori, were nevertheless called kings: and Tacitus says, that among the ancient Germans there were kings, who governed more by the influence of persuasion than by the authority of power. Livy too, speaking of king Evander, describes him as reigning more by personal authority than by his regal power; and Aristotle, Polybius, and Diodorus give the names of Kings to the Suffetes or judges of the Carthaginians. In the same manner Solinus also calls Hanno King of the Carthaginians. Strabo speaks of Scepsis in Troas, that having incorporated the Milesians into the state, it formed itself into a Democracy, leaving the descendants of the ancient kings the title, and something of the dignity of kings.

On the other hand, the Roman emperors, after they had exercised openly, and without any disguise, a most absolute monarchical power, were notwithstanding called Princes. And in some popular states the chief magistrates are graced with ensigns of royalty.

Again the states general, that is the convention of those who represent the people, divided into classes according to Gunther, consist of three orders, which are the Prelates, the Nobles, and Deputies of large towns. In some places, they serve as a greater council to the king, to communicate to him the complaints of his people, which might otherwise be kept from his cars; leaving him at the same time full liberty to exercise his own discretion upon the matters so communicated. But in other places they form a body with power to inquire into the prince's measures, and to make laws.

Many think that in order to know whether a prince be sovereign or not, it is proper to inquire whether his title to the crown is by election or inheritance. For they maintain that hereditary monarchies alone are sovereign. But this cannot be received as a general criterion. For sovereignty consists not merely in the TITLE to the throne, which only implies that the successor has a right to all the privileges and prerogatives that his ancestors enjoyed, but it by no means affects the nature or extent of his powers. For right of election conveys all the powers, which the first election or appointment conferred. Among the Lacedaemonians the crown was hereditary even after the institution of the Ephori. And Aristotle describing the chief power of such a state, says, "Of these kingdoms, some are hereditary, and others elective." In the heroic times most of the kingdoms in Greece were of this description, as we are informed by Thucydides The Roman empire, on the contrary, even after the power of the Senate and people was abolished, was given or confirmed by election.

**XI**. Another caution is necessary. For to inquire into the matter of a right is not the same thing as to examine the nature of its tenure. A distinction which takes place not only in corporeal but in incorporeal possessions. For a right of passage or carriage through a ground is no less a right than that which entitles a man to the possession of the land itself. Now some hold these privileges by a full right of property, some by an usufructuary, and others by a temporary right. Thus the Roman Dictator had sovereign power by a temporary right. In the same manner kings, both those who are the first of their line elected to the throne, and those who succeed them in the lawful order, enjoy an usufructuary right, or inalienable right. But some sovereigns hold their power by a plenary right of property; when for instance it comes into their possession by the right of lawful conquest, or when a people, to avoid greater evils, make an unqualified surrender of themselves and their rights into their hands.

The opinion of those can never be assented to, who say that the power of the Dictator was not sovereign, because it was not permanent. For in the moral world the nature of things is known from their operations. The powers attended with equal effects are entitled to equal names. Now the Dictator for the time being performed all acts with the same authority as the most absolute sovereign; nor could any other power annul his acts. The permanence therefore of uncertainty alters no the nature of a right, although it would undoubtedly abridge its dignity, and diminish its spelndour.

[**Translator's note:** The translation proceeds from hence to the second book of the original, which seems to follow this part without any material break in the chain of argument: the intermediate sections relating to instances in the Roman Republic, which do not directly apply to the practice of modern governments.]

# BOOK II

## CHAPTER 1: DEFENSE OF PERSON AND PROPERTY

*Causes of War — Defence of person and property — What are called justifiable causes of war — Justifiable causes of War are Defence, recovery of one's property or debt, or the punishment of offences committed War for defence of life, justifiable, and lawful — This kind of war lawful against an aggressor only — The danger must be present and real, not an imaginary danger — Lawful to kill any one attempting to maim one's person, or violate one's chastity — Occasions where this right may be lawfully waved — This right to be waved particularly with respect to the person of the Sovereign, which is sacred and inviolable — Homicide in defence of one's property allowed by the law of nature — How far homicides permitted by the law of Moses — Self-defence in public war — Not lawful to attack any power solely on account of its increasing greatness — The hostile measures of an aggressor, not to be justified on the plea of self-defence.*

**I**. THE causes of war by which are meant the justifiable causes, are now to be considered. For in some cases motives of interest operate distinctly from motives of justice. Polybius accurately distinguishes these motives from each other, and from the beginning of the war, or that which gave occasion to the first acts of hostility; as was he case when Ascanius wounded the stag, which gave rise to the war between Turnus and Aeneas. But though here is an actual distinction between the justifiable causes, he pretexts, and the beginning of war; yet the terms used to express them are often confounded. For what we call justifiable causes, Livy, in the speech which he as put into the mouth of the Rhodians, calls beginnings. he Rhodian deputies said, "You Romans profess to believe that your wars are successful, because they are just: or do you boast so much of their victorious issue, as of he just principles, upon which you make them.".

The principal drift of our argument rests upon these justifiable causes, to which the sentiment of Coriolanus in Dionysius of Halicarnassus, particularly applies, he says, "in the first place, I beseech you to consider how you may find pious and just pretexts for the war." And Demosthenes in his second Olynthiac, makes a similar observation, "I think, *says he*, that as in a ship, or house, or any other fabric, the lowest parts ought to be the strongest; so in all political measures the motives and pretexts ought to be laid deeply in the principles of truth and justice." The following language of Dion Cassius is no less applicable to the question. "Justice must be made the principal ground of our actions. For with such support there is the best hope of success to our arms. But without that, any point which may be gained for the moment has no firm ground to rest upon." To which may be added, the words of Cicero, who maintains those wars to be unjust, which are made without sufficient cause. And in another place, he reproves Crassus for having intended to pass the Euphrates, when there was no cause of war. Which is no less true of public than of private wars. Hence come the complaints of Seneca, "Why do we restrain homicide, and the murder of individuals, but glory in the crime of slaughter, which destroys whole nations? Avarice and cruelty know not any bounds. By decrees of the Senate, and of the people cruel acts are authorized, and measures, which are pursued by order of the state, are forbidden to individuals." Wars indeed undertaken by public authority are attended with certain effects of right, and have the sanction of opinion in their favour. But they are not the less criminal, when made without just cause. For which reason Alexander was not improperly styled a robber by the Scythian ambassadors, as may be seen in Quintus Curtius. Seneca and Lucan give him the same appellation; the Indian sages call him a madman; and a pirate once presumed to rank him with his own class. Justin speaks of Philip in the same terms, who, *says he*, in deciding a dispute between two rival kings, stripped both of their dominions with all the treachery and violence of a robber. Augustin has a pertinent remark on this subject. He says, what are unjustly acquired dominions, but the spoils of robbery? In the same strain, Lactantius says, "Men, captivated with the appearances of vain glory, give the names of virtues to their crimes." Injury, or the prevention of injury forms the only justifiable cause of war. "And, *in the language of the same Augustin*, all the evil consequences of war are to be laid at the door of the aggressor." Thus the Roman Herald in a declaration of war makes a solemn appeal against the aggressor, as having violated the laws of nations, and refused proper satisfaction.

**II.** The grounds of war are as numerous as those of judicial actions. For where the power of law ceases, there war begins. Now there are methods in law to prevent intended injuries, as well as actions for those actually committed. For CIVIL INJURIES various methods of redress, or prevention are appointed by the law; and by the same power securities are provided to prevent the commission of crimes and misdemeanors. In civil cases, the party aggrieved may recover damages for the injuries sustained; and in crimes, which are offences against the public, the aggressor must submit to actual punishment. Plato, in his ninth book on laws, very properly makes the same distinction, as Homer had done before him.

Now reparation or indemnity relates to what either does or did belong to us; which gives rise to real and personal actions. These ascertain our right to the damages, which are our due, either from an agreement, or from an injury received. A right which is termed in law a right by contract, or injury. Crimes, which are offences against society, are prosecuted by indictment, that is by an accusation in the name of the sovereign.

The justifiable causes generally assigned for war are three, defence, indemnity, and punishment, all which are comprised in the declaration of Camillus against the Gauls, enumerating all things, which it is right to defend, to recover, and the encroachment on which it is right to punish.

There is an omission in this enumeration, unless the word recover be taken in its most extensive sense. For recovering by war what we have lost, includes indemnity for the past, as well as the prosecution of our claim to a debt. Plato has not omitted to notice this distinction, for he has said, "that wars are made to punish not only oppression or robbery, but also fraud and deception." With whom Seneca agrees; for to command payment of what you owe, he calls, "an equitable sentence, stamped with the authority of the law of nations." Indeed the form which was prescribed for the Roman heralds to use in declarations of war, bears exactly the same import. For therein the aggressor is charged with having neither given, paid, nor done what was due. Sallust in one of his fragments, has made a Tribune, in his harangue to the people, say, "As a final settlement of all discussion; I demand restitution according to the law of nations."

St. Augustin, in defining those to be just wars, which are made to avenge injuries has taken the word avenge in a general sense of removing and preventing, as well as punishing aggressions. This appears to be his meaning from the following sentence of the passage, in which he does not enumerate the particular acts, which amount to injury, but adds, by way of illustration, that "the state or nation, which has neglected to punish the aggressions of its own subjects, or to make reparation for the losses occasioned by those aggressions, is a proper object of hostility and attack." Prompted by this natural knowledge of right and wrong, the Indian King, as we are informed by Diodorus, accused Semiramis of having commenced war against him without having received any injury, Thus the Romans expostulated with the Senones, that they ought not to attack a people who had given them no provocation. Aristotle in the second book and second chapter of his Analytics, says, war generally is made upon those who have first done an injury. Quintus Curtius describes the Abian Scythians, as the best acquainted with the principles of justice of any of the Barbarians. For they declined having recourse to arm; unless provoked by aggression. A just cause then of war is an injury, which though not actually committed, threatens our persons or property with danger.

**III.** It has already been proved that when our lives are threatened with immediate danger, it is lawful to kill the aggressor, if the danger cannot otherwise be avoided: an instance, as it has been shewn, on which the justice of private war rests. We must observe that this kind of defence derives its origin from the principle of self. preservation, which nature has given to every living creature, and not from the injustice or misconduct of the aggressor. Wherefore though he may be clear of guilt, as for instance a soldier in actual service, mistaking my person for that of another, or a madman in his frenzy, or a man walking in his sleep, none of these cases deprive me of the right of self-defence against those per. sons. For I am not bound to submit to the danger or mischief intended, any more than to expose myself to the attacks of a wild beast.

**IV**. It admits of some doubt, whether those, who unintentionally obstruct our defence, or escape, which are necessary to our preservation, may be lawfully maimed or killed. There are some, even Theologians, who think they may. And, certainly if we look to the law of nature alone, according to its principles, our own preservation should have much more weight with us, than the welfare of society. But the law of charity, especially the evangelical law, which has put our neighbour upon a level with ourselves, does not permit it.

Thomas Aquinas, if taken in a right sense, has justly observed, that in actual self-defence no man can be said to be purposely killed. Indeed, it may some times happen that there is no other way for a person to save himself, than by designedly doing an act, by which the death of an aggressor must inevitably ensue. Yet here the death of any one was not the primary object intended, but employed as the only means of security, which the moment supplied. Still it is better for the party assaulted, if he can safely do it, to repel or disable the aggressor than to shed his blood.

**V**. The danger must be immediate, which is one necessary point. Though it must be confessed, that when an assailant seizes any weapon with an apparent intention to kill me I have a right to anticipate and prevent the danger. For in the moral as well as the natural system of things, there is no point without some breadth. But they are themselves much mistaken, and mislead others, who maintain that any degree of fear ought, to be a ground for killing another, to prevent his SUPPOSED intention. It is a very just observation made by Cicero in his first book of Offices, that many wrongs proceed from fear; as when the person, who intends to hurt another, apprehends some danger to himself unless he tool, that method. Clearchus, in Xenophon, says, I have known some men, who partly through misrepresentation, and partly through suspicion, dreading one another, in order to prevent the supposed intentions of their adversaries, have committed the most enormous cruelties against those who neither designed, nor wished them any harm.

Cato in his speech for the Rhodians, says, "Are we to prevent them by doing first, what we say they intended to do to us?" On this subject there is a remarkable passage in Aulus Gellius, "When a Gladiator prepares to enter the lists for combat, such is his lot that he must either kill his adversary, or be killed himself. But the life of man is not circumscribed by the hard terms of such an over-ruling necessity, as to oblige him to do an injury to prevent him from receiving one." Quintilian has quoted a passage from Cicero, wherein the orator asks, "Whoever made such a decision, or to whom could such a point be yielded without the most imminent danger, that you have a right to kill the person, by whom you say, you fear that you shall afterwards be killed yourself?" To which this passage of Euripides, may be applied, "If your husband, as you say, intended to have killed you, you ought to have waited, till he actually did make the attempt." Conformably to which Thucydides, in the first book of his history, has expressed himself in the following terms, " The issue of war is uncertain, nor ought we to be so far transported by our fears, as to engage in immediate and open hostilities." The same writer too in his luminous description of the dangerous factions, that had arisen in the Grecian states, condemns the approbation bestowed on the person, that injured or destroyed another from whom he himself apprehended injury or destruction."

Livy says, "Men, to guard against their alarms, make themselves objects of terror; averting the danger from their own heads, by imposing upon others the necessity of either doing or suffering the evil which they them. selves fear." Vibius asked a person, that appeared armed in the forum, " Who gave you permission to shew your fear in this manner?" A question not inapplicable to the present subject, and much commended by Quintilian. Livia also in Dion says, that great infamy redounds to those, who by anticipation perpetrate the criminal act, which they fear.

Now if any one intend no immediate violence, but is found to have formed a conspiracy to destroy me by assassination, or poison, or by false accusation, perjury, or suborned witnesses, I have no right to kill him. For my knowledge of the danger may prevent it. Or even if it were evident that I could not avoid the danger without killing him; this would not establish my right to do so. For there is every presumption that my knowing it will lead me to apply for the legal remedies of prevention.

**VI.** and **VII.** The next thing to be considered is, what must be said upon the mutilation of a limb. Now, as the loss of a limb, especially that of a principal limb in the body, is a grievous detriment, and nearly equal to the loss of life, to which may be added the probability of death ensuing from such a calamity; the lawfulness of killing any one, who makes such an attempt, if the danger cannot otherwise be avoided, scarce admits of a doubt. Neither is there any more difficulty in allowing the same right for the personal defence of chastity, the preservation of which, both in the common estimation of men, and by the divine law, is deemed of equal value with life itself. We have an example of this in Cicero, Quintilian, and Plutarch, in the person of one of Marius's tribunes, who was killed by a soldier. Among the actions of women, who have defended themselves. Heliodorus records that of Heraclea, which he calls a just defence of her injured honour.

**VIII.** Though some, as it has been already said, admit the lawfulness of killing the person, who attempts with open violence to destroy one's life, yet they deem it more commendable to spare the life of another, even at the hazard of one's own. Yet to persons, in whose preservation the public interest is involved, they will grant an exemption from this rule of forbearance. Indeed it seems unsafe to impose upon ANY, whose lives are of importance to others, a rule of forebearance so contrary to all the principles of all law. This exemption therefore must be allowed to all vested with any public office, which makes them responsible for the safety of others; as the generals who conduct armies, or the rulers of the state, and many others in similar situations; to whom may be applied the lines of Lucan — "When the lives and safety of so many nations depend upon yours, and so great a portion of the world has chosen you for its head; it is cruelty to expose yourself willfully to death."

**IX.** On the other hand it may happen, that the aggressor may be one whose person is rendered sacred and inviolable by all divine, human, and natural laws; which is the case with respect to the person of the Sovereign. For the law of nature regards not only the principles of STRICT JUSTICE, but comprises other virtues also, as temperance, fortitude, and discretion, making the observance of them in certain cases, binding as well as honourable. To observe these we are bound also by the law of charity.

Nor is the truth of this argument at all weakened by what Vasquez has advanced, who maintains that the Sovereign who attempts the life of an individual loses, in reality, the character of Sovereign: a doctrine fraught with equal absurdity and danger. For sovereignty cannot any more than property be forfeited by any particular act of delinquency; unless it has been previously and expressly so enacted by the fundamental laws of the state, For such a rule of forfeiture, which would be productive of universal anarchy and confusion, never has been, or ever will be established among any civilized people. For the maxim, "that all government is framed for the benefit of the subject and not of the Sovereign," which Vasquez and many other writers lay down as a fundamental law, though it may be generally true in theory, is by no means applicable to the question. For a thing loses not its existence, by losing some part of its utility, Nor is there sufficient consistency in his observation, that every individual desires the safety of the commonwealth on his own account, and therefore every one ought to prefer his own safety to that of the whole state. For we wish for the public welfare not on our own account alone, but also for the sake of others.

The opinion of those who think that friendship arises from necessity alone, is rejected, as false, by the more sound Philosophers; as we feel a spontaneous and natural inclination towards friendly intercourse. Charity indeed often persuades, and in some instances commands us to prefer the good of many to our own single advantage. To which the following passage from Seneca is very applicable. "It is not surprising that princes, and kings, or whatever name the guardians of the public welfare may bear, should be loved with a veneration and affection, far beyond those of private friendship. For all men of sober judgment, and enlarged information deem the public interest of higher moment than their own. Their attachment therefore must be warmest to the person on whom the well being and prosperity of the state depends." And to the same effect, St. Ambrose in his third book of Offices, says, "every man feels a greater delight in averting public than private danger." Seneca, the writer already quoted, produces two instances, the one of Callistratus at Athens, and the other of Rutilius at Rome, who refused to be restored from banishment thinking it better for two individuals to suffer hardship, than for the public to be plunged into calamities.

[**Translator's note:** The tenth section is omitted in the translation, as the subject of Christian forbearance of which it treats, has already been discussed in the preceding book.]

**XI**. The next object to be considered, relates to injuries affecting our property. In strict justice, it cannot be denied that we have a right to kill a robber, if such a step is inevitably necessary to the preservation of our property. For the difference between the value of life and property is overbalanced by the horror which a robber excites, and by the favourable inclination felt by all men towards the injured and innocent. From whence it follows, that regarding that right alone, a robber may be wounded or killed in his flight with the property, if it -cannot otherwise be recovered. Demosthenes in his speech against Aristocrates, exclaims, "By all that is ,sacred, is it not a dreadful and open violation of law, not only of written law, but of that law which is the unwritten rule of all men, to be debarred from the right of using force against the robber as well as against the ,enemy; who is plundering your property?" Nor is it forbidden by the precepts of charity, apart from all consideration of divine and human law, unless where the property is of little value, and beneath notice; an exception, which some writers have very properly added.

**XII**. The sense of the Jewish law on this point is now to be considered. The old law of Solon, to which Demosthenes, in his speech against Timocrates, appeals, agrees with it. From hence the substance of the TWELVE TABLES, and Plato's maxim in his ninth book of laws were taken. For they all agree in making a distinction between a thief who steals by day, and the robber, who commits the act by night; though they differ about the REASON of this distinction. Some think this distinction arises from the difficulty of discerning by night, whether an aggressor comes with an intent to murder or steal, and therefore he ought to be treated as an assassin. Others think the distinction is made, because as it is difficult to know the person of the thief, there is less probability of recovering the goods. In neither case do the framers of laws seem to have considered the question in its proper light. Their evident intention is to prohibit the killing of any one, merely on account of our property; which would happen, for instance, by killing a thief in his flight in order to recover the goods he had stolen. But if our own lives are endangered, then we are allowed to avert the danger, even at the hazard of another's life. Nor is our having run into the danger any objection; provided it was done to preserve or to recover our goods, or to take the thief. For no imputation of guilt can attach to us in any of these cases, while we are employed in doing a lawful act, nor can it be said that we are doing wrong to another by exercising our own right.

The difference therefore made between a thief in the night and a thief in the day, arises from the difficulty of procuring sufficient evidence of the fact. So that if a thief is found killed, the person who says, that he was found by him with a destructive weapon, and killed by him in his own defence, will easily gain belief. For the Jewish law supposes this, when it treats of a thief in the act of piercing, or, as some translate it, with a stabbing instrument. This interpretation accords with the law of the twelve tables, which forbids any one to kill a thief in the day time, except he defend himself with a weapon. The presumption therefore against a thief in the night is that he defended himself in such a manner. Now the term weapon comprehends not only an instrument of iron, but as Caius interprets it is law, a club, or a stone. Ulpian on the other hand, speaking of a thief taken in the night, says that the person who kills him will incur no guilt, provided that in saving his property he could not spare his life, without en. dangering his own. There is a presumption, as it has been already observed, in favour of the person who has killed a thief taken in the night. But if there be evidence to prove, that the life of the person who killed the thief was in no danger; then the presumption in his favour fails, and the act amounts to murder.

The law of the twelve tables indeed required, that the person who took a thief either in the day time, or in the night, should make a noise that, if possible, the magistrates or neighbours might assemble to assist him and give evidence. But as such a concourse could more easily be assembled in the day time than in the night, as Ulpian observes upon the passage before quoted from Demosthenes, the affirmation of a person declaring the danger he was in during the night is more readily believed. To which an additional observation may be made, that, even under equal circumstances, the danger which happens by night can be less examined, and ascertained, and therefore is the more terrible. The Jewish law therefore, no less than the Roman, acting upon the same principle of tenderness forbids us to kill any one, who has taken our goods, unless for the preservation of our own lives.

[**Translator's note:** Sections XIII. XIV. and XV. of the original are omitted in the translation.]

**XVI**. What has been already said of the right of defending our persons and property, though regarding chiefly private war, may nevertheless be applied to public hostilities, allowing for the difference of circumstances. For private war may be considered as an instantaneous exercise of natural right, which ceases the moment that legal redress can be obtained. Now as public war can never take place, but where judicial remedies cease to exist, it is often protracted, and the spirit of hostility inflamed by the continued accession of losses and injuries. Besides, private war extends only to self-defence, whereas sovereign powers have a right not only to avert, but to punish wrongs. From whence they are authorised to prevent a remote as well as an immediate aggression. Though the suspicion of hostile intentions, on the part of another power, may not justify the commencement of actual war, yet it calls for measures of armed prevention, and will authorise indirect hostility. Points, which will be discussed in another place.

**XVII**. Some writers have advanced a doctrine which can never be admitted, maintaining that the law of nations authorises one power to commence hostilities against another, whose increasing greatness awakens her alarms. As a matter of expediency such a measure may be adopted, but the principles of justice can never be advanced in its favour. The causes which entitle a war to the denomination of just are somewhat different from those of expediency alone. But to maintain that the bare probability of some remote, or future annoyance from a neighbouring state affords a just ground of hostile aggression, is a doctrine repugnant to every principle of equity. Such however is the condition of human life, that no full security can be enjoyed. The only protection against uncertain fears must be sought, not from violence, but from the divine providence, and defensive precaution.

**XVIII**. There is another opinion, not more admissible maintaining that the hostile acts of an aggressor, may be considered in the light of defensive measures, because, say the advocates of this opinion, few people are content to proportion their revenge to the injuries they have received; bounds which in all probability the party aggrieved has exceeded, and therefore in return becomes himself the aggressor. Now the excess of retaliation cannot, any more than the fear of uncertain danger, give a colour of right to the first aggression, which may be illustrated by the case of a malefactor, who can have no right to wound or kill the officers of justice in their attempts to take him, urging as a plea that he feared the punishment would exceed the offense.

The first step, which an aggressor ought to take, should be an offer of indemnity to the injured party, by the arbitration of some independent and disinterested state. And if this mediation be rejected, then his war assumes the character of a just war. Thus Hezekiah when he had not stood to the engagements made by his ancestors, being threatened with an attack from the King of Assyria on that account, acknowledged his fault, and left it to the King to assign what penalty he should pay for the offence. After he had clone so, finding himself again attacked, relying on the justice of his cause, he opposed the enemy, and succeeded by the favour of God. Pontius the Samnite, after restoration of the prizes had been made to the Romans, and the promoter of the war delivered up into their hands, said, "We have now averted the wrath of heaven, which our violation of treaties had provoked. But the supreme being who was pleased to reduce us to the necessity of restoration, was not equally pleased with the pride of the Romans, who rejected our offer. What farther satisfaction do we owe to the Romans, or to Heaven, the arbiter of treaties? We do not shrink from submitting the measure of YOUR resentment, or of OUR punishment to the judgment of any people, or any individual." In the same manner, when the Thebans had offered the most equitable terms to the Lacedaemonians, who still rose higher in their demands, Aristides say, that the justice of the cause changed sides and passed from the Lacedaemonians to the Thebans.

## CHAPTER 2: THE GENERAL RIGHTS OF THINGS

*The general rights of things — Division of what is our own — The origin and progress of property — Some things impossible to be made the subject of property — The Sea of this nature, in its full extent, or in its principal parts — Unoccupied lands may become the property of individuals, unless they have been previously occupied by the people at large — Wild beasts, fishes, birds, may become the property of him who seizes them — In cases of necessity men have a right of using that which has already become the property of others — To sanction this indulgence, the necessity must be such that it cannot otherwise be avoided — This indulgence not allowed where the possessor is in an equal degree of necessity — The party thus supplying his wants from another's property, bound to make restitution whenever it is possible. The application of this principle to the practice of war — The right to use the property of another, provided that use be no way prejudicial to the owner — Hence the right to the use of running water — The right of passing through countries, and by rivers explained — An inquiry into the right of imposing duties on merchandise — The right of residing for a time in a foreign state — The right of exiles to reside in the dominions of a foreign state, provided they submit to its laws — In what manner the right of occupying waste places is to be understood — The right to certain articles necessary to the support of human society, and life — The general right of purchasing those articles at a reasonable price — The right to sell, not of equal force and extent — The right to those privileges which are promiscuously granted to foreigners — Inquiry whether it be lawful to contract with any people for the purchase of their productions on condition of their not selling the same to others.*

**I**. AMONG the causes assigned to justify war, we may reckon the commission of injury, particularly such as affects any thing which belongs to us. Now we establish this claim to any thing as our own either by a right COMMON to us as men, or acquired by us in our INDIVIDUAL capacity. But to begin with that which is the common right of all mankind; we may observe that it comprises what is called by legal authorities, Corporeal and Incorporeal rights.

Things corporeal are either unappropriated, or made the subjects of private property. Now the things unappropriated, are such that it may be either possible or impossible for them to be reduced to a state of private property. In order therefore to understand this more clearly, it will be necessary to take a survey of the origin of property.

**II** God gave to mankind in general, dominion overall the creatures of the earth, from the first creation of the world; a grant which was renewed upon the restoration of the world after the deluge. All things, as Justin says, formed a common stock for all mankind, as the inheritors of one general patrimony. From hence it happened, that every man seized to his own use or consumption what. ever he met with; a general exercise of a right, which supplied the place of private property. So that to deprive any one of what he had thus seized, became an act of injustice. Which Cicero has explained in his third book, on the bounds of good and evil, by comparing the world to a Theatre, in which the seats are common property, yet every spectator claims that which he occupies, for the time being, as his own. A state of affairs, which could not subsist but in the greatest simplicity of manners, and under the mutual forbearance and good-will of mankind. An example of a community of goods, arising from extreme simplicity of manners, may be seen in some nations of America, who for many ages have subsisted in this manner without inconvenience. The Essenes of old, furnished an example of men actuated by mutual affection and holding all things in common, a practice adopted by the primitive Christians at Jerusalem, and still prevailing among some of the religious orders. Man at his first origin, requiring no clothing, afforded a Proof of the simplicity of manners in which he had been formed. Yet perhaps, as Justin says of the Scythians, he might be considered as ignorant of vice rather than acquainted with virtue; Tacitus says, that in the early ages of the world, men lived free from the influence of evil passions, without reproach, and wickedness; and consequently without the restraints of punishment. In primitive times there appeared among mankind, according to Macrobius, a simplicity, ignorant of evil, and inexperienced in craft: a simplicity which in the book of Wisdom seems to be called integrity, and by the Apostle Paul simplicity in opposition to subtlety. Their sole employment was the worship of God, of which the tree of life was the symbol, as it is explained by the ancient Hebrews, whose opinion is confirmed by the Book of Revelation.

Men at that period subsisted upon the spontaneous productions of the ground: a state of simplicity to which they did not long adhere, but applied themselves to the invention of various arts, indicated by the tree of knowledge of good and evil, that is the knowledge of those things which may be either used properly, or abused; which Philo calls a middle kind of wisdom. In this view, Solomon says, God hath created men upright, that is, in simplicity, but they have sought out many inventions, or, in the language of Philo, they have inclined to subtlety. In the sixth oration of Dion Prusaeensis it is said, "the descendants have degenerated from the innocence of primitive times, contriving many subtle inventions no way conducive to the good of life; and using their strength not to promote justice, but to gratify their appetites." Agriculture and pasturage seem to have been the most ancient pursuits, which characterized the first brothers. Some distribution of things would necessarily follow these different states; and we are informed by holy writ, that the rivalry thus created ended in murder. At length men increasing in wickedness by their evil communications with each other, the race of Giants, that is of strong and violent men appeared, whom the Greeks denominate by a title, signifying those who make their own hands and strength the measure of justice.

The world in progress of time being cleared of this race by the deluge, the savage was succeeded by a softer and more sensual way of life, to which the use of wine proved subservient, being followed by all the evil consequences of intoxication. But the greatest breach in the harmony of men was made by ambition, which is considered in some measure, as the offspring of a noble mind. Its first and most eminent effects appeared in the attempt to raise the tower of Babel; the failure of which caused the dispersion of mankind, who took possession of different parts of the earth.

Still after this a community of lands for pasture, though not of flocks, prevailed among men. For the great extent of land was sufficient for the use of all occupants, as yet but few in number, without their incommoding each other. In the words of the Poet, it was deemed unlawful to fix a land mark on the plain, or to apportion it out in stated limits. But as men increased in numbers and their flocks in the same proportion, they could no longer with convenience enjoy the use of lands in common, and it became necessary to divide them into allotments for each family. Now in the hot countries of the East, wells would be objects of great importance, for the refreshment of their herds and flocks; so that in order to avoid strife and inconvenience, all would be anxious to have them as possessions of their own. These accounts we derive from sacred history, and they are found to agree with the opinions maintained upon this subject by Philosophers and Poets, who have described the community of goods, that prevailed in the early state of the world, and the distribution of property which afterwards took place. Hence a notion may be formed of the reason why men departed from the primeval state of holding all things in common, attaching the ideas of property, first to moveable and next to immovable things.

When the inhabitants of the earth began to acquire a taste for more delicate fare than the spontaneous productions of the ground, and to look for more commodious habitations than eaves, or the hollow of trees, and to long for more elegant cloathing than the skins of wild beasts, industry became necessary to supply those wants, and each individual began to apply his attention to some particular art. The distance of the places too, into which men were dispersed, prevented them from carrying the fruits of the earth to a common stock, and in the next place, the WANT of just principle and equitable kindness would destroy that equality which ought to subsist both in the labour of producing and consuming the necessaries of life.

At the same time, we learn how things passed from being held in common to a state of property. It was not by the act of the mind alone that this change took place. For men in that case could never know, what others intended to appropriate to their own use, so as to exclude the claim of every other pretender to the same; and many too might desire to possess the same thing. Property therefore must have been established either by express agreement, as by division, or by tacit consent, as by occupancy. For as soon as it was found inconvenient to hold things in common, before any division of lands had been established, it is natural to suppose it must have been generally agreed, that whatever any one had occupied should be accounted his own. Cicero, in the third book of his Offices says, it is admitted as an universal maxim, not repugnant to the principles of natural law, that every one should rather wish himself to enjoy the necessaries of life, than leave them for the acquisition of another. Which is supported by Quintilian, who says, if the condition of life be such, that whatever has fallen to the private use of any individual, becomes the property of such holder, it is evidently unjust to take away any thing which is possessed by such a right. And the ancients in styling Ceres a law-giver, and giving the name of Thesmophoria to her sacred rights, meant by this to signify that the division of lands had given birth to a new kind of right.

**III.** Notwithstanding the statements above made, it must be admitted that some things are impossible to be reduced to a state of property, of which the Sea affords us an instance both in its general extent, and in its principal branches. But as some are willing to make this concession with regard to individuals, but not with regard to nations, the position advanced in the beginning of this section may be proved from the following moral argument, that as in this ease the reason no longer subsists why men should hold all things in common, the practice ceases also. For the magnitude of the sea is such, as to be sufficient for the use of all nations, to allow them without inconvenience and prejudice to each other the right of fishing, sailing, or any other advantage which that element affords. The same may be said of air as common property, except that no one can use or enjoy it, without at the same time using the ground over which it passes or rests. So that the amusement of fowling cannot be followed, except by permission, without trespassing upon the lands of some owner, over which the birds fly.

The same appellation of COMMON may be given to the sand of the shore, which being incapable of cultivation, is left free to yield its inexhaustible supplies for the use of all.

There is a natural reason also, which renders the sea, considered in the view already taken, incapable of being made property: because occupancy can never subsist, but in things that can be confined to certain permanent bounds. From whence Thucydides gives the name of infinite space to unoccupied lands, and Isocrates speaking of that occupied by the Athenians calls it that which has been measured by us into allotted parts. But fluids, which cannot be limited or restrained, except they be contained within some other substance, cannot be occupied. Thus ponds, and lakes and rivers likewise, can only be made property as far as they are confined within certain banks. But the ocean as it is equal to, or larger than the earth, cannot be confined within the land: so that the ancients said the earth was bounded in by the sea like a girdle surrounding it. Nor can any imaginable division of it have been originally framed. For as the greatest part of it was unknown, it was impossible that nations far removed from each other could agree upon the bounds to be assigned to different parts.

Whatever therefore was the common property of all, and after a general division of all other things, retained its original state, could not be appropriated by division, but by occupancy. And the marks of distinction and separation by which its different parts were known, followed such appropriation.

**IV**. The next matters to be noticed are those things, which though not yet made property, may be reduced to that condition. Under this description come waste lands, desert islands, wild beasts, fishes, and birds. Now in these cases there are two things to be pointed out, which are a double kind of occupancy that may take place; the one in the name of the Sovereign, or of a whole people, the other by individuals, converting into private estates the lands which they have so occupied. The latter kind of individual property proceeds rather from assignment than from free occupancy. Yet any places that have been taken possession of in the name of a sovereign, or of a whole people, though not portioned out amongst individuals, are not to be considered as waste lands, but as the property of the first occupier, whether it be the King, or a whole people. Of this description are rivers, lakes, forests, and wild mountains.

**V**. As to wild beasts, fishes, and birds, it is to be observed that the sovereign of the respective lands, or waters where they are found, has a legal right to prohibit any one from taking them, and thereby acquiring a property in them. A prohibition extending to foreigner, as well as subjects. To foreigners; because by all the rules of moral law they owe obedience to the sovereign, for the time during which they reside in his territories. Nor is there any validity in the objection founded on the Roman Law, the Law of nature, or the Law of nations, which, it is said, declare such animals to be beasts of chance free to every one's hunting. For this is only true, where there is no civil law to interpose its prohibition; as the Roman law left many things in their primitive state, which by other nations were placed upon a very different footing. The deviations therefore from the state of nature, which have been established by the civil law, are ordained by every principle of natural justice to be obeyed by mankind. For although the civil law can enjoin nothing which the law of nature prohibits, nor prohibit any thing which it enjoins, yet it may circumscribe natural liberty, restraining what was before allowed; although the restraint should extend to the very acquisition of property, to which every man AT FIRST had a right by the law of nature.

**VI**. The next thing to be considered is the right, which men have to the common use of things, already appropriated; terms, in which at the first sight there appears to be some inconsistency, as it appears that the establishment of property has absorbed every right that sprung from a state of things held in common. But this is by no means the case. For the intention of those, who first introduce private property, must be taken into the account. And it was but reasonable to suppose, that in making this introduction of property, they would depart As little as possible from the original principles of natural equity. For if written laws are to be construed in a sense, approaching as nearly as possible to the laws of nature, much more so are those customs which are not fettered with the literal restrictions of written maxims. From hence it follows that in cases of extreme necessity, the original right of using things, as if they had remained in common, must be revived; because in all human laws, and consequently in the laws relating to property, the case of extreme necessity seems to form an exception.

Upon this principle is built the maxim that if in a voyage provisions begin to fail, the stock of every individual ought to be produced for common consumption; for the same reason a neighbouring house may be pulled down to stop the progress of a fire: or the cables or nets, in which a ship is entangled, may be cut, if it cannot otherwise be disengaged. Maxims, none of which were introduced by the civil law, but only explained by it according to the rules of natural equity.

Now among Theologians also it is a received opinion, that if in urgent distress, any one shall take from another what is absolutely necessary for the preservation of his own life, the act shall not be deemed a theft. A -rule not founded, as some allege, solely upon the law of charity, which obliges every possessor to apply some part of his wealth to relieve the needy; but upon the original division of lands among private owners, which was made with a reservation in favour of the primitive rights of nature. For if those who at first made the division had been asked their opinion upon this point, they would have given the same reason that has just been advanced. Necessity, says Seneca, the great protectress of human infirmity breaks through all human laws, and all those made in the spirit of human regulations. Cicero in his eleventh Philippic, says, that Cassius went into Syria, which might be considered as another's province, if men adhered to written laws, but if these were abolished, it would be considered as his own by the law of nature. In the sixth book and fourth chapter of Quintus Curtius, we find an observation, that in a common calamity every man looks to himself.

**VII**. Now this indulgence must be granted with precautions and restrictions, to prevent it from degenerating into licentiousness. And of these precautions, the first requires the distressed party to try every mode of obtaining relief, by an appeal to a magistrate, or by trying the effect of entreaty to prevail upon the owner to grant what is necessary for his pressing occasions. Plato allows any one to seek water from his neighbour's well, after having dug to a certain depth in his own without effect Solon limits the depth to forty cubits; upon which Plutarch remarks, that he intended by this to relieve necessity and difficulty, but not to encourage sloth. Xenophon in his answer to the Sinopians, in the fifth book of the expedition of Cyrus, says, "wherever we come, whether into a barbarous country or into any part of Greece, and find the people unwilling to afford us supplies, we take them, not through motives of wantonness, but from the compulsion of necessity."

**VIII**. In the next place this plea of necessity cannot be admitted, where the possessor is in an equal state of necessity himself. For under equal circumstances the owner has a better right to the use of his possessions. Though Lactantius maintains that it is no mark of folly to forbear thrusting another from the same plank in a shipwreck in order to save yourself. Because you have thereby avoided hurting another: a sin which is certainly a proof of wisdom to abstain from. Cicero, in the third book of his offices, asks this question, if a wise man, in danger of perishing with hunger, has not a right to take the provisions of another, who is good for nothing? To which he replies; By no means. For no one's life can be of such importance as to authorize the violation of that general rule of forbearance, by which the peace and safety of every individual are secured.

**IX**. In the third place, the party thus supplying his wants from the property of another, is bound to make restitution, or give an equivalent to the owner, whenever that is possible. There are some indeed, who deny this, upon the ground that no one is bound to give an indemnity for having exercised his own right. But strictly speaking, it was not a full and perfect right, which he exercised; but a kind of permission, arising out of a case of necessity, and existing no longer than while the necessity continued. For such a permissive right is only granted in order to preserve natural equity in opposition to the strict and churlish rigour of exclusive ownership.

**X**. Hence it may be inferred, that, in the prosecution of a just war, any power has a right to take possession of a neutral soil; if there be real grounds, and not imaginary fears for supposing the enemy intends to make himself master of the same, especially if the enemy's occupying it would be attended with imminent and irreparable mischief to that same power. But in this case the restriction is applied that nothing be taken but what is actually necessary to such precaution and security. Barely occupying the place is all that can be justified: leaving to the real owner the full enjoyment of all his rights, immunities, and jurisdiction, and all the productions of his soil. And this must be done too with the full intention of restoring the place to its lawful Sovereign, when. ever the necessity, for which it was occupied, may cease. The retaining of Enna, Livy says, was either an act of violence, or a necessary measure; by violence meaning the least departure from necessity. The Greeks, who were with Xenophon being in great want of ships, by Xenophon's own advice, seized upon those that were passing, still preserving the property untouched for the owners, supplying the sailors with provisions, and paying them wages. The principal right therefore, founded upon the original community of goods, remaining since the introduction of property, is that of necessity, which has just been discussed.

**XI**. There is another right, which is that of making use of the property of another, where such use is attended with no prejudice to the owner. For why, says Cicero, should not any one; when he can do it without injury to himself, allow another to share with him those advantages, which are useful to the receiver, and no way detrimental to the giver? Seneca therefore observes, that it is no favour to allow another to light his fire from your flame. And in the 7th book of Plutarch's Symposiacs, we find an observation, that when we have provisions more than sufficient for our own consumption it is wicked to destroy the remainder; or after supplying our own wants, to obstruct or destroy the springs of water; or after having finished our voyage, not to leave for other passengers the sea-marks, that have enabled us to steer our course.

**XII**. Upon the principles already established, a river, as such, is the property of that people, or of the sovereign of that people, through whose territories it flows. He may form quays, and buttresses upon that river, and to him all the produce of it belongs. But the same river, as a running water, still remains common to all to draw or drink it. Ovid introduces Latona thus addressing the Lydians, "Why do you refuse water, the use of which is common?" where he calls water a public gift that is common to men, taking the word public in a more general sense than as applied to any PEOPLE, a meaning in which some things are said to be public by the law of nations. And in the same sense Virgil has asserted water to be free and open to all men.

**XIII**. It is upon the same foundation of common right, that a free passage through countries, rivers, or over any part of the sea, which belongs to some particular people, ought to be allowed to those, who require it for the necessary occasions of life; whether those occasions be in quest of settlements, after being driven from their own country, or to trade with a remote nation, or to recover by just war their lost possessions. The same reason prevails here as in the cases above named. Because property was originally introduced with a reservation of that use, which might be of general benefit, and not prejudicial to the interest of the owner: an intention evidently entertained by those, who first devised the separation of the bounteous gifts of the creator into private possessions. There is a remarkable instance of this in the Mosaic history, when the leader of the children of Israel required a free passage for that people, promising to the King of Edom, and to the King of the Amorites, that he would go by the highway, without setting a foot upon the soil of private possessions, and that the people should pay the price of everything, which they might have occasion to use. Upon these equitable terms being rejected, Moses was justified in making war upon the Amorites. Because, says Augustin, an inoffensive passage, a right interwoven with the very frame of human society, was refused. The Greeks under the command of Clearchus, said, "we are upon the way to our home, if no one interrupt us; but every attempt to molest us, we are, with the assistance of heaven, determined to avenge."

Not unlike this answer of the soldiers under Clearchus is the question put to the different nations of Thrace by Agesilaus, who desired to know whether they wished him to pass through their country as a friend, or as an enemy. When the Boeotians hesitated upon some propositions made to them by Lysander, he asked them whether they intended that he should pass with erected or inclined spears, meaning by the expression in a hostile or a quiet manner. We are informed by Tacitus, that the Batavians, as soon as they came near the camp at Bonn, sent a message to Herennius Gallus, importing that "they had no hostile design; that if not obstructed, they would march in a peaceable manner; but if they met with op. position they would cut their way sword in hand." When Cimon in carrying supplies to the Lacedaemonians, had marched with his troops through some part of the Corinthian district, the Corinthians expostulated upon his conduct as a violation of their territory, because he had done it without asking their leave, at the same time observing, that no one knocks at another man's door, or presumes to enter the house without obtaining the master's leave. To whom he replied, you never knocked at the gates of Cleone and Megara, but broke them down, believing, I suppose, that no right ought to withstand the force of the mighty.

Now between these two extremes there is a middle course, requiring a free passage to be first asked; the refusal of which will justify the application of force. Thus Agesilaus in his return from Asia when he had asked a passage of the King of the Macedonians, who answered that he would consider of it, said, you may consider, if you please, but we shall pass in the mean time,

The fears, which any power entertains from a multitude in arms passing through its territories, do not form such an exception as can do away the rule already laid down. For it is not proper or reasonable that the fears of one party should destroy the rights of another. Especially, as necessary precautions and securities may be used, such as those, for instance, of requiring that the troops shall pass without arms, or in small bodies; a promise which the Agrippinians made to the Germans, and, as we are informed by Strabo, the practice still prevails in the country of the Eleans. Another security may be found in providing garrisons at the expense of the party, to whom the passage is granted; or in giving hostages; the condition, which Seleucus demanded of Demetrius, for permitting him to remain within his territories. Nor is the fear of offending that power which is the object of attack, a sufficient pretext for refusing the passage of the troops to the state that is engaged in a just war. Nor is it a proper reason to assign for a refusal, to say that another passage may be found; as every other power might allege the same, and by this means the right of passage would be entirely defeated The request of a passage therefore, by the nearest and most commodious way, without doing injury and mischief, is a sufficient ground upon which it should be granted. It alters the case entirely, if the party making the request is engaged in unjust war, and is marching with the troops of a power hostile to the sovereign of that territory; for in this instance, a passage may be refused. For the sovereign has a right to attack that power in his own territory, and to oppose its march.

Now a free passage ought to be allowed not only to persons, but to merchandise. For no power has a right to prevent one nation from trading with another at a remote distance; a permission which for the interest of society should be maintained. Nor can it be said that any one is injured by it. For though he may be thereby deprived of an exclusive gain, yet the loss of what is not his due, as a MATTER OF RIGHT, can never be considered as a damage or the violation of a claim.

**XIV**. But it will form a subject of inquiry, whether the sovereign of the country has a right to impose duties on goods carried by land, or upon a river or upon any part of the sea, which may form an accession to his dominions. It would undoubtedly be unjust for any burdens foreign to the nature of trade to be imposed upon such goods. Thus strangers merely passing through a country would have no right to pay a poll-tax, imposed to support the exigencies of the state. But if the sovereign incurs expence by providing security and protection to trade, he has a right to reimburse himself by the imposition of moderate and reasonable duties. It is the REASONABLENESS of them, which constitutes the justice of customs and taxes, Thus Solomon received tolls for horses and linen that passed over the Isthmus of Syria. Pliny, speaking of frankincense, observes that as it could not be transported but by the Gebanites, a duty upon it was paid to their king. In the same manner, as Strabo informs us in his fourth book, the people of Marseilles derived great wealth from the canal which Marius had made from the Rhone to the sea, by exacting tribute of all that sailed upon it to and fro with vessels. In the eighth book of the same writer, we are told that the Corinthians imposed a duty upon all goods, which, to avoid the dangerous passage of Cape Malea, were transported by land from sea to sea. The Romans too made the passage of the Rhine a source of tribute, and Seneca relates that a toll was paid for going over bridges. The works of legal writers abound in instances of this kind. But it frequently happens that extortion is practised in these matters, which Strabo forms into a subject of complaint against chiefs of the Arabian tribes, concluding that it would be unlikely for men of that lawless kind to impose upon the goods of merchants any duties that were not oppressive.

**XV**. Those going with merchandise or only passing through a country, ought to be allowed to reside there for a time, if the recovery of health, or any other just cause should render such residence necessary. For these may be reckoned among the innocent uses of our right. Thus Ilioneus in Virgil calls heaven to witness the injustice of the Africans in driving him and his shipwrecked companions from the hospitable use of the shore, and we are informed by Plutarch in his life of Pericles that all the Grecians approved of the complaint, which the Megarensians made against the Athenians, who had prohibited them from setting foot upon the soil of their territories, or carrying a vessel into their harbours. So the Lacedaemonians regarded this as the most sufficient grounds to justify the war.

From hence results the right of erecting a temporary hut, upon the shore, although, for instance, the same shore is allowed to be the property of the people of that place. For what Pomponius says of its being necessary to obtain the Praetor's leave, before a building can be raised upon the public shore, relates to structures of a permanent kind, when the massy piles of stone, as the Poet says, encroach upon the sea, and the affrighted fish feel their waves contracted.

**XVI**. Nor ought a permanent residence to be refused to foreigners, who, driven from their own country, seek a place of refuge. But then it is only upon condition that they submit to the established laws of the place, and avoid every occasion of exciting tumult and sedition. A reasonable rule, which the divine poet has observed, when he introduces Aeneas making an offer that Latinus, who had become his father-in-law, should retain all military and civil power. And in Dionysius of Halicarnassus, Latinus admits the proposal of Aeneas to be just; as he came through necessity in quest of a settlement. To drive away refugees, says Strabo, from Eratosthenes, is acting like barbarians; and a conduct like this in the Spartans was also condemned. St. Ambrose passes the same sentence of condemnation upon those powers, who refuse all admission to strangers. Yet settlers of this description have no right to demand a share in the government. A proposal of this kind made by the Minyae to the

Lacedaemonians, who had received them, is very properly considered by Herodotus as insolent, and unreasonable.

**XVII**. It is indeed but an act of common humanity in a sovereign to allow strangers, at their request, liberty to fix their residence upon any waste or barren lands within his dominions, still reserving to himself all the rights of sovereignty, Seven hundred acres of barren and uncultivated land, as Servius observes, were given by the native Latins to the Trojans. Dion Prusaeensis, in his seventh oration, says, that they commit no crime of trespass, who take upon them to cultivate waste lands. The refusal of this privilege made the Ansibarians exclaim, "the firmament over our heads is the mansion of the deity: the earth was given to man; and what remains unoccupied, lies in common to all." Yet that complaint did not apply exactly to their case. For those lands could not be called unoccupied, as they served to supply the Roman army with forage for their cattle, which certainly furnished the Romans with a just pretext for refusing to grant their request. And with no less propriety the Romans asked the Galli Senones if it were right to demand lands already possessed, and to threaten to take them by force.

**XVIII**. Since the COMMON RIGHT TO THINGS has been established, the COMMON RIGHT TO ACTIONS follows next in order, and this right is either absolute, or established by the supposition of a general agreement amongst mankind. Now all men have absolutely a right to do such or such acts as are necessary to provide whatever is essential to the existence or convenience of life. CONVENIENCE is included in this right; for there is no occasion here to imagine an existence of the same necessity as was requisite to authorize the seizing of another's property. Because the point of discussion here is not whether any act is done AGAINST THE WILL of an owner, but whether we acquire what is necessary for our wants ACCORDING TO THE TERMS to which the owner has agreed. Supposing there is nothing illegal in the contract, nor any willful intention on his part to make it null and void. For any impediment created by the owner in such trans. actions, is repugnant to the very principles of natural justice, which suppose an equality of upright dealing to subsist in both the parties concerned. St. Ambrose calls a fraudulent conduct of that kind, an attempt to deprive men of their share in the goods of a common parent, to withhold the productions of nature which are the birthright of all, and to destroy that commerce which is the very support of life. For we are not treating of superfluities and luxuries, but of those things, which are essential to life, as physic, food and cloathing.

**XIX**. From what has already been proved, it follows that all men have a right to purchase the necessaries of life at a reasonable price, except the owners want them for their own use. Thus in a great scarcity of corn, there would be no injustice in their refusing to sell. And yet in such a time of necessity foreigners, who have been once admitted, cannot be driven away; but as St. Ambrose shews in the passage already quoted, a common evil must be borne by all alike.

**XX**. Now owners have not the same right in the sale of their goods: for others are at full liberty to determine whether they will purchase certain articles or not. The ancient Belgians, for instance, allowed not wines and other foreign merchandise to be imported among them. The same rule, we are informed by Strabo, was practised by the Nabathaean Arabians.

**XXI**. It is supposed to be generally agreed among man. kind, that the privileges, which any nation grants promiscuously to the subjects of foreign powers or countries, are the common right of all. Consequently the exclusion of any one people from these rights would be considered as an injury to that people. Thus, wherever foreigners in general are allowed to hunt, to fish, to shoot, to gather pearls, to succeed to property by testament, to sell commodities, or to form intermarriages, the same privileges cannot be refused to any particular people, unless they have by misconduct forfeited their right. On which account the tribe of Benjamin was debarred from intermarrying with other tribes.

**XXII**. It has sometimes been a subject of inquiry whether one nation may lawfully agree with another to exclude all nations but herself from purchasing certain productions, which are the peculiar growth of her soil. An agreement which, it is evident, may be lawfully made; if the purchaser intends to supply other nations with those articles at a reasonable price. For it is a matter of indifference to other nations OF WHOM they purchase, provided they can have a reasonable supply for their wants. Nor is there any thing unlawful in allowing one people an advantage over another in this respect, particularly for a nation who has taken another under her protection and incurred expence on that account. Now such a monopoly, under the circumstances already mentioned, is no way repugnant to the law of nature, though it may be sometimes for the interest of the community to prohibit it by express laws.

## CHAPTER 3: ON MOVEABLE PROPERTY

*Specification of moveable property — The difference between sovereignty and property — The right to movables by occupancy may be superseded by law Rivers may be occupied — Right to seas — On the treaties binding a people not to navigate the seas beyond certain bounds — Inquiry into the nature of the change which a river, changing its course, makes in the adjoining territories — What determination is to be made, where the river has entirely changed its channel — Sometimes a whole river may accrue to a territory — Things deserted belong to the first occupier.*

**I.** AMONG the means of acquiring property, Paulus the Lawyer reckons one, which seems most natural, and that is, if by the ingenuity of art, or the exertions of labour we have given to any production its existence among the works of man. Now as nothing can naturally be produced, except from some materials before in existence, it follows that, if those materials were our own, the possession of them under any new shape, or commodity is only a CONTINUATION of our former property; if they belonged to no one, our possession comes under the class of title by occupancy: but if they were another's, no improvement of ours can by the law of nature give us a right of property therein.

**II.** Among those things, which belong to no one, there are two that may become the subjects of occupancy; and those are jurisdiction, or sovereignty and property. For jurisdiction and property are distinct from each other in their effects. The objects over which sovereignty may be exercised are of a twofold description, embracing both persons and things. But this is not the case with property, the right of which can extend only to the irrational and inanimate part of the creation. Though it might originally, for the most part, be the same act by which sovereignty and property were acquired, yet they are in their nature distinct. SOVEREIGNTY, says Seneca, belongs to PRINCES and PROPERTY to INDIVIDUALS. The sovereignty therefore, not only over subjects at home, but over those in the Prince's foreign dominions passes with the hereditary descent of the crown.

**III.** In places, where sovereignty is already established, the right to movables by occupancy, and indeed every, original right must give way to the superior sanction of law. And what any man before held by any such right, he would afterwards be considered as holding by the laws of the country. For those original rights were PERMISSIONS of the law of nature, and not commands that were to be PERPETUALLY enforced. For the continued establishment of such a right as that by prior occupancy, so far from promoting the welfare, would operate to the very destruction of human society. Although it may be said by way of objection, that the law of nations seems to admit of such a right, yet we may answer that if such a rule either is or has been commonly received in any part of the world, it has not the force of a general c in. pact binding upon different independent nations; but may be considered as one branch of the civil law of many nations, which any state has a right to continue, or repeal according to its own pleasure or discretion. There are many other things indeed which legal writers, in treating of the division and acquisition of property, consider as forming a part of the law of nations.

**IV**. Rivers may be occupied by a country, not including the stream above, nor that below its own territories. But the waters which wash its lands form an inseparable part of the current, making its way to the main sea. For to constitute the right to a property in its channel, it is sufficient that its sides, inclosed by the banks of that territory form its greatest part, and that the river itself compared with the land, makes but a small portion.

**V**. In the same manner, the sea appears capable of being made a property by the power possessed of the shore on both sides of it; although beyond those limits it may spread to a wide extent, which is the case with a bay, and with a straight beyond each of its outlets into the main sea or ocean. But this right of property can never take place where the sea is of such a magnitude, as to surpass all comparison with that portion of the land which it washes. And the right, which one people or prince possesses, may also be shared by a great number of states, among whose respective territories the sea flows. Thus rivers separating two powers may be occupied by both, to each of whom their use and advantages may be equal.

**VI**. Instances may be found of treaties by which one nation binds itself to another, not to navigate particular seas beyond certain bounds. Thus between the Egyptians and the Princes inhabiting the borders of the Red Sea, it was agreed, in ancient times, that the former should not enter that sea with any ship of war, nor with more than one merchant ship. In the same manner, in the time of Cimon, the Persians were bound by a treaty, made with the Athenians, not to sail with any ship of war between the Cyanean rocks and the Chelidonian islands; a prohibition, which, after the battle of Salamis, restricted any Persian armed vessel from sailing between Phaselis and the above named rocks. In the one year's truce of the Peloponnesian war, the Lacedaemonians were prohibited from sailing with any ships of war whatever, or indeed with any other ships of more than twenty tons burden. And in the first treaty, which the Romans, immediately after the expulsion of their kings, made with the Carthaginians, it was stipulated that neither the Romans, nor their allies should sail beyond the promontory of Pulchrum, except they were driven thither by stress of weather, or to avoid being captured by an enemy. But in either case they were to take nothing more than necessaries, and to depart before the expiration of five days. And in the second treaty, the Romans were prohibited from committing any acts of piracy, or even from trading beyond the promontory of Pulchrum, Massia and Tarscius.

In a treaty of peace between the Illyrians and Romans, the latter required that they should not pass beyond the Lissus with more than two frigates, and those unarmed. In the peace with Antiochus, he was bound not to sail within the capes of Calyeadnius and Sarpedon, except with ships carrying tribute, ambassadors, or hostages. Now the instances alluded to do not prove the actual occupancy of the sea, or the right of navigation. For it may happen that both individuals and nations may grant as a matter of favour or compact, not only what they have a competent right to dispose of, but that which is the common right of all men as well as of themselves. When this happens, we may say as Ulpian did on a like occasion, where an estate had been sold with a reservation, that the purchaser should not fish for Tunny to the prejudice of the seller. He observed that the sea could not be rendered subject to a service, but still the purchaser and those who succeeded to his possession, were bound in honour to observe that part of the contract.

**VII**. Whenever a river has changed its course, disputes have arisen between neighboring states to decide whether such an alteration creates any change in the adjoining territories, and to whom any addition of land occasioned by that change accrues. Disputes which must be settled according to the nature and manner of such acquisition. Writers, who have treated of the division of land, have described it as of a threefold nature: one kind they name DIVIDED and ASSIGNED land, which Frontinus the Lawyer calls LIMITED, because it is marked out by artificial boundaries. By land ASSIGNED, is meant that which has been appropriated to a whole community, comprehending a certain number of families; a hundred for instance: from whence it has derived that name. And those portions are called hundreds. There is another division called ARCIFINIUM, which is applied when the land is defended against an enemy by the natural boundaries of rivers or mountains. These lands Aggenus Urbicus calls OCCUPATORY, being such as have been occupied either by reason of their being vacant, or by the power of conquest. In the two first kinds of lands, because their extent and bounds are fixed and determined, though a river should change its course, it occasions no change of territory, and what is added by allusion will belong to the former occupant.

In arcifinious lands, where the bounds are formed by nature, any gradual change in the course of the river makes a change also in the boundaries of territory, and whatever accession is given by the river to one side, it will belong to the possessor of the land on that side. Because the respective nations are supposed originally to have taken possession of those lands, with an intention of making the MIDDLE of that river, as a natural boundary, the line of separation between them. Thus Tacitus in speaking of the Usipians and Tencterians, who border on the Cattians, says, "their territory lies on the banks of the Rhine, where that river, still flowing in one regular channel, forms a sufficient boundary."

**VIII**. Decisions like those above can only take place in instances, where the river has not altered its channel. For a river, dividing territories, is not to be considered barely as so much water, but as water flowing in a PARTICULAR CHANNEL, and inclosed WITHIN CERTAIN BANKS. For which reason an addition, a decrease, or such a change of small portions, as leaves the ancient appearance, upon the whole, nearly the same, allows us to consider the river as still the same. But if the whole face of the river is changed, the case will be entirely altered. For as a river may be entirely destroyed by the erection of dams upon the higher parts of its stream, or by digging canals, which carry off its waters in another direction: so by the desertion of its old channel, and breaking out for itself another course, it will not continue to be same river it was before, but will be completely a new one. In the same manner if a river has been dried up, the middle of its channel will remain as the boundary between neighbouring states, who in taking possession of the neighbouring territory originally intended the middle of such a river to be the line of separation, and under all changes to preserve the same as a permanent limit. But in doubtful cases, the territories bordering upon a river ought to be considered as arcifinious, because nothing can be a more apt mark of distinction than those impassable bounds assigned by nature. It very seldom indeed happens, that the artificial or civil admeasurements of territory can be regulated by such natural bounds, as they are, in general, the effect of original acquisition, or have been ceded by treaty.

**IX**. Although in doubtful cases, it has been said that the territories on each side of a river are determined by the middle of the channel; yet it may happen, and has happened, that the sole right to a river may belong to the territories on one side of it. Because that on the opposite side was of later occupancy, and subsequent to the possession of that river by the other power: or because this sole right may have been so settled by treaty.

**X**. It is not unworthy of observation that things which have had an owner, but have ceased to have one, become subject to the right by original acquisition. They are supposed to have been abandoned from the want of an owner, and therefore have returned to the original state of common stock. But at the same time it is proper to observe, that some times the original acquisition may have been made by a people or their sovereign, in such a manner as to give them or him not only those pre-eminent rights which constitute prerogative, but also the full title of property.

And this property again may be divided into smaller grants, and those again subdivided into other portions, to be held as dependent upon the original grantor, the Sovereign, or the Lord. Though the land may not be held by base service, or vassalage, yet it is possessed by some conditional tenure. For things are occupied by many kinds of right; among which may be reckoned the right of a person who expects property to be left to him under the condition of a trust. Seneca says, that an owner's being debarred from selling his lands, committing waste upon them, or even making improvements, is not to be taken as a proof that the property is not his. For that is a man's own, which he holds under any certain conditions. Since then property distributed in the manner above named is held of the sovereign, or of some inter. mediate Lord, who himself is tenant of the sovereign, it follows that any thing which wants an owner does not become the property of him, who can first seize it, but reverts to the state or to the sovereign.

## CHAPTER 4: TITLE TO DESERT LANDS BY OCCUPANCY, POSSESSION, AND PRESCRIPTION.

*Why Usucaption or Prescription cannot subsist between independent States, and Sovereigns — Long possession alleged as a ground of right — Inquiry into the intentions of men, which are not to be judged of by words alone — Intention to be judged of by acts — Intentions also to be judged of by omissions — How far length of time, silence, and non-possession, may confirm the conjecture of an abandoned right — Time immemorial generally thought to bar any claim — What constitutes time immemorial — Objections to a presumed desertion of property, considered without any conjecture, time immemorial appears to transfer and constitute a property — Inquiry whether persons yet unborn may thus be deprived of their right — Rules of civil law respecting Usucaption and Prescription as applied to the case of Sovereign Princes, explained.*

**I.** A GREAT difficulty arises here respecting the right to property by uninterrupted possession for any certain time. For though time is the great agent, by whose motion all legal concerns and rights may be measured and determined, yet it has no effectual power of itself to create an express title to any property. Now those rights were introduced by the civil law; and it is not their long continuance, but the express provisions of the municipal law, which gives them their validity. They are of no force therefore, in the opinion of Vasquez, between two independent nations or sovereigns, or between a free nation and a sovereign: between a sovereign and an individual who is not his subject, or between two subjects belonging to different kings or nations. Which indeed seems true; and is actually the case; for such points relating to persons and things, are not left to the law of nature, but are settled by the respective laws of each country. As the -unqualified admission of this principle would lead to great inconvenience, and prevent the disputes of kings and nations respecting the bounds of territory from ever being adjusted; in order to eradicate the seeds of perpetual warfare and confusion, so repugnant to the interests and feelings of every people; the settlement of such boundaries is not left to the claims of prescriptive right; but the territories of each contending party are, in general, expressly defined by certain treaties.

**II.** To disturb any one in the actual and long possession of territory, has in all ages been considered as repugnant to the general interests and feelings of man. kind. For we find in holy writ, that when the King of the Ammonites demanded the lands situated between the rivers Arnon and Jabok, and those extending from the deserts of Arabia to the Jordan, Jepthah opposed his pretentions by proving his own possession of the same for three hundred years, and asked why he and his ancestors had for so long a period neglected to make their claim. And the Lacedaemonians, we are informed by Isocrates, laid it down for a certain rule admitted among all nations, that the right to public territory as well as to private property was so firmly established by length of time, that it could not be disturbed; and upon this ground they rejected the claim of those who demanded the restoration of Messena.

Resting upon a right like this, Philip the Second was induced to declare to Titus Quintius, "that he would restore the dominions which he had subdued himself, but would upon no consideration give up the possessions which he had derived from his ancestors by a just and hereditary title. Sulpitius, speaking against Antiochus, proved how unjust it was in him to pretend, that because the Greek Nations in Asia had once been under the subjection of his forefathers, he had a right to revive those claims, and to reduce them again to a state of servitude. And upon this subject two historians, Tacitus and Diodorus may be referred to;

the former of whom calls such obsolete pretentions, empty talking, and the latter treats them as idle tales and fables. With these opinions Cicero, in his 2nd book of Offices, agrees, asking "what justice there can be in depriving an owner of the land, which he has for many ages quietly possessed?"

**III**. Can it be said, in order to justify the disturbance of long enjoyed possessions, that the rightful owner INTENDED to assert his claim, when he never manifested such intention by any outward visible act? The effect of right which depends upon a man's intentions can never follow from a bare conjecture of his will, unless he has declared and proved it by some express and visible act. For actions being the only evidence of intentions, intentions can never of themselves alone without such acts be the object of human laws. No conjectures indeed respecting the acts of the mind can be reduced to mathematical certainty, but only to the evidence of probability at the utmost. For men by their words may express intentions different from their real ones, and by their acts counterfeit intentions which they have not. The nature of human society, however, requires that all acts of the mind, when sufficiently indicated, should be followed by their due effects. Therefore the intention, which has been sufficiently indicated, is taken for granted against him who gave such indication.

**IV**. But to proceed to proofs derived from actions. A thing is understood to be abandoned, when it is cast away; except it be under particular circumstances, as throwing goods overboard in a storm to lighten a ship, where the owner is not supposed to have abandoned all intention of recovery, should it ever be in his power. Again, by giving up or canceling a promissory note, a debt is deemed to be discharged. Paulus the Lawyer, says, a right to property may be renounced not only by words, but also by actions, or any other indication of the will. Thus, if an owner knowingly make a contract with any one who is in possession, treating him as if he were the rightful proprietor, he is naturally supposed to have relinquished his own pretensions. Nor is there any reason, why the same rule may not take place between sovereign princes, and independent states, as between individuals. In the same manner, a Lord by granting certain privileges to his Vassal, which he could not legally enjoy without a release from his former obligations, was supposed by such act to have given him his freedom. A power derived not from the civil law only, but from the law of nature, which allows every man to relinquish what is his own, and from a natural presumption that a person designed to do the act which he has given manifest proofs of his intention to do. In this sense, Ulpian may be rightly understood, where he says, that ACCEPTILATION or the verbal discharge of a debt is founded upon the law of nations.

**V**. Even omissions, taking all proper circumstances into consideration, come under the cognizance of the law. Thus the person, who knowing of an act, and being present at the commission of it, passes it over in silence, seems to give his consent to it; this was admitted by the Mosaic Law. Unless indeed it can be shewn that the same person was hindered from speaking either by fear or some other pressing circumstance. Thus a thing is accounted as lost when all hope of recovering it is given up; as for instance, if a tame animal, which was in our possession, be seized and carried off by a wild beast Goods too lost by shipwreck, Ulpian says, cease to be considered as our own, not immediately, but when they are lost beyond all possibility of being reclaimed, and when no proofs of the owner's intention to reclaim them can be discovered.

Now the case is altered, if persons were sent to inquire after the lost goods, or property, and a reward was promised to the finder. But if a person knows his property to be in the possession of another, and allows it to remain so for a length of time, without asserting his claim, unless there appear sufficient reasons for his silence, he is construed to have entirely abandoned all pretentious to the same. And to the same purpose he has said else. where, that a house is looked upon to be abandoned on account of the long silence of the proprietor.

The Emperor Antoninus Pius, in one of his rescripts, said there was but little justice in claiming interest upon money after a long period; for the length of time elapsed was an indication that the debtor had been excused from payment, from some motive of kindness.

There appears something similar to this in the nature of custom. For apart from the authority of civil laws, which regulate the time and manner of custom, and its introduction, it may arise from the indulgence of a sovereign to a conquered people. But the length of time from which custom derives the force of right, is not defined, but left to the arbitrary decision of what is sufficient to indicate general consent. But for silence to be taken as a valid presumption that property is deserted, two things are requisite: it must be a silence with a knowledge of the fact, and with a perfect freedom of will in the person concerned. For a silence founded in ignorance can have no weight; and where any other reason appears, the presumption of free consent must fail.

**VI**. Although the two requisites already named maybe produced, yet other reasons have their weight; among which length of time is not the least important. For in the first place, it can scarcely happen, that for a great length of time a thing belonging to any one should not some way or other come to his knowledge, as time might supply many opportunities. Even if the civil law did not interpose to bar remote pretensions, the very nature of things would shew the reasonableness of a shorter period of limitation being allowed to present than to absent claimants. If impressions of fear were pleaded by any one in excuse, yet their influence would not be of perpetual duration, and length of time would unfold various means of security against such fears, either from resources within himself, or from the assistance of others. Escaping beyond the reach of him he dreaded, he might protest against his oppression, by appealing to proper judges and arbitrators.

**VII**. Now as time immemorial, considered in a moral light, seems to have no bounds, silence for such a length of time appears sufficient to establish the presumption that all claim to a thing is abandoned, unless the strongest proofs to the contrary can be produced. The most able Lawyers have properly observed, that time according to the memory of man is not an hundred years, though probably it may not fall far short of that space. For a hundred years are the term beyond which human existence seldom reaches; a space, which in general completes three ages or generations of men. The Romans made this objection to Antiochus, that he claimed cities, which neither he himself, his father, nor his grandfather had ever possessed.

**VIII**. From the natural affection which all men have for themselves, and their property, an objection may be taken against the presumption of any one's abandoning a thing which belongs to him, and consequently negative acts, even though confirmed by a long period of time, are not sufficient to establish the above named conjecture.

Now considering the great importance deservedly attached to the settlement of CROWNS, all conjectures favourable to the possessors ought to be allowed. For if Aratus of Sicyon thought it a hard case, that PRIVATE possessions of fifty years' standing should be disturbed, how much weightier is that maxim of Augustus, that it is the character of a good man and a good subject to wish for no change in the present government, and, IN THE WORDS, WHICH THUCYDIDES HAS ASSIGNED TO ALCIBIADES, to support the constitution, under which he has been born? But if no such rules in favour of possession could be adduced, yet a more weighty objection might be found against the presumption, drawn from the inclination of every one to preserve his own right, which is the improbability of one man's allowing another to usurp his property for any length of time, without declaring and asserting his own right.

**IX**. Perhaps it may reasonably be said, that this matter does not rest upon presumption only, but that it is a rule, introduced by the voluntary law of Nations, that uninterrupted possession, against which no claim has been asserted, will entirely transfer such property to the actual possessor. For it is most likely that all nations by consent gave their sanction to such a practice, as conducive to their common peace. The term uninterrupted possession therefore has been very properly used to signify, as Sulpitius says in Livy, "that which has been held by one uniform tenour of right, without intermission." Or as the same author, in another place, calls it, I perpetual possession, that has never been called in question." For a transitory possession creates no title, And it was this exception which the Numidians urged against the Carthaginians, alleging that as opportunity offered, sometimes the Kings of the Numidians had appropriated to themselves the disputed possessions, which had always remained in the hands of the stronger party.

**X**. But here another question, and that of considerable difficulty, arises, which is, to decide, whether, by this desertion, persons yet unborn may be deprived of their rights. If we maintain that they MAY NOT, the rule already established would be of no avail towards settling the tranquillity of kingdoms, and security of property. For in most things some thing is due to the interests of posterity. But if we affirm that they MAY, it then seems wonderful that silence should prejudice the rights of those, who were unable to speak, before they had any existence, and that the act of OTHERS should operate to their injury. To clear up this point, we must observe that no rights can belong to a person before he has any existence, as, in the language of the schools, there can be no accident without a substance. Wherefore if a Prince, from urgent motives of policy, and for the advantage of his own native dominions, and subjects, should decline to accept an additional sovereignty, or for the same reasons, should relinquish that, which he had al. ready accepted, he would not be charged with injuring his heirs and successors, then unborn, who could have no rights before they had a natural existence.

Now as a sovereign may EXPRESSLY declare a change of his will respecting such dominions, so that change may. in certain cases, be implied without such declaration.

In consequence of such a change either expressed or implied, before the rights of heirs and successors can be supposed to have any existence, the possession may be considered as entirely abandoned. The case here has been considered according to the LAW OF NATURE: for the civil law, among other fictions, introduced that of the law's personating those, who are not yet in being, and so preventing any occupancy from taking place to their prejudice; a regulation of the law established upon no slight grounds in order to preserve estates in families, although every means of PERPETUATING property to individuals, which prevents its transfer from hand to hand, may in some measure be detrimental to the public interest. From whence it is a received opinion, that length of time will give a property in those fees, which were originally conveyed, not by right of succession, but by virtue of primitive investiture. Covarruvias, a lawyer of great judgment, supports this opinion with the strongest arguments in favour of primogeniture, and applies it to estates left in trust. For nothing can prevent the civil law from instituting a right, which, though it cannot be lawfully alienated by the act of one party without consent of the other, yet, to avoid uncertainty in the tenure of present proprietors, may be lost by neglect of claim for a length of time. Still the parties thus deprived may maintain a personal action against those, or their heirs, through whose neglect their right has been forfeited.

**XI**. It is an inquiry of importance whether the law of usucaption and prescription, if it prevail in a prince's dominions, can be applied to the tenure of the crown, and all its prerogatives. Many legal writers, who have treated of the nature of sovereign power according to the principles of the Roman civil law, seem to affirm that it may be so applied. But this is an opinion to which we cannot accede in its full extent. For to make a law binding upon any one, it is requisite that the legislator should possess both power and will. A legislator is not bound by his law, as by the irrevocable and unchangeable controul of a superior. But occasions may arise that will demand an alteration or even a repeal of the law which he has made. Yet a legislator may be bound by his own law, not directly as a legislator, but as an individual forming part of the community: and that too according to natural equity, which requires that all the component parts should bear a reference to the whole. We find in holy writ, this rule observed by Saul in the beginning of his reign.

Now that rule does not take place here. For we are considering the lawgiver, not as a part but as the REPRESENTATIVE and SOVEREIGN of the whole community. Nor indeed can any such intention in the lawgiver be pre. sumed to have existed. For legislators are not supposed to comprehend themselves within the rule of the law, except where the nature and subject of it are general, But sovereignty is not to be compared with other things; it so far surpasses them in the nobleness of its end, and the dignity of its nature. Nor is any civil law to be found which either does, or designs to comprehend sovereign power within the rules of prescription.

[**Translator's note:** The translation proceeds from the fourth to the ninth Chapter of the Second book of the original. The intermediate chapters, being chiefly a repetition of the author's former arguments, respecting the rights of the seas and rivers, and other kinds of dominions; and that relating to the rights of persons, being so fully treated in the first volume of Judge Blackstone's Commentaries, it seemed unnecessary to give them in the present work.]

## CHAPTER 9: IN WHAT CASES JURISDICTION AND PROPERTY CEASE.

*Jurisdiction and property cease, when the family of the owner bar, become extinct — In what manner the rights of a people may become extinct — A people becomes extinct when its essential parts are destroyed — A people does not become extinct by emigration — The existence of separate states not destroyed by a federal union.*

**I.** and **II**. AFTER the preceding inquiries into the manner in which private property as well as sovereign power may be acquired and transferred, the manner, in which they cease, naturally comes next under consideration. It has been shewn before that the right to property may be lost by neglect; for property can continue no longer than while the will of ownership continues. There is also another manner in which property may cease to exist, without any express or implied alienation: and that is where the family either of a sovereign, or an owner, becomes extinct, a contingency for which provision must be made somewhat similar to a succession to the property of one who dies intestate. Wherefore if any one die, without any declaration of his will, and have no relations by blood, all the right, which he had, becomes extinct, and reverts, if a sovereign, to the hands of the nation, except where express provisions of law have been made to the contrary.

**III**. The same mode of reasoning applies to a nation. Isocrates, and after him the Emperor Julian, has said that states are immortal, or may be so. For a people is one of that kind of bodies which are formed of distinct parts, following each other in regular succession, and supplying the place of the deceased. This body goes under one name, forming, as Plutarch says, one constitution; or, in the language of Paulus the Lawyer, one spirit. Now the spirit or constitution in a people is the full and perfect harmony of civil life, from which emanates the sovereign power, the very soul of all government, and, as Seneca says, the vital breath which so many thousands draw.

These artificial bodies bear a close resemblance to the natural body, which, notwithstanding the alteration of its component particles, loses not its identity, so long as the general form remains. And therefore in the passage of Seneca, where he says, that no one is the same in his old age that he was in his youth, he means only as to natural substance. In the same manner Heraclitus, as cited by Plato in Cratylus, and Seneca in the place already quoted, has said, that we cannot descend TWICE into the same river. But Seneca afterwards corrects himself, adding, that the river retains its name, though the watery particles of which it is composed are perpetually changing. So Aristotle, too, in comparing nations to rivers, has said that the rivers are always called by the same name, though their several parts are fluctuating every moment. Nor is it the name alone which continues, but that principle also which Conon calls the constitutional system of the body, and Philo the spirit, that holds it together. So that a people, as Alphenus and Plutarch, in speaking of the late, but unerring approach of divine vengeance, maintain, though not one of its members of a former period be now living, is the same at present that it was a hundred years ago, as long as the spirit, which first framed and afterwards kept the body together, preserves its identity.

Hence has originated the custom, in addressing a people, of ascribing to them, who are now living, what happened to the same people many ages before; as may be seen both in profane historians, and in the books of holy writ. So in Tacitus, Antony the First serving under Vespasian, reminds the soldiers of the third legion of what they had done in former times, how under Mark Antony they had beaten the Parthians, and under Corbulo the Armenians. There was more of prejudice, therefore, than truth in the reproach, which Piso cast upon the Athenians of his own time, refusing to consider them as Athenians since they had become extinct by so many disasters, and were nothing more than a base mixture of all nations of the earth. We say there was more of prejudice than truth in this reproach. For though such a mixture might diminish the dignity, it could not destroy the existence of a people. Nor was he himself ignorant of this. For he reproaches the Athenians of his own day with their feeble efforts in former times against Philip of Macedon, and their ingratitude to their best friends. Now as a change of its component parts cannot destroy the identity of a people, not even for a thousand years or more; so neither can it be denied that a people may lose its existence in two ways; either by the extinction of all its members, or by the extinction of its form and spirit.

**IV**. A body is said to die, when its essential parts, and necessary form of subsistence are destroyed. To the former case may be referred the instance of nations swallowed up by the sea, as Plato relates, and others whom Tertullian mentions: or if a people should be destroyed by an earthquake, of which there are many instances in history, or should destroy themselves, as the Sidonians and Saguntines did. We are informed by Pliny, that in ancient Latium, fifty-three nations were destroyed without a single trace of them remaining.

But what, it may be said will be the case, if out of such a nation so few remain that they cannot form a people? They will then retain that property, which they had before as private persons, but not in a public capacity. The same is the case with every community.

**V**. A people loses its form, by losing all or some of those rights, which it had in common; and this happens, either when every individual is reduced to slavery, as the Mycenaeans, who were sold by the Argives; the Olynthians by Philip, the Thebans by Alexander, and the Brutians, made public slaves by the Romans: Or when, though they retain their personal liberty, they are deprived of the rights of sovereignty. Thus Livy informs us respecting Capua, that the Romans determined, though it might be inhabited as a city, that there should be no municipal body, no senate, no public council, no magistrates, but that deprived of political deliberation, and sovereign authority, the inhabitants should be considered as a multitude; subject to the jurisdiction of a Praefect sent from Rome. Therefore Cicero, in his first speech against Rullus, says that there was no image of a republic left at Capua. The same may be said of nations reduced to the form of Provinces, and of those subjugated by another power; as Byzantium was to Perinthus, by the Emperor Severus, and Antioch to Laodicea, by Theodosius.

**VI**. But if a nation should emigrate, either spontaneously, on account of scarcity or any other calamity, or if by compulsion, which was the case with the people of Carthage in the third Punic war, while she retains her form, she does not cease to be a people; and still less so, if only the walls of her cities be destroyed, and therefore when the Lacedaemonians refused to admit the Messenians to swear to the peace of Greece, because the walls of their city were destroyed, it was carried against them in the General Assembly of the Allies.

Nor does it make any difference in the argument, whatever the form of government may be, whether regal, aristocratical, or democratical. The Roman people for instance was the same, whether under kings, consuls, or emperors. Even indeed under the most absolute form, the people is the same that it was in its independent state, while the king governs it as head of that people, and not of any other. For the sovereignty which resides in the king as the head, resides in the people likewise as the body of which he is the head; and therefore in an elective government, if the king or the royal family should become extinct, the rights of sovereignty, as it has been already shewn, would revert to the people.

Nor is this argument overthrown by the objection drawn from Aristotle, who says that, if the form of government is changed, the state no longer continues to be the same, as the harmony of a piece of music is entirely changed by a transition from the Doric to the Phrygian measure.

Now it is to be observed, that an artificial system may possess many different forms, as in an army under one supreme commander there are many subordinate parts, and inferior powers, while in the operations of the field it appears but as one body. In the same manner, the union of the legislative and executive powers in a state gives it the appearance of one form, while the distinction between subject and sovereign, and their still mutual relation give it another. The executive power is the politician's concern; the judicial, the lawyer's. Nor did this escape the notice of Aristotle. For he says it belongs to a science different from that of politics to determine whether, tinder a chancre in the form of government, the debts contracted under the old system ought to be discharged by the members of the new. He does this, to avoid the fault which he blames in many other writers, of making digressions from one subject to another.

It is evident that a state, which from a commonwealth has become a regal government, is answerable for the debts incurred before that change. For it is the same people, possessing all the same rights, and powers, which are now exercised in a different manner, being no longer vested in the body, but in the head. This furnishes a ready answer to a question some times asked, which is, what place in general assemblies of different states, ought to be assigned to a sovereign, to whom the people of a commonwealth have transferred all their power? Undoubtedly the same place which that people or their representatives had occupied before in such councils. Thus in the Amphictyonic council, Philip of Macedon succeeded to the place of the Phocensians. So, on the other hand, the people of a commonwealth occupy the place assigned to sovereigns.

[**Translator's note:** Section VII of the original is omitted in the translation.]

**VIII**. Whenever two nations become united, their rights, as distinct states, will not be lost, but will be communicated to each other. Thus the rights of the Albans in the first place, and afterwards those of the Sabines, as we are informed by Livy, were transferred to the Romans, and they became one government. The same reasoning holds good respecting states, which are joined, not by a federal UNION, but by having one sovereign for their head.

**IX**. On the other hand, it may happen that a nation, originally forming but one state, may be divided, either by mutual consent, or by the fate of war; as the body of the Persian Empire was divided among the successors of Alexander. When this is the case, many sovereign powers arise in the place of one, each enjoying its independent rights, whatever belonged to the original state, in common, must either continue to be governed as a common concern, or be divided in equitable proportions.

To this head may be referred the voluntary separation, which takes place when a nation sends out colonies. For thus a new people as it were is formed, enjoying their own rights; and as Thucydides says, sent out not upon terms of slavery, but equality, yet still owing respect and obedience to their mother-country. The same writer, speaking of the second colony sent by the Corinthians to Epidamnus, says, "they gave public notice that such as were willing to go should enjoy equal privileges with those that staid at home."

## CHAPTER 10: THE OBLIGATION ARISING FROM PROPERTY

*Origin and nature of the obligation to restore what belongs to another — Obligation to restore to the rightful owner the profits that have accrued from the unjust possession of his personal or real property — A bona-fide possessor not bound to restitution if the thing has perished — Such bona-fide possessor bound to the restitution of the profits remaining in his hands — Bound to make reparation for the consumption occasioned by his possession — A possessor not bound to make a recompence for a gift, with an exception — The sale of any thing that has been bought, obliges the seller to make restitution, with a certain exception — In what cases a bona-fide purchaser of what belongs to another may retain the price, or a part of it — He who has purchased a thing of one who is not the real owner, cannot return it to that seller — The possessor of a thing whose real owner is unknown, not bound to give it up to any one — A person not bound to restore money received upon a dishonest account, or for service done — Opinion that the property of things valued by weight, number and measure, may be transferred without consent of the owner, refuted.*

I. HAVING explained in the preceding part the nature and rights of property, it remains for us to consider the obligation which we incur from thence.

Now this obligation proceeds from things either in existence, or not in existence, comprehending, under the name of things, the right also over persons, as far as is beneficial to us. The obligation, arising from things in existence, binds the person, who has our property in his power, to do all he can to put us again into possession of it. We have said to do all he can: for no one is bound to an impossibility, nor to procure the restoration of a thing at his own expence. But he is obliged to make every discovery which may enable another to recover his own property. For as in a community of things, it was necessary that a certain equality should be preserved, to prevent one man from having an undue share of the common stock; so upon the introduction of property, it became, as it were, a kind of established rule of society among the owners, that the person, who had in his possession. anything belonging to another should restore it to the lawful proprietor. For if the right of property extended no farther than barely to enable the owner to make a demand of restitution without ENFORCING it by LEGAL PROCESS, it would rest upon a very weak foundation, and scarce be worth the holding. Nor does it make any difference, whether a person has fairly or fraudulently obtained possession of a thing not belonging to him. For he is equally bound to restore it, both by the positive obligations of law, and by the principles of natural justice. The Lacedaemonians had nominally cleared themselves of the crime, by condemning Phaebidas, who, in violation of their treaty with the Thebans, had seized upon the citadel of Cadmea, but in reality they were guilty of injustice, by retaining the possession. And Xenophon has remarked that, such a singular act of injustice was punished by the signal providence of God, For the same reason Marcus Crassus, and Quintus Hortensius, are blamed for having retained part of an inheritance left them by a will, the making of which had been procured upon false pretences, but in the management of which they had no share. Cicero blames them, because it is understood to be settled by general agreement, that all men are to restore what they are possessed of, if another is proved to be the rightful owner. A principle by which property is firmly secured, and upon which all special contracts are founded, and any exceptions to this rule, contained in them, must be expressly named as such. This throws light upon the passage of Tryphoninus. "If a robber, *says he*, has spoiled me of my goods, which he has deposited with Seius, who knows nothing of the fact; the question is, whether he ought to restore them to the robber or to me. If we consider him as giving and receiving on his own account, GOOD FAITH requires that the deposit should be restored to him who gave it, If we consider the equity of the whole case, including all the persons concerned in the transaction, the goods should be restored to me, as the person unjustly deprived of them." And he properly adds, "I prove it to be strict justice to assign to every one his due, without infringing on the more just claims of another." Now it has be n shewn that the justest title on which any one can claim, is that which is coaeval with the property itself. From whence the principle laid down by Tryphoninus, that if any one unknowingly received goods as a deposit, and afterwards discovers them to be his own, he is not bound to restore them. And the question, which the same author puts a little before respecting goods deposited by one, whose property had been confiscated, is better settled by this principle, than by what he says elsewhere on the utility of punishment. For as to the nature of property, it makes no difference, whether it arises from the law of nations, or from the civil law; as it always carries with it peculiar qualities, among which may be reckoned the obligation, under which every possessor lies to restore a thing to its rightful owner. And hence it is said by Martian, that according to the law of nations, restitution may be demanded, of those, who have no legal title to the possession. From the same origin springs the maxim of Ulpian, that whoever has found a thing belonging to another, is bound to restore it, even without claiming or receiving a reward for finding it. The profits also are to be restored, with a deduction only of reasonable charges.

**II.** Respecting things, non-existent, or whose identity cannot be ascertained, is a principle generally received among mankind, that the person, who has become richer by that property, of which the rightful owner has been dispossessed, is bound to make him reparation in proportion to the benefit, which he has derived from his property. For the true proprietor may be justly said to have lost, what HE has gained. Now the very introduction of property was intended to preserve that equality, which assigns to every one his own.

Cicero has said, that it is contrary to natural justice, for one man to improve his own advantage at the expence of another, and in another place, that nature does not allow us to increase our resources, riches, and power, from the spoils of others. There is so much of equity in this saying, that many legal writers have made it the basis of their definitions, to supply the deficiency of the strict letter of the law, always appealing to equity as the most sure and clear rule of action.

If any one employ a slave, as his factor, to trade for him, he is bound by the acts of that factor, unless he has previously given notice that he is not to be trusted. But even if such notice has been given, where the factor has a property in the concern, or the master a profit, the notice shall be deemed a fraud. For, says Proculus, whoever makes an advantage from the loss of another is guilty of a fraud; a term implying every thing repugnant to natural justice and equity. He, who, at the instance of a mother, has put in bail for her son's advocate, has no action on the case against the advocate for what is called an assumpsit or undertaking. For it was not strictly his business, which the advocate managed; the bail was put in at the INSTANCE of the MOTHER. Yet according to the opinion of Papinian, an action on the case for the assumpsit, or undertaking will lie against the advocate, because it is with the bailor's money that he is discharged from the risque of the costs.

So a wife who has given to her husband money, which she may by law demand again, has a personal action of recovery against him, or an indirect action upon any thing purchased with the money. Because, as Ulpian says, it cannot be denied, that the husband has been made richer by it, and the question is, whether what he possesses belongs to his wife?

If I have been robbed by my slave, and any one has spent the money under the supposition that it was the slave's own property, an action may be maintained against that person, as being unjustly in possession of my property. According to the Roman laws, minors are not answerable for money borrowed. Yet if a minor has become richer by the loan, an indirect action will lie against him, or, if anything, belonging to another, has been pawned and sold by a creditor, the debtor should be released from the debt in proportion to what the creditor has received. Because, says Tryphoninus, what. ever the obligation may be, since the money raised accrued from the debt, it is more reasonable that it should redound to the benefit of the debtor than the creditor. But the debtor is bound to indemnify the purchaser, for it would not be reasonable that he should derive gain from another's loss. Now if a creditor, holding an estate in pledge for his money, has received from it rents and profits amounting to more than his real debt; all above that shall be considered as a discharge of so much of the principal.

But to proceed with other cases. If you have treated with my debtor, not supposing him to be indebted to me, but to another person, and have borrowed my money of him, you are obliged to pay me; not because I have lent you money; for that could only be done by mutual consent; but because it is reasonable and just, that my money, which has come into your possession, should be restored to me.

The later writers on the law have adduced this kind of reasoning in support of similar cases. Thus, for instance, if the goods of any one, who has been cast through default, have been sold, if he can make any good exception to the decision, he shall be entitled to the money arising from such sale. Again, when any one has lent money to a father for the maintenance of his son; if the father should become insolvent, he may bring an action against the son, provided the son is possessed of any thing through his mother.

These two rules being perfectly understood, there will be no difficulty in answering the questions often proposed by Lawyers and Theologians on such subjects.

**III**. In the first place it appears, that a person who has obtained possession of goods by fair means, is not bound to restitution, if those goods have perished, because they are no longer in his possession, nor has he derived any advantage from them. The case of unlawful possession which is left to the punishment of the law is entirely out of the question.

**IV**. In the next place a bona-fide possessor of a thing is bound to a restitution of the fruits or profits thereof remaining in his hand. The FRUITS or PRODUCE of the THING ITSELF are here meant. For the benefit derived from a thing owing to the industry bestowed upon it by the occupier thereof, cannot belong to the thing itself, though originally proceeding from it. The reason of this obligation arises from the institution of property. For the true proprietor of a possession is naturally proprietor of the fruits or produce of the same.

**V**. Such possessor in the third place is bound to make restitution of the thing, or reparation for the consumption of it occasioned by his possession. For he is conceived to have been made the richer thereby. Thus Caligula is praised for having, in the beginning of his reign, restored to different Princes along with their crowns, the intermediate revenues of their kingdoms.

**VI**. In the fourth place, an occupier of lands, for instance, is not bound to make a compensation for the produce thereof which he has not reaped, For if dispossessed, he has neither the thing itself, nor any thing in the place of it.

**VII**. In the fifth place, a possessor who has granted to a third person a thing of which a gift had been made to himself, is not bound to make a recompence to the original giver, unless he received it under stipulation, that if he granted it to a third person, and thereby spared his own property, he should make a return proportionable to such gain.

**VIII**. Sixthly, if any one has sold a thing which he has bought, he is not bound to restitution of more than the surplus arising from the sale. But if he had received it under stipulation to sell, he is bound to make restitution of the whole price, unless, in transacting the sale he has incurred an expence, amounting to the whole price, which he would not otherwise have done.

**IX**. Seventhly, a bona-fide purchaser of what belongs to another is obliged to make restitution to the real owner, nor can the price he paid be recovered. To this however there seems to be one exception, which is, where the owner could not have recovered possession without some expence; so for instance, if his property were in the hands of pirates. For then a deduction may be made of as much as the owner would willingly have spent in the recovery. Because the actual possession, especially of a thing difficult to be recovered, may be ascertained, and the owner deemed so much the richer by such recovery. And therefore, though in the ordinary course of law, the purchase of what belongs to one's self can never constitute a bargain, yet Paulus the Lawyer says, that it may do so, if it has been originally agreed that we are to pay for the re-possession of what another has belonging to us in his hands.

Nor is it in the least material, whether a thing has been bought with an intention of restoring it to the owner; in which case, some say, that an action for costs may be maintained, whilst others deny it, For an action on the case, to recover a compensation for business done arises from the artificial rules of CIVIL LAW and not solely from the simple dictates of natural justice; which are here the principal subject of inquiry.

Not unlike to this is what Ulpian has written on funeral expences, in which he says, that a compassionate judge will not rigidly regard the bare labour that has been given, but allowing some relaxation in favour of equity, will shew indulgence to the feelings of human nature.

The same writer, in another place has said, that if any one has transacted my business, not out of regard to me, but for his own interest, and has incurred expence on my account, he may bring an action on the case, not for what he has given, but for what I have gained by his labour and expence.

In the same manner, owners, by throwing whose goods overboard a ship has been lightened, may recover a compensation from others whose goods were by that means saved. Because those persons are considered so much the richer by the preservation of what would otherwise have been lost.

**X**. Eighthly, the person that has bought a thing of one, who is not the owner, cannot return it to that seller; because from the time that the thing came into his possession, he incurred an obligation to restore it to the lawful owner.

**XI**. Again, if any one is in possession of a thing, whose real owner is unknown, be is not naturally, and necessarily bound to give it to the poor; although this may be considered as an act of piety, a custom very properly established in some places. The reason of which is founded on the introduction of property. For, in consequence of that, no one except the real owner, can claim a right to any thing. To the person therefore, who cannot discover such an owner, it is the same as if there really were none.

**XII**. Lastly, a person is not obliged by the law of nature to restore money, which has been received upon a dishonest account, or for the performance of a legal act, to which that person was of himself bound. However it is not without reason that some laws have required restitution in such cases. The reason of this is, because no one is bound to part with any thing unless it belongs to another. But here the property is voluntarily transferred by the first owner.

The case will be altered, if there be any thing iniquitous in the manner of acquiring the thing; as if, for instance, it be gained by extortion. This gives rise to the obligation of submitting to penalties, which is not immediately to the present purpose.

**XIII**. The present subject may be concluded with a refutation of Medina's false opinion, that a property in things, belonging to another, may be transferred without consent of the owner; provided the things are such as are usually valued by weight, number and measure. Because things of that nature can be repaid in kind, or by an equivalent. But this is only, where such a mode of repayment has been previously agreed upon; or where it is understood to be established by law or custom; or where the thing itself has been consumed, and cannot be identically restored. But without such consent, either expressed or implied, or excepting the impossibility just mentioned, the things themselves must be restored.

## CHAPTER 11: ON PROMISES

*Opinion, that the obligation to fulfil promises is not enacted by the law of nature, refuted — A bare assertion not binding — A promiser bound to fulfil his engagements, though no right to exact the performance of them, is thereby conveyed to another — What kind of promise gives such right — The promiser should possess the right use of reason — Difference between natural and civil law with respect to minors — Promises made under an error, or extorted by fear, how far binding — Promises valid, if in the power of the promiser to perform them — Promise made upon unlawful considerations, whether binding — Manner of confirming the promises made by others, and the conduct of Ambassadors who exceed their instructions, considered — Owners of ships, how far bound by the acts of the masters of such vessels, and merchants by the acts of their factors — Acceptance requisite to give validity to a promise — Promises sometimes revokable — The power of revoking a promise, explained by distinctions — Burdensome conditions annexed to a promise — Means of confirming invalid promises — Natural obligation arising from engagements made for others.*

I. THE course of the subject next leads to an inquiry into the obligation of promises. Where the first object, that presents itself, is the opinion of Franciscus Connanus, a man of no ordinary learning. He maintains an opinion that the law of nature and of nations does not enforce the fulfillment of those agreements, which do not include an express contract.* Yet the fulfillment of them is right, in cases, where, even without a promise, the performance would be consonant to virtue and equity. In support of his opinion, he brings not only the sayings of Lawyers, but likewise the following reasons. He says, that the person, who makes, and he who believes, a rash promise, are equally to blame. For the fortunes of all men would be in imminent danger, if they were bound by such promises, which often proceed from motives of vanity rather than from a settled deliberation, and are the result of a light and inconsiderate mind. Lastly, the performance of whatever is any way just in itself, ought to be left to the free will of every one, and not exacted according to the rigid rules of necessity. He says that it is shameful not to fulfil promises; not because it is unjust, but because it argues a levity in making them.

*[**Editor's note:** All the reasonings of Grotius, on this, and on every other point, are intended to apply not only to the transactions of individuals, but to the conduct and affairs of nations.]

In support of his opinion, he appeals also to the testimony of Tully, who has said, that those promises are not to be kept, which are prejudicial to the person to whom they are made, nor, if they are more detrimental to the giver than beneficial to the receiver. But if the performance of an engagement is begun upon the strength of a promise, but not finished, he does not require a complete fulfillment of the promise, but only some compensation to the party for the disappointment. Agreements, he continues, have no intrinsic force of obligation, but only what they derive from the express contracts, in which they are included, or to which they are annexed, or from the delivery of the thing promised. From whence arise actions, on the one side, and exceptions on the other, and bars to all claims of recovery.

But it is through favour of the laws alone, which give the efficacay of obligation to what is only fair and equitable in itself, that obligatory agreements, such as express covenants and other things of that kind, derive their force.

Now there is no consistency in this opinion, taken in the general sense intended by its author. For in the first place it immediately follows from thence, that there is no force in treaties between kings and different nations, till some part of them be carried into execution, especially in those places, where no certain form of treaties or compacts has been established. But no just reason can be found, why laws, which are a kind of general agreement among a people, and indeed are called so by Aristotle, and Demosthenes, should be able to give the force of obligation to compacts, and why the will of an individual, doing every thing to bind himself, should not have the same power; especially where the civil law creates no impediment to it. Besides, as it has been already said that the property of a thing may be transferred, where a sufficient indication of the will is given. Why may we not then convey to another the right to claim a transfer of our property to him, or the fulfillment of our engagements, as we have the same power over our actions, as over our property?

This is an opinion confirmed by the wisdom of all ages. For as it is said by legal authorities, that since nothing is so consonant to natural justice, as for the will of an owner, freely transferring his property to another, to be confirmed, so nothing is more conducive to good faith among men, than a strict adherence to the engagements they have made with each other. Thus a legal decision for the payment of money, where no debt has been incurred, except by the verbal consent of the party promising, is thought conformable to natural justice. Paulus the Lawyer also says, that the law of nature and the law of nations agree in compelling a person, who has received credit, to payment. In this place the word, COMPELLING, signifies a moral obligation. Nor can what Connanus says be admitted, which is, that we are supposed to have credit for a full performance of a promise, where the engagement has been in part fulfilled. For Paulus in this place is treating of an action where nothing is due; which action is entirely void, if money has been paid, in any way, whether according to the manner expressly stipulated, or any other. For the civil law, in order to discourage frequent causes of litigation, does not interfere with those agreements which are enforced by the law of nature and of nations.

Tully, in the first book of his Offices, assigns such force to the obligation of promises, that he calls fidelity the foundation of justice, which Horace also styles the sister of justice, and the Platonists often call justice, TRUTH, which Apuleius has translated FIDELITY, and Simonides has defined justice to be not only returning what one has received, but also speaking the truth.

But to understand the matter fully, we must carefully observe that there are three different ways of speaking, respecting things which ARE, or which, it is supposed, WILL be in our power.

**II**. The first of these ways is, where an assurance is given of future intentions, and if the assurance be SINCERE at the time it is given, though it should not be carried into effect, no blame is incurred, as it might afterwards not be found expedient. For the human mind has not only a natural power, but a right to change its purpose. Wherefore if any blame attaches to a change of opinion, or purpose, it is not to be imputed to the BARE ACT OF CHANGING, but to the CIRCUMSTANCES, under which it happens, especially when the former resolution was the best.

**III**. The second way is, when future intentions are expressed by outward acts and signs sufficient to indicate a resolution of abiding by present assurances. And these kind of promises may be called imperfect obligations, but conveying to the person to whom they are given no RIGHT to exact them. For it happens in many cases that we may be under an obligation of duty, to the performance of which another has no right to compel us. For in this respect the duty of fidelity to promises, is like the duties of compassion and gratitude. In such kinds of promises therefore the person to whom they are made, has no right, by the law of nature to possess himself of the effects of the promiser, as his own, nor to COMPEL him to the performance of his promise.

**IV**. The third way is, where such a determination is confirmed by evident signs of an intention to convey a peculiar right to another, which constitutes the perfect obligation of a promise, and is attended with consequences similar to an alienation of property.

There may be two kinds of alienation, the one of our property, the other of a certain portion of our liberty. Under those of the former kind we may class the promises of gifts, and under the latter the promises of doing certain actions. On this subject we are supplied with noble arguments from the divine oracles, which inform us, that God himself, who can be limited by no established rules of law, would act contrary to his own nature, if he did not perform his promises. From whence it follows that the obligations to perform promises spring from the nature of that unchangeable justice, which is an attribute of God, and common to all who bear his image, in the use of reason. To the proofs of scripture here referred to, we may add the judgment of Solomon, "My son if thou hast been surety for thy friend, thou hast tied up thy hands to a stranger; thou art ensnared by the words of thy mouth, then art thou taken by the words of thine own mouth." Hence a promise is called by the Hebrews a bond or chain, and is compared to a vow. Eustathius in his notes on the second book of the Iliad, assigns a similar origin to the word □□□□□□□□□□ or engagement. For he who has received the promise, in some measure takes and holds the person, that has made the engagement. A meaning not ill expressed by Ovid in the second book of his Metamorphoses, where the promiser says to him, to whom he had promised, "My word has become yours."

After knowing this, there remains no difficulty in replying to the arguments of Connanus. For the expressions of the lawyers, respecting BARE PROMISES refer only to what was introduced by the Roman laws, which have made a FORMAL STIPULATION the undoubted sign of a deliberate mind.

Nor can it be denied that there were similar laws among other nations. For Seneca, speaking of human laws, and promises made without proper solemnities, says, "What law, *of any country, we may add*, obliges us to the performance of bare promises?" But there may naturally be other signs of a deliberate mind, besides a formal stipulation, or any other similar act which the civil law requires, to afford grounds for a legal remedy. But what is not done with a deliberate mind, we are inclined to believe does not come under the class of perfect obligations; as Theophrastus has observed in his book on laws. Nay, even what is done with a deliberate mind, but' not with an intention of conceding our own right to another; though it cannot give any one a natural right of exacting its fulfillment, yet it creates an obligation not only in point of duty, but in point of moral necessity. The next matter to be considered is, what are the requisites to constitute a perfect promise.

**V**. The use of reason is the first requisite to constitute the obligation of a promise, which idiots, madmen, and infants are consequently incapable of making. The case of minors is somewhat different. For although they may not have a sound judgment, yet it is not a permanent defect, nor sufficient of itself to invalidate all their acts. It cannot be certainly defined at what period of life reason commences. But it must be judged of from daily actions, or from the particular customs of each country. Amongst the Hebrews a promise made by a male at the age of thirteen, and by a female at the age of twelve, was valid. In other nations, the civil laws, acting upon just motives, declare certain promises made by wards and minors to be void, not only among the Romans, but among the Greeks also, as it has been observed by Dion Chrysostom in his twenty-fifth oration. To do away the effect of improvident promises, some laws introduce actions of recovery, or restitution. But such regulations are peculiar to the civil law, and have no immediate connection with the law of nature and of nations, any farther than that wherever they are established, it is consonant to natural justice that they should be observed. Wherefore if a foreigner enter into an agreement with a citizen or subject of any other country; he will be bound by the laws of that country, to which, during his residence therein, he owes a temporary obedience. But the case is different, where an agreement is made upon the open sea, or in a desert island, or by letters of correspondence. For such contracts are regulated by the law of nature alone, in the same manner as compacts made by sovereigns in their public capacity.

**VI**. The consideration of promises, made under an error, is a subject of some intricacy. For it, in general, makes a difference, whether the promiser knew the full extent of his promise, and the value of the thing promised, or not, or whether the contract, which was made, originated in fraudulent intention, or not, or whether one of the parties was privy to the fraud; and whether the fulfillment of it was an act of strict justice, or only of good faith. For according to the variety of these circumstances, writers pronounce some acts void and others valid, leaving the injured party a discretionary power to rescind or amend them.

Most of these distinctions originate in the ancient civil, and praetorian Roman law. Though some of them are not strictly founded in reason and truth. But the most obvious and natural way of discovering the truth is by referring to laws, which derive their force and efficacy from the general consent of mankind; so that if a law rests upon the presumption of any fact, which in reality has no existence, such a law is not binding. For when no evidence of the fact can be produced, the entire foundation, on which that law rests must fail. But we must have recourse to the subject, to the words and circumstances of a law, to determine when it is founded on such a presumption.

The same rule applies to the interpretation of promises. For where they are made upon the supposition of a fact, which in the end proves not to be true, they lose the force of obligations. Because the promiser made them upon certain conditions only, the fulfillment of which becomes impossible. Cicero, in his first book on the talents and character of an orator, puts the case of a father, who, under the supposition or intelligence that his son was dead, promised to devise his property to his nephew. But the supposition proving erroneous, and the intelligence false, the father was released from the obligation of the promise made to his relative. But if the promiser has neglected to examine the matter, or has been careless in expressing his meaning, he will be bound to repair the damage which another has sustained on that account. This obligation is not built on the strength of the promise, but on the injury, which it has occasioned. An erroneous promise will be binding, if the error was not the OCCASION of the promise. For here there is no want of consent in the party, who made it. But if the promise was obtained by fraud, the person so obtaining it shall indemnify the promiser for the injury sustained, if there has been any partial error in the promise, yet in other respects it shall be deemed valid.

**VII**. Promises extorted by fear are a subject of no less intricate decision. For here too a distinction is usually made between a well founded and a chimerical fear, between a just fear and a bare suspicion, and between the persons who occasion it, whether it be the person to whom the promise is given, or some other. A distinction is also made between acts purely gratuitous, and those in which both parties have an interest. For according to all this variety of circumstances some engagements are considered as void, others as revocable at the pleasure or discretion of the maker, and others as warranting a claim to indemnity for the inconvenience occasioned. But on each of these points there is great diversity of opinion.

There is some shew of reason in the opinion of those who, without taking into consideration the power of the civil law to annul or diminish an obligation, maintain that a person is bound to fulfil a promise which he has given under impressions of fear. For even in this case there was CONSENT, though it was extorted; neither was it conditional, as in erroneous promises, but absolute. It is called CONSENT. For as Aristotle has observed, those who consent to throw their goods overboard in a storm, would have saved them, had it not been for the fear of shipwreck. But they freely part with them considering all the circumstances of time and place.

**VIII**. To render a promise valid, it must be such as it is in the power of the promiser to perform. For which reason no promises to do illegal acts are valid, because no one either has, or ever can have a right to do them. But a promise, as was said before, derives all its force from the right of the promiser to make it, nor can it extend beyond that.

If a thing is not now in the power of the promiser, but may be so at some future time; the obligation will remain in suspense. For the promise was only made under the expectation of some future ability to fulfil it. But if a person has a controul over the condition upon which the promise is made, to realise it or not, he lies under a moral obligation to use every endeavour to fulfil it. But in obligations of this kind also, the civil law, from obvious motives of general utility, occasionally interposes its authority to make them void: obligations, which the law of nature would have confirmed.

**IX**. The next general inquiry, for the most part, refers to the validity of promises made upon any immoral or unlawful consideration; as if, for instance, any thing is promised to another on condition of his committing a murder. Here the very promise itself is wicked and unlawful, because it encourages the commission of a crime. But it does not follow that every FOOLISH or IMPROVIDENT promise loses the force of an obligation, as in the confirmation of imprudent or prodigal grants, for no further evil can result from a confirmation of what has been already given: and the invalidity of promises would be a greater evil than any that could result from a confirmation of the most improvident. But in promises made Upon IMMORAL and UNLAWFUL considerations, there is al. ways a criminality remaining, even while they continue unfulfilled. For during the whole of that time, the expectation of fulfillment carries with it the indelible mark of encouragement to the commission of a crime.

[**Translator's note:** Sections X, and XI of the original are omitted in the translation.]

**XII**. We are obliged to confirm the engagements made by others, acting in our name, if it is evident that they had special, or general instructions from us to do so. And in granting a commission with full powers to any one, it may so happen that we are bound by the conduct of that agent, even if he exceed the secret instructions which he has received. For he acts upon that ostensible authority, by which we are bound to ratify whatever he does, although we may have bound him to do nothing but according to his private instructions. This rule, we must observe, applies to the promises made by ambassadors in the name of their sovereigns, when, by virtue of their public credentials, they have exceeded their private orders.

**XIII**. From the preceding arguments, it is easy to understand how far owners of ships are answerable for the acts of the masters employed by them in those vessels, or merchants for the conduct of their factors. For natural equity will qualify the actions brought against them, according to the instructions and powers which they give. So that we may justly condemn the rigour of the Roman law, in making the owners of ships absolutely bound by all the acts of the masters employed. For this is neither consonant to natural equity, which holds it sufficient for each party to be answerable in proportion to his share, nor is it conducive to the public good. For men would be deterred from employing ships, if they lay under the perpetual fear of being answerable for the acts of their masters to an unlimited extent. And therefore in Holland, a country where trade has flourished with the greatest vigour, the Roman law has never been observed either now or at any former period. On the contrary, it is an established rule that no action can be maintained against the owner for any greater sum than the value of the ship and cargo.

For a promise to convey a right, acceptance is no less necessary than in a transfer of property. And in this case there is supposed to have been a precedent request, which is the same as acceptance. Nor is this contradicted by the promises which the civil law implies every one to have made to the state, WITHOUT ANY REQUEST OR FORMAL ACCEPTANCE.

**XIV**. A reason which has induced some to believe that the sole act of a promiser, by the law of nature, is sufficient. Our first position is not contradicted by the Roman law. For it no where says, that a promise has its full effect before acceptance, but only forbids the revocation of it which might prevent acceptance: and this effect results, not from NATURAL but from purely LEGAL rules.

**XV**. Another question is, whether the acceptance alone of a promise is sufficient, or whether it ought to be communicated to the promiser before it can be made binding.

It is certain that a promise may be made two ways, either upon condition of its being fulfilled, if accepted, or upon condition of its being ratified, if the promiser is apprised of its being accepted. And in cases of mutual obligation, it is presumed to be taken in the latter sense; but it is better to take promises that are purely gratuitous in the former sense, unless there be evidence to the contrary.

**XVI**. From hence it follows, that a promise may be revoked, without the imputation of injustice or levity, BEFORE ACCEPTANCE, as no right has yet been conveyed; especially if ACCEPTANCE were made the condition of its being fulfilled. It may be revoked too if the party to whom it was made, should die before acceptance. Be. cause it is evident that the power to accept it or not, was conferred upon Him, and not upon his HEIRS. For to give a man a right, which may POSSIBLY descend to his heirs, is one thing, and to express an intention of giving it to his heirs is another. For it makes an essential difference upon what person the favour is conferred. This is understood in the answer made by Neratius, who said, that he did not believe the prince would have granted to one who was dead, what he granted, supposing him still alive.

**XVII**. A promise may be revoked, by the death of the person appointed to communicate to a third the intention of the promiser. Because the obligation to the third person rested upon such communication. The case is different, where a public messenger is employed, who is not himself the obligatory instrument, but only the means through which it is conveyed. Therefore letters indicating a promise, or consent may be conveyed by any one. Yet there is a distinction to be made between a minister appointed to communicate a promise, and one appointed to make the promise in his own name.

For in the former case, a revocation will be valid, even though it has not been made known to the minister employed; but in the latter case, it will be entirely void, because the right of promising was committed to the minister, and fully depended upon his will; therefore the obligation of the promise was complete, as he knew of no intended revocation. So also in the former case, where a second person is commissioned to communicate the intentions of a donor to a third; even if the donor should die, the acceptance of the gift will be deemed valid, all that was requisite being performed on one part; though till that period the intention was revocable, as is evident in the case of bequests. But in the other case, where a person has received a full commission to execute a promise during the LIFE of the donor, should the donor die before the execution of it, and the person employed be apprised of his death; the commission, the promise, and the acceptance of it will then, at once, become void.

In doubtful cases, it is reasonable to suppose that it was the intention of the promiser, that the commission which he gave should be executed, unless some great change, as for instance, his own death should occur. Yet reasons in favour of a contrary opinion may easily be found and admitted, especially with respect to pious donations, which, at all events, ought to stand good. And in the same manner may be decided the long disputed question, whether an action on account of such a bequest could be brought against the heir. Upon which the author of the second book to Herennius says, that Marcus Drusus the praetor decided one way, and Sextus Julius another.

**XVIII**. The acceptance of a promise for a third person is a matter subject to discussion, in which there is a distinction to be observed between a promise made to a person of a thing, which is to be given to another, and a promise made directly to the person himself, on whom the former is to be conferred. If a promise is made to any one, where his own personal interest is not concerned, a consideration introduced by the Roman law, by acceptance he seems naturally to acquire a right which may be transferred to another for His acceptance, and this right will pass so fully, that in the mean time the promise cannot be revoked by the person who gave, though it may be released by him who received it. For that is a meaning by no means repugnant to the law of nature, and it is entirely conformable to the words of such a promise; nor can it be a matter of indifference to the person, through whom another is to receive a benefit.

But if a promise is made directly to one, on whom a thing is to be conferred, a distinction must be made, whether the person receiving such a promise has SPECIAL commission for acceptance, or one SO GENERAL as to include acceptance, or has it not. When a commission has been previously given, no farther distinction is necessary, whether the person be free or not, a condition which the Roman laws require. But it is plain that from such an acceptance, let the condition of the person be what it will, the promise is complete: because consent may be given and signified through the medium of another, For a person is supposed to have fully intended, what be has put into the power of another to accept or refuse.

Where there is no such commission, if another, to whom the promise was not directly made, accepts it with the consent of the promiser, the promise will be so far binding, that the promiser will not be at liberty to revoke it, before the person, in whose favour it was made has ratified, and afterwards chosen to release the engagement. Yet, in the mean time, the accepter cannot release it, as having derived no peculiar right from it himself, but only been used as an instrument in promoting the kind intentions and good faith of the promiser. The promiser therefore himself, by revoking it, is not doing violence to the perfect right of another, but only acting in contradiction to his own good faith.

**XIX**. From what has been said before, it is easy to conceive what opinion ought to be entertained of a burdensome condition annexed to a promise. For it may be annexed at any time, till a promise has been completed by acceptance, or an irrevocable pledge to fulfil it has been given. But the condition of a burden annexed to a favour intended to be conferred upon a third per. son, through the medium of any one, may be revoked before the person has confirmed it by his acceptance, On this point there is great difference of opinion. But upon impartial consideration the natural equity of any case may be easily seen without any great length of arguments.

**XX. XXI. XXII.** Another point of discussion relates to the validity of an erroneous promise, when the person, who made it, upon being apprised of his error is willing to adhere to his engagement. And the same inquiry applies to promises, which, arising out of fear or any other such motive, are prohibited by the civil law. What, it may be asked, will become of these promises, if that fear, or that motive has been removed?

To confirm such obligations, some think an internal consent of the mind alone in conjunction with some previous external act is sufficient. Others disapprove of this opinion, because they do not admit that an external act is a real sign of a subsequent intention. Therefore they require an express repetition of the promise and acceptance. Between these two opinions, the truth is most likely to be found. There may be an external act expressive of a promise, though unaccompanied with words; where one party's accepting and retaining a gift, and the other's relinquishing his right in it are sufficient to constitute a full consent.

To prevent civil laws from being confounded with natural justice, we must not omit noticing, in this place, that promises though founded in no EXPRESS motive, are not, any more than gifts, void by the law of nature.

Nor is a person who has engaged for another's performing any thing, bound to pay damages and interest for neglect, provided he has done every thing that was necessary on his part towards obtaining its accomplishment. Unless the express terms of the agreement, or the nature of the business require a stricter obligation, positively declaring that, under all circumstances whatever, the thing shall be performed.

## CHAPTER 12: ON CONTRACTS

*Human actions divided into simple or mixed — Gratuitous, or accompanied with mutual obligation — Acts by way of exchange, adjustment of what is to be given or done — Partnership — Contracts — Previous equality — As to knowledge of all circumstances — As to freedom of consent, requisite in contracts of exchange, of sale, of commission and loan — Price of things in what manner to be rated — Transfer of property by sale — What kind contrary to the law of nature — Money — Its use as the standard value of all things — No abatement in the rent or hire of a thing on account of ordinary accidents — Increase or diminution of just salaries — Usury, by what law forbidden — Interest not coming under the name of usury*

*— Insurance — Partnerships of Trade, Naval Associations — Inequality in the terms of a contract no way repugnant to the law of nations.*

**I.** and **II.** OF ALL human actions, wherein the interest of others is concerned, some are simple, and some are mixed. In those of the former description all service is purely gratuitous, but in the latter it is a traffic of exchange. In the one case the service is granted without a requital, but in the other it is accompanied with an obligation on both sides. Gratuitous services are either immediate in their effect, or to take place at some future time. A beneficial service may be said to be immediately performed, when it confers an advantage, to which the person so benefitted has no direct or absolute right. As a gift transfers property, where there is no previous right. A subject, which has been already discussed. And promises may be said to relate to some future gift, or action, of which a full and sufficient explanation has before been given.

Services accompanied with mutual obligation are those where the use of a thing is allowed to any one without a complete alienation, or where labour is given in expectation of some valuable consideration. Under the first of these heads we may reckon the loan and use of all consumable or inconsumable property: and under the latter we may place all commissions to transact business, or all trusts to preserve the property of another. Similar to which are all promises of something to be done, except that they regard a future time. And in this view we may consider all the actions, which are now to be explained.

**III.** In all acts of exchange, there is either an adjustment of shares, or the profits are regarded as a common stock. And such adjustments are made by the Roman Lawyers in the following terms, "I give this to receive that in return, I do this in order for you to do that, or I do this for you to give me that."* But the Romans exclude from that adjustment certain kinds of contracts, which they call EXPRESS ENGAGEMENTS. Not because they are entitled to any such peculiar name more than the simple acts of exchange already mentioned: but because from frequent use they have naturally derived a character similar to that of the original contract, from which they are named, though they are not attended exactly with the same circumstances, nor expressed directly in the same terms. Whereas in other contracts less frequently in use, the form was confined to an exact statement of all the circumstances of the case. An action upon which was therefore called by the Roman law an ACTION IN PRESCRIBED WORDS.

For the same reason, if those contracts, which are in general use, be accompanied with any of the requisite formalities, as in a bargain or sale, if the price had been agreed upon, though no part of the agreement had been performed by either of the parties, the civil law enforced an obligation to fulfil them. But as it considers those contracts which are seldom used, more in the light of voluntary engagements, depending upon the good faith of the respective parties, than upon legal obligation, it leaves both sides at liberty to relinquish them at any time prior to their being naturally performed.

Distinctions of this kind are unknown to the law of nature, which gives SIMPLE AGREEMENTS equal authority with those, that are included by civilians in the class of EXPRESS CONTRACTS, And on the score of antiquity their pretensions are far superior. It is therefore perfectly conformable to the principles of nature to reduce the adjustment of all agreements, without any regard to the distinction between SIMPLE and EXPRESS CONTRACT, to the three species already named. Thus, for instance, one thing is given for another, which constitutes barter, the most ancient kind of traffic; the next step in the progress of commercial intercourse is where one kind of money is given for another, a transaction which by mer. chants is called exchange; and a third species of contract is where money is given for any thing, as in the acts of selling and buying. Or the USE of one thing may be given for that of another; money also may be given for the USE of a thing, which last method constitutes the acts of letting and hiring.

The term use is to be understood here as applied not only to the bare unproductive use of a thing, but to that which is attended with profit, whether it be temporary, personal, hereditary or circumscribed, as was the case among the Hebrews with regard to transfers, which could be made for no longer a time than till the year of jubilee. The very essence of a loan consists in a return of the same kind of thing after a stated period. A return which can take place only in things regulated by weight, number, or measure, whether it be in commodities or money. But the exchange of labour branches out into various kinds of recompence or return. As, for instance, a person gives his labour for money, which in the daily transactions of life is called hire or wages: where one undertakes to indemnify another for accidental losses or damages, it is called insurance: a species of contract scarce known to the ancients, but now forming a very important branch in all mercantile and maritime concerns.

**IV**. Acts of communication are those, where each contributes a share to the joint stock. Perhaps on one side, money, and on the other, skill and labour may be given, But in whatever way these concerns are regulated, they come under the denomination of partnerships. With this class we may rank the alliances of different states in war. And of the same description are those naval associations of individuals, so frequently formed in Holland for protection against pirates or other invaders, which is generally called an ADMIRALTY, and to which the Greeks gave the name of a joint fleet.

**V**. and **VI**. Now mixed actions are either such in themselves, or made so by some adventitious circumstance, Thus if I knowingly give one person a greater price for a thing than I can purchase it for of another, the excess of price may be considered partly as a gift, and partly as a purchase. Or if I engage a goldsmith to make me any article with his own materials, the price which I give will be partly a purchase, and partly wages. The feudal system too might be considered as a train of mixed contracts. Where the grant of the fee might be considered as a beneficial act; but the military service required by the Lord, in return for his protection, gave the fee the nature of a contract, where a person did one thing expecting for it the performance of another. But if any payment is attached to it by way of acknowledgement, it partakes of the nature of a quit rent. So money sent to sea by way of venture is something compounded of a contract, of a loan, and of an insurance.

**VII**. All acts beneficial to others, except those that are purely gratuitous, come under the denomination of contracts.

**VIII**. In all contracts, natural justice requires that there should be an equality of terms: insomuch that the aggrieved party has an action against the other for overreaching him. This equality consists partly in the performance, and partly in the profits of the contract, applying to all the previous arrangements, and to the essential consequences of the agreement.

**IX**. As to an equality of terms previous to the contract, it is evident that a seller is bound to discover to a purchaser any defects, which are known to him, in a thing offered for sale; a rule not only established by civil laws, but strictly conformable to natural justice. For the words of agreement between contracting parties are even stronger than those, on which society is founded. And in this manner may be explained the observation of Diogenes the Babylonian, who in discussing this topic said, it is not every degree of silence, which amounts to concealment; nor is one person bound to disclose every thing, which may be of service to another. Thus for instance, a man of science is not strictly bound to communicate to another that knowledge, which might redound to his advantage. For contracts, which were invented to promote a beneficial intercourse among mankind, require some closer and more intimate connection than bare good-will to enforce their obligation. Upon which Ambrose has justly remarked, "that, in contracts, the faults of things exposed to sale ought to be made known, of which unless the seller has given intimation, though he may have transferred the right of property by sale, yet he is liable to an action of fraud."

But the same cannot be said of things not coming under the nature of contracts. Thus if any one should sell his corn at a high price, when he knows that many ships laden with grain are bound for that place, though it would be an act of kindness in him to communicate such intelligence to the purchasers, and though no advantage could be derived to him, from withholding the communication, but at the expence of charity, yet there is nothing unjust in it, or contrary to the general rules of dealing. The practice is vindicated by Diogenes in the passage of Cicero alluded to, he says, "I carried my commodities and offered them to sale, in selling them I demanded no greater price than others did; if the supply had been greater I would have sold them for less, and where is the wrong done to any one?" The maxim of Cicero therefore cannot generally be admitted, that, knowing a thing yourself, to wish another, whose interest it is to know it also, to remain ignorant of it, merely for the sake of your own advantage, amounts to a fraudulent concealment. By no means; for that only is a fraudulent concealment which immediately affects the nature of the contract: as for instance, in selling a house, to conceal the circumstance of its being infected with the plague, or having been ordered by public authority to be pulled down. But it is unnecessary to mention, that the person, with whom a seller treats, ought to be apprised of every circumstance attending the thing offered for sale; if it be lands, whether the tenure be subject to a rent-charge, or service of any kind, or be entirely free.

**X.** and **XI.** Nor is the equality that has been explained confined solely to the communication of all the circumstances of the case to the contracting parties, but it includes also an entire freedom of consent in both.

In the principal act itself, the proper equality requires that no more should be demanded by either party than what is just. Which can scarce have a place in gratuitous acts. To stipulate for a recompence in return for a loan, or for the service of labour or commission is doing no wrong, but constitutes a kind of mixed contract, partaking of the nature of a gratuitous act, and an act of ex. change. And in all acts of exchange, this equality is to be punctually observed. Nor can it be said that if one party promises more, it is to be looked upon as a gift. For men never enter into contracts with such intentions, nor ought the existence of such intentions ever be presumed, unless they evidently appear. For all promises or gifts, in these cases, are made with an expectation of receiving an equivalent in return." When, in the *words of Chrysostom*, in all bargains and contracts, we are anxious to receive MORE and give LESS than is due, what is this but a species of fraud or robbery?" The writer of the life of Isidorus in Photius, relates of Hermias, that when any thing, which he wished to purchase was valued at too low a rate, be made up the deficiency of the price, thinking that to act otherwise was a species of injustice, though it might escape the observation of others. And in this sense, may be interpreted the law of the Hebrews.

**XII.** There remains another degree of equality to be considered, arising out of the following case. It may happen in contracts that although nothing is concealed, which ought to be made known, nor more exacted or taken by one party than is due, yet there may be some inequality without any fault in either of the parties. Perhaps, for instance there might be some unknown defect in the thing, or there might be some mistake in the price. Yet, in such cases, to preserve that equality, which is an essential requisite in all contracts, the party suffering by such defect or mistake, ought to be indemnified by the other. For in all engagements it either is, or ought to be a standing rule, that both parties should have equal and just advantages.

It was not in every kind of equality that the Roman law established this rule, passing over slight occasions, in order to discourage frequent and frivolous litigation. It only interposed its judicial authority in weighty matters, where the price exceeded the just value by one half. Laws indeed, as Cicero has said, have power to compel, or restrain men, whereas philosophers can only appeal to their reason or understanding. Yet those, who are not subject to the power of civil laws ought to comply with whatever reason points out to them to be just: So too ought they, who are subject to the power of human laws, to perform whatever natural and divine justice requires, even in cases, where the laws neither give nor take away the right, but only forbear to enforce it for particular reasons.

**XIII**. There is a certain degree of equality, too, in beneficial or gratuitous acts, not indeed like that prevailing in contracts of exchange, but proceeding upon a supposition of the hardship, that any one should receive detriment from voluntary services, which he bestows. For which reason a voluntary agent ought to be indemnified for the expence or inconvenience, which he incurs, by undertaking the business of another. A borrower too is bound to repair a thing that has been damaged or destroyed. Because he is bound to the owner not only for the thing itself, by virtue of the property which he retains in it, but he owes a debt of gratitude also for the favour of the loan; unless it appears that the thing so lent would have perished, had it even remained in possession of the owner himself. In this case, the owner loses nothing by the loan. On the other hand, the depositary has received nothing but a trust. If the thing therefore is destroyed, he cannot be bound to restore what is no longer in existence, nor can he be required to make a recompence, where he has derived no advantage; for in taking the trust he did not receive a favour, but conferred one. In a pawn, the same as in a thing let out for hire, a middle way of deciding the obligation may be pursued, so that the person taking it is not answerable, like a borrower, for every accident, and yet he is obliged to use greater care, than a bare depositary, in keeping it safe. For though taking a pledge is a gratuitous acceptance, it is followed by some of the conditions of a contract. All these cases are conformable to the Roman law, though not originally derived from thence, but from natural equity. Rules, all of which may be found among other nations. And, among other works, we may refer to the third book and forty-second chapter of the GUIDE FOR DOUBTFUL CASES, written by Moses Maimonides, a Jewish writer.

Upon the same principles the nature of all other contracts may be explained; but the leading features in those of certain descriptions seemed sufficient for a treatise like the present.

**XIV**. The general demand for any thing, as Aristotle has clearly proved, constitutes the true measure of its value, which may be seen particularly from the practice prevailing among barbarous nations of exchanging one thing for another. But this is not the only standard: for the humours and caprice of mankind, which dictate and controul all regulations, give a nominal value to many superfluities. It was luxury, says Pliny, that first discovered the value of pearls, and Cicero has somewhere observed , that the worth of such things can only be estimated by the desires of men.

But on the other hand, it happens that the plentiful supply of necessaries lowers their price. This Seneca, in the 15th chapter of his sixth book on benefits, proves by many instances, which he concludes with the following observation, " the price of every thing must be regulated by the market, and notwithstanding all your praises, it is worth nothing more than it can be sold for." To which we may add the authority of Paulus the Lawyer, who says, the prices of things do not depend upon the humours and interest of individuals, but upon common estimation, that is, as he explains himself elsewhere, according to the worth which they are of to all.

Hence it is that things are valued in proportion to what is usually offered or given for them, a rule admitting of great variation and latitude, except in certain cases, where the law has fixed a standard price. In the common price of articles, the labour and expence of the merchant in procuring them is taken into the account, and the sudden changes so frequent in all markets depend upon the number of buyers, whether it be great or small, and upon the money and marketable commodities, whether they be plentiful or scarce.

There may indeed be casualties, owing to which a thing may be lawfully bought or sold above or below the market price. Thus for instance, a thing by being damaged may have lost its original or common value, or that, which otherwise would not have been disposed of, may be bought or sold from some particular liking or aversion. All these circumstances ought to be made known to the contracting parties. Regard too should be had to the loss or gain arising from delay or promptness of payment.

**XV**. In buying and selling we must observe, that the bargain is completed from the very moment of the contract, even without delivery, and that is the most simple way of dealing. Thus Seneca says, that a sale is a transfer of one's right and property in a thing to another, which is done in all exchanges. But if it be settled that the property shall not be transferred immediately, still the seller will be bound to convey it at the stated period, taking in the mean time all the profits and losses.

Whereas the completion of bargain and sale, by giving the purchaser a right of possession and ejectment, and conveying to him the hazard with all the profits of the property, even before it is transferred, are regulations of the civil law not universally observed. Indeed some legislators have made the seller answerable for all accidents and damages, till the actual delivery of possession is made, as Theophrastus has observed in a passage in Stobaeus, under the title of laws, where the reader will find many customs, relating to the formalities of sale, to earnest, to repentance of a bargain, very different from the rules of the Roman law. And among the Rhodians, Dion Prusaeensis informs us that all sales and contracts were confirmed by being entered in a public register.

We must observe too that, if a thing has been twice sold, of the two sales the one is valid, where an immediate transfer of the property has been made, either by delivery of possession, or in any other mode. For by this means the seller gives up an absolute right, which could not pass by a promise alone.

**XVI**. It is not every kind of monopoly that amounts to a direct violation of the laws of nature. The Sovereign power may have very just reasons for granting monopolies, and that too at a settled price: a noble instance of which we find in the history of Joseph, who governed Egypt under the auspices of Pharaoh. So also under the Roman government the people of Alexandria, as we are informed by Strabo, enjoyed the monopoly of all Indian and Ethiopian goods.

A monopoly also may, in some cases, be established by individuals, provided they sell at a reasonable rate. But all combinations to raise the necessary articles of life to an exorbitant rate, or all violent and fraudulent attempts to prevent the market from being supplied, or to buy up certain commodities, in order to enhance the price, are public injuries and punishable as such. Or indeed ANY WAY of preventing the importation of goods, or buying them up in order to sell them at a greater rate than usual, though the price, UNDER SOME PARTICULAR CIRCUMSTANCES, may not seem unreasonable, is fully shewn by Ambrose in his third book of Offices to be a breach of charity; though it come not directly under the prohibition of laws.

**XVII**. As to money, it may be observed that its uses do not result from any value intrinsically belonging to the precious metals, or to the specific denomination and shape of coin, but from the general application which can be made of it, as a standard of payment for all commodities. For whatever is taken as a common measure of all other things, ought to be liable, in itself, to but little variation. Now the precious metals are of this description, possessing nearly the same intrinsic value at all times and in all places. Though the nominal value of the same quantity of gold and silver, whether paid by weight or coin will be greater or less, in proportion to the abundance or scarcity of the things for which there is a general demand.

**XVIII**. Letting and hiring, as Caius has justly said, come nearest to selling and buying, and are regulated by the same principles. For the price corresponds to the rent or hire, and the property of a thing to the liberty of using it. Wherefore as an owner must bear the loss of a thing that perishes, so a person hiring a thing or renting a farm must bear the loss of all ordinary accidents, as for instance, those of barrenness or any other cause, which may diminish his profits. Nor will the owner, on that account, be the less entitled to the stipulated price or rent, because he gave the other the right of enjoyment, which at that time was worth so much, unless it was then agreed that the value should depend upon such contingencies.

If an owner, when the first tenant has been prevented from using a thing, shall have let it to another, all the profits accruing from it are due to the first tenant, for it would not be equitable that the owner should be made richer by what belonged to another.

**XIX.** The next topic, that comes under consideration, is the lawfulness of taking interest for the use of a consurnable thing; the arguments brought against which appear by no means such as to command our assent. For as to what is said of the loan of consumable property being a gratuitous act, and entitled to no return, the same reasoning may apply to the letting of inconsumable property for hire, requiring a recompence for the use of which is never deemed unlawful, though it gives the contract itself a different denomination.

Nor is there any more weight in the objection to taking interest for the use of money, which in its own nature is barren and unproductive. For the same may be said of houses and other things, which are unproductive and unprofitable without the industry of man.

There is something more specious in the argument, which maintains, that, as one thing is here given in return for another, and the use and profits of a thing cannot be distinguished from the thing itself, when the very use of it depends upon its consumption, nothing more ought to be required in return for the use, than what is barely equivalent to the thing itself.

But it is necessary to remark, that when it is said the enjoyment of the profits of consumable things, whose property is transferred, in the use, to the borrower or trustee, was introduced by an act of the senate, this does not properly come under the notion of Usufruct, which certainly in its original signification answers to no such right. Yet it does not follow that such a right is of no value, but on the contrary money may be required for surrendering it to the proprietor. Thus also the right of not paying money or wine borrowed till after a certain time is a thing whose value may be ascertained, the delay being considered as some advantage. Therefore in amortgage the profits of the land answer the use of money. But what Cato, Cicero, Plutarch and others allege against usury, applies not so much to the nature of the thing, as to the accidental circumstances and consequences with which it is commonly attended.

**XX.** There are some kinds of interest, which are thought to wear the appearance of usury, and generally come under that denomination, but which in reality are contracts of a different nature. The five shillings commission which a banker, for instance, charges upon every hundred pounds, is not so much an interest in addition to five per cent, as a compensation for his trouble, and for the risk and inconvenience he incurs, by the loan of his money, which he might have employed in some other lucrative way. In the same manner a person who lends money to many individuals, and, for that purpose, keeps certain sums of cash in his bands, ought to have some indemnity for the continual loss of interest upon those sums, which may be considered as so much dead stock. Nor can any recompence of this kind be branded with the name of usury. Demosthenes, in his speech against Pantaenetus, condemns it as an odious act of injustice, to charge with usury a man, who in order to keep his principal undiminished, or to assist another with money, lends out the savings of his industry and frugal habits, upon a moderate interest.

**XXI.** Those human laws, which allow a compensation to be made for the use of money or any other thing, are neither repugnant to natural nor revealed law. Thus in Holland, where the rate of interest upon common loans was eight per cent, there was no injustice in requiring twelve per cent of merchants; because the hazard was greater. The justice and reasonableness indeed of all these regulations must be measured by the hazard or inconvenience of lending. For where the recompence exceeds this, it becomes an act of extortion or oppression.

**XXII.** Contracts for guarding against danger, which are called insurances, will be deemed fraudulent and void, if the insurer knows beforehand that the thing insured is already safe, or has reached its place of destination, and the other party that it is already destroyed or lost. And that not so much on account of the equality naturally requisite in all contracts of exchange, as because the danger and uncertainty is the very essence of such con. tract. Now the premium upon all insurances must be regulated by common estimation.

**XXIII**. In trading partnerships, where money is contributed by both parties; if the proportions be equal, the profits and the losses ought to be equal also. But if they be unequal, the profits and the losses must bear the same proportion, as Aristotle has shewn at the conclusion of the eighth book of his Ethics. And the same rule will hold good where equal or unequal proportions of labor are contributed. Labor may be given as a balance against money, or both labor and money may be given, according to the general maxim that one man's labour is an equivalent for another man's money.

But there are various ways of forming these agreements. If a man borrows money to employ his skill upon in trading for himself, whether he gains or loses the whole, he is answerable to the owner for the principal. But where a man unites his labor to the capital of another in partnership, there he becomes a partner in the principal, to a share of which he is entitled. In the first of these cases the principal is not compared as a balance against the labor, but it is lent upon terms proportioned to the risk of losing it, or the probable gains to be derived from it. In the other case, the price of labour is weighed, as it were, against the money, and the party who bestows it, is entitled to an equivalent share in the capital.

What has been said of labour may be applied to voyages, and all other hazardous - undertakings. For it is contrary to the very nature of partnerships for any one to share in the gain, and to be exempt from the losses. Yet it may be so settled without any degree of injustice. For there may be a mixed contract arising out of a contract of insurance in which due equality may be preserved, by allowing the person, who has taken upon himself the losses, to receive a greater share of the gain than he would otherwise have done. But it is a thing quite inadmissible that any one should be responsible for the losses without partaking of the gains; for a communion of interests is so natural to society that it cannot subsist without it.

What has been said by writers on the civil law, that the shares are understood to be equal where they are not expressly named, is true where equal quotas have been contributed. But in a GENERAL partnership the shares are not to be measured by what may arise from this or that article, but from the probable profits of the whole.

**XXIV**. In naval associations the common motive of utility is self-defence against pirates: though they may sometimes be formed from less worthy motives. In computing the losses to be sustained by each, it is usual to estimate the number of men, the number of ships, and the quantity of merchandise protected. And what has hitherto been said will be found conformable to natural justice.

**XXV**. Nor does the voluntary law of nations appear to make any alteration here. However, there is one exception, which is, that where equal terms have been agreed upon, if no fraud has been used, nor any necessary information withheld, they shall be considered as equal in an external point of view. So that no action can be maintained in a court for such inequality. Which was the case in the civil law before Dioclesian's constitution. So among those, who are bound by the law of nations alone, there can be no redress or constraint on such account.

And this is the meaning of what Pomponius says, that in a bargain and sale, one man may NATURALLY overreach another: an allownace which is not to be construed, as a right, but is only so far a permission, that no legal remedy can be used against the person, who is determined to insist upon the agreement.

In this place, as in many others, the word natural signifies nothing more than what is received by general custom. In this sense the Apostle Paul has said, that is naturally disgraceful for a man to wear long hair; a thing, in which there is nothing repugnant to nature, but which is the general practice among some nations. Indeed many writers, both sacred and profane, give the name of NATURAL to what is only CUSTOMARY and HABITUAL.

# CHAPTER 13: ON OATHS

*Efficacy of oaths among Pagans — Deliberation requisite in oaths — The sense, in which oaths are understood to be taken, to be adhered to — To be taken according to the usual meaning of the words — The subject of them to be lawful — Not to counteract moral obligations — In what sense oaths are an appeal to God — The purport of oaths — To be faithfully observed in all cases — The controul of sovereigns over the oaths of subjects — Observations on our Saviour's prohibition of oaths — Forms substituted for oaths.*

**I.** THE sanctity of an oath with regard to promises, agreements, and contracts, has always been held in the greatest esteem, in every age and among every people. For as Sophocles has said in his Hippodamia, "The soul is bound to greater caution by the addition of an oath. For it guards us against two things, most to be avoided, the reproach of friends, and the wrath of heaven." In addition to which the authority of Cicero may be quoted, who says, our forefathers intended that an oath should be the best security for sincerity of affirmation, and the observance of good faith. "For, *as he observes in another place*, there can be no stronger tie, to the fulfillment of our word and promise, than an oath, which is a solemn appeal to the testimony of God."

**II.** The next point, to be considered, is the original force and extent of oaths.

And in the first place the arguments, that have been used respecting promises and contracts, apply to oaths also, which ought never to be taken but with the most deliberate reflection and judgment. Nor can any one lawfully take an oath, with a secret intention of not being bound by it. For the obligation is an inseparable and necessary consequence of an oath, and every act accompanied with an obligation is supposed to proceed from a deliberate purpose of mind. Every one is bound likewise to adhere to an oath in that sense, in which it is usually understood to be taken. For an oath being an appeal to God, should declare the full truth in the sense in which it is understood. And this is the sense upon which Cicero insists that all oaths should be performed and adhered to in that sense, in which the party imposing them intended they should be taken. For although in other kinds of promises a condition may easily be implied, to release the promiser; yet that is a latitude by no means admissible in an oath. And on this point an appeal may be made to that passage, where the admirable writer of the Epistle to the Hebrews has said, GOD WILLING more abundantly to shew unto the heirs of the promise the immutability of his counsel confirmed it by an oath: that by two immutable things, in which it was impossible for God to deceive, we might have a strong consolation. In order to understand these words, we must observe that the sacred writers, in speaking of God, often attribute to him human passions, rather in conformity to our finite capacities, than to his infinite nature. For God does not actually change his decrees, though he may be said to do so, and to repent, whenever he acts otherwise than the words seemed to indicate, the occasion, on which they. were delivered, having ceased. Now this may easily be applied in the case of threats, as conferring no right; sometimes too in promises, where a condition is implied. The Apostle therefore names two things denoting immutability, a promise which confers a right, and an oath, which admits of no mental reservations.

From the above arguments it is easy to comprehend what is to be thought of an oath fraudulently obtained. For if it is certain that a person took the oath upon a supposition, which afterwards was proved to have no foundation, and but for the belief of which he would never have taken it, he will not be bound by it. But if it appears that he would have taken it without that supposition; he must abide by his oath, because oaths allow of no evasion.

**III.** The meaning of an oath should not be stretched beyond the usual acceptation of words. Therefore there was no breach of their oath in those, who, having sworn that they would not give their daughters in marriage to the Benjamites, permitted those that had been carried off to live with them. For there is a difference between giving a thing, and not recovering that which is lost.

**IV**. To give validity to an oath, the obligation, which it imposes ought to be lawful. Therefore a sworn promise, to commit an illegal act, to do any thing in violation of natural or revealed law, will be of no effect.

**V**. Indeed if a thing promised upon oath be not actually illegal, but only an obstruction to some greater moral duty, in that case also the oath will not be valid. Because it is a duty which we owe to God not to deprive ourselves of the freedom of doing all the good in our power.

**VI**. Oaths may differ in form, and yet agree in sub. stance. For they all ought to include an appeal to God, calling upon him to witness the truth, or to punish the falsehood of their assertions, both of which amount to the same thing. For an appeal to the testimony of a superior, who has a right to punish, is the same as requiring him to avenge an act of perfidy. Now the omniscience of God gives him power to punish, as well as to witness every degree of falsehood.

**VII**. It was a custom with the ancients to swear by persons or beings expressly distinct from the supreme creator, either imprecating the wrath of those by whom they swore, whether it were the sun, the heavens, or the earth; or swearing by their own heads, by their children, their country or their prince, and calling for destruction upon THEM, if there were any falsehood in their oaths.

Nor was this practice confined to Heathen nations only, but, as we are informed by Philo, it prevailed among the Jews. For he says that we ought not, in taking an oath upon every occasion, to have recourse to the maker and father of the universe, but to swear by our parents, by the heavens, the earth, the universe. Thus Joseph is said to have sworn by the life of Pharaoh, according to the received custom of the Egyptians. Nor does our Saviour, in the fifth chapter of St. Matthew's Gospel, intend, as it is supposed by some, to consider these oaths to be less binding than those taken expressly by the name of God. But as the Jews were too much inclined to make use of, and yet disregard them, he shews them that they are real oaths. For, as Ulpian has well observed, he who swears by his own life, seems to swear by God, bearing a respect and reference to his divine power. In the same manner Christ shews that he, who swears by the temple, swears by God who pre. sides in the temple, and that he who swears by Heaven, swears by God, who sits upon the Heavens. But the Jewish teachers of that day thought that men were not bound by oaths made in the name of created beings, unless some penalty were annexed, as if the thing, by which they swore, were consecrated to God. For this is the kind of oath implied in the words BY A GIFT, And it is this error of theirs, which Christ refutes.

**VIII**. The principal effect of oaths is to cut short disputes. "An oath for confirmation, as the inspired writer of the Epistle to the Hebrews has said, is the end of all strife." So too we find in Diodorus Siculus, that an oath was regarded among the Egyptians as the surest pledge of sincerity that men could give. So that every one, in taking an oath, should express the real purpose of his mind, and render his actions conformable to those expressions. There is a beautiful passage on this subject, in Dionysius of Halicarnassus, who says, "the last pledge among men, whether Greeks or Barbarians, and it is a pledge, which no time can blot out, is that which takes the Gods, as witnesses to oaths and covenants."

**IX**. The substance of an oath too should be such, and conceived in such words, as to include not only the divine, but the human obligations, which it implies. For it should convey to the person, who receives it, the same security for his right, as he would derive from an express promise or a contract. But if either the words bear no reference to a person so as to confer upon him a right, or if they do refer to him but in such a manner that some opposition may be made to his claim, the force of the oath will, in that case, be such as to give that person no right from it; yet he who has taken it must still submit to the divine obligation, which the oath imposes. An example of which we have in a person, from whom a sworn promise has been extorted by fear. For here the oath conveys no right, but what the receiver ought to relinquish, for it has been obtained to the prejudice of the giver. Thus we find the Hebrew Kings were reproved by the prophets, and punished by God for not observing the oaths, which they had taken to the kings of Babylon.

**X**. The same rule applies not only to transactions between public enemies, but to those between any individuals whatsoever. For he, to whom the oath is taken, is not the only person to be considered; but a solemn regard must be paid to God, in whose name the oath is taken, and who possesses authority to enforce the obligation. For which reason it is impossible to admit the position of Cicero, that it is no breach of an oath to refuse paying to robbers the sum stipulated for having spared one's life; because such men are not to be ranked in the number of lawful enemies, but treated as the common enemies of all mankind, so that towards them no faith ought to be kept, nor even the sanctity of an oath observed.

**XI**. The power of superiors over inferiors, that is of sovereigns over subjects, with respect to oaths, is the next topic that comes under consideration. Now the act of a superior cannot annul the perfect obligation of an oath, which rests upon natural and revealed law. But as we are not, in a state of civil society, entirely masters of our own actions, which in some measure depend upon the direction of the sovereign power, which has a twofold influence with respect to oaths, in the one case applying to the person who takes, and in the other, to the person who receives them. This authority may be exercised over the person taking the oath, either by declaring, before it is taken, that it shall be made void, or by prohibiting its fulfillment, when taken. For the inferior or subject, considered as such, could not bind himself to engagements, beyond those allowed by the sovereign legislature. In the same manner, by the Hebrew Law, husbands might annul the oaths of wives, and fathers those of children, who were still dependent.

**XII**. In this place we may cursorily observe, that what is said in the precepts of Christ, and by St. James, agains swearing at all, applies not to an oath of affirmation, many instances of which are to be found in the writings of St. Paul, but to promissory oaths respecting uncertain and future events. This is plain from the opposition in the words of Christ. " You have heard it hath been said by them of old time, thou shalt not forswear thyself, but shalt perform unto the Lord thine oath. But I say to you, swear not at all." And the reason given for it by St. James, is that I you fall not into hypocrisy," or be found deceivers; for so the word HYPOCRISY signifies in the Greek.

Again it is said by St. Paul, that all the promises of God in Christ are YEA and AMEN, that is are certain and undoubted. Hence came the Hebrew phrase, that a just man's YEA is YEA, and his NO is NO. On the other hand, persons, whose actions differ from their affirmations, are said to speak YEA and NO, that is their affirmation is a denial, and their denial an affirmation.

In this manner St. Paul vindicates himself from the charge of lightness of speech, adding that his conversation had not been YEA, and NO.

**XIII**. Affirmations are not the only modes of obligation. For in many places signs have been used as pledges of faith; thus among the Persians giving the right hand was considered the firmest tie. So that where any form is substituted for an oath, the violation of it will be an act of perjury. It has been said of Kings and Princes in particular, that their faith is the same as an oath. On which account Cicero, in his speech for Dejotarus, commends Caesar no less for the vigour of his arm in battle, than for the sure fulfillment of the pledge and promise of his right hand.

[**Translator's note:** The nature of oaths, contracts and promises having been so fully discussed in the preceding chapters, the translation proceeds from the thirteenth to the fifteenth chapter of the original, the fourteenth being in a great measure only a repetition of our author's former arguments upon the subject.]

# CHAPTER 15: ON TREATIES AND ON ENGAGEMENTS MADE BY DELEGATES EXCEEDING THEIR POWER.

*Public Conventions — Divided into treaties, engagements, and other compacts — Difference between treaties and the engagements made by delegates exceeding their powers — Treaties founded on the law of nature — Their origin — Treaties founded on still more extensive principles — Treaties with those, who are strangers to the true religion, prohibited neither by the Jewish nor Christian law — Cautious respecting such treaties — Christians bound to unite against the enemies of the Christian religion — Among a number of Allies in war, which of them have the first pretensions to assistance — Tacit renewal of treaties — The effect of perfidy in one of the contracting parties considered — How far the unauthorized engagements of delegates are binding, when the sovereigns refuse to ratify them — The Caudian Convention considered — Whether the knowledge and silence of the Sovereign makes those unauthorized conventions binding — The Convention of Luctatius considered.*

**I.** ULPIAN has divided conventions into two kinds, public and private, and he has not explained a public convention upon the usual principles, but has confined it to a treaty of peace, which he alleges as his first example, and he has made use of the engagements entered into by the generals of two contending powers, as an instance of private conventions. By public conventions therefore he means those, which cannot be made but by the authority and in the name of the sovereign power, thus distinguishing them not only from the private contracts of individuals, but ALSO from the PERSONAL contracts of sovereigns themselves. And indeed private injuries and contracts, no less than public treaties frequently prove the origin of wars. And as private contracts have been already so amply discussed, the higher order of contracts, which come under the denomination of treaties, will necessarily form the leading part in our farther inquiries.

**II.** and **III.** Now public conventions may be divided into treaties, engagements, and other compacts.

The ninth book of Livy may be consulted on the distinction between treaties and engagements, where the historian informs us, that treaties are those contracts, which are made by the express authority of the sovereign power, and in which the people invoke the divine vengeance on their heads, if they violate their engagements. Among the Romans the persons employed in declaring war and making peace, were in the conclusion of these solemn treaties, always accompanied by the principal herald, who took the oath in the name of the whole people. A sponsio, or ENGAGEMENT, is what was made by persons, who had no express commission for that purpose from the sovereign power, and whose acts consequently required a further ratification from the sovereign himself.

The Senate of Rome, we are informed by Sallust, judged very properly in passing a decree, that no treaty could be' made without their consent and that of the people. Livy relates that Hieronymus, king of Syracuse, having entered into a convention with Hannibal, sent afterwards to Carthage to have it converted by the state into a league. For which reason Seneca the elder has said, applying the expression to persons invested with a special commission for that purpose, that a treaty, negotiated by the general, binds the whole of the Roman people, who are supposed to have made it.

But in monarchies, the power of making treaties belongs to the king alone, a maxim which the language of poetry, no less than the records of history, shews to have been held in all ages. Euripides, whose sentiments are always conformable to nature, and popular opinion, in his Tragedy of the Suppliants, says, "It rests with Adrastus to take the oath, to whom, as sovereign, the sole right of binding the country by treaties belongs."

No subordinate magistrates have such a power of binding the people; nor will the acts of a smaller portion bind the greater, an argument used in favour of the Romans against the Gauls. For there was a majority of the people with Camillus, the dictator.

But it remains to be considered how far the acts of those, who have engaged for the people, without any public authority, are binding. Perhaps it may be said that the contracting parties have discharged their responsibility when they have done all in their power towards the fulfillment of their obligation. That might be the case in promises, but the obligation in public contracts is of a stricter kind. For the party contracting requires something in return for the engagements he makes. Hence the civil law, which rejects all promises made by one person for the performance of some act by another, renders him who engages for the ratification of a thing liable to pay damages and interest.

**IV**. The most accurate distinction in treaties, is that which makes the foundation of some rest purely upon the law of nature, and others upon the obligations, which men have either derived from the law of nature, or added to it. Treaties of the former kind are, in general, made, not only between enemies, as a termination of war; but in ancient times were frequently made, and, in some degree, thought necessary among men in the formation of every contract. This arose from that principle in the law of nature, which established a degree of kindred among mankind. Therefore it was unlawful for one man to be injured by another. And this natural justice universally prevailed before the deluge. But after that event, in process of time, as evil dispositions and habits gained ground, it was by degrees obliterated. So that one people's robbing and plundering another, even when no war had been commenced or declared, was deemed lawful. Epiphanius calls this the Scythian fashion. Nothing is more frequent in the writings of Homer than for men to be asked, if they are robbers? A question, as Thueydides informs us, by no means intending to convey reproach, but purely for information. In an ancient law of Solon's mention is made of companies formed for robbery: and, we find from Justin, that, till the times of Tarquin, piracy was attended with a degree of glory.

In the law of the Romans it was a maxim, that nations, which had not entered into terms of amity, or into treaties with them were not to be considered as enemies. But if any thing belonging to the Romans fell into their hands, it became theirs; or any citizen of Rome, taken by them, became a slave; and the Romans would treat any person belonging to that nation, in the same manner. In this case the right of postliminium is observed. So at a remote period, before the times of the Peloponnesian war, the Corcyraeans were not considered as enemies by the Athenians, though there was no treaty of peace subsisting between them, as appears from the speech of the Corinthians given by Thucydides. Aristotle commends the practice of plundering barbarians, and in ancient Latium an enemy signified nothing but a foreigner.

In the class of treaties referred to in this section may be ranked those made between different states for the mutual preservation of the rights of hospitality and commerce, as far as they come under the law of nature. Arco makes use of this distinction, in his speech to the Achaeans, as reported by Livy, where he says he does not require an offensive and defensive alliance, but only such a treaty as may secure their rights from infringement by each other, or prevent them from harbouring the fugitive slaves of the Macedonians. Conventions of this kind were called by the Greeks, strictly speaking, PEACE in opposition to TREATIES.

**V**. Treaties founded upon obligations added to those of the law of nature are either equal, or unequal Equal treaties are those, by which equal advantages are secured on both sides. The Greeks call them ALLIANCES, and sometimes alliances upon an equal scale. But treaties of the latter kind are more properly leagues than treaties, and where one of the parties is inferior in dignity, they are called INJUNCTIONS, or INJUNCTIONS ANNEXED TO COVENANTS. Demosthenes in his speech on the liberty of the Rhodians says, all nations ought to guard against forming such leagues, as approaching too near to servitude.

Treaties of both kinds, whether of peace or alliance are made from motives of some advantage to the parties. By equal treaties of peace, the restoration of prisoners, the restoration or cession of conquered places, and other matters providing for its due maintenance, are settled, a subject that will be more fully treated of hereafter, in stating the effects and consequences of war. Treaties of alliance upon equal conditions relate either to commerce, or to contributions for the joint prosecution of a war, or to other objects of equal importance. Equal treaties of commerce may vary in their terms. For instance it may be settled that no duties shall be imposed upon the goods of the subjects, belonging to each of the contracting powers: or that the duties upon their respective commodities shall be lower than the duties upon those of any other nation. The first of these examples may be found in an ancient treaty between the Romans and Carthaginians, in which there is a clause, making an exception of what is given to the notary and public crier. Or it may be settled that no higher duties than those existing at the time the treaty is made shall be imposed, or that they shall not be augmented beyond a certain rate.

So in alliances of war the contracting parties are required to furnish equal numbers of troops or ships, a kind of alliance which, as Thueydides explains it, calls upon the united powers to hold the same states for common enemies or friends: we find, in many parts of Livy, alliances of this description among states, for the mutual defence of their territories or for the prosecution of some particular war, or against some particular enemy, or against all states excepting their respective allies. Polybius has given a treaty of this kind, made between the Carthaginians and Macedonians. In the same manner the Rhodians bound themselves by treaty to assist Atigonus Demetrius against all enemies except Ptolemy. There are. other objects too for which equal treaties are made. Thus one power may bind another to build no forts in their neighbourhood which might prove an annoyance, to give no encouragement to rebellious subjects, to allow the troops of an enemy no passage through their country.

**VI**. From equal treaties, the nature of unequal treaties may easily be understood. And where two powers contract, this inequality may be on the side either of the superior, or of the inferior power. A superior power may be said to make an unequal treaty, when it promises assistance without stipulating for any return, or gives greater advantages than it engages to receive. And on the part of the inferior power this inequality subsists when, as Isocrates says in his PANEGYRIC, her privileges are unduly depressed; so that engagements of this kind may be called injunctions or commands rather than treaties. And these may, or may not, be attended with a diminution of their sovereign power.

Such a diminution of sovereign power followed the second treaty between the Carthaginians and Romans, by which the former were bound to make no war but with the consent of the Roman people; so that from that time, Appian says, the Carthaginians were compelled by treaty to comply with the humour of the Romans. To this kind may be added a conditional surrender, except that it leads not to a DIMINUTION, but to an ENTIRE TRANSFER of the sovereign dignity and power.

**VII**. The burdens attached to unequal treaties, where no diminution of sovereignty takes place, may be either transitory or permanent.

TRANSITORY burdens are those, by which the payment of certain sums of money is imposed, the demolition of certain works and fortifications, the cession of certain countries and the delivery of ships or hostages are required. But PERMANENT conditions are those, which require the tribute of homage and submission from one power to another.

Nearly approaching to such treaties are those, by which one power is debarred from having any friends or enemies, but at the pleasure of another, or from allowing a passage and supplies to the troops of any state, with whom that power may be at war. Besides these there may be conditions of an inferior and less important kind; such as those, which prohibit the building of forts in certain places; maintaining armies, or having ships beyond a certain number; navigating certain seas, or raising troops in certain countries; attacking allies or supplying enemies. Some conditions indeed go so far as to prohibit a state from admitting refugees, and to demand annulling all former engagements with every other power. Numerous examples of such treaties are to be found in historians both ancient and modern.

Unequal treaties may be made not only between the conquerors and the conquered but also between mighty and impotent states, between whom no hostilities have ever existed.

**VIII**. In considering treaties, it is frequently asked, whether it be lawful to make them with nations, who are strangers to the Christian religion; a question, which, according to the law of nature, admits not of a doubt. For the rights, which it establishes, are common to all men without distinction of religion.

The gospel has made no change in this respect, but rather favours treaties, by which assistance in a just cause may be afforded even to those, who are strangers to religion. For to embrace opportunities of doing good to all men is not only permitted as laudable, but enjoined as a precept. For in imitation of God, who makes his sun to rise upon the righteous and the wicked, and refreshes them both with his gracious rain, we are commanded to exclude no race of men from their due share of our services. Yet, in equal cases, it admits of no doubt, that those within the pale of our own religious communion have a preferable claim to our support.

**IX**. In addition to the foregoing arguments we may observe that as all Christians are considered as members of one body, which are required to feel for the pains and sufferings of each other, this precept applies not only to individuals, but to nations and kings in their public capacity. For the rule of duty is not to be measured by the inclination of individuals, but by the injunctions of Christ. And in some cases the ravages of an impious enemy can only be opposed by a firm alliance among Christian kings, and governments. And it is a duty from which nothing, but inevitable necessity, and their immediate attention being engrossed by the prosecution of other wars, can excuse them.

**X**. Another question frequently arises, which is, when two states are engaged in war with each other, to which of them a power, equally allied to both, ought in preference to give assistance. Here too we must observe there can be no obligation to support unjust wars. On which account that confederate power, which has justice on its side, will have a claim to preference, if engaged in war with another not comprehended in the number of confederates, or even if engaged with one of the confederates themselves.

But if two powers engage in a war, equally unjust on both sides, a third power, united in confederacy with both, will prudently abstain from interference. Again, if two powers allied to us are engaged in a just war against others, with whom we have no connection; in the supplies of men or money that we furnish to either we ought to follow the rule, observed in the case of personal creditors.

But if personal assistance, which cannot be divided, is required of the contracting party, in that case the preference must be given to the engagements of the longest standing. However the case of a subsequent treaty, which makes the engagements of a more binding and extensive nature, will form an exception to this rule.

**XI**. The tacit renewal of a treaty ought not to be presumed upon at the expiration of the period, limited for its continuance, unless certain acts be performed, which can expressly be construed as a renewal of it, and can be taken in no other sense.

**XII**. If one of the parties violates a treaty, such a violation releases the other from its engagements. For every clause has the binding force of a condition. And as an example of this, a passage from Thucydides may be quoted, where that historian says that "for one power to accede to a new confederacy, and to desert an ally who has neglected to fulfil his engagements, is no breach of a treaty; but not to assist another power in conformity to sworn engagements amounts to a violation thereof." And this is generally true, except where it has been agreed to the contrary, that a treaty shall not be null and relinquished for trifling disgusts and miscarriages.

**XIII**. Conventions are as various and numerous as treaties, and the distinction made between them is owing more to the difference of power in those by whom they are made, than to any real difference in their own nature. But there are two particular points of inquiry materially connected with all conventions, the first of which relates to the extent of the negotiator's obligation, when the sovereign or the state refuses to ratify a convention, whether he is bound to make an indemnity to the other party for the disappointment, to restore things to the situation they were in before he treated, or to deliver up his own person. The first opinion seems conformable to the Roman civil law, the second to equity as it was urged by the tribunes of the people, L. Livius, and J. Melius, in the dispute about the peace of Caudium; but the third is that most generally adopted, as was done respecting the two famous conventions of Caudium and Numantia. But there is one caution particularly to be observed, and that is, that the sovereign is no way bound by such unauthorised conventions, until he has ratified them. In the convention alluded to, if the Samnites had intended to bind the Roman people, they should have retained the army at Caudium, and sent ambassadors to the senate and people at Rome, to discuss the treaty, and learn upon what terms they chose to redeem their army.

**XIV**. Another question is, whether the knowledge and silence of the sovereign bind him to the observance of a convention. But here it is necessary to make a distinction between an absolute convention, and one made upon condition of its being ratified by the sovereign. For as all conditions ought to be literally fulfilled, such a condition, on failure of fulfillment, becomes void.

This principle was very properly observed in the convention made between Luctatius and the Carthaginians; to which the people refused to accede, as it had been made without their consent. A new treaty therefore was made by public authority.

The next thing to be considered is, whether there may not be some act of consent besides silence. For without some visible act, silence is not of itself sufficient to warrant a probable conjecture of intention. But if certain acts are done which can be accounted for upon no other grounds than those of consent, they are supposed to ratify a treaty. Thus if the convention of Luctatius had contained many clauses, some of them relinquishing certain rights, and those clauses had been always duly observed by the Romans, such observance would be justly taken for a ratification of the treaty.

## CHAPTER 16: THE INTERPRETATION OF TREATIES

*The external obligation of promises — Words where other conjectures are wanting to be taken in their popular meaning — Terms of art to be interpreted according to the acceptation of the learned in each art, trade, and science — Conjectures requisite to explain ambiguous or seemingly contradictory terms — Interpretation of treaties from the subject-matter — From consequences, from circumstances and connection — Conjectures taken from motives — The more strict or more extensive interpretation — Treaties favourable, odious, mixed or indifferent — The good faith of kings and nations in treaties of equal validity with law — Rules of interpretation formed from the above named distinctions — Whether the word allies, in a treaty, is limited to those, who were such at the time of making it, or applies to all who are, or hereafter may become such — Interpretation of the prohibition of one party's making war without the consent or injunction of the other — Of the freedom granted to Carthage — Distinction between personal and real treaties — A treaty made with a king continues even during his expulsion by an usurper, such a treaty extends not to an invader — What kind of promises ought to have the preference — The extent of obvious conjectures — The performance of a commission by doing something equivalent — Interpretation restricted more closely than the bare signification of the words implies — From an original defect of intention — From failure of the sole motive — From a defect in the subject — Observations on the last named conjectures — Emergencies repugnant to the original intention, by rendering it unlawful or burdensome — Conjectures taken from a comparison of one part of the writings with another Rules to be observed — In dubious cases, writings not absolutely requisite to the validity of a contract — Contracts of Sovereigns not to be interpreted by the Roman law — Whether the words of the person accepting or offering the engagement ought to be most regarded — This explained by a distinction.*

**I.** IF WE consider the promiser alone, be is naturally bound to fulfil his engagements. Good faith, observes Cicero, requires that a man should consider as well what he intends, as what lie says. But as acts of the mind are not, of themselves visible it is necessary to fix upon some determinate mark, to prevent men from breaking their engagements, by allowing them to affix their own interpretation to their words. It is a right, which natural reason dictates, that every one who receives a promise, should have power to compel the promiser to do what a fair interpretation of his words suggests. For otherwise it would be impossible for moral obligations to be brought to any certain conclusion. Perhaps it was in this sense that Isocrates, treating of agreements, in his prescription against Callimachus, maintains that the laws enacted on this subject are the common laws of all mankind, not only Greeks, but barbarians also. It is for this very reason, that specific forms have been assigned for treaties, which are to be drawn up in terms of unequivocal and certain meaning. The proper rule of interpretation is to gather the intention of the parties pledged, from the most* probable signs. And these are of two kinds, namely, words and conjectures, which may be considered either separately, or together.

**II.** Where we have no other conjecture to guide us, words are not to be strictly taken in their original or grammatical sense, but in their common acceptation, for it is the arbitrary will of custom, which directs the laws and rules of speech.* It was a foolish act of perfidy therefore in the Locrians, when they promised they would adhere to their engagements as long as they stood upon that soil, and bore those heads upon their shoulders, in order to evade their promise to cast away the mould, which they had previously put within their shoes, and the heads of garlick, which they had laid upon their shoulders. Acts of treachery like these, Cicero, in the third book of his Offices, has properly observed, instead of mitigating, tend to aggravate the guilt of perjury.

**III.** In terms of art which are above the comprehension of the general bulk of mankind, recourse, for explanation, must be had to those, who are most experienced in that art; thus from consulting legal writers, we may conceive the nature of particular crimes, or from the pages of the same authors, derive our notions of sovereign power.

It is a just remark of Cicero's, that the language of logic is not that of daily and familiar intercourse: the writers of that class have phrases peculiar to themselves: which indeed is the case with arts of every description. So in treaties, where military arrangements occur, an army is defined to be a number of soldiers capable of OPENLY invading a foreign, or an enemy's country. For historians everywhere make a distinction between the private incursions of robbers, and what is done by a lawful and regular army. What constitutes an army must be therefore judged of by the enemy's force. Cicero defines an army to consist of six legions and auxiliaries. Polybius says, that a Roman army in general amounted to sixteen thousand Romans, and twenty thousand auxiliaries. But a military force might be composed of a less number of troops than this. In the same manner the number of ships sufficient for any purpose will amount to a fleet, and a place able to hold out against an enemy may be called a fort.

**IV.** It is necessary to make use of conjecture, where words or sentences admit of many meanings: A mode of expression when included in one word, is called by Logicians, a synonymous term, and, when extending to two or more words, a doubtful phrase. In the same manner it is necessary to have recourse to conjecture whenever a seeming contradiction occurs in the expressions of a treaty. For in that case we must try to discover such conjectures, as will reconcile, if possible, one part with another. For if there be an evident contradiction, the contracting parties by their latter determinations, must have intended to abrogate their former; as no one can design to make contradictory resolutions at the same time. Indeed all acts depending upon the human will, as in the case of laws and testaments, which depend upon the will of one party, and in contracts and treaties, which depend upon that of two or more, all these acts are liable to changes, with a subsequent change of will in the parties concerned. In all such cases any obscurity in the language obliges us to have recourse to conjectures, which are sometimes so obvious, as to point out a meaning directly contrary to that of the words in their usual acceptation. Now the principal sources of conjecture are to be found in the subject-matter, the consequences, and the circumstances and connection.

**V**. From the subject or matter, as for instance, in the word day. Thus if a truce be made for thirty days, here civil and not natural days are meant.

So the word donation is sometimes used to signify a transfer, according to the nature of the business. In the same manner too the word arms, which in general signifies military instruments, is sometimes applied to troops, and may be taken in either sense, according to the particular occasion. Every interpretation must be given according to the intention understood. Thus the promise of a free passage given upon the evacuation of a town, implies also that the troops shall pass without molestation. If a number of ships are to be given up, perfect and not mutilated ships are meant. And in all similar cases a similar judgment must be formed according to the natural tenor of the words.

**VI**. Another source of interpretation is derived from the consequences, especially where a clause taken in its literal meaning would lead to consequences foreign or even repugnant to the intention of a treaty. For in an ambiguous meaning such an acceptation must be taken as will avoid leading to an absurdity or contradiction. The cavil of Brasidas therefore is highly abominable, who, promising that he would evacuate the Boeotian territory, said he did not consider that as Boeotian territory, which he occupied with his army; as if the ancient bounds were not intended, but only what remained unconquered, an evasion, which entirely annulled the treaty

**VII**. From the circumstances or context another source of interpretation is derived. No inconsiderable light maybe thrown upon the meaning of an expression from the circumstance of its being used by the same person to, express the same intentions on other similar occasions, and from its relation to what goes before, and what follows the place, where it stands. For in all doubtful cases, we have reason to suppose that the contracting parties mean to be consistent with their former opinions and intentions. Thus in Homer, in the agreement between Paris and Menelaus, that Helen should be given up to the conqueror, when compared with what follows, it is evident that by the conqueror is meant the combat. ant, who killed the other. This rule of interpretation, Plutarch illustrates by the conduct of judges, "who passing by what is obscure rest their decisions upon clear and unambiguous points."

**VIII**. As to the motives, which are sometimes taken for a rule of interpretation, there may be other substantial ones, besides those immediately expressed, for the passing of a law or the making of a treaty. Yet the strongest conjecture is that which arises from certain proof that the will was actuated by some reason, operating as a sole and sufficient motive. For there are frequently MANY motives, and sometimes the will is influenced by its own choice independent of any other reason. In the same manner a grant made, in contemplation of a marriage, will be void, if the marriage never takes place.

**IX**. It is further to be observed that many words have a variety of acceptations, some more limited and others more extensive; which may be owing either to the application of a general name to a particular class of things, as in the words kindred and adoption; or to the use of masculines to express animals both of the male and female kind, where nouns of a common gender are wanting. In terms of art too, words are often taken in a metaphorical or extended sense: thus in the civil law death signifies banishment; but in its popular acceptation a dissolution of the parts of the natural body.

**X**. In promises likewise, some things are of a favour. able, some an odious, and others of a mixed or indifferent description. Favourable promises are those which contain an equality of terms, or which bear some relation to the common good, the magnitude and extent of which increases the favour of the promise: so that all engagements more conducive to peace than to war are to be considered as those of a favourable complexion, and alliances for mutual defence are always regarded as a more laudable object than those for offensive war.

Treaties of an odious kind are those which lay greater burdens on one party than on the other, which contain penalties for non-performance, or which lead to an abrogation or infraction of former treaties. Whereas, though engagements of a mixed nature may create a deviation from former treaties, they may be taken either in a favourable or odious light, according to the magnitude, or object of the change produced. If it be for the sake of peace, it is better, taking all circumstances into consideration, to rank them with those of a favourable kind.

**XI**. The distinction made by the Roman law between acts of equity and those of strict justice, cannot GENERALLY be applied to the law of nations, though it may in some cases be adopted. Thus in any transaction between the subjects of two countries, in each of which the same form of legal proceeding is observed, the parties are supposed to treat without any intention of deviating from the common rule and form, unless they have expressly determined to the contrary. But in acts for which no common rule is prescribed, as in donations and free promises, there the parties are supposed to treat according to the strict letter of the agreement.

**XII**. After the establishment of the former positions, the subject naturally proceeds to the rules themselves, which are to be observed in the interpretation of treaties. And in the first place we may remark, that in things, which are not of an odious nature, words are to be taken strictly in their popular meaning, and where they admit of exceptions, or have more significations than one, it is lawful to use that which is most extensive. As it has been already observed, that both Logicians and Grammarians frequently use particular terms in a general sense. Thus Cicero in pleading for Caecina, justly maintains that the interlocutory decree, ordering THAT THE PERSON EJECTED FROM HIS INHERITANCE SHOULD BE REINSTATED IN THE POSSESSION, implies not only an ejectment, but extends to any forcible prevention of the owner's taking possession.

In things of a favourable nature, if the parties engaged are acquainted with the legal principles, upon which they proceed, or rest upon the judgment of those who are so, the words used may be taken in their most extensive signification, including even terms of art and of law. Again, we must never have recourse to a metaphorical interpretation, except where the literal meaning would lead to a direct absurdity, or would defeat the intention of a treaty.

On the other hand a passage may be interpreted in a more limited signification, than the words themselves bear, if such interpretation be necessary, to avoid injustice or absurdity. If no such necessity exist, but equity or utility manifestly require a restriction to the literal meaning, it must be most rigidly adhered to, except where circumstances compel us to do otherwise. But in things of an odious nature a figurative expression may be allowed in order to avoid inconvenience or injustice. Therefore, when any one makes a grant, or relinquishes his right, though he express himself in the MOST GENERAL terms, his words are usually RESTRICTED to that meaning, which it is probable he intended. And in cases of this kind, the hope of retaining a thing is sometimes taken for the act of possession. In the same manner it is understood that subsidies of men, promised by one party only, are to be maintained at the expence of the power, who requires them.

**XIII**. It is a famous question whether the word ALLIES includes only those who were such at the time of making the treaty, or those who might afterwards become so: as was the case in the treaty made between the Roman people and the Carthaginians at the conclusion of the war that had originated in a dispute about Sicily, by which treaty it was stipulated that both powers should forbear attacking the allies of each other. Hence the Romans inferred that although the convention made with Asdrubal, by which he was prohibited from passing the Iberus, had been of no service to them, as it had not been ratified by the Carthaginians, yet if the Carthaginians sanctioned the conduct of Hannibal in his attack upon the people of Saguntum with whom the Romans, after the making of that convention, had entered into an alliance, they should consider themselves as authorised to declare war against the Carthaginians for having violated a solemn treaty. Upon which Livy reasons in the following manner, "By the clause in favour of allies on both sides, there was sufficient security for the Saguntines. For there was no limitation of the words to those, who were allies at that time, nor were they such as to exclude either power from making new alliances. But if both sides were at liberty to make new alliances, who could think it just to deprive the new allies of that protection to which they would be entitled from treaties of amity? The exclusion could reasonably go no further than to declare that the allies of the Carthaginians should not be seduced to renounce their engagements, nor if they did so, be admitted into alliance with the Romans."

The last passage is taken, almost word for word, from the third book of Polybius. On which we may observe that the word ALLIES may strictly mean those, who were so at the time, when the treaty was made, and, without any forced interpretation, may also be extended to embrace those, who afterwards became such. To which of these interpretations the preference is to be given may be seen from the rules above given: and according to those rules, it will be found, that alliances formed after the making of the treaty will not be comprehended in it, because it relates to the breach of a treaty, the violation of which is an odious act, and tends to deprive the Carthaginians of the liberty of redressing themselves by force against those who were supposed to have injured them; a liberty sanctioned by the law of nature, and not to be abandoned on any slight occasion. Were the Romans debarred then by this rule from making any treaty with the Saguntines, and defending them after they became allies? No! they had a right to defend them, not by virtue of any treaty, but upon principles of natural justice, which no treaty can annul. The Saguntines therefore with respect to both powers were in the same situation, as if no engagement had been made in favour of allies. In this case, it was no breach of treaty for the Carthaginians, upon just grounds, to commence hostilities against the Saguntines, nor for the Romans to defend them. Upon the same principle, in the time of Pyrrhus, it had been stipulated, by treaty, between the Carthaginians and Romans, that if either of them afterwards entered into any engagement with Pyrrhus, the party so contracting should reserve to itself the right of sending succours to the other, if attacked by that king. Though in that case the war ON BOTH SIDES could not be just, yet it would involve no infraction of any treaty. This is an example of a case in equal treaties.

**XIV**. The case of an unequal treaty may be put, where it is agreed that one of the confederate parties shall not make war, without the consent, or by the injunction of the other, which was stipulated in the treaty between the Romans and Carthaginians, after the conclusion of the second Punic war. When the term WAR is applied to war of every description, particularly to offensive rather than defensive war; in a dubious case, it must be limited to its proper signification, lest the treaty should operate as too great a restraint upon the liberty of that power, which has engaged in the unequal treaty.

**XV**. Of the same kind is the promise given by the Romans, that Carthage should be free, which could never mean the enjoyment of complete independence, by a people, who had long before lost the right of making war, and many of their other privileges. Yet it left them some degree of liberty, so much at least, that they should not be obliged to remove the seat of their government at the command of any foreign power, and gave them a pledge that their city should not be disturbed. It was in vain then for the Romans to urge that it was only the city which was intended. Whereas those acquainted with the use of metaphorical language know that by the city is frequently meant the inhabitants, and government with its privileges, and not the mere walls and houses. For the term, BEING LEFT FREE, implies that the people should enjoy their own laws.

**XVI**. The nature of personal and real treaties is a frequent subject of inquiry, which may properly be examined in this place. Indeed in all transactions with a free people, the engagements entered into with them are of a real nature; because the subject of them is a permanent thing. So permanent, that, although a republican be changed into a regal government, a treaty will remain in force: for the political body continues the same, although the head be changed, and the sovereign power, which before was diffused among many members, is now centered in one. Yet this rule will admit of an exception, where it is evident that the specific form of government made an essential part of the treaty, as when two states make a federal union for the mutual preservation of their political systems. But if a treaty be made with a KING OR SOVEREIGN PRINCE, it does not consequently follow that it is to be considered only as a PERSONAL and not a REAL treaty. For the name of a person may be inserted in a treaty, not merely to give it the character of a personal treaty, but to point out the contracting parties. And this will be still more evident, if, as is usual in most treaties, a clause is annexed declaring it to be perpetual, or made for the good of the kingdom, or with the king himself, and his successors, and it will also be considered as a real treaty, even if it is stated to be passed for a definite time. The treaty between the Romans and Philip, King of the Macedonians, seems to have been of this description, which, upon the refusal of his son to continue it, gave rise to a war.

Other forms too besides those already named, and the subject itself, will frequently supply no improbable grounds of conjecture. But if the conjectures are equal on both sides, it will remain that favourable treaties are supposed to be real or permanent, and odious ones only personal. All treaties of peace or commerce are favourable. Yet all treaties of war are not odious, especially those of the defensive kind, such a character belonging only to offensive wars, from the contemplation of the calamities which they inflict. It is presumed too, that in the formation of treaties, the character of each party is taken into the account, and that both are persuaded that neither of them will commence hostilities, but from just and important causes.

What is usually said of societies terminating with the death of the parties, has no connection with this subject, but relates to private societies, the cognizance of which belongs to the civil law. Whether it was right or wrong therefore in the people of Fidenae, the Latins, Tuscans and Sabines, upon the death of Romulus, Tullus, Ancus, Priscus, Servius, to abandon the respective treaties made with those kings, it is impossible for us now to decide, those treaties being no longer extant. On the same point, Justin maintains a discussion, whether those states, which had been tributary to the Medes, were upon a change of government, released from their obligations. For the thing to be considered is, whether the convention with the Medes had been a voluntary act of their own. Indeed the argument of Bodinus can by no means be admitted, which is, that treaties made with kings extend not to their successors; For the obligation of an oath is limited to the person of him, who takes it. It is true that the oath itself can bind only the person who takes it; yet the engagements, which it confirms, will be binding upon his heirs. Nor is it to be taken for an established maxim, that oaths are the only foundation, on which treaties rest. The engagement itself is sufficiently binding, the oaths being only added to give it the greater sanctity. In the Consulship of Publius Valerius, the Roman people had taken an oath to muster at the command of the Consul. Upon his death, he was succeeded by Lucius Quintius Cincinnatus. Some of the tribunes began to quibble, pretending that the people were released from their obligation. Upon which Livy, in his third book, remarks, that "at that time they had not degenerated into the disregard of religious obligations, which marked his age: nor did every one allow himself a latitude in explaining oaths, and laws, but thought that he was bound to conform to their literal meaning."

**XVII.** A treaty made with a king continues in force, even though the same king or his successor should be banished from the kingdom by rebellious subjects. For the rights of a king, among which his alliances may be reckoned, remain unimpaired, during the temporary loss of his throne. A case to which the expression of Lucan may be applied, that "order never loses its rights under any change of circumstances."

**XVIII.** On the other hand, any war, if it be with the consent of the lawful sovereign, made upon the invader of his kingdom, or upon the usurper of a free people's rights before his usurpation has received public sanction, will be deemed no infraction of any former treaty with the established authorities of that kingdom or country, For acts of usurpation convey not immediately any right beyond that of bare possession. And this is what was said by Titus Quintius to Nabis, "We made no treaty of alliance and amity with you, but with the just and lawful king of the Lacedaemonians." For in treaties the characters of KING, SUCCESSOR, and the LIKE, carry with them an idea of a peculiar and lawful right, which must always render the cause of USURPERS odious.

**XIX.** It was a question formerly discussed by Chrysippus, whether a prize promised to him, who first reached the goal, could be given to two, who reached it at the same time, or to neither. But as rewards of merit are things of a favourable nature, it is the juster opinion that they should divide the prize. Although Scipio, Caesar and Julian acted more liberally, in giving the entire prizes to each of those who had ascended the walls together.

What has been already said upon the literal or figurative application of the words, in interpreting treaties, will be sufficient.

**XX.** There is also another kind of interpretation, arising from conjectures, which apply exactly to the signification of the words containing a promise or engagement; and that is of a twofold description, either extending or limiting the meaning. But it is more difficult to extend than to limit the acceptation of expressions. For as in all matters the want of one essential requisite is sufficient to defeat their effect; so in engagements, those conjectures, which extend the obligation are not readily to be admitted. And it is much more difficult here than in the case above mentioned; where words allow a more extensive but less familiar acceptation. For here it is seeking a conjecture to extend the words of a promise: the conjecture therefore, which is to create an obligation, ought to be very certain. Nor is it sufficient that there is some resemblance in the motives; for the motive produced to confirm an obligation must be exactly the same as that of the case under consideration. Neither is it always proper to allege a motive for extending an obligation; because, as it has been already said, motives, in actuating us to form engagements, may sometimes be swayed by the will which often acts independently of any just motive. To authorise therefore such an extension, it must be evident that the motive, produced as an example and authority, was the sole and effectual cause, which influenced the promiser, and that he considered it in the same extensive view; for otherwise it would have been unjust and prejudicial. The ancients in their treatises on rhetoric follow the same rule, when, in speaking of the LETTER and DESIGN, they give us one invariable form of expressing the same sentiment, but in their syllogisms or arts of reasoning they point out a way of interpreting what is not written, by what is written. In the same manner too legal writers lay down rules for avoiding frauds. Now if at a time, when there was no other mode of fortifying towns, than by surrounding them with walls, it were stipulated that a certain place should not be so surrounded, it is evident that to employ any other means of fortification would be a breach of that treaty.

As in the above case the interpretation must be extended to guard against every possible evasion, so in the following example, the prohibition to assemble an armed force to assail us includes all kinds of violence and force, by which our lives and security may be endangered.

[**Translator's note:** The case of a promise made on the supposition of a posthumous child's dying, instanced by our author in this place, bears so near a resemblance to that of a father's bequeathing his property to another, believing his son to be dead, that it is omitted in this chapter having been already given under the head of erroneous promises in the xi. chapter and 6th section of this book.]

**XXI**. Hence may be solved the question to be found in Gellius, respecting a commission, whether it can be fulfilled by doing, not the immediate act required, but some thing equivalent to it, or in a manner more beneficial than in the form prescribed. For this deviation from the written rule may be proper and lawful, where the prescribed form is not essential towards attaining the object, or where, by departing from it, that object can be better accomplished, according to the answer given by Scaevola, that the person required to be bail and security for another, may give an order to a third person to pay that money to the creditor. But where such a latitude of interpretation is not evidently admissible, we must adhere to what Gellius has said in the same place, that it would be a dissolution of all trusts, if the party acting in commission were, in all cases, left to his own discretion, rather than bound by his written instructions..

**XXII**. An interpretation, restricted more closely than the literal signification of the words containing a promise absolutely requires, may arise either from some original defect in the intention of the promiser, or from some sub. sequent emergency repugnant to such intention. Thus if it were evident that an absurdity would follow the fulfillment of a promise, this would be sufficient to prove an original defect in the intention, because no man can be supposed to have deliberately intended doing an absurd act. Or if the sole and effectual reason, by which the promise was influenced, should have ceased, the obligation also would be void, the sole ground on which it rested being no longer in existence.

**XXIII**. In the next place, where any sufficient reason can evidently be assigned for a promise or engagement, it is not the substance of the promise itself, which is to be considered, so much as the reason for which that promise was given.

**XXIV**. Thirdly, the contending parties must always be supposed to have in contemplation the subject, and nothing but the subject, however extensive a signification the words may seem to bear. This method of interpretation also is handled by the ancient rhetorical writers, in speaking of expression and design, and they place it under the head of VARIATIONS IN OPINION.

**XXV**. In speaking of motives and reasons, it is proper to observe, that they some times comprehend things, considered not according to their actual existence, but according to their moral consequences: in which case it is by no means right to limit the words of a treaty to their literal meaning, but the utmost extent of interpretation is allowable, in order to maintain the spirit as well as the letter of such treaties. Thus if it be stipulated that no troops or ships shall be brought to a certain place, or within a certain distance, the prohibition excludes ALL ships or troops from being brought thither, even under the fairest and most harmless pretences. For the purport of the treaty is to guard not only against actual mischief but even against remote danger.

It is a point often disputed, whether the continuance of things in their present state is a tacit condition, on which the fulfillment of all promises is founded. A position that can by no means be maintained, unless it appears that such continuance was the sole motive upon which the treaties were made. As in many parts of history, we read of ambassadors having relinquished their missions, and returned home, upon finding the state of things so changed that the object of their embassies was at an end.

**XXVI**. When an emergency arises repugnant to the general intention of an act, it is explained by the ancient masters of rhetoric under the head of expression and design. Now this variation between the emergency and the intention is of a twofold nature. For the will and its intention are to be collected either from natural reason or from some outward sign. In judging of the will by natural reason, Aristotle, who has treated the subject with great accuracy, makes the MIND the SEAT OF JUDGMENT, and the WILL the SEAT OF EQUITY, which he nobly defines to be the correction of that, wherein the law, by reason of its universal nature is defective.

And upon this principle all wills and treaties ought to be interpreted. For as all cases could neither be foreseen nor expressed by the lawgiver, it is necessary to leave a power of excepting the cases, which he himself would have excepted if he were present. Yet this is not to be done upon light grounds; for that would be exercising a controul over the acts of another; but is only to be established upon the clearest evidence and strongest proofs. The clearest proof we can have of a want of equity, is where following the literal meaning of the words would be unlawful, that is, repugnant to natural or divine precepts. For such things, as are incapable of obligation, are necessarily to be excepted. Quintilian the elder, says, " some things although comprehended within the meaning of no law form a natural exception." Thus any one, who has promised to return a sword, that has been given up to him, ought not to return it into the hands of a madman, as danger might result from it to himself or to other innocent persons. Likewise a thing, which has been deposited with any one, ought not to be returned to the hands of the person, who gave the pledge, if the real owner demands it. I prove this says Triphonius to be justice, which assigns to every one his own without disturbing the still juster claims of another. For the reason, it has been already observed, is founded on the institution of property, which makes it unjust not to return a thing when the real owner is known.

**XXVII**. The need of equity too will appear in cases, where following the literal meaning of the words will not be absolutely unlawful, yet, upon a fair estimation, will be found too hard and intolerable. It might impose a hardship inconsistent with the general condition of human nature, or, upon comparing the person and matter under consideration with each other, it might be found at variance with the general intent of all law, which is to prevent evil and to redress injury. Thus, if a person has lent a sum of money, or any other thing, for a CERTAIN time, he may justly require the repayment or restoration of it WITHIN that time, if he has great need of it himself: for acts of kindness are of such a nature, that no one can be supposed intentionally to bind himself thereby to manifest inconvenience or prejudice. In the same manner a sovereign, who has promised assistance to an ally, will, IN EQUITY, be excused from fulfilling his engagement, if he wants all his strength at home to ward off danger or hostilities. The grant also of immunities or privileges in ORDINARY cases, cannot be pleaded as an exemption or exception from the services, which the state in PARTICULAR emergencies requires.

From the above instances it appears that Cicero has too loosely worded his proposition, "that such promises, as are prejudicial to the person, to whom they are given, are not to be kept, nor, if they are more prejudicial to the party giving, than beneficial to the person receiving them. "For it should not be left to the promiser to judge, whether the fulfillment of his engagement will be serviceable to the party receiving it, except in the case of the madman cited above: nor is any TRIVIAL or IMAGINARY prejudice that might result from it, sufficient to release the obligation. But it ought to be such, as, according to the nature of the act, would necessarily be supposed to form an exception. Thus any one, having promised his assistance to a neighbour at a certain period, would not be bound to his engagement, if he were detained at home by the sickness of a father or a child. A case, which Cicero, in his first book of offices, has put in the following terms, "If any one has undertaken to manage a cause, and, in the mean time, his son is taken ill, it will be no breach of duty in him not to perform what he has promised." There is a passage in the fourth book of Seneca, ON BENEFITS, to the same effect. "I am liable, *says he*, to be charged with levity, and a breach of faith, if, things continuing as they were, when I made a promise, I do not perform my engagement. But if any change has taken place, it leaves me at liberty to reconsider the matter, and releases the obligation. I promised my support in court, and it afterwards appeared that the cause would be prejudicial to my own father. I promised to take a journey, but afterwards heard that the road was infested with robbers. I promised my presence on some particular occasion, but was prevented from attending by the sickness of a son. In all these cases, to bind me to my engagement, the circumstances ought to re. main exactly the same as they were when I made the promise."

**XXVIII**. It has been said that there are other indications of intention, which require an equitable exception in favour of the present case. And among such proofs there can be nothing stronger than the same words used in another place, not where they directly oppose the present meaning, for that would amount to a contradiction, but where they clash with it, owing to some unexpected emergency, which the Greek Rhetoricians call a circumstantial disagreement.

**XXIX**. When there is any accidental collision between one part of a written document and another, Cicero, in the second book of his treatise ON INVENTION, has given rules for deciding which of them ought to have the preference. Though his arrangement is not very accurate, yet it is by no means to be neglected. To supply therefore this defect of accuracy, the rules may be digested in the following order.

In the first place, a PERMISSION ought to give way to a COMMAND: because a permission appears to be granted only in case there is no weightier objection than its being an exception to a positive precept, nor any preponderance in favour of an opposite determination. Consequently, as the writer to Herennius says, what is positively prescribed is more powerful than a bare permission.

In the next place what is required to be one at a FIXED time should have the preference to what may be done at ANY time. From whence it follows that the PROHIBITIONS of a treaty are generally of more weight than its INJUNCTIONS: because the prohibitory power operates at ALL times. But it is not so with injunctions, unless an express time for their fulfillment is named, or they contain a tacit prohibition.

Among those treaties, which, in the above named respects, are equal, the preference is given to such as are more particular, and approach nearer to the point in question. For where particulars are stated, the case is clearer, and requires fewer exceptions than general rules do.

Those prohibitions which have a penalty annexed to them, are of greater weight than those, which have not; and those with a greater penalty are enforced in preference to those that have a less. Those engagements also which are founded -upon causes of less magnitude and importance ought to give way to those which have more laudable and useful objects in view.

Lastly it is to be observed that a subsequent law or treaty always repeals a former.

From what has been said an inference may be drawn in favour of sworn treaties or agreements that they ought to be taken in the most usual acception of the words, rejecting all implied limitations and exceptions, and such as are not immediately necessary to the subject. Consequently in a case, where a sworn treaty or engagement may happen to clash with another not enforced by the obligation of an oath, the preference ought to be given to the former.

**XXX**. It is often asked whether in doubtful points, a contract should be deemed perfect, before the writings are made and delivered. We find in Appian's history of the Mithridatic war, that it was upon this very ground Murena objected to the convention between Sylla and Mithridates. However it appears plain, unless it has been settled to the contrary, that writing ought to be considered admissible as evidence of a contract, though not as part of the substance, otherwise it is usually expressed, as in the truce with Nabis, which was to be ratified from the clay the terms were WRITTEN and DELIVERED to him.

**XXXI**. We can by no means admit the rule laid down by some writers, who maintain, that all engagements of kings, and states, ought to be explained, as far as it is possible, upon the principles of the Roman law: unless indeed it can be made to appear that among some states, in their intercourse with each other, the CIVIL LAW is received as the LAW OF NATIONS; a presumption which ought not to be hastily granted.

**XXXII**. As to the doubt, which Plutarch advances in his Symposiacs, whether the words of the party offering, or those of the one accepting a condition ought to be most attended to, it appears that where the party accepting the terms is the promiser, the nature and substance of the transaction will depend upon his words, if they are absolute and unqualified. For if the offer is regarded as a positive engagement to do certain acts, then the full extent of it will be seen by the necessary repetition of the same words in the promise. But before a condition is accepted, it is evident, as was seen in the chapter on promises, that the promiser is not bound to its fulfillment; for no right has been conferred by the one party, or acquired by the other. Therefore the offer of a condition of this kind does not amount to a perfect promise.

## CHAPTER 17: ON DAMAGES OCCASIONED BY INJURY AND THE OBLIGATION TO REPAIR THEM.

*On Damages occasioned by injury, and the obligation to repair them — Every misdemeanor obliges the aggressor to repair the loss — By loss is meant any thing repugnant to right strictly so called — Distinction between fitness and strict right — Loss or diminution of possession includes every injury done to the produce as well as the property itself — Loss estimated from the time that gain ceases Injuries done by principals — By accessories — Injuries done by the neglect of principal or of secondary agents — What persons are implicated in those charges, and in what degrees — The parties engaged answerable for all consequences — The case where homicide or any other act of violence ensues — Case of robbery — Or theft — Promises obtained through fraud or unjust fear — In what cases the consequences are imputable to the suffering party — How far the law of nations authorises states to take advantage of an enemy's fear — How far sovereigns are answerable for any acts of violence committed by their subjects — The case where subjects in violation of their sovereign's permission and orders commit acts of piracy upon allied or neutral states — No one answerable by the law of nature for the mischief done by his cattle, his slaves, or his ship — Damages allowed for injuries done to reputation or honour — What kind of reparation allowed.*

**I**. IT HAS been said above that the rights due to us arise from three sources, which are contract, injury and law. It is unnecessary here to dwell upon the nature of contracts which has been already so fully discussed. The next point therefore to which we proceed is an inquiry into the rights resulting to us from injuries received. Here the name of crime or misdemeanor is applied to every act of commission or neglect repugnant to the duties required of all men, either from their common nature or particular calling. For such offences naturally create an obligation to repair the loss or injury that has been sustained.

**II**. By loss is meant a diminution of what any one possesses, whether it be a right derived to him purely from the law of nature, or from the addition of human authority, that is from the law of property, contract, or civil law. God has given life to man, not to destroy, but to preserve it; assigning to him for this purpose a right to the free enjoyment of personal liberty, reputation, and the controul over his own actions. The manner, in which property and contracts convey to any one a right to things, as well as to the service of another, has been shewn in the preceding part of this treatise. In the same manner from the law every man derives his peculiar right; because the law has the same, if not greater power over persons and things than individuals themselves have. Thus by the appointment of law, a ward has a right to demand the strictest diligence of a guardian, the state of a magistrate, and not only the state, but every subject has a right to require it; where the law expressly declares or evidently implies that certain acts shall be performed. But the bare circumstance of an action being fit or proper gives not the right of POLITICAL justice to demand its performance, nor does the neglect of it entitle the party suffering to any legal redress. Because it does not follow that a thing must belong to a person because it is fit or beneficial for him. Thus, as Aristotle says, there is no actual injustice, though it may be illiberal to refuse assisting another with money. To the same purpose Cicero, in his speech for Cneius Plancus, says, that giving their votes to whom they please, or withholding them if they think proper, is the true characteristic of a free people. He afterwards, indeed, corrects his assertion by adding, that they may happen to do what they like, rather than what they ought to do, taking the word OUGHT to signify propriety.

**III**. A precaution is necessary here, in order to avoid confounding things of a different kind.

Now those who are entrusted with the power of appointing magistrates, are bound, from motives of public good, to chuse the properest persons, and this is what the state has a RIGHT to require of them. They are bound therefore to repair any loss which the state may sustain by the choice of improper persons. So any subject who is not disqualified, though he has no peculiar right to an office, has an equal right with others to endeavour to obtain it. In the exercise of which right, if, he is obstructed by violence or fraud, he may recover damages, not to the full value of the office which he sought, but according to the probable loss which he may reasonably be supposed to have suffered. Similar to which is the right of a legatee, when a testator has been prevented by fraud or violence from making a bequest. For the capability of receiving a legacy is a kind of right, which to obstruct a testator from conferring, is undoubtedly an injury.

**IV**. The loss or diminution of any one's possessions is not confined to injuries done to the SUBSTANCE alone of the property, but includes every thing affecting the produce of it, whether it has been gathered or not. If the, owner himself had reaped it, the necessary expence of reaping, or of improving the property to raise a produce, must also be taken into the account of his loss, and form part of the damages. For it is an established maxim that no one ought to derive benefit from the loss of another.

**V**. Damages are to be computed too, not according to any ACTUAL gain, but according to the REASONABLE expectation of it. Which in the case of a growing crop may be judged of by the general abundance or scarcity of that particular season.

**VI**. But besides the person immediately doing an injury, others may be bound also to repair the losses of the suffering party. For as a person may be guilty of offences by negligence as well as by the commission of certain acts, so they may be done also by accessories, as well as principals. Now a principal in any crime or offence is one, that urges to the commission of it, that gives all possible consent, that aids, abets, or in any shape is a partner in the perpetration of it.

**VII**. An accessory is one who gives his counsel, approbation, and assent. For where is the difference, says Cicero, in his second Philippic, between advising an act, and approving of it?

**VIII**. and **IX**. The obligation to repair the losses suffered by negligence may be considered in a two-fold light. Firstly, when any person, whose peculiar office it is, neglects either to forbid the commission of an injury, or to assist the injured party. And secondly, when the person, who ought to do it, either does not dissuade from the commission of an offence, or passes over in silence, what he is bound to make known. In these cases, when it is said that a person OUGHT to do, or to forbear doing certain actions, it is meant that he is bound by that right, which strict justice requires, whether that duty arises from law, or from the capacity, which the person bears. For though it may be wrong to omit any duty enjoined by the law of charity, there can be no redress for such omission, but every LEGAL REMEDY must be founded on some PECULIAR RIGHT.

**X**. It is to be observed also that all the parties above mentioned, if they have been the real occasion of loss to any one, or have abetted the person doing him the injury, are so far implicated in the guilt, as to be liable to full damages, or, at least, proportionably to the part they have taken. For it may and often does happen that a crime would have been committed by an offender, even without the aid of other principals or accessories. In which case he alone is answerable. Yet neither principals nor accessories will be allowed to plead as an excuse, that if they had not aided or abetted, others would have been found to assist and encourage the perpetrator in the commission of the act. Especially, if it appears that without such assistance from them the crime would never have been committed. For those other imaginary abettors would themselves have been answerable, if they had given their advice or aid.

**XI**. In the scale of implication the first degree applies to those, who by their authority, or other means have compelled or urged any one to the commission of an offence. On failure of these the perpetrator himself has the greatest share of guilt, and next to him, others who have been concerned. In short, all individuals, whose hands have been engaged in the perpetration, are guilty, though they have not been the sole authors of the act.

**XII**. Now he who is answerable for an act, is answerable for all the injurious consequences attending it. Seneca in one of his controversies, treating upon this point, puts the case of a plane-tree set on fire, by which a house was burnt, and he subjoins the following remark, "although the mischief went further than was intended, yet the person doing it was answerable for the WHOLE, as much, as if he had done it by design. For any one that puts his defence upon the plea of UNINTENTIONAL INJURY, ought to have abstained from all mischief whatsoever." When Ariarathes, king of Cappadocia had wantonly obstructed the channel of the river Melas, which discharges itself into the Euphrates, the swell of waters bursting the mounds, the Euphrates rose to such a height, as to occasion excessive damage to the Cappadocians, the Galatians, and the Phrygians. Upon which the decision of the matter being left to the Romans, they imposed upon him a fine of three hundred talents.

**XIII**. **XIV**. **XV**. and **XVI**. But to proceed with other instances of injury, which render the parties committing them liable to repair the losses occasioned thereby. The case of excusable homicide may be alleged as one, wherein the person, who has committed it, is bound to make every reasonable compensation to the family, dependents, and connections of the deceased party, in proportion to the loss, which they have sustained from his death. As Michael the Ephesian in the fifth book of Aristotle's Ethics has observed, that the compensation made to the parents, the wife or children of the deceased is nearly the same as if it could be made to himself. The writer is here speaking of excusable homicide, that is, when the person by whom it is committed, does it not in the immediate discharge of some legal duty. Wherefore if any one, in defending himself, has killed another from whom he might have escaped, though he may have violated the law of charity, yet he has not incurred the penalty of a capital offence.

Upon the same principle the person, who has maimed or mutilated another, will be bound to make him a compensation, proportionably to the means of subsistence which he is deprived of by such a calamity.

A thief or a robber is bound to restore what has been taken, and to return it with all the improvements it may have acquired, or to make reparation to the owner, in proportion to the gain, which the privation has prevented him from making, or to the actual value of the thing itself. If the thing has been irretrievably consumed, the estimation of damages must be made, according to a medium between the highest and the lowest value.

To this class of offences and due reparation may be referred all frauds upon the public revenue, all unjust decisions, or all false evidence, by which states or individuals are injured.

**XVII**. Contracts, or promises obtained by fraud, violence or undue fear entitle the injured party to full restitution. For perfect freedom from fraud or compulsion, in all our dealings, is a RIGHT which we derive from natural law and liberty.

With the same class of offenders we may rank all men in office, who are unwilling to discharge their duty without a bribe.

**XVIII**. When a person has HIMSELF been the occasion of the fraud or violence, the consequences are imputable to his own conduct. For where a voluntary act gives rise to INVOLUNTARY consequences, those consequences, considered in a moral light, are to be deemed the fruits growing out of the exercise of a free will.

**XIX**. But to connect the preceding cases and arguments with public and national concerns, it is necessary to observe, that it is a maxim introduced and established by the consent of all nations that the wars which are declared and conducted by the authority of the sovereign power on both sides are alone entitled to the denomination of just wars: And the enemy has no right to demand restitution for what the prosecution of such wars has reduced him to abandon through fear. It is upon this principle we admit the distinction which Cicero has made between an enemy, towards whom the consent and law of nations oblige us to observe many common rights, and between robbers and pirates. For any thing given up to pirates or robbers, through fear, is no lawful prize: but it may be recovered, unless a solemn oath of renunciation has been taken. This is not the case with the captures made in just war.

The justification which Polybius makes for the Carthaginians, in the second Punic war, carries with it an appearance of equity, though it is not a question immediately founded upon the law of nations. They alleged as a reason for their making that war, that, when they were engaged in quelling a mutiny of their own mercenaries, the Romans had declared war, seized upon Sardinia, and levied contributions of money.

**XX**. Sovereign Princes and States are answerable for their neglect, if they use not all the proper means within their power for suppressing piracy and robbery. And on this account the Scyrians were formerly condemned by the Amphictyonic council.

When some of the states of the united Provinces had, on a particular occasion, granted commissions to many privateers, and those adventurers plundered friends and enemies alike, and became general pirates, it was a subject of great discussion, whether those states were justified in having made use of the services of desperate and abandoned men, without exacting sufficient security for their good conduct. At that time, it was maintained that they were bound to nothing more, than to punish or deliver up the offenders, if they could be found, and to see justice done by a forfeiture of their property. For they themselves had neither authorised those UNJUST acts of plunder, nor shared in the fruits of them. They had even strictly prohibited the privateers from molesting the subjects of friendly powers. As to their taking securities, there was no obligation to do that: for they had a right to grant a GENERAL commission to all their subjects to seize upon the enemy's property: a thing, which had frequently been done. Nor could that particular commission be considered as an act of injustice against either allies or neutrals; since even without such permission individuals might have fitted and sent out armed vessels. The states could not foresee, nor consequently provide against the misconduct of those adventurers, who had exceeded their commission; and if nations were to decline using the assistance of wicked men, no army could ever be collected. And it has been confirmed by the authority both of France and England, that a sovereign cannot answer for every injury done to the subjects of a friendly power by his naval or military forces; especially if it is plain that they acted in violation of his orders.

But in what cases any one is released from being answerable for what is done by his subordinate agents, is a point not so much for the law of nations, as for the municipal law, and particularly the maritime code of each country to decide. In a case similar to that alluded to, a decision of the supreme court of judicature was made against the Pomeranians two centuries at least before.

**XXI**. It is the CIVIL law too, which makes an owner answerable for the mischief or damage done by his slave, or by his cattle. For in the eye of natural justice he is not to blame. So neither is the person, whose ship, by running foul of another, has damaged it, though by the laws of many nations, and of ours among the rest, the damages are usually divided between both parties, owing to the difficulty of deciding, who was in fault.

**XXII**. Damages are allowed too for any injury done to our honour or reputation, by assault, slander, or various other ways. In which, as well as in theft and other crimes the nature of the offence is to be estimated by its consequences. For the reparation in such cases answers to the penalty imposed for crimes. And that reparation is made some times by acknowledging the injured party's innocence; and some times by a compensation in money, which is a standard value of all things.

## CHAPTER 18: ON THE RIGHT OF EMBASSIES.

*Right of Embassies, an obligation arising out of the law of nations — Where it obtains — Whether Embassies are always to be admitted — Dismissal or punishment of ambassadors engaging in plots not to be considered as a harsh measure, but an act of self-defence — A power to whom no ambassador has been sent, not bound to respect the rights of embassy — An enemy to whom an ambassador is sent bound to respect his rights — The law of retaliation no plea for ill treatment of an ambassador — This right of protection extends to an ambassador's suite, if he thinks proper to claim it — To his moveable property — Examples of obligation without the right of compulsion — Importance of the sacred character of ambassadors.*

I. HITHERTO the pursuit of our inquiries has led us to examine those rights to which we are entitled by the law of nature, occasionally touching upon those points where its authority is farther confirmed by the voluntary law of nations. And that voluntary law as it is called, gives rise to certain obligations, which now remain for our discussion, and in which the rights of embassadors form a leading feature. Almost every page of history offers some remark on the inviolable rights of ambassadors, and the security of their persons, a security sanctioned by every clause and precept of human and revealed law. Nor is it surprising that the persons of those should be deemed inviolable, who form the principal link in that chain, by which sovereigns and independent states maintain their intercourse with each other. To offer violence to them is not only an act of INJUSTICE, but, as Philip in his letter to the Athenians says, is acknowledged by all to be an act of IMPIETY.

II. But whatever rights the law of nations may confer upon ambassadors, it is necessary in the first place to observe, that none are entitled to them, but those, who are sent by the sovereigns of independent countries to each other. For the privileges of provincial, or municipal deputies sent to the states general of any country are regulated by the particular laws of that country and not by the law of nations.

Thus we find, in the first book of Livy, an ambassador styling himself a public messenger of the Roman People; and, in the sixth book of the same historian, we have a declaration of the senate, confining the rights of embassies to the intercourse between foreign powers, and excluding citizens from the same privileges in their transactions with each other. Upon this topic, the authority of Cicero may be cited, who, in order to shew the impropriety of sending ambassadors to Antony, observes, that they are not dealing with a Hannibal or a foreign enemy, but with one of their own citizens.

Now Virgil has so clearly explained WHO are to be reckoned FOREIGNERS, that we need not have recourse to lawyers, to understand what is so well expressed by the poet, who says, "I look upon every country as foreign, which owns not the sway of our sceptre." Aen. vii. 369.

A state therefore connected with another though by an unequal treaty, if it retain its independence, will have a right of sending embassies. The Princes of Germany, who were in some respects subject to the Emperor, as their head, being Sovereign Princes possessed the right of sending ambassadors to foreign states. But Kings who have been entirely subdued in just war, and stripped of their dominions, have, with all their other sovereign rights, lost that of sending ambassadors. It was for this reason, that Paulus Aemilius made prisoners of the messengers sent to him by Perseus, whom he had conquered.

In civil wars necessity sometimes gives birth to new rights in violation of former rules. When for instance, a kingdom is so equally divided between two parties, that it is a matter of doubt which of them constitutes the nation, or in a disputed succession between two claimants of the crown; the kingdom may be considered as forming two nations at the same time. Tacitus, considering each party in such cases, as entitled to the rights of the law of nations, condemns the Flavians for having, in the rage of civil dissensions, violated, in the persons of the Vitellian ambassadors, those privileges, which are respected even among FOREIGN nations. Pirates and robbers, as they form no civil community, cannot rest any claim to protection and support upon the law of nations. Tiberius, as we are informed by Tacitus, when Tacfarinas sent ambassadors to him, spurned at the idea of treating with a robber, as with a lawful enemy. Yet sometimes a pledge of public faith, and the rights of embassy are allowed to men of that description, which was done by Pompey to the fugitives from the Pyrenean forest.

**III**. There are two points upon which the privileges granted by the law of nations to ambassadors turn. In the first place, they have a right to be admitted into any country, and secondly to be protected from all personal violence. Respecting the former of these points, there is a passage in the eleventh book of Livy, where Hanno, a Carthaginian senator inveighs against Hannibal for not having admitted into his camp ambassadors, who came from the allies, and on their behalf; as he had thereby overturned the law of nations.

But this rule by no means compels nations to give an UNQUALIFIED admission to all ambassadors. For that is what the law of nations can never intend: it only prohibits the refusal of admission without sufficient grounds.

There are various motives which may afford a sufficient plea for such refusal. There may be an objection to the power who offers to treat, to the person sent upon the embassy, or perhaps to the object of his mission. Thus at the suggestion of Pericles, Melesippus, the Lacedaemonian ambassador, was sent out of the territories of Athens; because he came from an enemy, who had no pacific intentions. The senate of Rome said, that they could receive no embassy from Carthage, as long as the Carthaginian army remained in Italy. The Achaeans refused to admit the ambassadors of Perseus, who were secretly MEDITATING war against the Romans. Upon the same grounds Justinian rejected an embassy from Totilas, and the same was done by the Goths at Urbino to messengers from Belisarius. Polybius relates in the third book of his history, that every power drove away the ambassadors of the Cynethensians, as they were so infamous a people.

We have an instance of the second kind, where the objection is made to the PERSON sent on an embassy, in the case of Theodore, who was called the atheist, and whom Lysimachus refused to receive in the character of an ambassador sent from Ptolemy, and the same thing has frequently happened to others, against whom peculiar motives of aversion have existed.

In the third place, there may be sufficient grounds for refusing to admit an ambassador, if the object of his mission be of a suspicious kind, as was the case with that of Rhabsbakeh the Assyrian, whom Hezekiah had reason to suspect of coming with a design to excite his people to rebellion. Or the refusal may be justified, where it is not consistent with the dignity or circumstances of one power to enter into any treaty, or intercourse with another. For this reason the Romans sent a declaration to the Aetolians, that they should send no embassy, but with the permission of their general, and Perseus was not allowed to send one to Rome, but to Licinius. Jugurtha's ambassadors too, as Sallust informs us, were ordered to leave Italy within the space of ten days, unless they came with offers from that prince to surrender himself, and his kingdom.

There may often be the best reasons for a sovereign's refusing to allow of a RESIDENT minister at his court; a practice, so general in the present day, but totally unknown to the ages of antiquity.

**IV**. As to the personal exemption of ambassadors from arrest, constraint, or violence of any kind, it is a subject of some difficulty to determine, owing to the varieties of opinion entertained by the most celebrated writers on the question. In the consideration of this matter, our attention is directed in the first place to the personal privileges and exemptions of ambassadors themselves, and next to those of their attendants, and their goods. With respect to their persons, some writers are of opinion, that it is ONLY from UNJUST VIOLENCE, and ILLEGAL CONSTRAINT, that the law of nations protects ambassadors. For they imagine that their privileges are to be explained according to the common principles of the law of nature. Others again suppose that ambassadors are not amenable to punishment for ALL offences, but only for such as amount to a transgression of the law of NATIONS, the principles of which are of such general extent, as to include the law of nature: consequently there can be no offences for which an ambassador is not punishable, except for those actions that are made such by the positive rules of MUNICIPAL or CIVIL LAW.

Others again consider these public representatives of states and crowned heads, as only liable to punishment for offences affecting the dignity or governments of the sovereigns to whom they are sent. While, on the other hand, there are some writers who maintain that for any state to punish an ambassador for ANY CRIME WHATEVER is highly dangerous to the independence of foreign powers; but that all offenders of that description ought to be left to the laws of their respective countries, to be punished or not, according to their deserts, upon due complaint being made to the sovereigns by whom they were sent

Some few writers, indeed, in laying down the rule to be observed in such cases, have decided that an appeal should be made to other independent and disinterested powers, which may be considered rather as a matter of DISCRETION, than Of ABSOLUTE RIGHT. But the advocates of all these various systems have come to no definite conclusion in support of their favourite opinions. For this is a right which cannot, like the law of nature, be established upon unchangeable rules, but derives all its efficacy from the will of nations. Nations if they had thought proper, certainly might have laid down ABSOLUTE rules of security for ambassadors, or coupled them with certain exceptions. The argument is supported on one side by the urgent necessity of heinous crimes being punished, and on the other, the utmost latitude of exemption is favoured on account of the utility of embassies, the facility of sending which ought to be encouraged by every possible privilege, and security. To settle the point therefore, we must consider how far nations have agreed among themselves upon these principles; the proofs of which can only be found in the evidence of history.

Many instances may be produced in favour of both opinions. And in cases like this, the opinions of those celebrated for their judgment and knowledge will be of no small weight, but in some cases we must rest upon conjectures- On this subject the two eminent historians, Livy and Sallust, may be quoted as authorities, the former of whom, in mentioning the ambassadors of Tarquin, who had been guilty of fomenting treasonable conspiracies at Rome, says, " that although they deserved to be treated as enemies for their guilty conduct, yet the privilege, which they derived from the law of nations, prevailed over every other consideration. "Here we see that the rights of ambassadors could not be annulled even by the most criminal acts of hostility. But the observation made by Sallust, — relates rather to those who come in the train of an embassy than to ambassadors themselves. The law of nations surely then will not deny the same privilege to a principal, which it evidently allows to those who form but a subordinate part in the public mission. The historian says, that "Bomilcar was arraigned and tried rather upon principles of equity and natural justice, than in conformity to the law of nations, as he belonged to the train of Jugurtha; who had come to Rome under the pledge of public faith."

Equity and natural justice require punishment to be inflicted on ALL offenders, whereas the law of nations makes an exception in favour of ambassadors, and those who have the public faith for their protection. Wherefore to try or punish ambassadors, is contrary to the law of nations, which prohibits many things, that are permitted by the law of nature.

The law of nations, thus deviating from the law of nature, gives rise to those interpretations and conjectures, which reconcile with the principles of justice a greater extension of privileges than the law of nature strictly allows. For if ambassadors were protected against nothing more than violence and illegal constraint, their privileges would confer no extraordinary advantage. Besides, the security of ambassadors is a matter of much greater moment to the public welfare than the punishment of offences. Because reparation for the misconduct of an ambassador may be looked for from the sovereign, by whom he is sent, unless that sovereign chuses to expose himself to hostilities by approving of his crimes. An objection to such privileges is made by some, who assert, that it is better for one person to be punished than for whole nations to be involved in war. But if a sovereign has SECRETLY given his sanction to the misconduct of his ambassador, his APPARENT intentions to punish that ambassador will not deprive the injured power of the right to seek redress by commencing hostilities.

On the other hand, the right of ambassadors would rest upon a very slippery foundation if they were accountable, for their actions, to any one but their own sovereigns. For as the interests of powers sending, and of those receiving ambassadors, are in general different, and some times even opposite, if a public minister were obliged to consult the inclinations of both, there would be no part of his conduct, to which they might not impute some degree of blame. Besides although some points are so clear, as to admit of no doubt, yet universal danger is sufficient to establish the equity and utility of a general law. For this reason it is natural to suppose, that nations have agreed, in the case of ambassadors, to dispense with that obedience, which every one, by general custom, owes to the laws of that foreign country, in which, at any time, he resides. The character, which they sustain, is not that of ordinary individuals, but they represent the Majesty of the Sovereigns, by whom they are sent, whose power is limited to no local jurisdiction. As Cicero, in his eighth Philippic, speaking of a certain ambassador, says, "he carried with him the Majesty of the Senate, and the authority of the State." From hence it is concluded, that an ambassador is not bound by the laws of the country, where he resides. If he commit an offence of a trivial nature, it may either be suffered to pass unnoticed, or he may be ordered to leave the country.

Polybius relates an instance of an ambassador, who was ordered to leave Rome, for having assisted some hostages in making their escape. Hence it is obvious why the Romans inflicted corporeal punishment upon an ambassador of Tarentum, because the Tarentines were at that time their own subjects, by right of conquest.

If a crime is of a notorious nature, affecting the government, an ambassador may be sent home, and his sovereign required to punish, or deliver him up, as we read of the Gauls having done to the Fabians. But, as we have before occasionally observed, all human laws are framed upon such principles, as, in cases of extreme necessity, to admit of equitable relaxations, among which the privileges of ambassadors may be reckoned. But these extreme cases of necessity may, according to the law of nations, as will be seen hereafter, in discussing the effects of just and solemn war, prevent punishment in CERTAIN cases, though not in ALL. For it is not the act of punishment itself, which is objected to, either in respect to time, or manner, but the exemption is created to prevent the greater public evil, which might arise from the punishment of the offender. To obviate therefore any imminent danger, if no other proper method can be devised, ambassadors may be detained and interrogated.

Thus the Roman Consuls seized the ambassadors of Tarquin, previously taking care to secure their papers, to prevent the evidence, which they might afford, from being destroyed. But if an ambassador excites and heads any violent insurrection, he may be killed, not by way of punishment, but upon the natural principle of self-defence, The Gauls therefore might have put to death the Fabii, whom Livy calls violators of the law of nature.

**V.** Mention has before been frequently made of the exemptions, by which ambassadors are protected from all personal constraint and violence, and it is understood that all powers are bound by a tacit agreement, as it were, from the time of admitting an ambassador, to respect these exemptions. It MAY and indeed sometimes DOES happen, that one power gives notice to another that no ambassador will be received, and if one is sent, that he will be treated as an enemy. A declaration to this effect was made by the Romans to the Aetolians, and, on another occasion, the Vejentian ambassadors were ordered to leave Rome, with a menace, if they refused to comply, of being treated in the same manner as the Roman ambassadors had been treated by their king Tolumnius, who had put them to death. The Samnites too forbade the Romans to go to any council in Samnium, under pain of forfeiting their lives, or, at least, their personal safety.

The above law does not bind a power, through whose territories ambassadors pass without leave. For, if they are going to an enemy of that power, or returning from him, or are engaged in any hostile design, they may lawfully be treated as enemies; which was done by the Athenians in the case of the messengers passing between the Persians and Spartans, and by the Illyrians in that of those, who carried on the intercourse between the Essians and Romans. Xenophon maintains that in certain cases they may be made prisoners, as Alexander made those, who were sent from Thebes and Lacedaemon to Darius, and the Romans those, whom Philip sent to Hannibal, and Latius those of the Volseians. For to treat ambassadors with any degree of rigour, EXCEPT UPON THOSE SUFFICIENT GROUNDS, would be deemed not only a breach of the law of nations, but a personal offence against the sovereigns, to whom they are going, or by whom they are sent. Justin informs us, that Philip II. king of Macedon, sent an ambassador to Hannibal with credentials, empowering him to make an alliance, and that, when this ambassador was seized and carried before the Senate of Rome, they dismissed him without farther molestation, not out of respect to the king, but to prevent a doubtful enemy from becoming a decided one.

**VI**. But if an embassy, admitted by an ENEMY is en. titled to all the privileges of the law of nations, much more so is one, admitted by a power UNFRIENDLY, but not engaged in ACTUAL HOSTILITIES. Diodorus Siculus says, that a messenger with a flag of truce claims all the security of peace, even in the midst of war. The Lacedaemonians, who had murdered the heralds of the Persians, were said by that act to have confounded every distinction between right and wrong, as it is acknowledged by all nations. For legal writers lay it down as a rule, that to offer personal violence to ambassadors, whose characters are deemed sacred, is a defiance of the law of nations, and Tacitus calls the privileges we are now discussing, the rights of embassy, sanctified by the law of nations.

Cicero, in his first speech against Verres, asks, if ambassadors ought not to be safe in the midst of an enemy's country, or even in his camp? Innumerable other instances of this kind might be produced from the highest authorities both ancient and modern. And it is with reason that such privileges are revered, for in the midst of war many circumstances arise, which cannot be decided but through ambassadors, and it is the only channel through which proposals of peace can be made, and confirmed.

**VII**. It is frequently made a subject of inquiry, whether the ambassador of a sovereign, who has exercised any act of cruelty or rigour, will be subject to the law of retaliation. History furnishes many instances, in which punishment has been inflicted in such a manner. But history is sometimes nothing more than a catalogue of actions marked with injustice, and ungovernable fury. Whereas the law of nations, by its privileges, designs to secure the dignity not only of sovereigns themselves, but also that of the ambassadors whom they employ. Consequently there is a tacit agreement understood to be made with the latter, that HE shall be exempt, not only from any ill treatment, that may affect the principal, but from such likewise, as may affect himself. So that it was a magnanimous answer, conformable to the law of nations, which Scipio made, when the Roman ambassadors had been ill-treated by the Carthaginians, and the Carthaginian ambassadors were brought before him, upon his being asked, in what manner they should be treated, he replied, not as the Roman ambassadors had been by the Carthaginians. Livy adds, that he said, he would do nothing unbecoming the character and laws of the Roman people. Valerius Maximus assigns the same language to the

Consuls, on an occasion similar, but prior to this. In addressing Hanno, they said, "the pledge of faith, which our state has given, releases you from any such fear." For even at that time, Cornelius Asina, in violation of his public character, had been arrested and thrown into prison by the Carthaginians.

**VIII**. The train too of an ambassador, and all the plate belonging to him are entitled to a peculiar kind of protection. Which gave rise to the passage in the ancient song of the Heralds, "O Sovereign, do you make me a royal messenger from the Roman citizens? and do you confer the same privileges on my train and every thing, which belongs to me?" And by the Julian law, an injury affecting not only ambassadors, but even their attendants, is pronounced to be a violation of public right.

But these privileges of attendants are only granted so far as an ambassador himself may think proper: so that if any of them has committed an offence, he must be required to deliver up the offender to punishment. He must be REQUIRED to give him up. Because no violence, in taking an offender of that description must be -used. When the Achaeans had arrested some Lacedaemonians, who were along with the Roman ambassadors, the Romans raised a great outcry against the act, as a violation of the law of nations. Sallust's opinion in the case of Bomilcar has already been referred to.

But should the ambassador refuse to give up such offender, redress must be sought in the same manner, as would be done with respect to the ambassador himself. As to his authority over his household, and the asylum, which he may afford in his house to fugitives, these depend upon the agreement made with the power, to whom he is sent, and do not come within the decision of the law of nations.

**IX**. Neither can the moveable property of an ambassador, nor any thing, which is reckoned a personal appendage, be seized for the discharge of a debt, either by process of law, or even by royal authority. For, to give him full security, not only his person but every thing belonging to him must be protected from all compulsion. If an ambassador then has contracted a debt, and, as is usual, has no possession in the country, where he resides: first of all, courteous application must be made to himself, and, in case of his refusal, to his sovereign. But if both these methods of redress fail, recourse must be had to those means of recovery, which are used against debtors residing out of the jurisdiction of the country.

**X**. Nor is there, as some think, any reason to fear, that if such extensive privileges were established, no one would be found willing to enter into any contract with an ambassador, or to furnish him with necessary articles. For the same rule will hold good in the case of ambassadors, as in that of Kings. As sovereigns, who for the best of reasons, are placed above the reach of legal compulsion, find no difficulty in obtaining credit.

**XI**. The importance of such exemptions maybe easily inferred from the innumerable instances, in which both sacred and profane history abound, of wars undertaken on account of the ill-treatment of ambassadors. The war which David made against the Ammonites, on that account, affords us a memorable instance from holy writ, and as a profane writer, Cicero may be cited, who deemed it the most justifiable ground of the Mithridatic war.

## CHAPTER 19: ON THE RIGHT OF BURIAL

*Right of burying the dead founded on the law of nations — Origin of this right — Due to enemies — Whether due to those guilty of atrocious crimes — Whether to those, who have committed suicide — Other rights also authorised by the law of nations.*

**I**. THE right of burying the dead is one of those originating in the voluntary law of nations. Next to the right of ambassadors Dion Chrysostom places that of burying the dead, and calls it a moral act, sanctioned by the unwritten law of nature: And Seneca, the elder, ranks the law, which commands us to commit the bodies of the dead to their parent earth, among the UNWRITTEN precepts, but says, they have a stronger sanction than the RECORDED laws of all ages can give. For, in the language of the Jewish writers, Philo and Josephus, they are marked with the seal of nature, and under the name of nature, we comprehend the customs, that are common to all mankind, and agreeable to natural reason.

We find it some where said by Aelian, that our common nature calls upon us to cover the dead, and some writer, in another place, observes that all men are reduced to an equality by returning to the common dust of the earth. Tacitus informs us, in b. vi. of his Annals, that, when Tiberius made a general massacre of all, who had been connected with Sejanus, and that he forbad them the rites of burial, every one was struck with horror to see the last offices of humanity refused; offices, which Lysias the orator calls the common hopes of our nature.

As the ancients measured the moral character of every people by their observance or neglect of these rights, in order to give them a greater appearance of sanctity, they ascribed their origin to the authority and institutions of their Gods; so that in every part of their writings we meet with frequent mention of the rights of ambassadors, and the rights of burial, as founded upon divine appointment.

In the Tragedy of the Suppliants, Euripides calls it the law of the Gods, and in the Antigone of Sophocles, the heroine makes the following reply to Creon, who bad forbidden any one under pain of death, to give the rites of burial to Polynices, "A prohibition, like this, was not revealed by the supreme will, nor by that heaven-born justice, which has established those laws of respect for the dead: nor did I think that you could command mortals to transgress the unwritten and inviolable laws of God, They were not established to-day, nor yesterday, but from all eternity and will for ever be in force. Their sources are unknown. Am I through fear of a mortal, and by obeying his unjust commands, to incur the wrath of Heaven?"

The authority of Isocrates, and of Herodotus, and that of Xenophon, in the sixth book of his Grecian History, may be appealed to in support of the honours, that have at all times been paid to the dead. In short, these offices of humanity are recommended by the conspiring testimony of the orators, historians, poets, philosophers and divines of all ages, who have dignified them with the names of the most splendid virtues.

**II.** There seems to be no general agreement of opinion upon the origin of funeral rites, and the variety of ways, in which they were performed. The Egyptians EMBALMED, and most of the Greeks BURNED the bodies of the dead before they committed them to the grave. Cicero, in the 22d chapter of his second Book on Laws, speaks of the interment alone, which is now in use, as the most ancient method, and that, which is most congenial to nature, and in this he is followed by Pliny.

Some think that men paid it as a VOLUNTARY debt of nature, which they knew that, AT ANY RATE, they would be obliged to discharge. For the divine sentence, that the body should return to the dust, from which it was taken, was not passed upon Adam only, but, as we find it acknowledged by the writings of Greece and Rome, extended to the whole human race, Cicero, from the Hypsipyle of Euripides, says, "Earth must be returned to earth," and in the twelfth chapter of Solomon's Ecclesiastes, there is a passage to the same purport, that "the dust shall return to the earth as it was, but the spirit to God, who gave it." Euripides has enlarged on this subject in the character of Theseus in his Suppliants, I Suffer the dead to be laid in the lap of the earth; for every thing returns to its original state, the spirit to heaven, and the body to the earth: Neither of them is given in plenary possession, but only for a short use: The earth soon demands back the bodies, to which she had given birth and nourishment." In the same manner Lucretius calls the earth "a prolific parent and a common grave." Pliny also describes the earth, as receiving us at our birth, cherishing our growth, supporting us to the very last, and, when all the other parts of nature have forsaken us, taking us to her maternal bosom, and covering us with a mantle.

There are some, who think that the custom of burial was bequeathed to us by our first parents as a testamentary hope of a resurrection. For we are instructed by Democritus to believe, that our bodies are preserved in the earth under the promise of a restoration to life. And Christians in particular have frequently ascribed the custom of decent burial to the same hope. Prudentius, a Christian poet says, "What can be the meaning of hallowed rocks, or splendid monuments, except that they are the depositories of bodies, consigned not to death, but to a temporary sleep?"

But the most obvious explanation is to be found in the dignity of man, who surpassing other creatures, it would be a shame, if his body were left to be devoured by beasts of prey. It is an act of compassion then, said Quintilian, to preserve the bodies of men from ravages of birds and beasts. For to be tore by wild beasts, as Cicero observes in his first book ON INVENTION, is to be robbed of those honours, in death, which are due to our common nature. And the Roman Poet, makes a lamentation over one of his heroes, that he had no pious mother to lay his body in the grave, but he would be left a prey to birds, or thrown into the river as food for fishes. Aen. x. 557-560.

But to speak from still higher authority, God, by the mouth of his prophets, threatens the wicked that they shall have burial like that of the brutes, and that the dogs shall lick their blood. Such a menace denounced against the wicked, as a punishment, shews that it is an indignity done to out nature, when, in the words of Lactantius, the image of God is cast out, to the insults of beasts of prey. But in such indignity if there was even nothing repugnant to the feelings of men, still the nakedness and infirmities of our perishable nature should not be exposed to the eye of day.

Consequently the rights of burial, the discharge of which forms one of the offices of humanity, cannot be denied even to enemies, whom a state of warfare has not deprived of the rights and nature of men. For, as Virgil observes, all animosity against the vanquished and the dead must cease. Aen. xi. 104. Because they have suffered the last of evils that can be inflicted. " We have been at war, I grant, *says Statius*, but our hatred has fallen, and all our enmity is buried in the grave." And Optatus Milevitanus assigns the same reason for reconciliation. "If there have been struggles among the living, your hatred surely must be satisfied with the death of an adversary. For the tongue of strife is now silenced."

**III**. Upon the principles advanced above, it is agreed by all that public enemies are entitled to burial. Appian calls it the common right of war, with which, Tacitus says, no enemy will refuse to comply. And the rules, respecting this, are, according to Dio Chrysostom, observed, even while the utmost rage of war still continues. "For the hand of death, *as the writer just quoted observes*, has destroyed all enmity towards the fallen, and protected their bodies from all insult." Examples to this purpose may be found in various parts of history. Alexander ordered those of the enemy, that were killed at the battle of Issus to be honoured with the rites of burial, and Hannibal did the same to Caius Flaminius, Publius Aemilius, Tiberius Gracchus, and Marcellus, the Roman Generals. So that you would suppose, says Silius Italicus, he had been paying these honours to a Carthaginian General. The Romans treated Hanno, and Pompey Mithridates in the same manner. If it were necessary to quote more instances, the conduct of Demetrius on many occasions, and that of Antony to king Archelaus might be named.

When the Greeks were at war with the Persians, in one part of their military oath they swore to bury all the dead belonging to the ALLIES, and when they were victorious, to bury even the BARBARIANS. After a battle, it was -usual for both sides to obtain leave to bury the dead. Pausanias, in his account of the Athenian affairs, mentions the practice of the Athenians who buried the Medes, regarding it as an act of piety due to all men. We find from the Jewish writers, that for the same reason, their high priests, who were forbidden to come near a dead body, if they found one, were obliged to bury it. But Christians deemed BURIAL an act of such importance, that they would allow their church-plate to be melted down, and sold to defray the expences as they would have done to maintain the poor, or to redeem captives.

There are some few instances to the contrary, but they are reprobated by the universal feelings of mankind, and such cruelty deprecated in the most solemn terms. Claudian calls it a bloody deed to plunder the dead, and still more so to refuse them the covering of a little sand.

**IV**. Respecting those, who have been guilty of atrocious crimes, there is reason to entertain some doubt, whether the right of burial is due to them.

The divine law indeed, that was given to the Hebrews, and which is fraught with every precept of virtue and humanity, ordered those, who were crucified, which was the most ignominious kind of punishment that could be inflicted, to be buried on the same day. Owing to this law, as Josephus observes, the Jews paid such regard to burial, that the bodies of those, who were executed publicly as criminals, were taken away before sun-set, and committed to the ground. And other Jewish writers are of opinion that this was intended as a degree of reverence to the divine image, after which man was formed.

To allow burial to criminals must have been the practice in the time of Homer: for we are told, in the third book of the Odyssey, that Egisthus, who had added the crime of murder to that of adultery, was honoured with funeral ceremonies by Orestes, the son of the murdered king. It was the custom with the Romans, as may be seen from Ulpian, never to refuse giving the bodies of criminals to their relatives, to bury. The Emperors, Diocletian, and Maximian, in a rescript, declared, that they did not refuse to deliver up, for burial, those, who had deservedly been put to death for their crimes.

In reading the history of civil wars; we find more frequent instances of indignities offered to the dead, than in the accounts of any foreign wars. In some cases, the bodies of executed criminals are exposed to public view, and hung in chains, a custom the propriety of which is very much doubted both by Theological and Political writers. So far from approving of the practice, we find such writers bestowing praises upon many, who had ordered funeral honours to be paid to those, who would not themselves have allowed the same to others. An action of this kind was done by Pausanias the Lacedaemonian, who, being urged by the people of Aegina to retaliate upon the Persians for their treatment of Leonidas, rejected the advice, as unbecoming his own character and the Grecian name. The Pharisees allowed burial even to King Jannaeus Alexander, who had treated the dead bodies of their countrymen with every kind of insult. Though indeed on certain occasions, God may have punished some offenders with the loss of such a right, he did so by virtue of his own prerogative, which places him above the restrictions of all law. And when David exposed the head of Goliah, it was done to one, who was an alien, and a despiser of God, and might be justified by that law, which confined the name and privileges of neighbour to the Hebrews.

**V**. There is one thing not improper to be observed, that the rule prevailing among the Hebrews with respect to burying the dead, contained an exception, as we are informed by Josephus, excluding those, who had committed suicide. Nor is it surprising that a mark of ignominy should be affixed to those, on whom death itself cannot be inflicted as a punishment. Aristotle in the fifth book of his Ethics, speaks of the infamy universally attached to suicide. Nor is the observation at all weakened by the opinions of some of the Grecian poets, that as the dead are void of all perception, they cannot be affected either by loss or shame. For it is a sufficient reason to justify the practice, if the living can be deterred from committing actions, for which they see a mark of infamy set upon the dead.

In opposition to the Stoics, and others, who admitted the dread of servitude, sickness, or any other calamity, or even the ambitious love of glory to be a just cause of voluntary death, in opposition to them, the Platonists justly maintain, that the soul must be retained in the custody of the body, from which it cannot be released, but at the command of him, who gave it. On this subject there are many fine thoughts in Plotinus, Olympiodorus, and Macrobius on the dream of Scipio.

Brutus, following the opinions of the Platonists, had formerly condemned the death of Cato, whom he himself afterwards imitated. He considered it as an act of impiety for any one to withdraw himself from his allegiance to the supreme being, and to shrink from evils, which he ought to bear with fortitude. And Megasthenes, as may be seen, in Strabo book xv. remarked the disapprobation, which the Indian sages expressed of the conduct of Calanus: for it was by no means agreeable to their tenets, that any one, through impatience, should quit his post in life. In the fifth book of Quintus Curtius, there is an expression of King Darius to this effect, that he had rather die by another's guilty hand than by his own. In the same manner the Hebrews call death a release, or dismission, as may be seen not only in the Gospel of St. Luke, ch. ii. v. 19, but in the Greek version of the Old Testament, Gen. xv. 2, and Numb. xx, towards the conclusion: and the same way of speaking was used by the Greeks. Plutarch, in speaking of consolation, calls death the time, when God shall relieve us from our post.

**VI**. There are certain other rights too, which owe their origin to the voluntary law of nations, such as the right of possession from length of time, the right of succession to any one who dies intestate, and the right resulting from contracts, though of an unequal kind. For though all these rights, in some measure, spring from the law of nature, yet they derive their confirmation from human law, whether it be in opposition to the uncertainty of conjecture, or to certain other exceptions, suggested by natural reason: points, all of which have been slightly touched upon in our discussions on the law of nature.

## CHAPTER 20: ON PUNISHMENTS.

*Definition and origin of punishment — In what manner punishment relates to strict justice — The right of punishing allowed by the law of nature, to none, except to those, who are innocent of the crimes and misdemeanours to be punished — Difference of motive between human and divine punishment — In what sense revenge is naturally unlawful — The advantages of punishment, threefold — The law of nature allows any one to inflict punishment upon an offender, yet with a distinction — The regard which the law of nations pays to the benefit of the injured party, in the infliction of punishment — General utility of punishments — What is determined by the law of the Gospel, in this respect — Answer to the objections founded upon the mercy of God, as displayed in the Gospel — Capital punishments objected to as cutting off all possibility of repentance — Not safe for private Christians to inflict punishments, even when allowed to do so, by the law of nations — Prosecutions, for certain offences, to be carried on in the name of the public and not of individuals — Internal acts not punishable by man — Open acts, when inevitable through human infirmity not punishable — Actions, neither directly nor indirectly injurious to society, not punishable by human laws — The reasons of that exemption — The opinion, that pardon can never be granted, refuted — Pardon shewn to be allowable before the establishment of penal law — But not in all cases — Allowable also subsequently to the establishment of penalties — Internal and external reasons — Opinion, that there can be no just reason for dispensing with laws, except where such dispensation can be implied as authorised by the law, examined and refuted — Punishment estimated by the desert of the offender — Different motives compared — Motives which ought to restrain men from sin — Scale of offences according to the precepts of the Decalogue — Capacity of the offender — Punishment mitigated from motives of charity, except where there are stronger motives of an opposite kind — Facility or familiarity of crimes aggravates their nature — Clemency, proper exercise of — Views of the Jews and Romans in inflicting punishment — War considered as a punishment — Whether hostilities can justly be commenced for intended aggressions — Whether Kings and Nations are justified in making war to punish offences against the law of nature, not immediately affecting themselves or their subjects — The opinion, that jurisdiction is naturally necessary to authorise punishment, refuted — Distinction between the law of nature, and civil customs, and the divine voluntary law — The question, whether war can be undertaken to punish acts of impiety considered — The being of God, whence known Refusal to embrace the Christian religion not a sufficient cause of war — Cruel treatment of Christians, justifiable cause of war — Open defiance of religion punishable.*

**I**. IN THE preceding part of this treatise, where the causes, for which war may be undertaken, were explained, it was considered in a two-fold light, either as a reparation for injuries, or as a punishment. The first of these points having been already cleared up, the latter, which relates to punishments, remains to be discussed, and it will require a more ample investigation; for the origin and nature of punishment, not being perfectly understood, has given rise to many errors.

Punishment taken in its most general meaning signifies the pain of suffering, which is inflicted for evil actions. For although labour may some times be imposed instead of punishment; still it is considered in that case, as a hardship and a grievous burden, and may therefore properly be classed with sufferings. But the inconveniences, which men are some times exposed to, by being excluded from the intercourse of society and the offices of life, owing to infectious disorders, or other similar causes, which was the case with the Jews on account of many legal impurities, these temporary privations are not to be strictly taken for punishments: though from their resemblance to each other, they are often, by an abuse of terms, confounded.

But among the dictates laid down by nature, as lawful and just, and which the ancient Philosophers call the law of Rhadamanthus, the following maxim may be placed, THAT IT IS RIGHT FOR EVERY ONE TO SUFFER EVIL PROPORTIONED TO THAT WHICH HE HAS DONE.

Which gave occasion to Plutarch, in his book on exile, to say that "justice is an attribute of God, avenging all transgressions of the divine law; and we apply it as the rule and measure of our dealings with each other. For though separated by the arbitrary or geographical bounds of territory, the eye of nature looks upon all, as fellow subjects of one great empire." Hierocles gives a fine character of justice, calling it the healing remedy of all mischief. Lactantius in speaking of the divine wrath calls it "no inconsiderable mistake in those, who degrade human or divine punishment with the name of cruelty or rigour, imagining that some degree of blame must always attach to the punishment of the guilty." What has been said of the inseparable connection of a penalty with every offense is similar to the remark of Augustin, "that to make a punishment JUST, it must be inflicted for some crime." He applies the expression to explain the divine justice, where through human ignorance, the offence is often undiscoverable though the judgment may be seen.

**II**. There are diversities of opinion whether punishment comes under the rank of ATTRIBUTIVE or that of STRICT justice. Some refer it to justice of the attributive kind, because offences are punished more or less, in pro. portion to their consequences, and because the punishment is inflicted by the whole community, as it were, upon an individual.

It is undoubtedly one of the first principles of justice to establish an equality between the penalty and the of. fence. For it is the business of reason, says Horace, in one of his Satires, to apply a rule and measure, by which the penalty may be framed upon a scale with the of. fence, and in another place, he observes, that it would be contrary to all reason to punish with the rack a slave, who deserved nothing more than the whip. I. Sat. iii. v. 77, and 119. The divine law, as may be seen from the xxv. Chapter of Deuteronomy, rests upon the same principle.

There is one sense, in which all punishment may be said to be a matter of strict justice. Thus, when we say that punishment is due to any one, we mean nothing more than that it is right he should be punished. Nor can any one inflict this punishment, but the person, who has a right to do so. Now in the eye of the law, every penalty is considered, as a debt arising out of a crime, and which the offender is bound to pay to the aggrieved party. And in this there is something approaching to the nature of contracts. For as a seller, though no EXPRESS stipulation be made, is understood to have bound himself by all the USUAL, and

NECESSARY conditions of a sale, so, punishment being a natural consequence of crime, every heinous offender appears to have VOLUNTARILY incurred the penalties of law. In this sense some of the Emperors pronounced sentence upon malefactors in the following manner, "you have brought this punishment upon Yourselves." Indeed every wicked action done by design was considered as a voluntary contract to submit to punishment. For, as Michael the Ephesian observes on the fifth book of Aristotle's Nicomachean Ethics, the ancients gave the name of contract, not only to the voluntary agreements which men made with each other, but to the obligations arising from the sentence of the law.

**III.** But to whom the right of punishing properly belongs, is a matter not determined by the law of NATURE. For though reason may point out the necessity of punishing the guilty, it does not specify the PERSON, to whom the execution of it is to be committed.

Natural reason indeed does so far point out the person, that it is deemed most SUITABLE for a SUPERIOR ONLY to be invested with the power of inflicting punishment. Yet this demonstration does not amount to an ABSOLUTE NECESSITY, unless the word superior be taken in a sense implying, that the commission of a crime makes the offender inferior to every one of his own species, by his having degraded himself from the rank of men to that of the brutes, which are in subjection to man; a doctrine, which some Theologists have maintained. Philosophers too agreed in this. For Democritus supposed that power -naturally belonged to superior merit, and Aristotle was of opinion that both in the productions of nature and art the inferior were provided for the use of the superior parts.

From this opinion there arises a necessary consequence, that in a case where there are equal degrees of guilt in two parties, the right of punishment belongs to neither.

In conformity to, which, our Saviour, in the case of the woman taken in adultery, pronounced that whoever of the accusers was without sin, meaning sins of equal enormity, should cast the first stone. John viii. 7. He said so for this reason, because in that age the manners of the Jews were so corrupt, that, under a great parade of sanctity, the most enormous vices, and the most wicked dispositions were concealed. A character of the times which the Apostle has painted in the most glowing colours, and which he closes with a reproof similar to what his divine master had given, "therefore thou art inexcusable, O man, whosoever thou art that judgest: for wherein thou judgest another thou condemnest thyself; for thou that judgest doest the same things." Rom, ii. 1. Applicable to which there is a remark of Seneca's, that "no sentence, which is passed by a guilty person can have any weight." And in another place, the same writer observes, that " if we look into ourselves and consider whether we have been guilty of the offences we are going to condemn, we shall be more moderate in our judgments."

**IV.** Another part of our inquiry respects the end pro. posed by punishment. For by what has hitherto been said, it was only meant to shew that in punishing the guilty no injury is done to them. Still the absolute necessity of punishment does not follow from thence. For the pardon of the guilty on many occasions has been considered as the most beauteous feature in the divine and human character. Plato is celebrated for his saying that "justice does not inflict punishment for the evils that are done and cannot be retrieved; but to pre. vent the same from being clone for the time to come." From Thucydides we find that Diodorus in addressing the Athenians on the conduct of the Mitylenaeans, advises them "to forbear punishing their avowed injustice, unless it was probable that the punishment would be attended with some good effect."

These maxims may be true with regard to human punishments: for one man being so nearly allied to another by blood, no degree of suffering should be inflicted, but for some consequent good. But the case is different with respect to God, to whom Plato injudiciously applies the above sentiments. For though the divine counsels will undoubtedly have the good of men in view, as the end of all punishment, yet the bare reformation of the offender cannot be the sole object. Since the divine justice, though tempered with mercy must adhere to the truth of the revealed word, which threatens the wicked with punishment or destruction.

The honour therefore of God, as well as the example held up to men, will be a consequence resulting from his punishment of the wicked.

**V**. A dramatic writer has said that "the pain of an enemy is a hearing remedy to a wounded spirit," in which he agrees with Cicero and Plutarch: in the opinion of the former "pain is mitigated by the punishment of an adversary," and in that of the latter "satisfaction is a sweet medicine to a troubled mind."

But a disposition like this, when stripped of all disguise and false colouring, will be found by no means suitable to the reasonable soul of man, whose office it is to regulate and controul the affections. Nor will that disposition receive any sanction from the law of nature, who in all her dictates, inclines to unite men in society by good will, rather than to separate them by cherishing animosity. For it is laid down by reason, as a leading axiom in her code of laws, that no man shall do any thing which may hurt another, unless it be for the purpose of some evident and essential good. But the pain of an enemy considered solely of such, is no benefit to us, but a false and imaginary one, like that derived from superfluous riches or things of the same kind.

In this acceptation revenge is condemned both by Christian teachers and heathen philosophers. In this respect, the language of Seneca approaches very near to the perfection of Christian morals. He calls revenge, in its usual and proper acceptation, a term of inhumanity, differing from injury only in degree. For retaliation of pain can be considered as nothing better than excusable sin. Juvenal, after describing the different tempers, over which revenge exercises the most powerful dominion, and shewing the amiable characters over which it has no influence, concludes it to be the pleasure of a little and infirm mind.

From the preceding arguments it is plain that punishment cannot justly be inflicted from a spirit of revenge. We proceed therefore to consider the advantages attending its just infliction.

**VI**. This seems the most proper place for reviewing those distinctions in the motives of punishment, which have been used by Plato in his Gorgias, and by Taurus the philosopher in a passage quoted by Gellius in the fourteenth chapter of his fifth book. These distinctions seem to result naturally from the end of all punishment. Plato indeed considers the amendment of the offender, and the example given to others, as the two principal motives: but Taurus has added a third, which he calls satisfaction, and which is defined by Clemens Alexandrinus, to be repayment of evil, contributing to the benefit of both the aggrieved and avenging party. Aristotle passing over example as a motive, confines the object of punishment to the amendment or correction of the offender. But Plutarch has not made the same omission: for he has said, that "where immediate punishment follows the execution of a heinous crime, it both operates to deter others from committing the same crime, and administers some degree of consolation to the injured and suffering person." And this is what Aristotle calls commutative justice. But these matters require a more minute inquiry. We may observe therefore that there is nothing contrary either to human or divine law, in punishments, which have the good of the offender, or that of the injured party, or of any persons whatsoever in view.

The three proper ends are obtained by that kind of punishment, which some philosophers have called correction, some chastisement, and others admonition. Paulus the Lawyer, has given it the name of correction; Plato styles it a lesson of instruction, and Plutarch a medicine of the soul, reforming and healing the sufferer, while it operates as a painful remedy. For as all deliberate acts, by frequent repetition, produce a propensity, which ripens into habit, the best method of reforming vices in their earliest stage is to deprive them of their sweet savour by an infusion of subsequent pain. It is an opinion of the Platonists, repeated by Apuleius, that "impunity and the delay of reproof are more severe and pernicious to an offender than any punishment whatsoever," and, in the words of Tacitus, "violent disorders must be encountered with remedies proportionably strong."

**VII**. The power of inflicting the punishment, subservient to this end, is allowed by the law of nature to any one of competent judgment, and not implicated in similar or equal offences. This is evident as far as verbal reproof goes, from the maxim of Plautus, that "to bestow merited reproof upon a friend is useful, upon certain occasions, though by no means a grateful office." But in all kinds of constraint and compulsion, the difference made between the persons, who are allowed, and who are not allowed to exercise it is no appointment of natural law, but one of the positive institutions of the civil law. For no such natural distinction could be made, any farther than that reason would intrust parents with the peculiar use of such an authority, in consideration of their affection. But laws, in order to avoid animosities, have, with respect to the authority of punishing, passed over the common kindred subsisting among mankind, and confined it to the nearest degrees of relation: as may be seen in many records, and particularly in the code of Justinian, under the title of the POWER OF RELATIVES TO CORRECT IN ORDER TO REFORM OFFENDERS. And Cyrus, in the v. book and viii. chapter of Xenophon's history of the Expedition, addresses the soldiers to the following purport, "If I punish any one for his good, I am willing to submit to justice; but would it not be equally reasonable that parents and masters should submit to justice, for having corrected children, or the Surgeon be responsible for having used the incision-knife, where the patient's case required it?"

But this kind of corrective punishment does not extend to death, which cannot be considered, as a benefit in itself, except INDIRECTLY and By WAY OF REDUCTION, as it is called by Logicians, who, in order to confirm negatives, reduce them to things of an opposite kind. Thus, in Mark xiv. 21, when our Saviour says, that it were better for some, they had never been born, so, for incurable dispositions, it is better, that is would be a less evil, to die than to live; since it is certain that by living they will grow worse. Plutarch calls such men a pest to others, but the greatest pest to themselves. Galen says that capital punishments are inflicted to prevent men from doing harm by a longer course of iniquity, and to deter others by the fear of punishment, adding that it is better men should die, when they have souls so infected with evil, as to be incurable.

There are some, who think that these are the persons meant by the Apostle John, who describes them as sinning a sin unto death. But as their arguments are not satisfactory, charity requires that no one should be deemed incorrigible, except upon the clearest grounds. So that punishment with such an end in view can only be inflicted for important causes.

**VIII**. The benefit accruing to an injured person from the punishment of an offender consists in his being secured in future against a recurrence of the same injury from that offender, or from others. There are three ways of preventing this recurrence-by removing the offender — by depriving him of the power of doing harm, or lastly by compelling him to better habits of thought or action, which is the reformation produced by the punishment already spoken of. It is not every kind of punishment, which can produce such effects; it must be open and conspicuous, to operate as an example, that may deter others from the commission of the same crimes. A vindictive punishment, inflicted by an injured individual, or by any other person, when it is restrained by bounds and limitations of this kind, has nothing unlawful in it considering the law of nature by itself, apart from all human and divine institutions, and every adventitious circumstance, that may create a deviation from the primitive dictates of nature. We have said that it may be inflicted by any other individual, as well as by the injured person: for it is comformable to nature, that one man should assist another. But as our judgment is apt to be biassed by our affections, in cases, where our interest is concerned; since the formation of families into states, judges have been appointed, and invested with the power of punishing the guilty, whereby the natural liberty of personal redress, originally allowed to individuals, was abolished, or at least abridged. And it is only in places, on the seas for instance, where no judicial remedy can be obtained, that this natural liberty continues in force. There is a circumstance related of Julius Caesar, applicable to this subject. While he was only in a private station, being taken prisoner by some pirates, after he had redeemed himself by a sum of money, he applied to the proconsul for redress. But his application being neglected, he fitted out a certain number of ships, attacked and defeated the pirates, and ordered them all to be crucified.

The practice of private individuals, exercising punishment, was the origin of single combats, so familiar to the Germans before the introduction of Christianity, and not yet sufficiently laid aside. We are informed by Velleius Paterculus, in his second book, that the Germans were surprised to see the forms of Roman jurisprudence, and those disputes, which they themselves decided by the sword, settled by law. By the Jewish law, the nearest in blood to the deceased were allowed to k ill a murderer, if taken beyond the places of refuge. And the Jewish interpreters observe, that in GENERAL the infliction of punishment, as a retaliation for murder, it intrusted to no hand, but that of the judge: as it is difficult for an individual in his own case to moderate his resentment. The same custom of allowing individuals to avenge their own wrongs prevailed among the ancient Greeks, as we find from the words of Thecelymenes, in Homer's Odyssey. But it prevailed most in countries, where public courts of justice were not established. From hence St. Augustin defines those wars to be just, which are intended to avenge injuries. And Plato, in his twelfth book ON A COMMONWEALTH, justifies the prolongation of hostilities, till the aggressor is reduced to submit to just, and equitable terms.

**IX**. GENERAL Utility which was considered as the third end proposed by punishment, may be divided into the same number of parts, as the benefit accruing from thence to individuals. For these are the objects in view, either to prevent the individual, who has injured one person, from doing injury to others: an object which can be accomplished only by removing the offender, disarming him of the means of farther injury, or by reforming him: or it may be inflicted to deter others from being allured, by an example of impunity, to commit acts of molestation or enmity. And the infliction of punishment, for such reasons, is a RIGHT granted by the law of nature to every individual. Upon this principle, Plutarch observes in the life of Pelopidas, that good men are designed by nature for the office of perpetual magistracy, and superiority belongs to those, in whom the characters of truth and justice unite.

But as it requires a painful degree of patience to examine into facts, and no inconsiderable share of skill and equity to affix the extent of punishments; in order to prevent quarrels from arising through the presuming conceit, which every man entertains of his own wisdom, and to which others are averse to yield; in all well regulated communities, it has been usual to select for the tribunals of justice those, who were deemed worthy of such honour, or likely to become so, from their integrity and wisdom. Democritus has said, there would have been no occasion for laws to prevent every man from living according to his own humour, if one had not done injury to another. For envy was the origin of strife. But as we have just observed, that it happens, in the case of revenge, so in this kind of punishment, inflicted for the sake of example, there are traces and remains of ancient law, in those places, and among those persons, that are subject to no CIVIL jurisdiction; and in certain other cases besides. Thus any Hebrew, according to the customs of that people, if he should turn away from God, or from the law of God, or should seduce others to false worship, might immediately be put to death by any one whatsoever. The Hebrews call that an act of ZEAL, which was first done by Phinehas, and which afterwards became a custom. Thus Mattathias slew a Jew, who was polluting himself with Grecian rites. In the same manner, in the book commonly called the third book of Maccabees, it is related that three hundred other Jews were put to death by their own countrymen. Nor could any other pretext be assigned for stoning Stephen, and conspiring against Paul. Philo, and Josephus abound in instances of this kind. There are many countries where we may trace the remains of primitive law, in the plenary power al. lowed to masters over their slaves, and to parents over their children, extending even to inflict the punishment of death. So the Ephori of Sparta might put a citizen to death without the formality of trial. From what has been said, it is easy to infer what punishment the law of nature authorises, and how far it has remained in force.

**X**. We come now to consider whether the law of the Gospel has confined that liberty within closer bounds. It has been observed in another part of this treatise, that it is not surprising that some things, which are allowed by natural and civil law, should be forbidden by the divine law, owing to its great perfection, and the superiority of its rewards over any thing that human nature can bestow. To the attainment of which it is not unreasonable that virtues should be required, far exceeding the simple precepts of nature. Those kinds of correction that leave neither any mark of infamy, nor any permanent injury, but are suited to the age, or other circumstances of the sufferer, if inflicted by those, who derive such a permission from human laws, for instance by parents, guardians, or masters, contain nothing repugnant to the precepts of the Gospel, as may be clearly understood from the nature of the thing itself. For they are remedies to the mind no less harmless than medicines ungrateful to the palate are to the body. But as to revenge the case is different For the infliction of punishment, only to gratify resentment, so far from being conformable to the Gospel, has been shewn above to be repugnant even to the law of nature.

The Jewish law indeed not only forbids the cherishing of hatred against a neighbour, that is, one of the same country and people, but requires certain common acts of kindness to be bestowed even upon enemies of that description. The Gospel therefore, comprehending all men under the appellation of neighbour, not only forbids us to hurt our enemies, but commands us to do them good; a commandment clearly stated in the Gospel of St. Matthew. Yet the law permitted the Jews to seek revenge for injuries of a more grievous kind, not with their own hands, but by appealing to the judge. But Christ does not give us the same permission, as appears from that opposition which he makes between the permissions of former times, and those of his own law. "You have heard that it was said an eye for an eye — but I say unto you, love your enemies, etc."

For although what follows relates peculiarly to the repelling of injury, and, in some measure, abridges this permission, yet it passes a much greater censure upon revenge, rejecting it as an indulgence suitable only to a more imperfect, and carnal state.

To inflict punishment by way of retaliation was disapproved of even by those of the Jews, who were distinguished for their worth and wisdom; because they regarded not only the LETTER, but the PURPOSE and SPIRIT of the law. This appears from Philo, in whose writings we find the Jews of Alexandria, upon the calamity of Flaccus, their persecutor, addressing themselves to God in the following language, "We do not rejoice, 0 Lord, in the calamity or punishment of an enemy, being taught by thy holy laws to feel for the miseries of men." And in this case we may apply that general command given by Christ to forgive all who have offended or injured us, that is, neither to do, nor to wish them evil, through resentment of the evil they have done to us. But what can be said of revenge, not as regarding the past, but as providing security for the future? Here too Christ requires of his followers the same disposition to pardon injuries, particularly, if the offender shews any probable signs of repentance. Luke xvii. 3. Eph. iv. 32. Col. iii. 13. In those passages a full remission is intended, such a remission as restores the offender to his former situation of friendship or confidence: and consequently nothing can be required of him under the name of punishment. Besides, if there were no such marks of repentance, the reparation of a loss is not to be pursued with to much rigour; a doctrine inferred from the precept of Christ enjoining us to give up the garment along with the cloak.

But if it is likely that connivance at an offence will be attended with imminent inconvenience and even danger to ourselves, we should be contented with such securities as may be effectual, and at the same time operate with as little prejudice as possible to the offender. For even among the Jews, the law of retaliation was not in use, as we are informed by Josephus, and other writers of that nation. But in addition to the expence incurred, which the law treats of as a separate point, the injured party usually received a pecuniary fine instead of retaliation; the repayment of expences being considered simply as a restitution, and not a penalty.

It remains now to consider punishment, as providing for the PUBLIC and not INDIVIDUAL security, which is accomplished either by removing the guilty person out of the way or by restraining him from doing farther mischief, or by deterring others through the severity of example, none of which means it has been clearly proved were abolished by Christ; for in giving his precepts be affirmed that he destroyed no part of the law. The law Of MOSES indeed, which in these respects was to remain in force as long as the Jewish Polity existed, strictly enjoined magistrates to punish murder and other similar crimes. But if the precepts of Christ could exist in conjunction with the law of Moses, as far as it imposed capital punishments, surely they may exist in conjunction with human laws, which in this respect are but an imitation of the divine laws.

**XI**. Some, in support of an opposite opinion, allege the supreme mercy of God, as it is displayed in the new covenant, and which is given as an example for men, and for magistrates, in particular, to follow, who, in the exercise of authority, execute the laws of the Deity. This opinion may in some measure be true, but not to that extent, which the authors of it intend. For the great mercy of God displayed in the new covenant has a peculiar reference to offences against the primitive law, or even against the law of Moses, before the time that men had received a knowledge of the Gospel. For offences committed after the promulgation of the Gospel, especially if they are accompanied with a hardened obstinacy, are treated with much severer judgments than any that were declared by Moses. For God punishes sins of that kind not only in a future state, but in the present life. But for sins of that kind, to obtain the act of mercy and indulgence, the offender must inflict punishment upon himself, not in a slight or trivial manner, but with a heartfelt sorrow, and resolution to sin no more.

In the same manner it is maintained that if men are actuated by repentance, they are ENTITLED to impunity. We do not say that men are never actuated by sincere repentance; but it is not every kind of avowal or acknowledgment, by which God is moved to remit the WHOLE of a punishment, as appears from the case of David. As the supreme judge therefore might dispense with the full penalty of the law, inflicting death, and yet exercise no inconsiderable severity upon offenders, so now he may dispense with the sentence of eternal death, at the same time leaving the sinner to find an early grave by the stroke of some calamity, or by the hand of human justice.

**XII**. and **XIII**. Another objection made against capital punishments is that such a kind of sentence and execution is cutting off a criminal from all possibility of repentance. But those, who make the objection, must know, that in cases of that kind, venerable and upright judges use the greatest precautions, and suffer no one to be hurried away to execution, without a reasonable time allowed for reflection and deep abhorrence of his crime: a repentance, which though prevented by the interposing hand of death from producing the fruits of righteousness, we have reason to suppose, from the case of the thief pardoned on the cross, may be accepted with God.

But if on the other hand it be said that longer life might have been of more avail to serious repentance, we may observe that, in some cases, the reply of Seneca may be made, that to men of that description death is often the greatest blessing which can be bestowed; for, in the words of Eusebius, their career of wickedness cannot otherwise be shortened, or reformed. These in addition to the preceding arguments in the former part of this treatise may be deemed a sufficient answer to those, who assert that all capital punishments, and even all punishments, without exception, are abolished by the precepts of our Saviour. The Apostle, consigning to the office of kings the use of the sword, as an exercise of his divine commission to avenge all wrongs, instructs us to pray for kings, that, as true Christians, in their royal capacity, they may be a protection to the innocent. An end, which even after the introduction of the gospel, could not easily be obtained, owing to the depravity of mankind, if the violence of some were not restrained by the exemplary punishment, of others. Such authority is the more necessary, when even in the midst of so many examples and punishments, the lives of the innocent are scarcely secure. There have been indeed, it cannot be denied, happy instances where the sentence of death was changed for that of perpetual labour, a practice, as we are informed by Diodorus, followed by Sabacon, king of Egypt, a prince renowned for his piety. Balsamon observes that the penal laws of Rome, inflicting death, were most of them changed by the Christian emperors of later times, and other kinds of punishment were substituted, that the guilty might receive deeper impressions of repentance, and their punishment operate as a more durable example.

**XIV**. From what has been said, it may be inferred, how unsafe it is for a private Christian, whether from motives of personal interest, or from those of the public good, to take upon himself the punishment of an offender, and particularly to inflict death. Although, as it has been said before, it may, IN SOME CASES, be allowed by the law of nations. A permission, that has given rise to the laudable practice, prevailing in some countries of furnishing adventurers with public instructions and commissions to chase and capture pirates, wherever they may be found. But those adventurers may be considered as discharging a public duty rather than as acting upon their own authority.

**XV**. A custom not unlike to which prevails in many places, of not allowing individuals to bring criminal charges against others at their own pleasure: that office belonging to persons invested with public authority to undertake it. So that no one can contribute towards shedding the blood of another, but as an act of necessary duty. In reference to this custom, a canon of the council of Eliberis excluded from the communion any believer who had been instrumental in causing the proscription or death of another.

[**Translator's note:** Sections XVI and XVII of the original, relating only to the refutation of certain abstruse opinions, are omitted in the translation.]

**XVIII**. It is proper now to consider whether all wicked acts are of that kind, which are punishable by human laws. In reply to which we may answer that they certainly are not. In the first place, mere acts of the mind, or criminal intentions, though by subsequent confession, or some other accident, they may come to the knowledge of others, are not punishable by human laws. Because, as it was proved in a former part of this treatise, it is not consonant to the law of nature, that INTENTIONS ONLY should give rise to any right, or obligation amongst men. And in this sense the maxim of the Roman law is to be taken, THAT NO ONE DESERVES PUNISHMENT FOR MERE THOUGHTS. Yet this does not prevent intentions, when they have an influence upon the conduct, from being considered as actual deeds, and equally deserving of punishment.

**XIX**. In the second place, even outward acts, cannot be punished by men where they arise through some inevitable infirmity of human nature. For although there can be no sin, except where there is a freedom of will, yet to be at all times free from all infirmity and sin, is more than can be expected from the condition of man. So that Sopater, Hierocles and Seneca among the Philosophers; Philo among the Jews; Thucydides among the historians; and innumerable writers among Christians have maintained that sin is interwoven with our very nature. Nay indeed, a doubt may be entertained whether such acts can rightly and properly be called sins. For though seeming to be voluntary actions, they will be found, when minutely considered, not to proceed from a free and deliberate exercise of the will. "Laws, *says Plutarch in the life of Solon*, should be framed to suit possible cases, the legislator may obtain every beneficial end by punishing a few offenders, where the indiscriminate punishment of multitudes would be attended with no good effect."

There are some actions, which though not imputable to human nature itself, are inevitable consequences of the influence of bodily habits on the mind. Actions like these are punishable in human courts, owing to the criminality of voluntary contracting, or of not sufficiently guarding against, those habits.

**XX**. In the third place, human courts of justice cannot take cognizance of those offences, which neither directly nor indirectly, affect the public or individuals. For no reason can be assigned, why such offences should not be left to the judgments of God, whose all-seeing eye must know them, whose equity will weigh them, and whose power can punish them. It would be unnecessary therefore, and presumptuous in human tribunals to assume such decisions. However we must except from this rule those corrective kinds of punishment,, designed for the reformation of offenders, even where their conduct is no way injurious to others.

Neither are those actions punishable, which are directly opposite to the virtues of compassion, liberality, or gratitude, in the performance of which virtues natural justice allows of no compulsion.

**XXI**. The point, necessarily to be considered next, is the opinion, whether it is lawful some times to grant pardon. For the Stoics maintain it not to be lawful, as may be seen from a fragment in Stobaeus, under the title of MAGISTRACY, from Cicero's speech for Murena, and towards the conclusion of Seneca's books on Clemency; but their arguments are fallacious, and unsubstantial. They say "that pardon is the remission of a penalty, that OUGHT to be paid; but a wise man does every thing, which he OUGHT to do." Here the fallacy lies in the use of the word OUGHT. For if it means that an offender owes a penalty, that is, that he may be punished without injustice, it will not necessarily follow that the person who does not punish him, is doing what he ought not to do. But if the word be taken to imply that a good man, or a wise man, ought at all events, to exact the penalty, it may be observed in reply that THIS does not always hap. pen, and therefore, in this sense, the penalty or punishment may be considered, not as a debt, but only a permission. And this will hold good, both before and after the establishment of penal laws.

**XXII**. Before the establishment of penal laws, punishment, beyond all doubt, might be inflicted; because by the law of nature, every offender made himself subject to punishment; but it is not a natural and inevitable consequence of its being lawful, that it should be enforced. For this depends upon the connection between the ends, for which punishments were established, and the punishments themselves. If the ends proposed therefore are not immediately necessary, in a moral point of view, or if other ends of a different kind, but not less wise and salutary should be devised, or that the ends originally designed may be obtained by some other means, in all these cases, the right of punishment may be saved, there being no immediate occasion to inflict it. Thus for instance, where an offence is known to very few, there can be no immediate occasion for a public punishment, by way of exemplary exposure, which in some cases might be even injurious to society rather than productive of advantage. Upon which Cicero in a letter to his brother makes a pertinent remark, respecting one Zeuxis, observing that "had he once been brought into court, he could not have been released, but there was no necessity that a search should be made for him, in order to bring him to trial." — In the next place the right and end of punishment may be dispensed with, where a man's own services, or those of his family are sufficient to outweigh the consideration of his offences. "For, *in the words of Seneca*, an act of kindness eclipses the fault of an injury." — And in the last place, where reproof operates upon an offender, as a means of correction and amendment, or where the injured party is satisfied with an acknowledgment of the offence, the occasion for punishment is done away. It was this motive to clemency, which the son of David had in view, where he observes that it behoves the righteous to be merciful. For as all punishment, especially of the more severe cast, has in it some thing, which tho' not repugnant to justice, is at variance, at least, with charity, reason easily suffers us to forbear inflicting it, unless that forbearance is opposed by some weightier, juster, and more undeniable motive of charity.

**XXIII**. Cases may occur where it is absolutely necessary to inflict punishment, as upon notorious, and atrocious criminals, or where it is for the public good, to dispense with that severity, or where the judicial authorities may use their own discretion in mitigating or enforcing the sentence of the law. Upon which Seneca pertinently remarks, that the exercise of lenity should always be an act of free deliberation. As to the disputes of the Stoics on these points, they are, in the opinion of Cicero and others, debates upon words rather than things: consequently they are less worthy of philosophical contemplation.

**XXIV**. There seems to be a greater difficulty in deciding what is to be done, subsequently to the establishment of penal laws; because a legislator is bound, in some measure, by his own laws. But this, as it was proved in a former part of this treatise, is only true with respect to the legislator, in his individual capacity, as a private member of the state, but not in his public character, in which he represents the whole Majesty and Authority of the state itself. As such, he can entirely repeal the law: for it is the nature of all human laws, to depend upon the will of the maker, not only for their origin, but also for their duration. Yet a lawgiver ought not, upon trivial grounds, to repeal a statute, for, in so doing he would be acting against the rules of sovereign justice. But as the legislator has power to repeal the whole of a law, so in the case of some particular person, or individual action, he may relax its rigour, allowing it to remain in other respects, as it stood before. As an example of this, the actions of the Deity may be cited, who, according to the testimony of Lactantius, in enacting his laws, did not deprive himself of the exercise of his mercy, to grant pardons. "The Emperor, says Augustin, may recall his sentence, pardon and release a criminal; because, as he further explains it, the person who has power to make laws, is not INVARIABLY bound to observe them." Yet this privilege of departing from the letter must never be used but for the most important reasons. Although such reasons cannot be precisely defined, yet it is certain that, since the establishment of civil law, more weighty ones are required to authorise such pardons, than before that period. Because punishments have derived an additional sanction from the authority of the law, which ought to be respected and observed.

**XXV**. The reasons for releasing any one from the penalties of the law, are of two kinds, either internal or external.

An internal reason, to justify a departure from the sentence of the law, must be one, where the punishment is severe when compared with the offence.

**XXVI**. An external reason is one arising from some favourable circumstance in the character of the offender, or some fair hopes that may be entertained of his future conduct. And these reasons will have the most weight n cases, where the particular motives for making the law cease to operate. For although a general reason unopposed by any other of a weightier kind, may sufficiently authorise the enaction of a law; yet where the peculiar reason, for which that law was made, has ceased to exist, the relaxation of it, or even a total dispensation will be attended with less danger to the universal authority of law in general.

Such a dispensation indeed is most allowable, where an offence has been committed through ignorance, though the party so committing it is not entirely free from blame, or through some invincible infirmity of mind, in all which cases, a Christian ruler will have an eye to the example of God, who, under the old covenant, appointed many such offences to be atoned for by certain expiatory offerings: Levit. iv. and v.: and, in the New Testament, he has expressly declared his intention to pardon such offences, upon due repentance. Luke xxiii. 34. ; Heb. iv. 15. and V. 2.; 1 Tim. 1. 13. And Chrysostom observes, that Theodosius, impressed with those words of our Saviour, "Father, forgive them, for they know not what they do, I was led to grant a pardon to the people of Antioch.

**XXVII**. And hence it is evident, how mistaken Ferdinand Vasquez is in his judgment, when he maintains that there can be no just reason for dispensing with a law, that is, for releasing any one from its obligations, except where the lawgiver, upon being consulted, expressly declares that he never intended it should be observed to its full extent. For he does not make the proper distinction between an equitable interpretation, and the entire relaxation of a law. For which reason, in another place, he reproves Thomas, and Sotus, because they say that a law is binding although the particular reason of its being made may have ceased, as if they supposed that the mere letter of the law was the source of its obligation, an opinion which they never did entertain. So far from every relaxation coming under the idea of equity, properly so called; those relaxations may be freely granted or refused, which could not be done in matters of equity, to which even acts of charity or those of reasonable policy do not strictly belong. For there is a great difference between the repeal of a law upon fair or urgent grounds, and a legislator's declaring that at the time of passing the law he had not the particular offence or case in contemplation.

Having thus far considered the nature of dispensations, we proceed to a review of the merits upon which they may be granted.

**XXVIII**. From what has been said above, it appears that in punishments, two things are to be regarded, the offence, and the object for which they are inflicted. It is consonant to justice that no one should receive greater punishment than he deserves; upon which Cicero, in one of his letters, observes, that, "the same moderation, which is commended in all other things, ought to be observed in punishments." Papinian therefore calls punishment an estimation of demerit; but this equality established between crime and punishment, says Demosthenes in his Letter in behalf of the children of Lycurgus, is not the only thing to be considered: the object and intention also of the delinquent must be weighed and taken into the account. But, if care be taken to inflict no more punishment than is due for an offence; it may be greater or less, in proportion to the utility to be de. rived from thence.

**XXIX**. In examining the different degrees of guilt, we ought to take into the account the motives which impelled the offender to commit the act -the motives, which ought to have restrained him therefrom, and how far he was capable of yielding to either. Scarce any one does a wicked action without some motive, or so far strips himself of the nature of man, as to delight in such acts from pure malignity. Most men are led away by the indulgence of their appetites, which engender sin. Under the name of appetite also may be comprehended the strong desire of avoiding evil, which is the most consonant to nature, and therefore to be reckoned amongst the most laudable of all desires. So that offences committed for the sake of avoiding death, imprisonment, pain, or extreme want are generally deemed the most excusable.

Which gave occasion to Demosthenes to say, I that we are justly more exasperated against those, who, abounding in riches, commit evil actions, than against those, who are impelled by want to do the same. Humane judges are always ready to make allowance for necessity: but where wealth is united with injustice, no pre. text can be pleaded in excuse." On this score, Polybius excuses the Acarnanians, for having neglected, when threatened with impending danger themselves, to fulfil the terms of a defensive treaty made with the Greeks against the Aetolians.

Besides the desire of avoiding evil there are other desires tending to some good, either real or imaginary. Real advantages, considered apart from virtues, and those actions, which have a virtuous tendency, are either such as give delight themselves, or, like abundance of riches, can procure those things, which administer to pleasure. Among advantages purely imaginary, we may reckon that of desiring to excel others, from a spirit of rivalry, rather than from any laudable intention, or the power of gratifying resentments, which the farther they deviate from natural justice the more shocking they are to natural feeling. These appetites the Apostle has described in terms of marked censure, calling them, the "lust of the flesh, the lust of the eye, the pride of life." Here the first member of the sentence expresses the love of pleasure, the second implies the insatiable love of riches, and the third comprehends the pursuit of vain glory, and the desire of revenge.

**XXX**. The very injustice of all offences ought to be a GENERAL motive with men, to restrain them from the commission of them. For at present we are not considering sins of any kind, but those, which extend their consequences beyond the offender himself, and affect others. And injustice is the more heinous and criminal in proportion to the greatness of the injury, which it inflicts.

In the highest rank of crimes and misdemeanours therefore, we may place those, which are carried into complete execution: and lower in the scale we find those criminal designs, which have proceeded some degrees, but not to the last stage of completion. For the aggravation of a criminal intent is measured by the length to which it goes. In either class that kind of injustice, is most notorious, which tends to disturb the common peace of society, and therefore is injurious to greater numbers. Private wrongs follow in the next degree. The greatest of which are those affecting life, and very great, though somewhat inferior in the degrees of enormity, are those, that disturb the peace of families, which is founded on the marriage -contract. And the last description of wrongs are those affecting the property of individuals, either by taking it with open violence, or obtaining or injuring it by fraudulent means.

Some are of opinion that a more accurate order of division might have been used; but that which is here followed is the same used by God himself in the delivery of his commandments. For under the name of parents are included not only those, who are naturally such, but sovereign princes, magistrates, and rulers of every description, whose authority is the key-stone of the fabric of society. Next follows the prohibition of murder; the prohibition of adultery, as a violation of the marriage bond; the prohibition of theft, and false evidence: and the catalogue of offences concludes with the prohibition of criminal desires. Among the immediate causes to restrain the commission of a crime, not only the cruelty of the act itself, but all the remote and possible consequences should be taken into the account. If a fire is begun, or the barriers, that keep out the waves, are broken down, the perpetrator brings upon his own head the blood of thousands, and all the guilt of that ruin by which they perish.

In addition to the general characters of injustice above described, we may annex the crime of being undutiful to parents, unkind to relatives, or ungrateful to benefactors, which are each of them a violation of natural, and in some respects of civil law. The repetition of these offences too aggravates their enormity: because wicked habits are sometimes worse than wicked actions. Hence we may comprehend the natural justice of that rule, which the Persians followed, comparing the past life of an offender with his present transgression. And this ought to have some weight in cases where a crime does not originate from habit, but from a momentary occasion. But not so, where a course of former rectitude has been changed into an unvaried course of wickedness. For in such cases, God himself has declared by the mouth of his prophet Ezekiel, that he has no regard to the former life. Even profane writers have the same clear views upon the subject; for Thueydides observes, that degeneracy from a righteous to a wicked course incurs double punishment: for offences are least pardonable in those, who know the difference between right and wrong. In this respect all praise and admiration are due to the wisdom of the primitive Christians, who, in estimating the magnitude of offences, weighed the preceding and the subsequent conduct of a transgressor against the action, for which he was to be punished, as may be seen from the council of Ancyra, and other councils. It heightens the enormity of an offence, where it is committed in violation of an express prohibition of the law. For, in the language of Tacitus, "the fear of prohibition may sometimes operate as a restraint, but where men once act in defiance of that, fear and shame have lost all their force."

**XXXI**. The capacity of the person too, with respect to judgment, disposition, age, education, and every other circumstance must be taken into consideration, when we look for resistance, or submission to the suggestions of wicked inclinations. The thought of immediate danger augments fear, and recent, unallayed pain inflames anger; so that in either case the calm dictates of reason cannot be heard. Offences therefore springing from the influence of such impressions, are of a less odious complexion than those arising from the love of pleasure, or the indulgence of hatred. Because there is less excuse for actions of the latter kind, the delay, or total forbearance of which could occasion no serious inconvenience. For it must always be kept in mind, that where there are more powerful impediments to the exercise of judgment, and more urgent persuasives to natural feeling, the criminality of an offence is proportionably softened. And these are the rules for measuring the degrees of pardon or punishment.

**XXXII**. The Pythagoreans maintain that justice lies in proportioning the punishment to the offence: a rule which cannot be admitted to the full extent of requiring an aggressor to suffer nothing more than a bare requital of the injury he has occasioned. For this is at variance with the most perfect laws, which in cases of theft sometimes require fourfold, and sometimes fivefold restitution to be made. And the Athenian law, besides compelling a thief to pay double the value of what he had taken sentenced him to many days' imprisonment. Among the Indians, as we are informed by Strabo, the person, who had maimed another, was condemned, in addition to the penalty of retaliation, to lose his hand. Nor is it right, as Philo, in explaining the punishment of murder, justly observes, for the suffering of an innocent and guilty person to be exactly the same. And hence it is easy to see why certain crimes not carried into actual execution, and therefore less injurious than those, which are so, are punished only proportionably to the design. In this manner false witnesses were treated by the Jewish law; and by the Roman law, those who walked ready armed to commit murder. Consequently a greater degree of punishment is due, where the criminal intention is completed But as death is the severest punishment that can be inflicted, and one that can never be repeated; the sentence of all human law rests there: though by the custom of some countries death is accompanied with torture, in cases of extreme atrocity.

**XXXIII**. In many instances, the magnitude of a punishment can only be measured by the situation of the person on whom it is to be inflicted. Thus a fine imposed upon the poor would be a heavy sentence, though it would scarcely affect the rich; and a man of high rank would feel the weight of a disgrace, that would but lightly touch an ignoble person. Such distinctions are frequently used by the Roman law, often degenerating into acts of partiality; a fault from which the law of Moses is entirely free. And the above rules may be considered as the scale for estimating the different degrees of punishment.

**XXXIV**. Though punishment does not exceed the bounds of justice, yet in certain cases it may be mitigated in favour of a criminal, from motives of mercy, except where such lenity to the guilty is deemed cruelty to the innocent, whose safety is thereby endangered. For the escape of a criminal is often an encouragement to his own perseverance in iniquity, and to that of others, who are encouraged by the example. Necessity indeed requires the sharpest remedies for the suppression of crimes; especially, where the incentives of habit and a facility to commit them prevail.

**XXXV**. The divine law given to the Hebrews punished the stealing of cattle from a pasture with more severity than breaking into a house, on account of the ease with which the former of those crimes might be committed. Exod. xxii. 1-9. Justin in speaking of the Scythians, describes them as "punishing theft with more severity than any other crime; for as they have no covered habitations to protect their flocks, and herds from depredations, what could be safe, if thieving were allowed?" Though the FAMILIARITY of certain crimes may prevent us from being surprised at their perpetration, it by no means diminishes their atrocity, or demands a mitigation of punishment. But, as Saturninus says, "the giant-strides of crimes must be impeded with the strongest bands." In trials for offences, clemency may be indulged, but in the passing of laws severity should be regarded: For the GENERAL nature of law requires that offences should be pursued with rigour: but in trials, in which individuals are the objects concerned, there may be circumstances to aggravate or diminish the offence: which leaves room for the discretionary exercise of rigour or lenity.

**XXXVI**. and **XXXVII**. The inclination to mitigate penalties, where the urgent motives to enforce them no longer exist, is a point of compassion perfectly distinct from the abolition of punishment altogether.

Nor has any thing been omitted, that might tend to clear up this difficult and delicate question. But every point, we trust, has been examined in its proper place, either respecting the magnitude of crimes, as measured by the injury done, the habitual commission of such offences, or the influence of the motives, sufficient to encourage or restrain them. Indeed the character of the offender affords the most conclusive means for judging of his capacity to commit the crime; and that of the sufferer often contributes something towards enabling us to estimate the due proportion of the penalty. The circumstances of the time, when-the place, where-or the facility, with which a crime is perpetrated, tend to aggravate, or lessen its enormity. The length of time intervening between a criminal design and its execution gives us some opportunity to examine how far the perpetrator was actuated by a malicious purpose. But the true complexion of a crime is to be discovered, partly from the nature of those appetites, to which it owes its birth; and partly, on the other hand, from the nature of the motives which ought to have restrained them. By this class of appetites the magnitude of a crime may be judged of; and the consequences are the motives which should operate to restrain them.

**XXXVIII**. It has been shewn before, and it is a truth founded upon historical fact, that wars are undertaken, as acts of punishment, and this motive, added to that of redress for injuries, is the source, from which the duties of nations, relating to war, take their rise. But it is not every injury, that can be construed into a just ground of war. For laws, whose vengeance is meant to protect the innocent, and to fall upon the guilty, do not regard every case, as a sufficient warrant for their exertion. So that there is much truth in the opinion of Sopater, who says that there are trivial and common offences, which it is better to pass over unnoticed, than to punish.

**XXXIX**. The maxim laid down by Cato, in his speech in defence of the Rhodians, that it is not right any one should be punished upon the bare suspicion of his having intended to commit aggression or injury, was well applied in that place; because no positive decree of the people of Rhodes could be alleged against them, nor was there any other proof beyond the CONJECTURE of their wavering in their policy. But this maxim is not universally true.

For where intention has proceeded to any outward and visible signs of insatiable ambition and injustice, it is deemed a proper object of jealousy, and even of punishment. Upon this principle, the Romans, as may be seen from Livy's account in the X1ii. book and xxx. chapter of his history, thought themselves justified in declaring war against Perseus, King of Macedon, unless he gave satisfactory proof, that he had no hostile intentions against them, in the naval and military armaments, which he was preparing. And we are informed by the same historians, that the Rhodians urged it as a rule established by the laws and customs of all civilized states; that if any one wished the destruction of an enemy, he could not punish him with death, unless he had actually done something to deserve it.

But it is not every unjust design, though indicated by some outward act, which can authorize and direct hostilities. For if the actual commission of crimes and aggressions is, in some cases, proper to be overlooked, much more will it be a mark of deliberate caution to use the same forbearance, where nothing further than the pure design of aggression appears. A forbearance which Cicero justifies upon the possibility that the enemy may have repented of his design, before the execution of it. No conclusive inference can be drawn from the severity of Mosaic Law against all intended acts of impiety and murder. For, in comparing human laws with the divine counsels, whose depths we cannot sound, we are liable to run into error; and the impulse of anger, where it is attended with no fatal consequence, is a case in which the infirmity of human nature calls for pardon. For altho' the precepts of the decalogue are designed to lay a restraint upon unlawful desires as well as upon unlawful actions, yet in addition to the spiritual sense, that which is called the carnal, or external commandment applies to those dispositions that are manifested by some open act. This interpretation may be deduced from a passage in the gospel of St. Mark, c. x. 19, where the prohibition to defraud is immediately preceded by the injunction not to steal. So that intended aggressions are not to be punished by force of arms, except in cases of atrocity, where the very design threatens consequences of the greatest danger. All punishment therefore must have in view either security against future aggressions, reparation for the injury done to national or private honour, or it must be used as an example of awful severity.

**XL.** It is proper also to observe that kings and those who are possessed of sovereign power have a right to exact punishment not only for injuries affecting immediately themselves or their own subjects, but for gross violations of the law of nature and of nations, done to other states and subjects. For the liberty of inflicting punishment for the peace and welfare of society, which belonged to individuals in the early ages of the world, was converted into the judicial authority of sovereign states and princes; a right devolving upon them not only as rulers of others, but as subject to the controul of no earthly power. For that is a right, which can belong to no subject. It is never safe to leave the entire assertion of a man's own rights, or the punishment of his wrongs, to his own judgment; for he cannot be entirely disinterested in his own cause. Partiality will make him fall short of, or prejudice will make him exceed the bounds of justice. It was the theme of praise bestowed upon the heroes of antiquity, that in their most arduous undertakings they avenged the wrongs of others rather than their own. Upon this principle there can be no hesitation in pronouncing all wars to be just, that are made upon pirates, general robbers, and enemies of the human race. So far this opinion agrees with that of Innocentius and others, who maintain all war to be lawful against those who have renounced the ties and law of nature. An opinion directly the reverse is held by Victoria, Vasquez, Azorius, Molina, and others, who deem an aggression done to a prince, his government, or his subjects, or civil jurisdiction over the aggressor, the only justifiable warrant for inflicting punishment, particularly the punishment of hostilities. For they suppose punishment to be an effect purely arising from the authority of civil law, whereas, according to the proofs established in the beginning of this treatise, it was shewn to be a right resulting entirely from the law of nature.

If the opinion of those, from whom we differ, be admitted, no enemy will have a right to punish another, by the prosecution of a just war; a right, which notwithstanding is allowed and confirmed by the practice of all nations, not only after the defeat of an enemy, but during the continuance of a war; and that too, not from any civil jurisdiction, but from a natural right, which prevailed long before the foundation of states, and which still exists in all its force, in places, where the community consists of families distinct, and united as the subjects of one sovereign.

**XLI.**, **XLII.**, **XLIII**. But certain precautions are necessary to prevent us from being carried away by an opinion that civil customs, though founded upon just reasons, and received among many nations, are to be reckoned as a part of the law of nature. And in the next place, it is necessary to guard against enumerating as prohibitions of natural law, things which are not proved to be so, as certain kinds of marriages the taking of interest for the use of money, and other positive injunctions of the divine, or Mosaic law. The third rule is, to make an accurate distinction between general principles, such as the duty of living according to the dictates of reason, and those of a more particular though not less obvious meaning; as the duty of forbearing to take what belongs to another. To which many truths may be added though not quite so easy of apprehension: among which may be named the cruelty of that kind of punishment, which consists in revenge, delighting in the pain of another. This is a method of proof similar to that which occurs in mathematics, the process of which rises from self-evident truths to demonstrations, the latter of which, though not intelligible to all alike, upon due examination obtain assent.

As then in matters of civil law, ignorance is deemed an excuse, so with respect to the law of nature, wherever infirmity of understanding forms an invincible obstruction to the knowledge of its rules, such infirmity may be alleged as a vindication. For as, in cases of unavoidable ignorance a great degree of the guilt of sin is removed; so it is in some measure softened wherever this ignorance subsists, though it may be owing to former negligence. And for this reason, Aristotle compares barbarians, in their rude, unformed state, to persons, whose appetites are rendered sickly by disease. Plutarch also observes that there are certain infirmities and disorders, which naturally infect the soul. Once for all, by way of conclusion we may add that wars undertaken to inflict punishment may be suspected of injustice, except there be manifest and enormous aggressions, with other conspiring causes, to vindicate nations for having recourse to arms.

**XLIV**. The progress of the work has necessarily led to the consideration of offences against God; the propriety or impropriety of punishing which by force of arms is a fit subject of inquiry.

Admitting the affirmative part of the question, we may observe that as in ecclesiastical affairs Bishops are intrusted with a Catholic, or general power; so kings, besides the care of their own immediate states and subjects, may be regarded as protectors of the human race. The best argument, on the negative side of the question, against the justice of such wars, is the sufficiency of the divine omnipotence to avenge its own wrongs. Yet the same may be said of other offences. For the Deity possesses sufficient power to punish them, although he leaves them to the sentence of human tribunals. Some will urge and maintain that other kinds of offences are punished only in cases, where others are uninjured or endangered by the commission of them. On the other hand, it may be said that men punish not only offences, which directly hurt others, but even those, which affect them indirectly, as suicide and other similar crimes.

Although religion is a concern between the soul of man and his Maker alone, its influence on human morals is of no inconsiderable importance. So that Plato had reason to call it the bulwark of authority and law, and the bond of every thing venerable in social order and discipline. Every false opinion in divine things, says Plutarch, is pernicious, betraying itself in the disorders of the imagination, wherever it takes root, and springs up into action. So that Aristotle reckons the care and support of religion the first of public concerns. This is a truth applying not to any particular state, but to all governments, and to human society in every shape. An avowal which Xenophon makes the characteristic of a great and wise prince, attributing to Cyrus a declaration of his firm persuasion that the more his subjects feared God, the more obedient he should find them to his laws, and the more attached to his person. But once remove the motives of religion, says Tully, and you destroy faith, the intercourse between man and man, and justice the most excellent of all virtues.

The opinions of Epicurus afford a sufficient proof of this: for in banishing the providence of God from his system, he made justice nothing but an empty name, springing from human conventions, founded on self-interest, and restraining men from the commission of crimes by no other principle but that of fear.

But there is a wider sphere, than the internal welfare of independent states, on which religion operates. In the separate society, which every kingdom, state, or country forms within itself, the place of religion may occasionally be supplied by the influence and execution of municipal laws. But in all the transactions of the great community at large, where civil laws are silent, and tribunals give way to the decision of the sword, the law of nature and of nations, founded upon the fear of God, and obedience to his will, is the standard of right to which

Kings and Sovereign states appeal; a violation of which is regarded as a violation of the divine law.

**XLV**. But to take a closer view of the subject, we must observe that true religion, which is the same at all periods of time, rests upon four evident and universally acknowledged truths. The first of which is the being and unity of God, — the second, that God is not any of the things, that can be seen, but of a nature too sublime to be the object of human conception, or of human sight, -the third is, that with the eye of his providence he regards the events of this world, and regulates them with the most equitable and unerring judgments, — the fourth is, that he is the creator of all things, except himself. And these four truths are unfolded and laid down in an equal number of commandments, the first of which plainly declares the unity of God-the second forbids any representation, by painting or image, to be made of that being, who is invisible to mortal eye. Tacitus bears testimony to the spiritual nature of the Jewish religion: for he says, that "the Jews have nothing but a mental conception of one God, and they look upon every attempt to represent him under the appearance of human form, as a profanation of his heavenly nature. " — From the third commandment we deduce his knowledge of all human transactions, even of our very thoughts; an omniscience upon which the obligation and sanctity of oaths is founded, For God is a witness even of the secret designs of the heart, so that every solemn oath is an appeal to his justice and his power, for the vindication of truth, and the punishment of falsehood. The fourth commandment presents us with an account of the creation of the world, to commemorate which God appointed the Sabbath, commanding it to be observed with a degree of reverence above every other sacred institution. For the violation of any other rites, such as those respecting forbidden meats, was left to the discretionary punishment of the law: but offences against the Sabbath were capital; because, considering the nature and design of its origin, such contempt implied a disbelief, that the world was created by God. Now the creation of the world by God affords a tacit proof of his goodness, wisdom, eternity and power: and the effect of this contemplative knowledge is the offering of honour, love, worship and obedience to God. So that Aristotle says that the man, who denies that God ought to be honoured, or parents loved, should be taught to renounce his error, not by reasoning, but by punishment. And, in another place, he observes that some actions are proper on certain occasions, but reverence for the majesty of God is requisite at all times, and in all places.

The truth of those contemplative opinions may undoubtedly be proved from the nature of things; the clearest of which proofs is the evidence of sense, shewing the existence of things, which naturally leads us to consider the time, when they had no being.

But as all are not able to understand these arguments and others of the same kind, it is sufficient to observe that in all ages and all countries of the world, with very few exceptions, these opinions have found a general reception with those who were too plain in their dealings, and ingenuous in their designs, to impose -upon others, and with many, who had too much sagacity to be deceived themselves, But when amid such variety of laws, customs, and opinions, there is so general an agreement upon one point; that agreement may be adduced as a proof, that such a belief owes its origin to the primitive ages of the world, from whence it has been derived to us: when we consider too that it has never been clearly refuted, it is a sufficient reason to establish our faith.

**XLVI**. There is no excuse therefore for the rejection of those opinions, even in cases, where there is no intuitive sagacity to discover new proofs, or to comprehend old ones: as there are so many guides both in nature and reason to lead men to the knowledge of those truths, and as no solid arguments have ever been produced to establish a contrary belief. But as human punishments form the subject of our present inquiry, it is right to make a distinction between opinions themselves, and the manner of deviating from them. The belief in a supreme being, and in the controul of his providence over human affairs, is one of those universal tenets to be found in all religions, whether true or false. And in reality to deny the being of a God, and to deny the interposal of his providence in human affairs, amounts in its moral consequences to the same thing. And it is for this reason these two opinions have been inseparably united in all ages, and among every civilized people. Consequently we find, that in all well governed states, wholesome laws have been enacted to restrain those, who disturb those opinions, which have always been regarded as the chief support of social order; and all contempt, shewn to those opinions, has always been considered as contempt shewn to society itself, and which it consequently has a right to punish.

**XLVII**. There are other truths not equally self-evident, such as these, that there are not more Gods than one; that no visible thing, neither the world, nor the heavens, nor the sun, nor the air is God; that the world, and the matter of which it is formed, have not existed from all eternity, but were made by God. So that we see the knowledge of these truths disfigured, and almost entirely obliterated among many nations by the lapse of time. And this might the more easily happen, as there were no legal provisions made to preserve the purity of these truths, which were not considered as essential to the very existence of all religion. The law indeed given to that people, who were instructed in the clear knowledge of these truths, by the mouths of the prophets, by miracles seen with their own eyes, or brought to their ears by the reports of the most undoubted testimony, that law, though it expresses the greatest abhorrence of the worship of false gods, does not inflict the punishment of death upon all convicted of that crime, but only in particular instances, where they have seduced others into idolatry, — or where a state has introduced the worship of unknown Gods, — or where the true worship of God, and obedience to his laws have been forsaken for the worship of the stars, which St. Paul calls serving the creature above the creator, an offence, which was, for some time, punished among the descendants of Esau. Those too who offered their children to Moloch, that is, to Saturn, were punished with death. Yet the Canaanites, and the neighbouring nations, who had long been sunk into the most depraved superstitions, were not consigned by God to immediate punishment, but were left to fill up the measure of their crimes. And there were other nations, where, in the language of Scripture, God winked at the times of this ignorance. Where men have had no means of arriving at the knowledge of a true God, as their superstitions and errors are excusable, so where, in despite of knowledge, they have deified Daemons, and vices, which they knew to be such, their superstitions are not to be called errors, but impieties. And no less impious is the supposed homage, that is paid to God with the blood of innocent human victims, and Darius king of the Persians, and Gelo king of Syracuse, are commended for abstaining from such practices. Plutarch informs us of some barbarians, who would have been punished by the Romans for offering human victims to the deity, had they not pleaded the antiquity of the custom, which was admitted as an excuse, though they were strictly enjoined not to follow the same custom in future.

**XLVIII**. From the kind of evidence on which Christianity rests, it is plain that no force should be used with nations to promote its acceptance. It is not merely by natural arguments it can gain assent; for it has made an addition of many things to natural religion. Its evidence rests upon the history of Christ's resurrection, and upon the miracles performed by himself and his Apostles. So that it is a matter of fact proved by the most undeniable evidence, and of great antiquity. Therefore a doctrine of this kind cannot be thoroughly received upon the first hearing of it, without the secret assistance of God: an assistance not given as a reward for the merit of works; so that wherever it is withheld or less copiously bestowed; it is done for reasons, which though just, are generally unknown to us, and therefore not punishable by human judgments. For it is the custom in the sacred writings to assign the divine pleasure as the cause of things unknown to us.

There is another reason of no less weight, which is that Christ being the author of a new law, will have no one brought to embrace his doctrine by the fear of human punishments. Nor is the reason at all weakened by the objection drawn from the parable of the marriage-supper, where it is said the messengers are commanded to compel the guests to come in. For the term, COMPEL, here signifies nothing more than an earnest entreaty, a sense, in which it is used in other parts of the New Testament, implying an earnest request made to any one.

**XLIX**. But to obstruct the teachers of Christianity by pains and penalties is undoubtedly contrary to natural law and reason: for the doctrine of Christ, apart from all the corruptions added by the inventions of men, contains nothing hurtful, but every thing beneficial to society. The thing speaks for itself, and even those who were strangers to the doctrine itself were obliged to acknowledge the truth of this. Pliny says that the Christians bound themselves by an oath to commit neither theft, nor robbery, nor to violate their word. It was a common saying " Caius Seius is a good man, but he is a Christian."

Nor indeed can any danger be apprehended from the spreading of doctrines, calculated to inspire greater sanctity of manners, and the purest principles of obedience to lawful sovereigns. Philo has recorded a beautiful saying of Augustus, who observed that the assemblies of the Jews were not Bacchanalian revels, or meetings to disturb the public peace, but schools of virtue.

**L**. It seems unjust to persecute with punishments those who receive the law of Christ as true, but entertain doubts or errors on some external points, taking them in an ambiguous meaning or different from the ancient Christians in their explanation of them. A point which is proved by what has been said above, and by the ancient example of the Jews. For, possessing a law, which allowed them to inflict temporal punishments, they never exercised that authority upon the Sadducees, who denied the doctrine of a resurrection: a doctrine of the greatest truth, though but faintly delivered in that law, and under a typical application of words and circumstances.

But if there should be any weighty error, that discerning judges could easily refute by an appeal to sacred authority, or to the opinions of antiquity; here too it would be necessary to make allowance for ingrafted opinions, that have grown up to form an inseparable part of the human mind, and for the zealous attachment of every one to his own tenents; an evil which Galen says is more difficult to be eradicated than any constitutional disease.

## CHAPTER 21: ON THE COMMUNICATION OF PUNISHMENT.

*How accessories are liable to punishment — Sovereign Princes or States answerable for the misconduct of their subjects, when they know it, and do not endeavour to prevent it — Sovereigns bound not to protect offending subjects, but to deliver them up or punish them — The rights of suppliants belong to the unfortunate and not to the guilty — Suppliants may be protected while the inquiry into their case is still pending — How far states are amenable to punishment — All the different exceptions stated — Children not answerable for the offences of parents — The moral government of God in this respect considered — Individuals not answerable for offences, to which they have not given consent — Heirs, how far answerable for the acts of their ancestors.*

**I**. THE next topic of inquiry relates to the communication of punishment, as inflicted upon accomplices, who, in that capacity, cannot be said to be punished for the guilt of others, but for their own. And from what has been said above upon the loss sustained from injury, it may be understood who are the persons, that come under this description. For the partnership in loss, and the partnership in guilt are regulated by nearly the same principles. Yet the obligation to repair a loss does not always imply guilt, except where there has been any notorious malice, in which case every damage renders the party, who has occasioned it, liable to make reparation. So that persons ordering the commission of any wicked or hostile act, giving the requisite consent to it, supplying the aggressor with assistance, or protection, or, in any other shape, partaking of the crime, by giving counsel, commendation, or assent to his act, or when they have power to forbid the commission of such an act, by forbearing to exercise their authority, or by refusing to afford the succour, which they are bound by the law of nature, or by treaty to give to the injured party, by not using with the offender that power of dissuasion, which they have a right to do, or lastly by concealing what they ought to make known, in all these cases, such persons are punishable as accomplices, if they are convicted of that degree of malice, which constitutes a crime, and merits punishment: points which have before been discussed.

**II**. The case will be made clearer by examples. A civil community is no more bound than any other society by an act of individual members, except that act be done by its express consent and authority, or it has neglected to disavow such a proceeding. Hence it is formally stipulated in almost all treaties that no acts or aggressions are to be ascribed to a state, except those, which are done in the name of the sovereign, and by persons acting expressly under the authority of his commission. So a father is not answerable for the misconduct of his children, a master for that of his servants, nor a ruler for the acts of those under him, unless there appears in any of these some connivance, or encouragement in promoting that misconduct, or those acts.

In the case of a sovereign's responsibility for the acts of his subjects, there are two things to be considered, which require minute inquiry, and mature deliberation, and those are the forbearance, and the encouragement or protection, which he has shewn to their transgressions.

As to forbearance, it is an acknowledged point, that when he knows of a delinquency, which he neither forbids nor punishes, when he is both able and bound to do so, he becomes an accessory to the guilt thereof. Cicero, in his speech against Piso, says, "it makes no great difference especially in a consul, whether he harasses the government by moving ruinous laws, and making mischievous speeches, or suffers others to do the same. If a slave has committed a murder with the knowledge of his master, the master becomes answerable for the entire deed, as it was done with his concurrence."

But, as we have said before, besides the knowledge of a deed, to constitute a participation in the guilt, the person so knowing it, must possess the power to prevent it. And this is what is meant by the legal phrase, that the knowledge of a crime, when it is ordered to be punished, is taken in the sense of forbearance or connivance, and it is supposed that the person, who ought to have prevented it, did not do so. In this place knowledge implies a concurrence of will, and connivance a concurrence of design. A master therefore is not bound by the act of a slave, who has claimed his freedom, and done any thing in despite of his master, because the knowledge of a crime without ability to prevent it, by disclosure or some other means, cannot be construed into an act of guilt. So parents are bound by the acts of children; but only in cases where they have the children under their authority.... On the other hand, altho' by having them in their power, they might have prevented their misconduct, they will not be answerable for it, unless they had a knowledge of it also. For there ought to be a concurrence of knowledge, and forbearance or encouragement to involve any one in the guilt of another's actions; circumstances all of which by a parity of reasoning maybe applied to the connection between sovereigns and subjects: a connection founded on principles both of natural and civil law.

**III**. The matter that necessarily comes next under consideration is the case of those, who screen delinquents from punishment. It was before observed that, according to the law of nature, no one could inflict punishment, but a person entirely free from the guilt of the crime which he was going to punish. But since established governments were formed, it has been a settled rule, to leave the offences of individuals, which affect their own community, to those states themselves, or to their rulers, to punish or pardon them at their discretion. But they have not the same plenary authority, or discretion, respecting offences, which affect society at large, and which other independent states or their rulers have a right to punish, in the same manner, as in every country popular actions are allowed for certain misdemeanors. Much less is any state at liberty to pass over in any of its subjects crimes affecting other independent states or sovereigns, On which account any sovereign state or prince has a right to require another power to punish any of its subjects offending in the above named respect: a right essential to the dignity and security of all governments.

**IV**. But as it is not usual for one state to allow the armed force of another to enter her territories under the pretext of inflicting punishment upon an offender, it is necessary that the power, in whose kingdom an offender resides, should -upon the complaint of the aggrieved party, either punish him itself, or deliver him up to the discretion of that party. Innumerable instances of such demands to deliver up offenders occur both in sacred and profane history. Thus the other Israelites required the Benjamites to deliver up offenders, Jud. xx. — And the Philistines demanded of the Hebrews the surrender of Samson, as a criminal, Jud. xv.-In the same manner the Gauls made a demand that the Fabii should be surrendered for having fought against them. Sylla too, as Sallust informs us, urged Bocchus to deliver up Jugurtha, and by so doing to relieve the Romans from the bitter necessity of implicating Him for his erroneous conduct in the same guilt with that most desperate villain. Yet all these instances are to be understood not as strictly binding a people or Sovereign Prince to the actual surrender of offenders, but allowing them the alternative of either punishing or delivering them up. For it was upon this ground, as we are informed, that the Eleans made war upon the Lacedaemonians, because the latter neglected to punish their subjects, who had committed aggressions upon that people; that is, they had neither punished nor delivered them up: for the obligation may be taken either way, that being left to the choice of the aggrieved person, or nation, in order to make the satisfaction the more complete.

The surrender here meant is nothing more than delivering up a citizen or subject to the power of another state to decide upon his punishment. But this permission neither gives nor takes away any right, it only removes an impediment to the prosecution of a right. Wherefore if that other people make no use of the permitted right, the offender, who has been delivered up, is in such a situation, that he either MAY or may NOT be punished: either of which may happen in the case of many offences. But the right of a state, as to the enjoyment of its own laws, and many other advantages, is not lost by any particular act without a formal decree and judgment, unless in any way it has been previously enacted, that certain acts, or certain omissions, shall amount to a forfeiture of some particular rights and privileges. In the same manner, goods, if surrendered, but not accepted, will remain the property of the former owner. But if the surrender of a citizen has been accepted, and, by some accident, the person so surrendered shall afterwards return home, he will no longer be a citizen, except by some new act of grace. What has been said of punishing or giving up aggressors, applies not only to those, who always have been subjects of the sovereign, in whose dominions they are now found, but to those also, who, after the commission of a crime, have fled to some place for refuge.

**V**. Nor do the so much talked of rights of suppliants, and the inviolable nature of asylums at all weaken the argument that has been advanced. For the advantages of such protection are designed only for those, who are the victims of unmerited persecution, not for those who have committed crimes injurious to mankind, and destructive to society. Gylippus, the Lacedaemonian, as may be seen in the xiii. book of Diodorus Siculus, speaking of the rights of suppliants, says, that they were originally introduced, as measures of compassion to the unfortunate, and not a screen for malicious and wanton offenders, who have nothing but punishment to expect. And a little after he says, when such men, prompted by malice, or rapacity have plunged into evils, they have no right to talk of misfortune or to wear the name of suppliants. For that is a privilege granted by the laws of nature to the innocent, who are beaten down by the hard and oppressive strokes of ill fortune. But the refuge of compassion is withheld, where every line of a life has been marked with cruelty and injustice. Thus according to that law, which partakes of the wisdom of its divine author, asylums were open to those who had killed any one by a weapon escaping from their hand: slaves too were allowed places of refuge, but deliberate murderers, or those, who had disturbed the peaceful order of the state, found no protection even from the altar of God. Philo, in explaining this law says, that even the temple affords no refuge to the impious.

The more ancient of the Greeks acted upon the same principle. It is said that the Chalcidians refused to deliver up Nauplius to the Grecians, and the reason alleged was his having cleared himself of the charges made against him. There was among the Athenians an altar dedicated to Mercy; it is mentioned by Cicero, Pausanias, Servius, and also by Theophilus, and it is described at full length by Statius in the xii. book of his Thebais. The poet explains to what description of men it afforded shelter: it was, he says, to those who were driven from their homes by the calamity of war, or stripped of their kingdoms by usurpers. Tacitus in the third book of his Annals, and 60th chapter, reprobates the custom, prevailing in his time among the cities of Greece, of making it an act of religion to protect offenders from the punishment due to their crimes. Such offenders therefore ought either to be punished, or delivered up, or, at least, ordered to withdraw. Perseus the Macedonian king, clearing himself to Martins from the charge of screening those, who had attempted the life of Eumenes; said, "as soon as I was apprised by you of their being in Macedonia, I ordered immediate search to be made for them, peremptorily commanding their perpetual banishment from my kingdom."

The right of demanding the surrender or punishment of criminals that have fled into other kingdoms, has, in most parts of Europe, during the present, and the immediately preceding centuries, been generally exercised in cases, where the crimes were such as affected the safety of the state, or were attended with notorious atrocity. It has been usual to pass over, with mutual connivance, crimes of an inferior kind, except where it has been agreed to the contrary by express treaty. Nor can it be concealed that where robbers and pirates have gained a truly formidable power, it has often been deemed an act of humane policy both in Sovereign Princes, and States to exercise forbearance towards them, rather than to drive them to greater acts of desperation by treating them with all the rigour, which they deserve.

**VI**. If the act, of which refugees and suppliants are accused, is not prohibited by the law of nature or of nations, the matter must be decided by the civil law of the country, from which they come. This was a received opinion in ancient times, as we find from the language of Aeschylus, in whose Tragedy of the Suppliants, the King of Argos, addressing a number of the daughters of Danaus, on their coming from Egypt, says, " If the sons of Egypt exercise controul over you, maintaining that they are authorised to do so by the law of the state, as being the nearest allied by blood, who can resist them? It is for you to prove that, according to the laws of your country, they have no authority over you."

**VII** and **VIII**. It has often been a celebrated topic of discussion, whether a whole community can be punished for misconduct. And this is the proper place for that inquiry.

It was shewn in a former part of this treatise, that a body politic though it may seem to vary by a succession of new members, continues the same, as long as it retains its form. In which case it seems liable to punishment no less than individuals. On the other hand bodies politic seem to possess many privileges peculiar to them. selves, such as having a common treasury, a common seal, laws, and other similar advantages. But there are some distinctions, which they particularly derive from the INDIVIDUALS of which they are composed. Thus we say that Universities are learned, or Garrisons brave, ac. cording to the number of learned or gallant men, which they respectively contain. Merit is a distinction of this kind, as being a gift of nature to individuals, or an individual acquirement, which no public body, OF ITSELF, can have. So that upon the death or departure of those meritorious individuals, the degree of merit, which any public society derived from their presence, must become extinct. In the same manner, the debt of punishment which is considered as arising from some act of demerit, must cease with the debt of the individual delinquents.

Arrian is justly commended for censuring the vengeance retorted upon the Persians by Alexander, at a time, when those, who had committed the original aggressions on the Greeks, had long been laid in their graves. He passes a like sentence upon the burning of Persepolis, as a retaliation for what the Persians had done at Athens. Such acts of retaliation, after a lapse of years, have been vindicated by some writers, as an imitation of the slow, but unerring progress of divine justice. But we must remember that the ways of God are not as our ways, nor is the exercise of his justice to be measured by our counsels- For if descendents can claim no merit for the actions of their FOREFATHERS, neither is it right they should be punished for THEIR transgressions. The consequences of merit indeed may be transmitted without injury, and therefore without injustice; but it is not so with punishments.

**IX**. Having thus shewn that a communication of punishment is necessarily connected with a participation in guilt, it remains to consider whether punishment can be extended to those, who are no way concerned in the crime. In order to understand this clearly, and to prevent the mistakes that may arise from a similarity of expression, where there is no similarity of facts, it will be necessary to make use of some precautions.

**X**. In the first place there is a difference between a loss DIRECTLY occasioned by any act, and one resulting but INDIRECTLY from it. Now it may be called a direct injury to deprive any one of what peculiarly belongs to him as his right. An indirect injury is that which prevents any one from possessing what he otherwise would have done, by destroying the condition or means, which gave him such a right. As an example, Ulpian says," if any one has opened a well in his own ground, by which the subterraneous streams of water, that would have passed to the lands of another, are cut off, here no fault is imputable to the person who has only exercised his own right." And in another place, he says, it makes a great difference, whether any one directly does an injury, or is only indirectly and unintentionally instrumental in preventing another from reaping advantages, which he would otherwise have enjoyed. And it is absurd, says Paulus, another legal authority, for men to be called rich before they possess the means of being so. Thus when the property of parents is forfeited, it is felt as an inconvenience by their children; though it can not be considered as a direct punishment inflicted upon them, because that property would never have been theirs, unless the parents had retained it to their last breath. On which Alphenus has made a just observation, in saying, that, by the punishment of the father, children lose that which would have come to them from him, but things, which they do not receive from him, such as the gifts of nature, or those derived from any other quarter, remain untouched. Cicero relates that in this manner the children of Themistocles were reduced to want, nor does he think it unjust that the children of Lepidus should share the same fate. And he says that it is an ancient custom, and the received usage of all states, the hardship of which nevertheless was greatly softened by the laws of Rome at a later period. Thus when a whole people is implicated in the misconduct of the majority, which holds the representative character of the state, and consequently loses its civil liberties, its fortifications, and other privileges, the loss affects innocent individuals, but only in those things, which they could not have enjoyed, except as belonging to that community.

**XI**. Besides, we must observe, that the offence of one man may sometimes occasion inconvenience or loss to another, and yet that offence may not be considered as the immediate cause of the action, which is grounded on the exercise of a right. This may be explained by an example. Thus if any one has engaged for another's debt, he brings himself into the dilemma named in the ancient proverb, that being bound for any one is the next stage to ruin; but it is a MAN'S OWN PROMISE, and NOT ANOTHER'S HAVING INCURRED A DEBT, that is the real cause of his obligation. For as a person, who has given security for a purchaser, is not, properly speaking, bound by the PURCHASE, but by his own PROMISE: so if any one has engaged to be responsible for a delinquent, it is his Own ENGAGEMENT, and not the ACT OF THAT DELINQUENT, which creates his obligation. And hence the inconvenience of that kind which any one incurs, must be measured not by the delinquency of another, but by his own power to enter into any such voluntary engagement. In consequence of which no one can give surety to suffer death for another; because no one has such power over his own life, as to take it away himself, or to be bound to forfeit it for another. Though the ancient Greeks and Romans thought otherwise, and therefore they maintained that a surety might be put to death for any one, as may be seen in the well known story of Damon and Pythias, and hostages were frequently punished in this manner.

What has been said of life may be applied to the limbs also, which no man has a right to part with, except for the preservation of the whole body. But if any one has engaged to suffer banishment, to submit to a pecuniary fine, or any other means of satisfying justice, any thing he suffers on this account will not, strictly speaking, be considered as a PERSONAL punishment, but as the performance of an agreement.

Something like this occurs in the right, which any one possesses dependent on another's will, both with respect to the right of individuals to private property, and to the more extensive right to demesnes possessed by a state, For if any one is deprived of such a thing owing to another's fault, here the executive power depriving that person, is not inflicting a punishment on Him, but only exercising a prior right.

**XII**. and **XIII**. Having laid down these distinctions, we may observe that it is impossible that an innocent person should suffer for another's crime. This does not proceed from the reasons given by Paulus, who maintains that punishment is designed for the reformation of the offender, For it seems possible that an example may be made, extending beyond the person of the criminal himself, when it affects, in its consequences, those, who are nearly related to him. So that it is not for the sake of example only that punishment is inflicted, but because the obligation thereto arises from the demerit of the offending party. Now every demerit must be of a personal nature, as it proceeds from a man's own will, over which he is supposed to exercise a perfect controul.

**XIV**. In the law given to the Hebrews, God threatens to avenge the impiety of fathers upon their children. But he has sovereign dominion over our lives and substance, as being his gift, which he may take away from any one, whenever he pleases, without assigning his reasons. Therefore if he thinks proper to take away by a premature or violent death the children of Achan, Saul, Jeroboam or Ahab, he is exercising over them the right of sovereignty, as well as that of punishment; imposing by that awful example the more severe penalty upon the parents. For if they survive their children, which was what the divine law had most in view, and therefore did not extend these threats beyond the time of great grand-children, a period to which the age of man might reach, it is certain that parents would be severely punished by such a sight, the most afflicting of any they could witness. Or if they should not survive such an event, to die under such an apprehension would be a great calamity.

But it is proper to remark that examples like those are never employed by God, except against crimes affecting his divine Majesty, as false worship, perjury or sacrilege. Indeed those threats of divine vengeance are not always enforced; especially where any extraordinary virtue shines in the characters and conduct of the children: as may be seen in the xviii. chapter of the prophesy of Ezekiel. Plutarch has discussed this topic with great eloquence in his book on the remote vengeance of God.

As the Gospel so clearly unfolds the future punishments of the wicked, all the threats contained in that new covenant terminate in the persons of the offenders themselves. But the ways of providence in these respects are not the rule which men can follow. For God, even without any reference to crime, is the sovereign lord and disposer of human life, a commission which man is only allowed to execute against the perpetrators of certain crimes. Wherefore as that same divine law forbids parents to be put to death for the offences of children, so it exempts children from the same punishment for the actions of their fathers: a lenity which is greatly commended by Josephus and Philo. The same commendation is bestowed by Isocrates upon the laws of Egypt; and by Dionysius of Halicarnassus upon those of Rome.

**XV**. But if it is unjust in human laws to punish the misconduct of parents in the persons of their children, how much more severe was the law of the Persians and Macedonians extending the penalties for crimes against the state to every branch of the offender's relatives, in the most remote degree, a law surpassing all others in rigour?

**XVI**. **XVII**. and **XVIII**. What has been said respecting the punishment of children for the offences of their fathers or forefathers, may be applied to the relation subsisting between sovereigns and subjects. For it is a relation springing from the contract of society, which makes the sovereign the essential head, life and soul of that body, in which his people form the members. As the civil community therefore with its sovereign or head forms but one body, there can be no separation of interests, but what affects one part must be prejudicial or serviceable to the whole.

**XIX**. Why should an heir, it has been sometimes asked, be bound by other debts of his ancester, and not feel the effects of his punishment for misconduct? to which answer may be given, that the heir represents the person of the deceased not in his merits or demerits, which are purely personal, but in his property; an artificial mode of preserving unbroken the chain of succession and descent.

**XX**. And hence it follows, that if in addition to the demerit of an offence, any new grounds of obligation should arise connected with the punishment, they must be discharged not properly as a punishment, but as a debt. Thus the heir will be liable to pay the costs awarded by a judgment after a contested suit, which is considered in the light of a contract.

## CHAPTER 22: ON THE UNJUST CAUSES OF WAR.

*Differences between real and colourable motives — War atrocious without either of these motives — Wars of plunder, under the most plausible pretexts, not justifiable — Causes apparently, but not really just — Unnecessary advantage — Desire of a better soil — Discovery of things belonging to others — Incapacity of the original owners — War not always justifiable under the pretext of asserting liberty or of imposing a beneficial government upon a people against their will — Emperor's pretensions to universal empire refuted — Pretensions of the Church — Imperfect obligations — Difference between wars originally unjust and those afterwards becoming so.*

**I**. IN a former part of this work, where the justice of war was discussed, it was observed that some wars were founded upon real motives and others only upon colourable pretexts. Thus Alexander made war upon Darius, under the pretence of avenging the former wrongs done by the Persians to the Greeks. But the real motive of that bold and enterprising hero, was the easy acquisition of wealth and dominion, which the expeditions of Xenophon and Agesilaus had opened to his view.

In the same manner, a dispute about Saguntum furnished the Carthaginians with COLOURABLE MOTIVES for the second Punic war, but, in REALITY, they could not brook the indignity of having consented to a treaty, which the Romans had extorted from them at an unfavourable moment; and more especially as their spirits were revived by their recent successes in Spain. The real causes assigned by Thucydides for the Peloponnesian war, were the jealousies entertained by the Lacedaemonians of the then growing power of the Athenians, though the quarrels of the Corcyreans, Potidaens, and other secondary states were made the ostensible reasons.

**II**. There are some who have neither ostensible reasons, nor just causes to plead for their hostilities, in which, as Tacitus says, they engage from the pure love of enterprise and danger. A disposition to which Aristotle gives the name of ferocity. And in the last book of his

Nicomachian Ethics, he calls it a bloody cruelty to convert friends into enemies, whom you may slaughter.

**III**. Though most powers, when engaging in war, are desirous to colour over their real motives with justifiable pretexts, yet some, totally disregarding such methods of vindication, seem able to give no better reason for their conduct, than what is told by the Roman Lawyers of a robber, who being asked, what right he had to a thing, which he had seized, replied, it was his own, because he had taken it into his possession? Aristotle in the third book of his Rhetoric, speaking of the promoters of war, asks, if it is not unjust for a neighbouring people to be enslaved, and if those promoters have no regard to the rights of unoffending nations? Cicero, in the first book of his Offices, speaks in the same strain, and calls the courage, which is conspicuous in danger and enterprise, if devoid of justice, absolutely undeserving of the name of valour. It should rather be considered as a brutal fierceness outraging every principle of humanity."

**IV**. Others make -use of pretexts, which though plausible at first sight, will not bear the examination and test of moral rectitude, and, when stripped of their disguise, such pretexts will be found fraught with injustice. In such hostilities, says Livy, it is not a trial of right, but some object of secret and unruly ambition, which acts as the chief spring. Most powers, it is said by Plutarch, employ the relative situations of peace and war, as a current specie, for the purchase of whatever they deem expedient.

By having before examined and established the principles of just and necessary war, we may form a better idea of what goes to constitute the injustice of the same. As the nature of things is best seen by contrast, and we judge of what is crooked by comparing it with what is straight. But for the sake of perspicuity, it will be necessary to treat upon the leading points.

It was shewn above that apprehensions from a neigh. bouring power are not a sufficient ground for war. For to authorize hostilities as a defensive measure, they must arise from the necessity, which just apprehensions create; apprehensions not only of the power, but of the intentions of a formidable state, and such apprehensions as amount to a moral certainty. For which reason the opinion of those is by no means to be approved of, who lay down as a just ground of war, the construction of fortifications in a neighbouring country, with whom there is no existing treaty to prohibit such constructions, or the securing of a strong hold, which may at some future period prove a means of annoyance. For as a guard or against such apprehensions, every power may construct, in its own territory, strong works, and other military securities of the same kind, without having recourse to actual war. One cannot but admire the character, which Tacitus has drawn of the Chauci, a noble and high-spirited people of Germany, "who, *he says*, were desirous of maintaining their greatness by justice, rather than by acts of ungovernable rapacity and ambition — provoking no wars, invading no countries, spoiling no neighbours to aggrandize themselves, — yet, when necessity prompted, able to raise men with arms in their hands at a moment's warning — a great population with a numerous breed of horses to form a well mounted cavalry-and, with all these advantages, upholding their reputation in the midst of peace."

**VI**. Nor can the advantage to be gained by a war be ever pleaded as a motive of equal weight and justice with necessity.

[**Translator's note:** Section V of the original is omitted in the translation.]

**VII**. and **VIII**. Neither can the desire of emigrating to a more favourable soil and climate justify an attack upon a neighbouring power. This, as we are informed by Tacitus, was a frequent cause of war among the ancient Germans.

**IX**. There is no less injustice in setting up claims, under the pretence of newly discovered titles, to what belongs to another.

Neither can the wickedness, and impiety, nor any other incapacity of the original owner justify such a claim. For the title and right by discovery can apply only to countries and places, that have no owner.

**X**. Neither moral nor religious virtue, nor any intellectual excellence is requisite to form a good title to property. Only where a race of men is so destitute of reason as to be incapable of exercising any act of ownership, they can hold no property, nor will the law of charity require that they should have more than the necessaries of life. For the rules of the law of nations can only be applied to those, who are capable of political or commercial intercourse: but not to a people entirely destitute of reason, though it is a matter of just doubt, whether any such is to be found.

It was an absurdity therefore in the Greeks to suppose, that difference of manners, or inferiority of intellect made those, whom they were pleased to call barbarians, their natural enemies. But as to atrocious crimes striking at the very root and existence of society, the forfeiture of property ensuing from thence is a question of a different nature, belonging to punishments, under the head of which it was discussed.

**XI**. But neither the independence of individuals, nor that of states, is a motive that can at all times justify recourse to arms, as if all persons INDISCRIMINATELY had a natural right to do so. For where liberty is said to be a natural right belonging to all men and states, by that expression is understood a right of nature, antecedent to every human obligation or contract. But in that case, liberty is spoken of in a negative sense, and not by way of contrast to independence, the meaning of which is, that no one is by the law of nature doomed to servitude, though he is not forbidden by that law to enter into such a condition. For in this sense no one can be called free, if nature leaves him not the privilege of chusing his own condition: as Albutius pertinently remarks, "the terms, freedom and servitude are not founded in the principles of nature, but are names subsequently applied to men according to the dispositions of fortune." And Aristotle defines the relations of master and servant to be the result of political and not of natural appointment. Whenever therefore the condition of servitude, either personal or political, subsists, from lawful causes, men should be contented with that state, according to the injunction of the Apostle, "Art thou called, being a servant, let not that be an anxious concern?"

**XII**. And there is equal injustice in the desire of reducing, by force of arms, any people to a state of servitude, under the pretext of its being the condition for which they are best qualified by nature. It does not follow that, because any one is fitted for a particular condition, another has a right to impose it upon him. For every reasonable creature ought to be left free in the choice of what may be deemed useful or prejudicial to him, provided another has no just right to a controul over him.

The case of children has no connection with the question, as they are necessarily under the discipline of others.

**XIII**. It would scarce have been necessary to refute the foolish opinion of some, who have ascribed to the Roman Emperors dominion over the most remote and unknown nations, if Bartolus, deemed a lawyer of the first eminence, had not pronounced it heresy to deny those pretensions. This opinion has been built upon the Roman Emperor's some times having styled himself Sovereign of the whole world; a term which it was not unusual for many people to apply to their own country. Thus in the scriptures we find Judea frequently called the whole inhabited earth; therefore when the Jews, in their proverbial expression, called Jerusalem the centre of the world, nothing more is to be implied than that it was situated in the middle of Judea.

As to the argument in favor of universal dominion from its being so beneficial to mankind, it may be observed that all its advantages are counterbalanced by still greater disadvantages. For as a ship may be built too large to be conveniently managed, so an empire may be too extensive in population and territory to be directed and governed by one head. But granting the expediency of universal empire, that expediency can not give such a right, as can be acquired only by treaty or conquest. There were many places formerly belonging to the Roman Empire, over which the Emperor has at present no controul. For war, treaty, or cession have made many changes, by which the rights of territory have passed to other states or sovereign princes, and the standards of different communities, whether kingdoms or commonwealths, now wave in places, which the Roman Eagle once overshadowed with his wings. These are losses and changes, that have been experienced by other powers no less than that, which was once mistress of the world.

**XIV**. But there have been some, who have asserted the rights of the church over unknown parts of the world, though the Apostle Paul himself has expressly said that Christians were not to judge those who were without the pale of their own community. And though the right of judging, which belonged to the Apostles, might in some cases apply to worldly concerns, yet in its general nature it was of a celestial rather than an earthly kind — a judgment not exercised by fire and sword, but by the word of God, proposed to all men and adapted to their peculiar circumstances — a judgment exercised by displaying or withholding the seals of divine grace, as it might be most expedient — lastly, it was a judgment exercised in supernatural punishments; in punishments proceeding from God, like the punishments of Ananias, Elymas, Hymenaeus, and others.

Christ himself, the spring', from whence all the power of the church was derived, and, whose life is the model for the church to follow, said, his kingdom was not of this world, that is, was not of the same nature, with other kingdoms, otherwise, like the rest of sovereigns, he would have maintained his authority by the power of the sword. For if he had pleased to call up the aid of Legions; he would have called up hosts of Angels and not of men. And every exercise of his right was performed by the influence of divine, and not of human power; even when he drove the sellers out of the temple. For the ROD was the EMBLEM and not the INSTRUMENT of divine wrath, as UNCTION was once a SIGN of healing, and not the HEALING POWER ITSELF. St. Augustin on the xviii Chapter of St. John, and 36 ver. invites Sovereign Princes into this kingdom, in these terms, "Hear, O Jews, and Gentiles, hear, O earthly Sovereigns, I will not obstruct your authority, for my kingdom is not of this world.. Be not alarmed, like Herod, who trembled, when he heard that Christ was born, and slew so many innocent children, hoping to include the Saviour in that calamity. His fear shewed itself in cruel wrath. But my kingdom, says Christ, is not of this world. Therefore enter this kingdom without fear. Come with faith, and provoke not the king to anger by your delay."

**XV**. There is a caution too necessary to be given, against drawing too close a parallel between ancient and modern times. For it is but seldom that any one can adduce a case exactly conformable to his own circumstances. To draw such pretexts from the interpretation of prophecy is the highest presumption. For no prophecy that is yet to be fulfilled can be unfolded without the aid of a prophetic spirit. The times even of events, that are certain, may escape our notice. Nor is it every pre. diction, unless it be accompanied with an express command from God, that can justify recourse to arms: sometimes indeed God brings his predicted designs to their issue by the means of wicked instrument.

**XVI**. As the imperfect obligations of charity, and other virtues of the same kind are not cognizable in a court of justice, so neither can the performance of them be compelled by force of arms. For it is not the moral nature of a duty that can enforce its fulfillment, but there must be some legal right in one of the parties to exact the obligation. For the moral obligation receives an additional weight from such a right. This obligation therefore must be united to the former to give a war the character of a just war. Thus a person who has conferred a favour, has not, strictly speaking, a RIGHT to demand a return, for that would be converting an act of kindness into a contract.

**XVII**. It is necessary to observe that a war may be just in its origin, and yet the intentions of its authors may become unjust in the course of its prosecution. For some other motive, not unlawful IN ITSELF, may actuate them more powerfully than the original right, for the attainment of which the war was begun. It is laudable, for instance, to maintain national honour; it is laudable to pursue a public or a private interest, and yet those objects may not form the justifiable grounds of the war in question.A war may gradually change its nature and its object from the prosecution of a right to the desire of seconding or supporting the aggrandizement of some other power. But such motives, though blamable, when even connected with a just war, do not render the war ITSELF unjust, nor invalidate its conquests.

## CHAPTER 23: ON DOUBTFUL CAUSES

*Origin of moral doubts — The dictates of conscience, though erroneous, not to be violated — Opposite opinions supported by argument, or by authority — In doubtful and important matters the safer side of the question to be followed — In such cases it is right to abstain from war — Disputes settled by conference or arbitration — Christian duties — Whether single combat is allowable in order to avoid war — In cases of equal doubt the claims of the present possessor to be preferred — Where neither party is in possession, claims to be divided — Whether a war can be just on both sides, explained by a distinction.*

**I**. THERE is much truth in Aristotle's observation that moral reasonings can never amount to the certainty of mathematical demonstration. Because in mathematical reasoning, all the figures are considered in the abstract, purely by themselves, and without relation to the circumstances of time or place, so that there is nothing to warp the judgment from the object immediately under consideration. Besides the figures in general form a direct contrast to each other. Thus, for instance, there is no intermediate line between a straight line and a curve.

But it is not so in morals, where the least circumstances vary the subject, and admit a latitude of interpretation, settling the points of truth and justice between two extremes. So that between what is right and what is unlawful there is a middle space, where it is easy to in. cline to the one side, or to the other. This occasions an ambiguity somewhat like the difficulty of deciding the precise moment, where the twilight begins, and where it ends. From hence Aristotle concludes that it is sometimes difficult to determine, between two extremes, what line of conduct ought to be chosen or rejected.

**II**. But it must be laid down as a necessary principle, that although an action may in reality be just, yet if the party doing it, after weighing every circumstance, cannot reconcile the act to his conscience, he incurs some degree of guilt. "For whatever is not of faith, *says the Apostle*, is sin;" where, by the term faith he means a deliberate judgment of the mind. For God has given conscience a judicial power to be the sovereign guide of human actions, by despising whose admonitions the mind is stupified into brutal hardness,, For it often happens that judgment can point out nothing certain, but hesitates; and when such doubts and hesitations cannot satisfactorily be cleared up, the rule of Cicero is a safe one to follow, who says, that it is an excellent injunction, which forbids us to do a thing of the rectitude or impropriety of which we entertain a doubt.

But this rule cannot be applied, where of two things, in the choice of which there is equal doubt, the one must be done, in which case that must be selected, which seems to be the least unjust. For on all occasions, where a choice cannot be avoided, the less of two evils assumes the appearance of a virtue.

**III**. But in doubtful cases, after examination, the mind seldom remains neuter, but inclines to one side, or the other, persuaded either by the merits of the case, or by respect for the judgment of those, who have delivered an opinion upon the question. Now the merits of the case are derived either from the causes, the effects, or other concomitant circumstances.

**IV**. To apprehend such distinctions properly, practice and penetration are necessary, and where men have not in themselves a capacity for the active exercise of judgment it behoves them to follow the maxims of others, who are distinguished by their wisdom and experience. For, in the opinion of Aristotle, those things are probably just, or true, which seem so to all, or to the greater part of men of worth. And this is the method of judging pursued by Sovereign Princes, whose engagements in the affairs of life allow them but little leisure for study and deliberation Thus the ancient Romans never undertook wars, till they had consulted the sacred college, established for that purpose, and the Christian Emperors scarcely ever did so without advising with the Bishops, in order to be apprized of any thing therein that might affect religion.

**V**. It may happen in many disputed points, that the intrinsic merits of the case, or the opinions of the learned, are equal on both sides. When that happens, if the matters in discussion are of no great importance, there is nothing to blame in the person, that makes his choice either way. But in matters of moment, where the lives of men are at stake, the decision should incline to the safer side, according to the proverbial maxim, which pronounces it better to acquit the guilty than to condemn the innocent.

**VI**. War then being an object of such weighty magnitude, in which the innocent must often be involved in the sufferings of the guilty, between wavering opinions the balance should incline in favour of peace.

There are three methods, by which independent nations may settle their disputed rights without coming to the decision of the sword.

**VII**. The first method is that of conference. For, in the words of Cicero, "there being two methods of deciding quarrels, the one by discussion and the other by force, the former, a peculiar characteristic of man, and the latter, of the brute creation: when the first of these methods fails, men are obliged to have recourse to the latter." Mardonius, in the Polyhymnia of Herodotus, blames the Grecians, who, being united in one language, might settle their quarrels by messengers of peace, by heralds, and negotiations, rather than by war.

**VIII**. The other method is that of compromise, which takes place between those, who have no common judge. Among innumerable instances of this kind in ancient history, we may select that given by Xenophon in his account of Cyrus, where that prince takes the king of the Indians for arbitrator between himself and the king of Assyria. The Carthaginians in their disputes with Masinissa prefer a settlement of this kind before a decision of war. Livy too informs us that the Romans themselves, in a dispute with the Samnites, made an appeal to the common allies of both.

The office of deciding wars and putting an end to the contentions of armies was assigned, according to Strabo, to the Druids of the Gauls, and upon the testimony of the same writer, it formed a part of the priestly functions among the Iberians.

Surely then it is a mode of terminating their disputes, balancing their powers, and settling their pretensions worthy to be adopted by Christian Kings and States. For if, in order to avoid trials before judges who were strangers to the true religion, the Jews and Christians appointed arbitrators of their own, and it was a practice recommended and enjoined by St. Paul, how much more ought such a practice to be recommended and enforced, to gain the still nobler end of preventing the calamities of war.

These and many other reasons of no less importance might be advanced for recommending to Christian powers general congresses for the adjustment of their various interests, and for compelling the refractory to submit to equitable terms of peace.

**IX**. A third method of terminating disputes, without hostilities, was by lot, a practice commended by Dion Chrysostom in his speech on the interposition of fortune in directing affairs, and it was commended long before him by Solomon in the xviii. chapter of his Proverbs.

**X**. Nearly related to the last named method is that of single combat, a practice recommended under the idea that by the risque of two lives a quarrel might be decided, which would otherwise have cost the blood of thousands. In Livy we find Metius addressing Tullus in the following terms, "let us try some method of determining to whom the pre-eminence shall belong, without wasting the blood of each people." Strabo says it was the practice of the ancient Greeks, and Aeneas proposed it to Turnus, as the most equitable way of settling their pretensions. It is described too as the custom of the ancient Franks.

**XI**. Although in doubtful cases, both sides are bound to devise every means of avoiding hostilities, yet it is a duty more incumbent upon the claimant than upon the immediate possessor of whatever may be the subject of dispute. For it is a rule not only of civil, but of natural law, that, where the pretensions are equal, those of the possessor are to be preferred.

To the foregoing remarks an additional observation may be made, that if any one, knowing his pretensions to be just, cannot produce sufficient proofs to convict the intruder of injustice, he cannot lawfully have recourse to arms, because he has no OSTENSIBLE RIGHT, by which he can compel the intruder to relinquish the possession.

**XII**. But where the right is ambiguous, and neither party has possession, the pretender, who refuses to divide the claims, may reasonably be charged with injustice.

**XIII**. From what has been said it will not be difficult to settle a much agitated question, whether, with respect to those, who are the principal movers of a war, there can be justice on both sides. For there are distinctions proper to be made in the various acceptations of the word JUST.

A thing is said to be just, either as to its causes, or its effects. The causes too may be confined either to justice in a PARTICULAR acceptation, or they may be extended so as to include under that name every kind of rectitude. Again, a particular acceptation may be divided into two kinds, one relating to the ACTION, and the other to the agent. An agent may be said to act justly, when, in what he does, he commits no breach of STRICT LAW, though his conduct may not be conformable to equity.

In a PARTICULAR acceptation of the word justice, with regard to a matter in dispute, it cannot in war, any more than in legal proceedings, apply to both sides. For there can be no moral principle, commanding us, under the same circumstances, both to Do, and to ABSTAIN from a particular action. It may happen indeed that neither of two belligerent powers may act unjustly. For no one can be charged with acting unjustly unless he knows that he is doing so; but there are many, who are not aware of the nature, extent, and consequences of their measures. Thus in a law-suit, both parties may sincerely believe that they have justice on their side. For many things both in law and fact, which would establish a right, may escape the notice of men.

In a GENERAL acceptation, an action may be called just, where the agent is free from every kind of blame. Yet in many cases an agent may deviate from the strict rules of legal justice, and be liable to no blame, when that deviation is owing to unavoidable ignorance, there having been neither time nor opportunity sufficient for him to know the substance, or perhaps existence of the law. So it may happen in law-suits, that both parties are free not only from the imputation of injustice, but from all blame, especially where either of them is litigating a matter not on his own, but on another's account; as for instance where a guardian is acting for his ward, he would not be authorized in abandoning even a doubted right. Aristotle says that in matters of disputed right neither side can be charged with injustice; conformably to which opinion Quintilian, observes that an upright pleader may be engaged on either side of the question. Aristotle further observes that passing a just judgment is an ambiguous term, signifying that a judge determines either according to the strict letter of the law, or according to the dictates of his own conscience. And, in another place, he has said that giving a wrong judgment through ignorance is no act of injustice.

But in matters of war and peace, where such weighty and varied interests on all sides are concerned, it would be difficult to obtain a judgment purely impartial, and abstracted from all personal motives, unless there be the most clear and undeniable evidence on the points in question.

If we denominate a thing to be just, from its effect in conferring certain rights, in this sense it is plain that in war there may be justice on both sides. In the same manner, a sentence not strictly legal, or a possession not perfectly just may nevertheless confer certain rights.

## CHAPTER 24: PRECAUTIONS AGAINST RASHLY ENGAGING IN WAR, EVEN UPON JUST GROUNDS.

*Relaxation of right in order to avoid war — particularly penalties — Self-preservation motive for forbearing hostilities — Prudential rules in the choice of advantages — Peace preferable to the extermination of hostile powers — Forbearance prudent in inferior powers — War not to be undertaken, but from necessity.*

**I**. Although it seems not to fall within the immediate province of a treatise, entitled the RIGHTS OF WAR, to enter into an investigation of other moral duties, which the relations of war and peace prescribe, yet it may not be improper slightly to touch upon certain errors, which it is necessary to obviate, in order to prevent any one from supposing, that, after establishing the right of war, he is authorized, INSTANTLY or at ALL TIMES, to carry his principles into action, and to reduce his theory to practice, So far from this, it frequently happens that it is an act of greater piety and rectitude to yield a right than to enforce it.

It was before shewn, in its proper place how honour. able it is to be regardless of our own lives, where we can preserve the lives, and promote the lasting welfare of others. A duty that should operate with greater force upon' Christians, who have before their eyes continually the example of him, who died to save us, while we were enemies and ungodly. An example which calls upon us, in the most affecting manner, not to insist upon the rigorous prosecution of our justest rights, where it can. not be done but by the calamities, which war occasions. If arguments and motives like these wanted authorities, abundance of authorities might be adduced for their support. II. Many reasons might be brought to dissuade us from urging the full infliction of a punishment. There is an obvious instance in the conduct of fathers, who connive at many faults in their children. But whoever, is authorized to punish another, assumes the character of a sovereign ruler, that is, of a father; in allusion to which St. Augustin, addressing Count Marcellinus, says, "O Christian judge, fulfil the office of a pious father."

Sometimes indeed men are so circumstanced, that to relinquish a right becomes not only a laudable act, but a debt of respect to that law, which commands us to love our enemies: a law to be respected and obeyed not only for its intrinsic value, but as being a precept of the gospel. By the same law, and for the same reasons, we are commanded to pray for and to promote the welfare and safety of Christian Princes and Kings, because their welfare and safety are so essential to the order, peace, and happiness of society.

**III**. With respect to the pardon of offences committed against ourselves, little need be said, as it is known to be a leading clause in the code of a Christian's duty, to which he readily and freely submits, knowing that God for Christ's sake has forgiven him. Thus revealed law adds a sanction to what was known by heathens to be an amiable precept. Cicero has drawn a fine character of Caesar, in which he commends the excellence of his memory that could recollect every thing but injuries. We find many noble examples of this excellent virtue in the writings of Moses and in various other parts of scripture. These, and these motives ALONE, when they can safely be complied with are sufficient to keep the sword within its scabbard. For the debt of love and forbearance to our enemies is an obligation, which it is honourable to discharge.

**IV**. It is often a duty, which we owe to our country and ourselves, to forbear having recourse to arms. After the college of heralds had pronounced a war to be just we are informed by Plutarch in the life of Numa, that the Senate further deliberated, whether it was expedient to undertake it. According to our Saviour's beautiful and instructive parable, a king, when he is obliged to go to war with another king, should first sit down, an expression implying an act of deliberation, and consider within himself, whether, with ten thousand men he is able to encounter one who is coming against him with twenty times that number: and if he finds himself unequal to the contest, before the enemy has entered his territories he will send an embassy to him offering terms of peace.

**V**. In all cases of deliberation, not only the ultimate but the intermediate objects leading to the principal ends are to be considered. The final object is always some good, or at least the evasion of some evil, which amounts to the same. The means are never to be considered by THEMSELVES, but only as they have a tendency to the proposed end. Wherefore in all cases of deliberation, the proportion, which the means and the end bear to each other, is to be duly weighed, by comparing them together: a mode of comparison, in which there are three rules -necessary to be observed.

The first thing, in a moral point of view, to be considered is, what tendency the desired object has to produce good or evil; and, if the former has the preponderancy, we are then at liberty to chuse it. — In the second place, if it appears difficult to decide, whether the good or the evil predominates, we may chuse the object, if, in the choice and use of our means, we can give a turn to affairs, that may throw the preponderance into the scale of advantage-or lastly if the good and the evil bear no proportion to each other, nor the means, AT THE FIRST VIEW, appear adequate to the end, if, in pursuing an object, the tendency to good, compared with the tendency to evil be greater than the evil itself when compared with the good; or if the good, in comparison of the evil, be greater than the tendency to evil, in comparison of the tendency to good, we may decide in favour of it, Cicero has treated these abstruse points in a more popular and pleasing manner than abstract reasoning would allow. Applying all the beauties of eloquence to elucidate moral truth, he says, " it is the height of folly and presumption UNNECESSARILY to expose ourselves to dangers. In encountering calamities we must imitate the conduct of physicians who use gentle remedies with weakly constitutions. But in constitutions of a stronger cast, especially, in virulent disorders, they must have recourse to more powerful, though more dangerous expedients. In the same manner, a skilful pilot would not attempt to face the wind directly, but would tack about in order to avoid its fury. "

**VI**. An example of evils, that ought by all possible means to be avoided, is furnished by the consultations among the states of Gaul, who, according to the account of Tacitus, deliberated, whether they should make choice of liberty or peace. By liberty is here meant civil liberty, that is, the right of governing themselves, and remaining independent states; and by peace is meant such a peace ,as would prevent the whole people from being exterminated, a calamity like that which befell the Jews, when their city was besieged by Titus.

In such cases reason itself dictates the choice of peace, as the only means of preserving life, which is the immediate gift of God, and the foundation of every blessing. So that the Almighty, as we read in his sacred volume, deems it a kindness, when instead of destroying a people, he permits them to be reduced to slavery. Therefore: he admonishes the Hebrews, by the mouth of his prophet, to surrender to the Babylonians, rather than to di6 by pestilence and famine.

What has been said of submitting to disadvantages, and some calamities for the preservation of life or liberty, may be applied to every object of dear value. As, Aristides says, it is a moral duty in a storm, to save the ship by casting overboard the goods, but not the crew.

**VII**. In exacting punishment it is necessary to use the precaution of avoiding hostilities with a power of equal strength. For to avenge a wrong, or to assert a right by force of arms requires a superiority of strength. So that not only prudence, but a regard for their subjects will at all times deter rulers from involving their people in the calamities of war. A principle of justice too, the sole directress of human affairs, binding sovereigns and subjects to each other by their mutual interests, will teach this lesson of precaution. For reparation must be looked for at the hands of those, who bring on the calamities of wanton and unnecessary war. Livy calls that a just, which is a necessary war, and it is a pious cause, when no hope is left, but in recourse to arms.

**VIII**. It is but now and then a cause of such imperious necessity occurs, as to demand the decision of the sword, and that is, when, as Florus says, the desertion of a right will be followed by calamities far more cruel, than the fiercest wars. Seneca says, "that it is right to meet danger, when equal harm would result from acquiescing in an injury," and in this, he is supported by Tacitus, who calls "war a happy exchange for a miserable and insecure peace," and the same animated writer in another place observes, that "an oppressed people may recover their liberty by daring enterprize, and, if defeated they cannot be reduced to greater subjection than before; " a sentiment, with which Livy accords, in naming "peace, when coupled with servitude, a far more grievous calamity, than all the horrors of war." But it is not so, as Cicero says, where defeat will be attended with proscription, and victory with bondage.

**IX**. Another necessary precaution relates to the TIME, when it is proper to undertake a war, which depends upon a due calculation, whether there are resources and strength,, sufficient to support our just pretensions. This is conformable to what was said by Augustus, that no war should be undertaken, but where the hopes of ad. vantage could be shewn to overbalance the apprehensions of ruin. Scipio Africanus, and Lucius Aemilius Paulus used to speak in terms not inapplicable to this subject, for they said "it was never right to try the event of battle, but under extreme necessity, or favourable circumstances."

The above precautions are of great use, where we hope by the dread and fame of our preparations to accomplish our object with little or no danger.

## CHAPTER 25: THE CAUSES OF UNDERTAKING WAR FOR OTHERS.

*Sovereigns may engage in war to support the rights of their subjects — Whether an innocent subject can be delivered up to an enemy to avoid danger — Wars justly undertaken in support of confederates upon equal, or unequal terms — For friends — or any men — Omission of this duty not blamable, from motives of self-preservation — Whether war may be justly undertaken in defence of another's subjects, explained by distinctions.*

**I**. IN SPEAKING of belligerent powers, it was shewn that the law of nature authorises the assertion not only of our own rights, but of those also belonging to others. The causes therefore, which justify the principals engaged in war, will justify those also, who afford assistance to others. But whether any one presides over an household, or a state, the first and most necessary care is the support of his dependents or subjects. For the household forms but one body with the master, and the people with the sovereign. So the people of Israel under the command of Joshua took up arms in support of the Gibeonites, whom they had subdued. Our forefathers, said Cicero to the Romans, often engaged in war to support the rights of merchants, whose vessels had been plundered. The same Romans who would refuse to take arms for a people who were only allies, did not hesitate to assert by force of arms the injured rights of the same, when they became their subjects.

**II**. Yet the cause of any subject, although it may be a just cause, does not always bind sovereigns or rulers to take arms: but only when it can be done without inconvenience to all, or the greater part of their subjects. For the interests of the whole community, rather than those of particular parts, are the principal objects of a sovereign's care; and the greater any part is, the nearer its claims and pretensions approximate to those of the whole.

**III**. Some have maintained the position, that if an enemy requires the surrender of a citizen, however innocent, the demand must unquestionably be complied with, if the state is too feeble to resist it. This opinion is strongly controverted by Vasquez, but if we attend to his meaning more than his words, we shall find it to be the drift of his argument, that such a citizen ought not to be rashly abandoned, while there remains any possible hope of protecting him. For as a case in point, he alleges the conduct of the Italian Infantry, who, upon receiving assurances of protection from Caesar, deserted Pompey, even before he was reduced to absolute despair: a conduct which he deservedly reprobates in the strongest terms.

But whether an innocent citizen may be given up into the hands of an enemy to avoid imminent destruction, which would otherwise fall upon the state, is a point that HAS BEEN formerly, and is still disputed by the learned, according to the beautiful fable, which Domosthenes told of the wolves, who demanded of the sheep the surrender of the dogs, as the only terms of peace. The lawfulness of this is denied not only by Vasquez, but by one, whose opinions that writer condemns, as bearing a near approach to perfidy. Sotus holds it as an established maxim, that such a citizen is bound to deliver himself up: this Vasquez denies, because the nature of civil society, which every one has entered into for his own advantage, requires no such thing.

No conclusion can be drawn from hence, except that a citizen is not bound to this by any RIGHT STRICTLY SO CALLED, while at the same time the law of charity will not suffer him to act otherwise. For there are many duties not properly included in the idea of strict justice. These are regarded as acts of good will, the performance of which is not only crowned with praise, but the omission of them cannot escape censure.

Such is the complexion of the following maxim, that every one should prefer the lives of an innumerable and innocent multitude to his own personal and private welfare. Cicero, in defending Publius Sextius, says, "If I were taking a voyage with my friends, and happening to meet with a fleet of pirates, they threatened to sink our little bark, -unless the crew surrendered me as the victim to appease their fury, I would sooner throw myself into the deep, than suffer my companions out of their affection to me to encounter sure death, or even imminent danger.

But after establishing this point, there remains a doubt, whether any one can be COMPELLED to do what he is BOUND to do. Sotus denies this, and in support of his argument quotes the case of a rich man, who, though bound from motives of charity to supply the wants of the needy, cannot be compelled to do so. But the transactions of equals with each other, must be regulated upon principles very different from those that regulate the mutual relations of sovereigns and subjects. For an equal cannot compel an equal to the performance of any thing, but what he is strictly bound by law to perform. But a superior may compel an inferior to the performance Of OTHER duties besides those of PERFECT OBLIGATIONS; for that is a right peculiarly and essentially belonging to the nature of superiority. Therefore certain legislative provisions may be made, enacting the performance of such duties, as seem to partake of the nature of benevolence. Phocion, as it is mentioned in Plutarch's lives, said that the persons, whom Alexander demanded, had reduced the commonwealth to such distress, that if he demanded even his dearest friend Nicocles, he should vote for delivering him up.

**IV**. Next to subjects, and even upon an equal footing with them, as to claims of protection, are allies, a name including, in its consequences and effects, both those, who have formed a subordinate connection with another power, and those who have entered into engagements of mutual assistance. Yet no such compacts can bind either of the parties to the support or prosecution of unjust wars. And this is the reason, why the Lacedaemonians, before they went to war with the Athenians, left all their allies at liberty to decide for themselves upon the justice of the quarrel. To which an additional observation may be made, that no ally is bound to assist in the prosecution of schemes, which afford no possible prospect of a happy termination. For this would be defeating the very end of alliances, which are contracted from motives of public advantage, and not for a participation in ruin. But any power is obliged to defend an ally even against those, with whom it is already connected by subsisting treaties, provided those treaties contain no express condition prohibiting such defence. Thus the

Athenians might have defended the Corcyraeans, IN A JUST CAUSE, even against the Corinthians, their more ancient allies.

**V**. A third case is that, where assistance has not been expressly promised to a friendly power, and yet is due on the score of friendship, if it can be given without inconvenience.

Upon this principle Abraham took arms in defence of his kinsman Lot: and the Romans charged the Antiates to commit no acts of piracy upon the Greeks, as being a people of the same kindred with the Italians. It was no unusual thing with the Romans to begin, or at least to threaten to begin wars not only in support of allies, to whom they were bound by treaty, but in support of any friendly powers.

**VI**. The last and most extensive motive is the common tie of one COMMON NATURE, which alone is sufficient to oblige men to assist each other.

**VII**. It is a question, whether one man is bound to protect another, or one people another people from injury and aggression. Plato thinks that the individual or state not defending another from intended violence is deserving of punishment. A case for which provision was made by the laws of the Egyptians.

But in the first place it is certain that no one is bound to give assistance or protection, when it will be attended with evident danger. For a man's own life and property, and a state's own existence and preservation are either to the individual, or the state, objects of greater value and prior consideration than the welfare and security of other individuals or states.

Nor will states or individuals be bound to risk their own safety, even when the aggrieved or oppressed party cannot be relieved but by the destruction of the invader or oppressor. For under some circumstances it is impossible successfully to oppose cruelty and oppression, the punishment of which must be left to the eternal judge of mankind.

**VIII**. Though it is a rule established by the laws of nature and of social order, and a rule confirmed by all the records of history, that every sovereign is supreme judge in his own kingdom and over his own subjects, in whose disputes no foreign power can justly interfere. Yet where a Busiris, a Phalaris or a Thracian Diomede provoke their people to despair and resistance by unheard of cruelties, having themselves abandoned all the laws of nature, they lose the rights of independent sovereigns, and can no longer claim the privilege of the law of nations. Thus Constantine took up arms against Maxentius and Licinius, and other Roman emperors either took, or threatened to take them against the Persians, if they did not desist from persecuting the Christians.

Admitting that it would be fraught with the greatest dangers if subjects were allowed to redress grievances by force of arms, it does not necessarily follow that other powers are prohibited from giving them assistance when labouring under grievous oppressions. For whenever the impediment to any action is of a personal nature, and not inherent in the action itself, one person may perform for another, what he cannot do for himself, provided it is an action by which some kind service may be rendered. Thus a guardian or any other friend may undertake an action for a ward, which he is incapacitated from doing for himself.

The impediment, which prohibits a SUBJECT from making resistance, does not depend upon the nature of the OCCASION, which would operate equally upon the feelings of men, whether they were subjects or not, but upon the character of the persons, who cannot transfer their natural allegiance from their own sovereign to another. But this principle does not bind those, who are not the liege-subjects of that sovereign or power. Their opposition to him or the state may sometimes be connected with the defence of the oppressed, and can never be construed into an act of treason. But pretexts of that kind cannot always be allowed, they may often be used as the cover of ambitious designs. But right does not necessarily lose its nature from being in the hands of wicked men. The sea still continues a channel of lawful intercourse, though sometimes navigated by pirates, and swords are still instruments of defence, though sometimes wielded by robbers or assassins.

# BOOK III

## CHAPTER 1: WHAT IS LAWFUL IN WAR.

*What is lawful in war — General Rules derived from the law of nature — Stratagems and lies — Arrangement of the following parts — First rule, all things necessary to the end lawful — Right resulting not only from the origin of a war, but from causes growing out of the same — Certain consequences justifiable, though not originally lawful — What measures are lawful against those who furnish an enemy with supplies — Stratagems — Negative — Positive — Sometimes allowable to use words in a sense different from the general acceptation — A lie according to the true notion of it injurious to the rights of others — Falsehood allowable in order to deceive children or madmen — Any one addressing another without intentions to deceive, not answerable for the misconceptions of a third person — A person not answerable for the willful mistakes of those to whom he speaks — The fictitious threats of a person in authority — Fiction allowable in order to save the lives of the innocent, or to promote other equally important purposes — Deception lawful against an enemy, but not including promises, or oaths — To forbear using this privilege an act of generosity and Christian simplicity — Not allowable to urge others to what is unlawful for them, but not for us to do — Allowable to use the services of deserters.*

**I**. HAVING, in the preceding books, considered by what persons, and for what causes, war may be justly declared and undertaken, the subject necessarily leads to an inquiry into the circumstances, under which war may be undertaken, into the extent, to which it may be carried, and into the manner, in which its rights may be enforced. Now all these matters may be viewed in the light of privileges resulting simply from the law of nature and of nations, or as the effects of some prior treaty or promise. But the actions, which are authorised by the law of nature, are those that are first entitled to attention.

**II** In the first place, as it has occasionally been observed, the means employed in the pursuit of any object must, in a great degree, derive the complexion of their moral character from the nature of the end to which they lead. It is evident therefore that we may justly avail ourselves of those means, provided they be lawful, which are necessary to the attainment of any right. RIGHT in this place means what is strictly so called, signifying the moral power of action, which any one as a member of society possesses. On which account, a person, if he has no other means of saving his life, is justified in using any forcible means of repelling an attack, though he who makes it, as for instance, a soldier in battle, in doing so, is guilty of no crime. For this is a right resulting not properly from the crime of another, but from the privilege of self-defence, which nature grants to every one. Besides, if any one has SURF and UNDOUBTED grounds to apprehend imminent danger from any thing belonging to another, he may seize it without any regard to the guilt or innocence of that owner. Yet he does not by that seizure become the proprietor of it. For that is not necessary to the end he has in view. He may DETAIN it as a precautionary measure, till he can obtain satisfactory assurance of security.

Upon the same principle any one has a natural right to seize what belongs to him, and is unlawfully detained by another: or, if that is impracticable, he may seize something of equal value, which is nearly the same as recovering a debt. Recoveries of this kind establish a property in the things so reclaimed; which is the only method of restoring the equality and repairing the breaches of violated justice. So too when punishment is lawful and just, all the means absolutely necessary to enforce its execution are also lawful and just, and every act that forms a part of the punishment, such as destroying an enemy's property and country by fire or any other way, falls within the limits of justice proportionable to the offence.

**III**. In the second place, it is generally known that it is not the ORIGIN only of a just war which is to be viewed as the principal source of many of our rights, but there may be causes growing out of that war which may give birth to additional rights. As in proceedings at law, the sentence of the court may give to the successful litigant other rights besides those belonging to the original matter of dispute. So those who join our enemies, either as allies or subjects, give us a right of defending ourselves against THEM also. So too a nation engaging in an unjust war, the injustice of which she knows and ought to know, becomes liable to make good all the expences and losses incurred, because she has been guilty of occasioning them. In the same manner those powers, who become auxiliaries in wars undertaken without any reasonable grounds, contract a degree of guilt and render themselves liable to punishment in proportion to the injustice of their measures. Plato approves of war conducted so far, as to compel the aggressor to indemnify the injured and the innocent.

**IV**. In the third place, an individual or belligerent power may, in the prosecution of a lawful object, do many things, which were not in the contemplation of the original design, and which in THEMSELVES it would not be lawful to do. Thus in order to obtain what belongs to us, when it is impossible to recover the specific thing, we may take more than our due, under condition of repaying whatever is above the real value. For the same reason it is lawful to attack a ship manned by pirates, or a house occupied by robbers, although in that ship, or that house there may be many innocent persons, whose lives are endangered by such attack.

But we have had frequent occasion to remark, that what is conformable to right taken in its strictest sense is not always lawful in a moral point of view. For there are many instances, in which the law of charity will not allow us to insist upon our right with the utmost rigour. A reason for which it will be necessary to guard against things, which fall not within the original purpose of an action, and the happening of which might be foreseen: unless indeed the action has a tendency to produce advantages, that will far outweigh the consequences of any accidental calamity, and the apprehensions of evil are by no means to be put in competition with the sure hopes of a successful issue. But to determine in such cases requires no ordinary penetration and discretion. But wherever there is any doubt, it is. always the safer -way to decide in favour of another's interest, than to follow the bent of our own inclination. "Suffer the tares to grow, says our divine teacher. least in rooting up the tares you root up the wheat also."

The general destruction, which the Almighty, in right of his supreme Majesty, has sometimes decreed and executed, is not a rule, which we can presume to follow. He has not invested men, in the exercise of power, with those transcendent sovereign rights. Yet he himself,

notwithstanding the unchangeable nature of his sovereign will, was inclined to spare the most wicked cities, if ten righteous persons could be found therein. Examples like these may furnish us with rules to decide, how far the rights of war against an enemy may be exercised or relaxed.

V. It frequently occurs as a matter of inquiry, how far we are authorised to act against those, who are neither enemies, nor wish to be thought so, but who supply our enemies with certain articles. For we know that it is a point, which on former and recent occasions has been contested with the greatest animosity; some wishing to enforce with all imaginary rigour the rights of war, and others standing up for the freedom of commerce.

In the first place, a distinction must be made between the commodities themselves. For there are some, such as arms for instance, which are only of use in war; there are others again, which are of no use in war, but only administer t o luxury; but there are some articles, such as money, provisions, ships and naval stores, which are of use at all times both in peace and war.

As to conveying articles of the first kind, it is evident that any one must be ranked as an enemy, who supplies an enemy with the means of prosecuting hostilities. Against the conveyance of commodities of the second kind, no just complaint can be made.- And as to articles of the third class, from their being of a doubtful kind, a distinction must be made between the times of war and peace. For if a power can not defend itself, but by intercepting the supplies sent to an enemy, necessity will justify such a step, but upon condition of making restoration, unless there be some additional reasons to the contrary. But if the conveyance of goods to an enemy tends to obstruct any belligerent power in the prosecution of a lawful right, and the person so conveying them possesses the means of knowing it; if that power, for instance, is besieging a town, or blockading a port, in expectation of a speedy surrender and a peace, the person, who furnishes the enemy with supplies, and the means of prolonged resistance, will be guilty of an aggression and injury towards that power. He will incur the same guilt, as a person would do by assisting a debtor to escape from prison, and thereby to defraud his creditor. His goods may be taken by way of indemnity, and in discharge of the debt. If the person has not yet committed the injury, but only intended to do so, the aggrieved power will have a right to detain his goods, in order to compel him to give future security, either by putting into his hands hostages, or pledges; or indeed in any other way. But if there are evident proofs of injustice in an enemy's conduct the person who supports him in such a case, by furnishing him with succours, will be guilty not barely of a civil injury, but his giving assistance will amount to a crime as enormous, as it would be to rescue a criminal in the very face of the judge. And on that account the injured power may proceed against him as a criminal, and punish him by a confiscation of his goods.

These are the reasons, which induce belligerent powers to issue manifestoes, as an appeal to other states, upon the justice of their cause, and their probable hopes of ultimate success. This question has been introduced under the article, which refers to the law of nature, as history supplies us with no precedent to deduce its establishment from the voluntary law of nations.

We are informed by Polybius, in his first book, that the Carthaginians seized some of the Romans, who were carrying supplies to their enemies, though they afterwards gave them up, upon the demand of the Romans. Plutarch says that when Demetrius had invested Attica, and taken the neighbouring towns of Eleusis and Rhamnus, he ordered the master and pilot of a ship, attempting to convey provisions into Athens, to be hanged, as he designed to reduce that city by famine: this act of rigour deterred others from doing the same, and by that means he made himself master of the city.

**VI**. Wars, for the attainment of their objects, it cannot be denied, must employ force and terror as their most proper agents. But a doubt is sometimes entertained, whether stratagem may be lawfully used in war. The general sense of mankind seems to have approved of such a mode of warfare. For Homer commends his hero, Ulysses, no less for his ability in military stratagem, than for his wisdom. Xenophon, who was a philosopher as well as a soldier and historian, has said, that nothing can be more useful in war than a well-timed stratagem, with whom Brasidas, in Thueydides agrees, declaring it to be the method from which many great generals have derived the most brilliant reputation. And in Plutarch, Agesilaus maintains, that deceiving an enemy is both just and lawful. The authority of Polybius may be added to those already named; for he thinks, that it shews greater talent in a general to avail himself of some favourable opportunity to employ a stratagem, than to gain an open battle. This opinion of poets, historians, and philosophers is supported by that of Theologians. For Augustin has said that, in the prosecution of a just war, the justice of the cause is no way affected by the attainment of the end, whether the object be accomplished by stratagem or open force, and Chrysostom, in his beautiful little treatise on the priestly office, observes, that the highest praises are bestowed on those generals, who have practised successful stratagems. Yet there is one circumstance, upon which the decision of this question turns more than upon any opinion even of the highest authority, and that is, whether stratagem ought to be ranked as one of those evils, which are prohibited under the maxim OF NOT DOING EVIL, THAT GOOD MAY ENSUE, or to be reckoned as one of those actions, which, though evil IN

THEMSELVES, may be so modified by particular occasions, as to lose their criminality in consideration of the good, to which they lead.

**VII.** There is one kind of stratagem, it is proper to remark, of a negative, and another of a positive kind. The word stratagem, upon the authority of Labeo, taken in a negative sense, includes such actions, as have nothing criminal in them, though calculated to deceive, where any one, for instance, uses a degree of dissimulation or concealment, in order to defend his own property or that of others. So that undoubtedly there is something of harshness in the opinion of Cicero, who says there is no scene of life, that will allow either simulation, or dissimulation to be practised. For as you are not bound to disclose to others all that you either know or intend; it follows that, on certain occasions, some acts of dissimulation, that is, of concealment may be lawful. This is a talent, which Cicero, in many parts of his writings, acknowledges that it is absolutely necessary for statesmen to possess. The history of Jeremiah, in the xxxviiith chapter of his prophecy, furnishes a remarkable instance of this kind. For when that prophet was interrogated by the king, respecting the event of the siege, he prudently, in compliance with the king's orders, concealed the real matter from the nobles, assigning a different, though not a false reason for the conference, which he had had. In the same manner, Abraham called Sarah, his sister, an appellation used familiarly at that time to denote a near relation by blood, concealing the circumstance of her being his wife.

**VIII.** A stratagem of a positive kind, when practised in actions, is called a feint, and when used in conversation it receives the name of a lie or falsehood. A distinction is made by some, between these two kinds of stratagems, who say, that words are signs of our ideas, but actions are not so. But there is more of truth in the opposite opinion, that words of themselves unaccompanied by the intention of the speaker, signify nothing more than the inarticulate cries would do of any one labouring under grief, or any other passion: which sounds come under the denomination of actions, rather than of speech. But should it be said that being able to convey to others the conceptions of his mind, by words adapted to the purpose, is a peculiar gift of nature, by which man is distinguished from other parts of the animated creation, the truth of this cannot be denied.

To which we may add that such communication may be made not only by words, but by signs or gestures, like those used to the dumb; it makes no difference, whether those signs or gestures have any natural connection with the thing they are intended to signify, or whether such a connection is only assigned to them by custom. Equivalent to such signs or gestures is handwriting, which may be considered, as a dumb language, deriving its force not merely from the words used, and the particular form of the letters, but from the real intention of the writer, to be gathered from thence: — to be gathered either from the resemblance between the characters and the intentions, as in the Egyptian hieroglyphics, or from pure fancy, as among the Chinese.

Here likewise another distinction is necessary to be applied in the same manner, as was done before, in order to remove all ambiguity in using the term Of THE LAW OF NATIONS. For it was there said, that the laws established by independent and separate states, whether or no those laws implied any mutual obligations, were denominated the LAW OF NATIONS. So that words, gestures, and signs, made use of to convey a meaning, imply an obligation, in all the persons concerned, to receive and employ them in their common acceptation. But the employment of OTHER MEANS, coming under NONE OF THOSE DESCRIPTIONS, cannot be construed into a violation of any social contract, although some may be deceived thereby. It is the REAL NATURE of the actions that is here spoken of, and not the ACCIDENTAL circumstances attending them: such actions for instance, as occasion no mischief; or if they do so, there is no guilt, where there is no treacherous design.

We have an instance of the former kind in the conduct of our Saviour, who, on the way to Emmaus, pretended to the disciples, that he was going further; here was a harmless stratagem, unless we interpret the words, as expressive of his intention to have gone further, if he had not been prevented by their efforts and entreaties to detain him. And in another part of the sacred history it is said, that he intended to have passed by the Apostles on the sea, that is, he intended to have done it, had he not been so earnestly importuned by them to go into the ship. There is another instance too in the conduct of Paul, who circumcised Timothy, though he knew the Jews would conclude from thence, that the ordinance of circumcision, which in reality had been abolished, was still binding upon the descendants of Israel, and that Paul and Timothy were of the same opinion. Whereas Paul had no such intention, but only hoped, by that means, to open for himself and Timothy a way to more familiar intercourse with the Jews. Neither could an ordinance of that kind, when the divine obligation was repealed, any longer be deemed of such importance, nor could the evil of a temporary error, resulting from thence, and afterwards to be corrected, be regarded as equivalent to the opportunity, which Paul thought to gain, of making it conducive to the introduction of Christian truth.

The Greek Fathers have given the name of ECONOMY, or MANAGEMENT to stratagems of this kind. On this subject there is an admirable sentiment in Clement of Alexandria, who, in speaking of a good man, says that "he will do many things for the benefit of his neighbour alone, which he would not otherwise have undertaken,"

One of these stratagems was practised by the Romans, who, during the time that they were besieged in the Capitol, threw some loaves of bread into the enemy's camp, that it might not be supposed they were pressed by famine. The feigned flight, which Joshua ordered his people to make, to assist him in his designs upon Ai, affords an instance of a stratagem of the second kind; the ensuing mischiefs of which may be considered, as some of the effects of lawful war. The ORIGINAL DESIGN of that pretended flight does not at all affect the question. The enemy took it for a proof of fear; and he was at liberty to do so, without debarring the other of his right to march this way, or that, with an accelerated or retarded motion, with a shew of courage, or an appearance of fear, as he might judge it most expedient.

History furnishes us with innumerable examples of deceptions practised with success upon an enemy, by assuming his arms, ensigns, colours, or uniforms; all which may be justified upon the same principle. For all these are actions, which any one may avail himself of at his pleasure, by departing from the usual course of his military system. For such points of 'discipline and system depend upon the will and fancy of the military commanders in each state, rather than upon any invariable custom, equally binding upon all nations.

**IX**. Those signs, by which the daily intercourse of life is maintained, form a subject of more weighty discussion, with which the consideration of lies or falsehood is necessarily interwoven.

All stratagems of this kind are so direct a violation of all moral principle, both in their nature and consequences, that almost every page of the revealed will of God declares their condemnation. Solomon describes a righteous, that is, a good man, as one, who holds every false word in detestation, deprecating the least appearance of deception: and the Apostle's injunction accords with these sentiments, instructing his disciples not to lie to one another.

Nor is it in the high standard of perfection alone, which the divine records present, that such a recommendation of fair, open, and sincere dealing is to be found. It is the theme of praise with poets and philosophers, and the angry hero of the Grecian poet declares, that he detests the man, as an infernal being, who utters one thing with his tongue, while he conceals another in his heart. But making some allowance for poetic fiction-we find even the grave, sober, and discerning, Stagirite describing falsehood, as a vile, and abominable refuge, and painting truth as a lovely object, that must extort the warmest praise.

These are all great and high authorities in favour of open dealing. Yet there are names of no less weight, both among sacred and profane writers, whose opinions are a vindication of stratagems, when used upon PROPER occasions. One writer speaks of a case, where stratagem may be used, even for the benefit of the person, on whom it is practised, and adduces the instances of a physician, who, by means of a deception, overcame the perverseness of a patient, and wrought a salutary cure.

**X**. To reconcile such a variety of discordant opinions, it may be necessary to devise some way of examining falsehood both in its more extensive, and more confined acceptation. Nor is speaking an untruth, UNAWARES, to be considered in the nature of a lie, but the falsehood, which comes within the limits here defined, is the KNOWN and DELIBERATE UTTERANCE of any thing contrary to our real conviction, intention, and understanding.

Words, or signs, importing the same meaning as words, are generally taken for conceptions of the mind, yet it is no lie for any man to utter a falsehood, which he believes to be true; but the propagation of a truth, which any one believes to be false, IN Him amounts to a lie. There must be in the use of the words therefore an INTENTION to deceive, in order to constitute a falsehood in the proper and common acceptation. Consequently, when any one single word, or the whole tenour of a discourse, admits of more significations than one, either by the use of some popular phrase, some term of art, or intelligible figure of speech, in that case if the speaker's intention correspond with any one of those meanings, he cannot be charged with using falsehood, although it is possible that a hearer may take his words in a very different sense. It is true that using such an ambiguous method of speaking on ALL OCCASIONS is not to be approved of, though there are particular circumstances under which it may be reconciled with honour and justice. In communicating knowledge, for instance, there is no harm in using a metaphor, an irony, or an hyperbole, figures of speech, tending either to adorn or to elucidate a subject. There are cases too, where by this doubtful mode of expression it may be proper to avoid an urgent and impertinent question. There is an instance of the former kind in our Saviour's saying, that "our friend Lazarus sleepeth," where the disciples understood him, as if he were speaking of the refreshing rest of an ordinary sleep: and when he spoke of restoring the temple, which he meant his own body, he knew that the Jews applied what he said to the MATERIAL EDIFICE Of the Temple. In the same manner he frequently addressed the multitudes in parables, which they could not understand by barely hearing, without that docility of mind, and attention, which the subject required. Profane history too furnishes us with an example of the second kind, in the conduct of Vitellius, who, as Tacitus informs us, gave Narcissus doubtful and ambiguous answers, in order to avoid his urgent questions; as any explicit declaration might have been attended with danger.

On the other hand, it may happen to be not only censurable, but even wicked to use such a manner of speaking, where either the honour of God or the welfare of mankind is concerned, or indeed any matter, which demands explicit avowals, and open dealing. Thus in contracts every thing necessary to their fulfillment ought to be fully disclosed to those concerned. There is an apposite expression of Cicero, who says, that every degree of deception ought to be banished from all contracts, and there is in the old Athenian Laws a proverb, conformable to this, which says, there must be nothing, but open dealing in markets.

**XI**. In strictness of speech such ambiguity is excluded from the notion of a lie. The common notion of a lie therefore is something spoken, written, marked, or intimated, which cannot be understood, but in a sense different from the real meaning of the speaker. But a lie, in this stricter acceptation, having some thing unlawful in its very nature, necessarily requires that a distinction should be made between it and that latitude of expression already explained. And if this acceptation be properly considered, at least according to the opinion prevailing in all nations, it seems, that no other explanation of it is necessary to be given, except that it is a violation of the existing and permanent rights of the person, to whom a discourse, or particular signs, are directed. It is a violation of the rights of ANOTHER; for it is evident, that no one can utter a falsehood with a view to impose upon himself. The rights here spoken of are peculiarly connected with this subject. They imply that liberty of judgment, which men are understood, by a kind of tacit agreement, to owe to each other in their mutual intercourse. For this, and this alone is that mutual obligation, which men intended to introduce, as soon as they began to use speech, or other signs of equal import. For without such an obligation the invention of those signs would have been perfectly nugatory. It is requisite too, that at the time a discourse is made, such a right or obligation should remain in full force.

A right may indeed have existed and afterwards have become obsolete, owing to the rise or occurrence of some new right: which is the case with a debt, that may be released by acquittance, or nonperformance of a condition. It is farther requisite, to constitute a VIOLATION OF THIS RIGHT, that the ensuing injury should immediately affect the PERSON ADDRESSED: as in contracts, there can be no injustice, but what affects one of the parties, or persons concerned.

And perhaps under the head of this right, it may not be improper to assign a place to that TRUE SPEAKING, which Plato, following Simonides, classes with justice, in order to form a more striking contrast with that falsehood, so often prohibited in Scripture, by the name of false witness to, or against, our neighbour, and which Augustin, in defining a lie, calls an intention to deceive. Cicero also in his offices lays down truth, as the basis of justice.

The right to a discovery of the whole truth may be relinquished by the express consent of the persons, who are engaged in a treaty: the one may declare his intention not to disclose certain points, and the other may allow of this reserve. There may be also a tacit presumption, that there are just reasons for such reserve which may perhaps be necessary out of regard to the rights of a third person: rights which, in the common judgment of all sober men, may be sufficient to counterbalance any obligation in either of the persons engaged in the treaty to make a full disclosure of his views and sentiments. These principles, duly considered, will supply many inferences to reconcile any seeming contradiction in the opinions, that have been advanced.

**XII**. In the first place, many things may be said to madmen, or children, the LITERAL MEANING of which may not be true, without incurring the guilt of willful falsehood. A practice which seems to be allowed by the common sense of all mankind. Quintilian, speaking of the age of puerility, says, it is a period of life, when many useful truths may be taught in the dress of fiction. Another reason given is, that as children and madmen possess no perfect power of judging, impositions of that kind can do no injury to their rights, in such respects.

**XIII**. Secondly, when a conversation is addressed to any one, who is not thereby deceived, although a third person, not immediately addressed, may misconceive the matter, there is no willful falsehood in the case. No WILFUL FALSEHOOD towards the person addressed: because he feels no greater injury from thence, than an intelligent hearer would do from the recital of a fable, or the use of a metaphor, irony, or hyperbole in speech. It cannot be said that an injury is done to the person, who accidentally and cursorily hears a matter, and misconceives it: for being no way concerned, there is no obligation due to him. As he misconceives a thing addressed to ANOTHER, and not to HIMSELF, he must take upon his own head all the consequences of the mistake. For, properly speaking, the discourse, WITH RESPECT TO HIM, IS no discourse, but an inexpressive sound that may signify one thing as well as another. So that there was nothing wrong in the conduct of Cato the Censor, who made a false promise of assistance to his confederates, nor in that of Flaccus, who informed others that Aemilius had taken the enemy's city by storm, although the enemy were deceived by it. Plutarch mentions an instance of the same kind in the life of Agesilaus. Here no communication was made to the enemy, and the prejudice he sustained was an accidental thing no way unlawful in itself, either to be wished for or procured.

**XIV**. In the third place, whenever it is certain that the person, on whom a deception is practised, discovers that the intent of it was to do him a service; he will not feel it as a grievance, nor can it come -under the strict denomination of a lie or falsehood. It will be no more an INJURY, than it would be a THEFT in any one, presuming upon an owner's consent, to take something belonging to that owner, in order to convert it to his use in a very beneficial way. For in cases of notorious certainty, a PRESUMPTION may be taken for express consent. But it is evident that no man would CONSENT to receive an INJURY.

From hence it appears, that a person is guilty of no treachery, who uses unfounded or fictitious motives to console a friend in distress, as Arria did to Paetus upon the death of his son, of which there is an account in Pliny's Epistles, or in a general, who in a perilous situation should avail himself of false intelligence, to encourage his troops, by which perhaps a victory might be gained.

It may be observed likewise, that the injury done to the freedom of judgment is, in such a case, of less consequence, because it is but momentary, and the real fact is soon discovered.

**XV**. There is a fourth case, which bears a near affinity to those above mentioned, and that is, when any one, possessing preeminent authority, orders another, in a subordinate capacity, to execute some device or stratagem, conducive either to his individual, or to the public welfare. Which Plato seems to have had particularly in view, in allowing those in authority to avail themselves of pretexts, or stratagems. The same writer is very correct in his notion of not making such a device a characteristic of that authority, which belongs to the supreme being. For all such devices, however justifiable they may be in CERTAIN CASES, strongly betray that imperfection, which is inseparable from all human systems.

The stratagem, which Joseph employed to obtain further discoveries without making himself known to his brethren, is much commended by Philo, as a mark of great policy, when, contrary to the convictions and feelings of his own mind, he accused them of being spies, and afterwards charged them with theft. It was by a stratagem of the same kind, that Solomon gave proof of his inspired wisdom, when he used the FICTITIOUS threat of dividing the living child in order to discover the real mother.

**XVI**. The fifth case, which allows a stratagem to be practised, is that, where it may be the ONLY means of saving the life of an innocent person, of obtaining some object of equal importance, or of diverting another from the perpetration of some horrid design. The heathen poet has given a beautiful illustration of this in his praises of Hypermnestra, whose conduct he calls "a splendid stratagem, ennobling the virgin to all posterity."

**XVII**. It is evident that many writers of acknowledged wisdom, and sober judgment, have carried the point farther than has been done in this treatise, in allowing the use of false representations to an enemy. In cases, where public enemies are concerned, they maintain, that it is lawful to deviate from those strict rules of avowing and disclosing all our intentions, which they prescribe, on all other occasions. Such is the opinion of Plato and Xenophon among the Greeks, of Philo among the Jews, and Chrysostom among Christians. It may not perhaps be amiss to cite, in this place, the message sent by the men of Jabesh Gilead to the Ammonites, by whom they were besieged, and also that of the prophet Elisha, and at the same time to mention the conduct of Valerius Laevinus, who boasted of having killed Pyrrhus.

The third, the fourth and fifth observations above made, may be illustrated from what is said by Eustratus, Archbishop of Nice, "An able and upright counsellor is not obliged to disclose the whole truth: for there may be occasions, when it may be necessary for him to recommend the means of deceiving an enemy, or to employ some stratagem towards a friend, where it may turn to his advantage."

**XVIII**. What has been said of false speaking must be understood as applied to affirmative declarations, which can be prejudicial to no persons, but public enemies: it can by no means be taken to include promises. For promises confer upon the person, to whom they are made, a peculiar right to claim their full performance. And this is a rule, which must take place, even between public enemies; a rule to which existing hostilities are not allowed to form an exception. It is a maxim proper to be enforced in TACIT, as well as in EXPRESS agreements:

as when a parley or conference is demanded, there is always an IMPLIED promise, that both sides shall attend it with perfect safety. But these are points reserved for the discussion of another part of this treatise.

**XIX**. It will be necessary to repeat an observation made before, with respect to oaths, both of the affirmative and promissory kind, where it was maintained that they exclude all exceptions, all mental reservations towards the person, to whom they are made, being regarded not merely as a solemn transaction with that individual, but as a steadfast appeal to God. Such an appeal to the supreme being demands the performance of an oath, even if it gave the individual no right to the same.

At the same time it was observed, that a sworn declaration is not like one of any other kind, where an application of terms different from their usual meaning may supply the speaker with an excuse for evading their import. But truth requires every declaration and promise to be made in terms, which it is supposed that every man of integrity and clear judgment will understand, spurning at the impious thought, that men may be deceived by oaths, as children are by toys and trifles.

**XX**. Some nations and individuals indeed have rejected the use of those stratagems, which even the law of nature allows to be employed as a means of self-defence against an enemy. But they did so, not from any opinion of their unlawfulness, but from a noble loftiness of mind, and from a confidence in their own strength. Aelian has preserved a saying of Pythagoras, "that there are two things, in which man approaches nearest to God, in always speaking the truth, and doing good to others." Aristotle, somewhere in his Ethics, calls speaking truth, the freedom of a great soul, and Plutarch says, that falsehood is the qualification of a slave. But an adherence to truth, in simplicity of heart, is not the only duty required of Christians, in this respect, they are commanded to abstain from all vain discourse, as having for their example him, in whose mouth there was found no guile.

**XXI**. With respect to the actions of men, there is another rule which may properly come under this head, and that is, the unlawfulness of urging or persuading any one to do an unlawful act. For instance, no subject has a right to lift his hand against his sovereign, to deliver up a town without public authority, or to despoil his neighbour of his goods. It would be unlawful then to encourage the subject of an enemy, as long as he continues his subject, to do any of these acts. For the person, who urges another to do a wicked act, makes himself a partner in his guilt. Nor can it be received as a just answer, that urging a subject to the perpetration of such a deed is nothing more than employing the lawful means of destroying an enemy. For though it may be necessary and just to destroy him, if possible, yet that is not the way, in which it should be done. Augustin has well observed, that it makes no difference whether any one should commit a crime himself, or employ another as his instrument.

But employing the spontaneous offers of a deserter's not contrary to the laws of war, and is a very different action from that of seducing a subject from his allegiance.

## CHAPTER 2: IN WHAT MANNER THE LAW OF NATIONS RENDERS THE PROPERTY OF SUBJECTS ANSWERABLE FOR THE DEBTS OF SOVEREIGNS. THE NATURE OF REPRISALS.

*No one but an heir bound by the act of another — Property of subjects answerable for the debts of sovereigns, according to the law of Nations — Capture of persons and property after satisfaction refused by the aggressor — Reprisals — Personal safety of subjects — Distinction made by the law of Nations in this respect.*

**I**. THE rights accruing from the law of Nations are the points next to be considered, which may be referred either to wars in GENERAL, or to those of a PARTICULAR description.

Wars in GENERAL are those, which properly first come under notice.

By the LITERAL law of nature, no one is bound by the actions of another, except the person, who succeeds to his property. For the introduction and establishment of property introduced and established also the power of transferring it with all its incumbrances. The Emperor Zeno however pronounces it repugnant to natural justice for one man to be molested for the debts of another. A principle, which gave rise to the distinctions in the Roman law, that the wife could not be sued for her husband, nor the husband for his wife, nor a son for his father, nor a father or mother for their son. Nor, as Ulpian clearly states it, could individuals be answerable for the debts of the community, and more especially if that community be possessed of property. Indeed if that were not the case individuals could only be obliged to contribute their due proportion, as members of that community.

Seneca says, "if any one lends money to my country, I am not to be considered as his debtor, nor to take the debt upon myself, though I am bound to pay my due proportion of it." There was a special provision made in the Roman law, that one peasant should not be bound for the debts of another, and it is laid down as a rule, that the goods of one person shall not be distrained for the debts of another, even if they be public debts; and in Justinian's Novels, pledges for others are forbidden, and the cause assigned for it is, because it is unreasonable that one person should incur the debt, and another be bound to the payment of it, an exaction to which the name of ODIOUS is given. King Theodoric Cassiodor, calls it a shocking licence for one man to be detained as a pledge for another.

**II** Although in the preceding observations there may be a great deal of truth, yet it is possible, and indeed appears actually to be the case, that the voluntary law of nations introduced the practice of rendering all the corporeal, and incorporeal property, belonging to the subjects of any state or sovereign, liable to the debts, which that state or sovereign may have incurred, either personally, or by refusing to make such reparation, as may be due for the injuries and aggressions, which they have committed.

Yet this is a practice, which nothing but necessity could justify; for, on any other ground, it would be opening a door to innumerable acts of wanton aggression and injustice against individuals. As the property of states and sovereigns cannot often so easily fall into an enemy's hand, as that belonging to individuals, who are more numerous, and whose property is consequently more exposed. So that rights of this kind are to be reckoned among those, which Justinian says, are the offspring of stern necessity, the calamities of men driving them to the use of such means.

But though a practice like this owes its introduction to NECESSITY, it is not so far at variance with the law of nature, as to exclude CUSTOM and TACIT agreement from having some share in its establishment. For we find that sureties are bound by no other tie, but that alone of having given their consent. Besides, it might easily be supposed, that it was the best method of redress against the subjects of another state, where the aggrieved persons could not so easily prosecute their rights, or obtain indemnities, the claims or injuries of strangers being but little understood, and perhaps still less regarded in a foreign land.

Subjects, being thus liable to the loss of their property, by the conduct of their fellow subjects, or by that of the state, might sometimes feel it a hardship, while on other occasions, it would prove their greatest security against aggressions from the subjects of another power.

That this was a received custom appears not only from the regular wars, carried on by one state against another, the rules observed in which are often named in the manifestoes issued on such occasions: the form of which may be seen in the first book of Livy, where it is said, "I declare war against the ancient nations of the Latins, and likewise against the respective individuals"; and the same writer, in his thirty first book, informs us, that, upon the question being put to the people, they were asked, whether it was their pleasure that war should be declared against Philip, and against the Macedonians, his subjects.- But the same custom also prevailed, even before the commencement of actual and open hostilities between two states, when mutual acts of aggression by the subjects of each power could be regarded as nothing but the eve, and prelude to a declaration of war. The words used by Agesilaus to Pharnabazus will serve to elucidate this point: he said; "While we were friends to the king of Persia, we treated him and his subjects in a friendly manner: now we are enemies, you can expect nothing from us but hostilities. Therefore, Pharnabazus, while you chuse to continue a vassal to the King, we wound him through your sides."

**III.** The Athenians had a method somewhat like this of seeking redress, a seizure of men's persons, which was laid down in the Attic law in the following terms, "if any one has been murdered in a foreign country, the nearest relatives of the deceased are authorized to seize any three subjects of that country, but not more than three, till the perpetrators of the deed be punished, or at least delivered up to the hands of justice for that purpose."

In this case we find that the personal liberty of subjects, which may be considered as a kind of incorporeal right, including the right of residing where they please, or doing whatever they may think proper, is made answerable for the debt of the state, who is bound to punish the criminal acts of her subjects: so that the subject suffers constraint, till the state has discharged the debt, which it is bound to pay; and by the payment of this debt is meant the punishment of the guilty. For although the Egyptians, as we learn from Diodorus Siculus, maintained that neither the person, nor liberty of any one ought to be bound or constrained for a debt, there is nothing in it repugnant to the law of nature, and by the practice not only of the Greeks, but of other nations, the opposite opinion seems to have been established.

Aristocrates, who was contemporary with Demosthenes had made a motion for a decree, that if any one killed Charidemus, it might be lawful to seize him, wherever he was to be found, and that any one, who attempted to rescue that person, should be deemed an enemy. Demosthenes finds fault with many parts of this decree For in the first place, Aristocrates had omitted making a proper distinction between murder and a lawful putting to death, the latter of which is an act of justice: in the next place, he has said nothing of bringing the per. son to a regular trial: besides, it was not the persons, among whom the murder had been committed, but those who afterwards received the murderer, that were to be declared enemies. Demosthenes says, that "the regular law prescribes, that if the persons in whose district a murder has been committed, neither punish, nor deliver up the perpetrator of the crime, three of their people shall be liable to be seized. But this decree, allowing the persons in whose district it has been committed to escape with impunity, not even naming THEM, passes sentence upon those, who in conformity to the common laws of humanity have received the fugitive, if they do not deliver him up, which would be a breach of the protection due to a suppliant."

The fourth point, in which he blames Aristocrates, is for having carried matters to the extremities of open and actual war, in a case, where the law only authorized the seizure and detention of particular persons. Of these arguments, the first, the second, and the fourth, are by no means destitute of weight. But the third argument, unless it be confined entirely to the circumstance of accidental death, or that necessarily occasioned by defending one's self, may be regarded more as an oratorical flourish than a just and solid reason. For the law of nations extends the privileges, and character of suppliants to those only, who have left their country on account of misfortune, and not owing to crimes. Indeed if the law of nations made no such distinction, the persons, among whom a crime has been committed, and who may be suspected of having countenanced the deed, and those who barely refuse to punish or deliver up the guilty fugitive, would be upon an equal footing as to right. So that it was either USAGE, which GRADUALLY introduced the above interpretation of that law, to which Demosthenes appeals, or it was afterwards more EXPRESSLY ESTABLISHED, in order to avoid such cavils. For no one can deny the truth of one of these positions who has attended to the observation of Julius Pollux, that "the seizure and detainder of persons can be enforced, whenever a power cannot obtain the surrender of fugitive murderers, which they demand. In this case the aggrieved power or individual may seize and detain any three of the people belonging to the state, which refuses to make that surrender."

It is upon the same principle that any power may detain the subjects of another state, in order to procure the release of any subjects of her own, unjustly seized, and imprisoned by that state.

**IV**. Another method of obtaining redress for any violation of persons, or property is by having recourse to what, in modern language, are called REPRISALS, which the Saxons and Angles denominated WITHERNAM, and to which the French gave the name of LETTERS OF MARQUE, and those were usually obtained from the crown.

**V**. It is generally understood that recourse may be had to this method of redress not only against a foreign aggressor, but also against a debtor, if justice cannot be obtained in due time: but in NOTORIOUS cases, which admit of no doubt, this right may be enforced even beyond the strict letter of the law. For even in DOUBTFUL matters, the presumption will always be in favour of judges appointed by public authority. For it is unlikely that they should GREATLY, or WANTONLY exceed their power; especially when, if so inclined, they have not the same means of enforcing their decrees against foreigners, as against their fellow subjects. Indeed even in disputes between subjects of the same country, they cannot annul a just debt. Paulus, the Lawyer, says that a REAL DEBTOR, though discharged, owing to some informality or inability of the law to enforce payment, still remains a debtor according to the law of nature.

And when, in consequence of a judicial sentence, a creditor, under pretext of seizing his own property, had taken from a debtor something which did not belong to him though it was in his possession: upon the discharge of the debt, a doubt arising whether the thing should be restored to the debtor, Scaevola maintained that it certainly ought to be restored.

There is a difference between the two cases. For subjects, AS SUCH, cannot make any violent resistance to the execution of a sentence, which they may not deem satisfactory, nor can they prosecute any right in opposition to the law. FOREIGNERS may use violent means to enforce a right: tho' they are not justified in using such means, while there is any possibility of obtaining redress in a legal, and peaceable manner.

It is on such grounds that reprisals are made upon the persons and property of the subjects, belonging to a power, who refuses to grant redress and reparation for injuries and aggressions. It is a practice not literally enacted by the law of nature, but generally received through custom. It is a practice too of the greatest antiquity: for in the eleventh book of the Iliad, we find Nestor giving an account of the reprisals, which he had made upon the Epeian nation, from whom he took a great number of cattle, as a satisfaction for a prize which his father Nelcus had won at the Elian games; and for debts due to many private subjects of the Pylian kingdom. Out of this booty the king having selected his own due, equitably divided the rest among the other creditors.

**VI**. It has been a received opinion with many nations, that reprisals might be made even upon the LIVES of innocent subjects, owing to the right, which it was supposed that every one had over his own life, and which might be transferred from the individual to the state. A doctrine, which, as it was proved in the first book of this treatise, can never be reconciled either to sound religion or morality. Indeed a person may ACCIDENTALLY, though not INTENTIONALLY be killed by us in attempting to prevent him from violently obstructing us in the prosecution of a lawful right. Yet if such an accidental calamity could be foreseen, the law of charity, setting so pre-eminent a value upon the life of man, would in such a case prescribe the forbearance of our right.

**VII**. But on this, as well as other points, we must take care not to confound the natural and fundamental law of nations, with the civil and conventional law of particular states.

By the law of nations all the permanent subjects, both natives and settlers, of an offending state or sovereign are 'liable to suffer reprisals: but the same rule does not bind those, who are passing through a country, or only residing in it for a time. For such reprisals are a kind of pledges, like public burdens, made answerable for the public debts, from which foreigners, being temporary residents, though owing obedience to the laws, are totally exempt.

In the same manner, Ambassadors, but not those sent from an enemy to our enemies, and their property, are exempt from such conditions by the law of nations. By the CIVIL LAW too Of many countries an exception is made in favour of women and children, of men of letters, and those who are travelling for the purposes of trade. But by the LAW OF NATIONS the goods of all are liable to reprisals, as was the case at Athens, respecting the seizure of persons. In many places, by the civil law, the right of making reprisals is obtained of the sovereign, and in others, of the judges.

By the law of nations the property of all captures is devoted to discharge the debt, and defray the expenses incurred, the remainder of which, after due satisfaction obtained, and peace concluded, should be restored. By the civil law the persons interested are summoned to appear, the property is sold by public authority, and the money, accruing from thence, divided among all who are entitled to a share of the same. But these and other points of the same kind are to be learned from civilians, who are conversant in such matters, and particularly from Bartolus, who has written upon reprisals. This subject may be closed with one observation, that will in some measure tend to soften the rigour of this stern, but necessary right, and that observation is, that such as by not discharging a debt, or granting redress. have occasioned reprisals to be made, are bound, in justice and honour, to make good the losses of those, who have thereby suffered.

## CHAPTER 3: ON JUST OR SOLEMN WAR ACCORDING TO THE LAW OF NATIONS ON DECLARATIONS OF WAR.

*Solemn war, according to the Law of Nations between different states — A people, though engaged in unjust war, to be distinguished from pirates and robbers — Change in the condition of belligerents — Formal war can be made by the Sovereign power alone — Declaration of war — The Law of Nature, Law of Nations, respecting the same — Declaration, conditional, absolute — Forms of declaration introduced by the civil law — War declared against a Sovereign includes his subjects, and allies — The reason why allies are included — Declarations, why necessary to establish certain effects — Whether actual warfare immediately follows a declaration, considered — Whether the violation of an Ambassador's rights to be a just ground of war.*

**I.** IN THE first book of this treatise it was observed, that according to the best writers, a war is defined to be just, not on account of the CAUSES solely, in which it originates, nor on account of the MAGNITUDE of its objects, but from certain, peculiar, effects of right, with which it is attended.

But to what kind of war such an appellation most duly belongs will be best understood by considering the definition, which the Roman Lawyers have given of a PUBLIC or NATIONAL enemy. Those, *says Pomponius*, are PUBLIC and LAWFUL ENEMIES, with whose STATE our own is engaged in war: but enemies of every other description, come under the denomination of pirates and robbers. With that opinion Ulpian entirely accords, making an additional observation, that "if any one be taken by robbers, as he is not a lawful prisoner of war, he cannot claim of his own state the right of postliminium. But if he be taken prisoner by a public enemy of the state, being considered as a prisoner Of war, he is entitled by the right of postliminium to be restored to his former condition. "

These opinions are supported by that of Paulus, who maintains, that persons captured by pirates still continue free, that is, are not to be considered as prisoners, for whom an exchange may be demanded. So that by the opinion of the Roman Lawyers it is evident, that no war is considered to be lawful, regular, and formal, except that which is begun and carried on by the sovereign power of each country. Cicero, in h s fourth Philippic, describes "a public and authorised enemy to be the person, who possesses the civil and military powers of the state, who can command the treasury, and the services of the people in support of his measures, and who, as occasions offer, has power to conclude treaties of peace and amity."

**II**. A state, though it may commit some act of aggression, or injustice, does not thereby lose its political capacity, nor can a band of pirates or robbers ever become a state, although they may preserve among themselves that degree of subordination, which is absolutely necessary to the subsistence of all society. For with the latter, the commission of crime is the SOLE bond of union, whereas the former, though not always free from blame, but occasionally deviating from the laws of, nature, which in many cases have been in a great measure obliterated, still regulate their conduct by the treaties, which they have made, and certain customs that have been established, being united among themselves for the mutual support of lawful rights, and connected with foreign states by known rules of standing polity.

The Scholiast, upon Thucydides, remarks that the Greeks, at the time when piracy was reckoned lawful, forebore committing massacres, or nightly depredations, and carrying off the oxen that were necessary for the plough. We are informed by Strabo, that other nations too, who lived by plunder, after they had returned home from their predatory voyages, sent messages to the owners, whom they had plundered, to know if they would redeem the captures at a fair price.

In morals, the whole system often derives its name from some one of the principal parts, as Cicero remarks, in the fifth book of his BOUNDS of GOOD and EVIL, and Galen observes that a mixture is often called by the name of its chief ingredient. So that Cicero is not altogether correct in saying, that a state is not merely diseased, but entirely destroyed, by the injustice of its component and leading members. For a morbid body is still a body, and a state, though dreadfully diseased, is still a political being, as long as its laws and tribunals and other necessary parts of its constitution remain, to administer justice and give redress to foreigners, no less than to private subjects in their actions against each other.

There is a beautiful observation in Dion Chrysostom, who compares the law of a state, particularly that branch of it relating to the law of nations, to the body animated by the soul, upon the departure of which the corporeal frame becomes a mass of lifeless clay: in the same manner political society cannot subsist without the guiding and controuling principle of law. Aristides, encouraging the Rhodians to harmony, observes, that even under a tyrannical government many good laws may be found.

These are points, which may be cleared up by examples. Thus Ulpian maintains that those who are captured by pirates cannot be considered as prisoners of war: but if captured by the Germans, for instance, or any national enemy, they lose their liberty for a time. But the Germans, as we are informed by Caesar, thought acts of plunder, if committed in a foreign territory, no disgrace. Tacitus says that the Cattians, a noble race of people in Germany, and the Garamantians were addicted to the same habits of plunder, yet still retained their rank among states. — Such is the difference between a national and political body, and a band of men uniting together SOLELY FOR THE COMMISSION OF CRIMES.

**III**. A change may occur not only in the situations of individuals, as in those of Jephthah, Arsaces, and Viriatus, who, from being leaders of voluntary bands, became lawful commanders; but the same has also happened with respect to whole communities, which being originally composed of nothing but freebooters have, by the gradual course and changes of time, risen to the rank and dignity of states.

**IV**. What has been said with respect to the right of making formal and lawful war, being vested in the sovereign power alone, includes those who have any share in the sovereign power, as the different communities forming the States General of many commonwealths. The same rule will hold good of those, who are not SUBJECTS of a superior state, but joined to it in confederacy by an unequal treaty: innumerable instances of which are to be found in history. This was the case between the Romans and their allies, the Volscians, the Latins, and the Spaniards: and all whom we read of being engaged in wars, which were considered as lawful and just.

**V**. But to make a war just, according to this meaning, it must not only be carried on by the sovereign authority on both sides, but it must also be duly and formally declared, and declared in such a manner, as to be known to each of the belligerent powers. Cicero, in the first book of his offices, points out "the equity of the rules prescribed by the Roman Law for the declaration of war, from whence it may be concluded that no war is regular or just, but such as is undertaken to compel restitution, and to procure indemnity for injuries, and that too accompanied with a formal declaration." Livy also in the same manner deems an observance of these rules requisite to form the characteristic of a just war. And describing an incursion of the Acarnanians into Attica, and their ravaging the country, he says that "those acts of irritation ended in a declaration Of JUST and REGULAR war on both sides."

**VI**. In order to understand all these points clearly respecting the declaration of war, an accurate distinction must be made between the principles, which are founded on the law of nature itself, and those, which, though not derived immediately from that source, are still found to be just: it will be necessary also to examine, what is required by the law of nations towards obtaining, IN WAR, all the consequences, privileges and effects of that law, and, at the same time, to investigate the consequences and rights arising from the peculiar laws and customs of particular nations.

To repel force, or to punish a delinquent, the law of nature requires no declaration. And, as Thucydides relates, Sthenelaidas, one of the Ephori, maintains that "where we have been injured, not by WORDS, but by ACTIONS, the matter cannot be decided by WORDS and FORMS." And Aelian, after Plato, observes that it is not the declaration of the Herald, but the voice and law of nature, which proclaim war, undertaken to repel force. Hence Dion Chrysostom, in addressing the Nicomedians, says that many wars are begun without any declaration.

Upon the same ground Livy condemns the conduct of Menippus, a general belonging to Antiochus for having killed some Roman citizens before any declaration of war had been made, or even before a sword had been drawn, or a drop of blood spilt, to shew that hostilities were intended. By this objection he proves that either a formal declaration, or some act indicative of hostilities was deemed requisite to justify actual warfare.

Neither, if we follow the law of nature, is there any more occasion for notice or declaration, where an owner intends to lay hands upon HIS OWN PROPERTY. But when. ever one thing is taken in return for another, or the property of a debtor is seized for the recovery of a debt, and, especially, if any one intends seizing the property of those, who are subjects to the debtor, a formal demand must be made, as a proof that recourse to such security is the only means left of obtaining redress and satisfaction. Such a demand is necessary because that is not a PRIMARY and ORIGINAL right, but a SECONDARY right, SUBSTITUTED in the place of the primary and original, by the artificial rules of civil law.

In the same manner to justify an attack upon a sovereign power for the aggressions and debts of its subjects, a previous remonstrance, and a proper demand of justice must be made to that power. For it is only by refusing to punish the guilty, or to grant indemnity to the injured, that states or sovereigns can be implicated in the misconduct of their subjects. But even where the law of nature does not directly prescribe that such a remonstrance or demand should be made, yet the common principles of humanity and equity will recommend the use of any means, that may prevent recourse to the calamities of war. The commandment given by God to the Hebrews, to send a message of peace to any state or city, before they began an intended attack, was designed as a special command to that people, yet some have confounded it with the general law of nations. For it was not ANY kind of peace that was meant by that in. junction, but only such a peace as imposed terms of SUBJECTION and TRIBUTE. We are informed by Xenophon, that when Cyrus went into the country of the Armenians, he sent messengers to the king, to demand the tribute and number of troops, which had been stipulated by treaty.

But to obtain the peculiar rights and consequences resulting from the law of nations, a declaration of war by one of the parties, at least, if not by both, is absolutely requisite in all cases.

**VII**. Those declarations are either conditional or absolute. A conditional declaration is that which is coupled with a demand of restitution or redress. Under the name of restitution, the FECIAL LAW of Rome, that is the LAW RESPECTING DECLARATIONS OF WAR, comprehended not only the claims, which OWNERSHIP established, but the prosecution Of EVERY right arising from criminal or civil causes.

Hence the declarations were couched in terms, requiring restoration, satisfaction, or surrender. Here, by the term, surrender, the party appealed to is understood to have the option either of punishing the offender, himself, or delivering him up to the aggrieved person. This manner of demanding restitution is, according to the testimony of Pliny, called CLARIGATION, that is, a LOUD and FORMAL DEMAND. Livy gives us an example of a conditional and qualified declaration, wherein the aggrieved power denounces "a determined resolution to prosecute her rights with the utmost violence, if the aggressor will not make reparation and atonement for the injury he has done." Tacitus also relates the substance of a dispatch sent to Caecina by Germanicus, wherein he declares, that "if the ringleaders of the mutinous and rebellious legions are not immediately punished, he will advance with his army, and put the whole to the sword. "

An ABSOLUTE declaration of war is issued, where any power has already begun hostilities, or committed acts which call for exemplary punishment. Sometimes indeed a conditional, is followed by an absolute war, though in such a case the latter is not actually necessary, but only a confirmation of the former. This gave rise to the form, which says, "an appeal is hereby made against such a people, as unjust and refusing to grant redress." There is another form also purporting, that "the principal herald of the Roman citizens has made known to the principal herald of the ancient Latins, and to the Latin people, that redress is demanded of them by just and lawful war, on account of all the disputes which they have refused to settle, and the indemnities which they have been bound to grant, and have refused; and that this is the only means remaining to recover all that has been unjustly detained." There is also a third mode of declaration, which runs in the following tenour; "Since the ancient people of the Latins have committed aggressions against the people of Rome, the people of Rome, with the advice and consent of the senate, declare war against them, and in the name of the senate and people of Rome their purpose is thus published."

But that in case Of RENEWED wars such a declaration is not absolutely necessary, appears from the circumstance of its being made in due form at the nearest garrison, and not PERSONALLY to the offender himself, according to the answer given by the heralds, when they were consulted in the case of Philip of Macedon, and afterwards respecting Antiochus. Whereas a declaration for the FIRST time should be made to the enemy himself. Indeed in the war against Pyrrhus the declaration was made to one of his soldiers, in the Flaminian Circus, where, as Servius observes in his notes on the sixth book of the Aeneid, he was commanded to purchase a piece of ground, as a handle for dispute. A proof also that IN SOME CASES a declaration is superfluous may be taken from the circumstance that war is frequently declared by BOTH SIDES, which was done by the Corcyraeans and Corinthians in the Peloponnesian war, though a declaration by one of the parties would have been sufficient.

**VIII**. As to the use of the caduceum, or staff with the figure of two snakes twisted around it, which ambassadors carried, when they sued for peace, it was a ceremony peculiar to the GREEKS, and not derived from the GENERAL law of nations. The ROMANS in the same manner had particular customs, such as using vervain in forming alliances, throwing a bloody spear, as a declaration of war, renouncing all former friendship and alliance at the expiration of thirty days, after satisfaction had been demanded and refused, and again throwing another spear. None of these PECULIAR customs ought to be confounded with the GENERAL law of nations. For Arnobius informs us, that in his time many of them had fallen into disuse, and even in the time of Varro some of them were omitted. The third Punic war indeed was not declared till the moment of its actual commencement

**IX**. A declaration of war, made against a sovereign, includes not only his own subjects, but all who are likely to become his associates, as thereby they make themselves accessories in the war. And this is what the modern lawyers mean, when they say that, in bidding defiance to a Prince, we bid defiance to all his associates. For they give the name of defiance to a declaration of war. By which is understood the war carried on with the power against whom it has been declared. Thus upon war being declared against Antiochus, there was no occasion for a separate declaration against the Aetolians, who had openly joined Antiochus. For, as the heralds in their answer justly observed, the Aetolians had, by that act voluntarily brought war upon themselves.

**X**. But if after the conclusion of such a war it should be deemed expedient to attack any other nation or king for having furnished supplies and assistance towards that war, a new declaration of war will be necessary. For that nation or king is then to be considered, not as an accessory, but as a principal enemy. And therefore it was with reason said, that the war of Manlius against the Galatians, and that of Caesar against Ariovistus, were not just wars according to the law of nations. For war was made upon them not as accessories, but as principals. So that for this purpose, as the law of nations would have required a declaration, in the same manner the Roman law would have required a new order of the Senate.

For on the motion being made for the war with Antiochus, the question was also put, whether it should not at the same time be made with his adherents. The same rule also being observed against King Perseus, it must be understood, as including the adherents during all the time that war with those princes continued; and implicating all, who in reality gave them support.

**XI**. The reason why a declaration is necessary to constitute what is deemed, according to the law of nations, a just war, is not that which some writers assign. For they allege that it is to prevent every appearance of clandestine and treacherous dealing: an openness, which may be dignified with the name of magnanimity, rather than entitled a matter of right. On this point, we are informed that some nations have gone so far, as to settle and make known the very time and place of a general engagement.

But waving all conjecture, a more satisfactory reason may be found in the necessity that it should be known for CERTAIN, that a war is not the PRIVATE undertaking of bold ADVENTURERS, but made and sanctioned by the PUBLIC and SOVEREIGN authority on both sides; so that it is attended with the effects of binding all the subjects of the respective states; — and it is accompanied also with other consequences and rights, which do not belong to wars against pirates, and to civil wars.

**XII**. There is much truth indeed in the observations, which some have made, and which they have produced examples to confirm, that even in wars of this kind all captures become the lawful prize of the captors.

Yet this is only partially true, and that too, according to the law of nature, and not according to the voluntary law of nations. For the latter only makes provision to secure the rights of nations, as WHOLE communities, and not of those, who, as in civil wars, form but ONE PART Of a nation.

The same writers are mistaken too in the supposition that defensive wars require no declaration. For it is no less necessary to shew by way of vindication that it is a defensive war, and at the same time by public declaration to give it the character of a national and lawful war, in order to establish those rights and consequences, that have been already mentioned, and which will hereafter be more fully explained.

**XIII**. They maintain another position also, which is by no means true, and that is, that a power ought not IMMEDIATELY to follow up a declaration of war with actual hostilities, as Cyrus did to the Armenians, and the Romans to the Carthaginians. For the law of nations requires the intervention of no DEFINITE time between the declaration and the commencement of war.

There may indeed be some cases, where natural justice will render such a delay proper. Thus, for instance, where reparation for injury, or the punishment of aggressors is demanded, it is but reasonable to wait till it can be known, whether the just demand will be complied with or rejected.

**XIV**. In order to establish the same consequences, a declaration will be equally necessary too, where the rights of Ambassadors have been violated. Yet it will be sufficient for it to be made in the manner, in which it may be done with the greatest safety. As in many other matters, in places which afford no security, satisfaction is demanded by denunciation or summons.

## CHAPTER 4: ON THE RIGHT OF KILLING AN ENEMY IN LAWFUL WAR, AND COMMITTING OTHER ACTS OF HOSTILITY.

*General explanation of the effects of formal war — Distinction between lawful and innocent impunity — Merit of the latter — Examples added to explain it — General effects of former war considered with respect to lawful impunity — The reason of their introduction — Historical testimonies — By this right all persons, found within an enemy's territory, objects of hostility — Also all going thither before the war — The subjects of an enemy liable to be seized everywhere, except protected by the laws of a neutral territory — Case of women and children — Case of prisoners — Of those whose voluntary offer of surrender is rejected — Unconditional surrender — Retaliation — Obstinate defence — Hostages.*

**I**. SERVIUS in his comment on the passage of Virgil, where that poet says that war "will authorise mutual acts of destruction and rapine," in tracing the fecial or herald's law to Ancus Martius, and even beyond him to a still more remote period, remarks that, "if ever the persons or property of subjects, belonging to the Roman state, were seized and carried off by any other nation, the principal Herald, or King at arms went out with the sacred ministers, who presided at the making of solemn treaties, and proceeding to the verge of the territories of the offending nation, declared with a loud voice the cause of the war, and the refusal of that nation either to restore what had been seized, or to deliver up the aggressors to justice. After this he threw a spear to indicate that war and all its consequences were from that moment begun."

The commentator had previously observed that the ancients gave the name of rapine to every act of hostility even where there was no act of plunder committed; and they likewise called every kind of restitution a satisfaction.

By this explanation we learn that whenever war is proclaimed between two states or sovereigns, it is accompanied with certain rights or consequences, which do not NECESSARILY belong to war itself. And this is perfectly conformable to the examples from the Roman Lawyers, which have been before produced.

**II**. But it will be proper to consider how far the lawfulness, which Virgil speaks of, extends. For the term lawful sometimes implies whatever is just and pious in all respects, although the pursuit of a different course may perhaps be more laudable: according to the expression of St. Paul, who says, "all things are lawful to me, but all things are not expedient." Ulpian is speaking of a seller, who, at the expiration of a certain period, is not answerable for the safety of goods, which a buyer has neglected to take away, says he, will yet think himself bound in EQUITY to preserve them with all imaginable care. On some occasions when it is said, that men may LAWFULLY do a thing, the expression only means that doing such act will not subject them to human and legal penalties, but it by no means indicates that the action is strictly conformable to the rule of religion and morality. Thus among the Lacedaemonians and Egyptians stealing was allowed: an indulgence that by no means took away the GUILT of theft.

Cicero in the fifth of his Tusculan questions, speaking of Cinna, beautifully and justly points out this abuse of the word, LAWFUL. He seems to me, says HE, a wretched man indeed for having done those acts, and for having been in a situation, where they might be thought lawful, It can never be lawful for any man to do wrong: but we fall into a great mistake in the use of that word: for we consider a thing to be lawful, which any one may do with impunity." This is the meaning, in which the term is generally understood, as the same orator, in addressing the judges in behalf of Rabirius Posthumus, observes, "it behoves you to consider, what is becoming your character, and not what the rigour of the law allows you to inflict. For if you consult the full extent of your authority, you may make away with any citizen you please."

In the same manner legislators, as it was proved in a former book of this treatise, are not accountable, in their legislative capacity, to any human tribunal, for the laws, which they make, yet they cannot, in a moral point of view, avail themselves of this transcendent power to enact a thing that is evidently unjust. In this sense we often meet with a distinction made between what is proper or right, and what is lawful. Thus Cicero, in his speech for Milo, makes the LAW OF NATURE the standard of what is RIGHT, and LEGAL AUTHORITY, the standard of what is lawful.

**III**. Thus qualified, the annoyance of an enemy, either in his person or property, is lawful. This right extends not only to the power engaged in a just war, and who in her hostilities confines herself within the practice established by the law of nature, but each side without distinction has a right to employ the same means of annoyance. So that any one taken in arms, even in another's territory, cannot be treated as a robber, malefactor, or murderer, nor can even that neutral power, in whose territory he is taken, treat him as an enemy, for being found in arms.

**IV**. This principle was established by nations to prevent others from interfering in their disputes, or giving the law to them respecting the rights of war. Besides, if this were not the case, neutral powers would frequently be involved in the wars of others. A reason which the people of Marseilles urged in the dispute between Caesar and Pompey. They alleged that they had neither sufficient judgment to determine on which side justice lay, nor, if they could determine, had they strength to give effect to their decisions.

A spectator indeed is but ill qualified to judge, how far, even in the most just war, self-defence, the attainment of indemnity, or the punishment of an aggressor, may be carried. These are points, which, on many, if not most, occasions must be left to the conscience and discretion of the belligerents themselves: a mode far preferable to that of appealing to the mediation, and decision of disinterested and neutral powers. Livy has given an address of the Achaeans to the senate, in which they ask, "how their availing themselves of the rights of war can ever be fairly called in question, or made a subject of discussion?"

Besides the impunity attending certain actions done in war, the acquisition of territory by the right of conquest is another topic of consideration, which will hereafter be examined.

**V**. The lawfulness of injuring or destroying the person of a public enemy is supported by the testimony of many of the best writers, both poets, moralists, and historians. In one of the tragedies of Euripides, there is a proverb, which says, that "to kill a public enemy, or an enemy in war is no murder." Therefore the custom of the ancient Greeks, which rendered it unlawful and impious to use the same bath, or to partake of the same festivities and sacred rites with a person who had killed another in time of peace, did not extend to any one who had killed a public enemy in war. Killing an enemy is in. deed everywhere called a right of war. "The rights of war, says Marcellus in Livy, support me in all that I have done against the enemy." And the same historian gives the address of Alcon to the Saguntines, where he says, "You ought to bear these hardships, rather than suffer your own bodies to be mangled, and your wives and children to be seized and dragged away before your eyes." Cicero in his speech in defence of Marcellus passes a high encomium upon the clemency of Caesar, who, "by the laws of war and the rights of victory, might have put to death all, whom he had spared and protected." And Caesar observes to the Eduans, that "it was an act of kindness in HIM, to spare those whom the laws of war would have authorised him to put to death."

But the rights of war, for which these writers plead, could not PERFECTLY JUSTIFY the putting prisoners to death, but could only grant IMPUNITY to those who availed them. selves of the barbarous custom. There is a wide difference however between actions like these, and destroying an enemy by proper means of hostility. For, as Tacitus says, "in the leisure hours of peace the merits and demerits of every case may be examined and weighed, but, in the tumult and confusion of war, the innocent must fall with the guilty": and the same writer, in another place, observes, that "there are many actions, which the principles of humanity cannot ENTIRELY approve, but which the policy of war requires." And it is in this, and no other sense that Lucan has said, "the complexion of right may be assigned to what is wrong."

**VI**. This right of making lawful what is done in war is of great extent. For in the first place it comprises, in the number of enemies, not only those who actually bear arms, or who are immediately subjects of the belligerent power, but even all who are within the hostile territories, as appears from the form given by Livy, who says, that "war is declared against the sovereign, and all within his jurisdiction." For which a very good reason may be assigned; because danger is to be apprehended even from THEM, which, in a continued and regular war, establishes the right now under discussion.

Reprisals do not come exactly under the same rule. For like taxes, they were introduced for the discharge of public debts, for no part of which temporary residents, or foreigners are answerable. Therefore Baldus is right in his observation, that, after war is actually begun, much greater latitude is allowed, than in the bare right of making reprisals. So that what is said of foreigners, who enter into an enemy's country, and reside there, after war is avowedly declared and begun, is undoubtedly true.

**VII**. But persons, who had gone to reside there before the war was begun, seem by the law of nations to be included in the number of enemies, unless within a reasonable time they chuse to withdraw. So that the Corcyraeans, when going to besiege Epidamnus, gave leave to all strangers to withdraw, denouncing that they would otherwise be treated as enemies.

**VIII**. But the persons of natural-born subjects, who owe permanent allegiance to a hostile power may, according to the law of nations, be attacked, or seized, wherever they are found. For whenever, as it was said before, war is declared against any power, it is at the same time declared against all the subjects of that power. And the law of nations authorises us to attack an enemy in every place: An opinion supported by most legal authorities: thus Marcian says "that deserters may be killed in the same manner as enemies, wherever they are found." They may be lawfully killed there, or in their own country, in the enemy's country, in a country belonging to no one, or on the sea. But as to the unlawfulness of killing, or violently molesting them in a neutral territory, this protection does not result from any personal privileges Of THEIR OWN, but from the rights of the SOVEREIGN Of that country. For all civil societies had an undoubted right to establish it as a standing maxim that no violence should be offered to any person within their territories, nor any punishment inflicted but by due process of law. For where tribunals retain their authority in full vigour, to try the merits of every offence, and, after impartial inquiry, to acquit the innocent, or condemn the guilty, the power of the sword must be restrained from inflicting promiscuous death.

Livy mentions the circumstance of seven Carthaginian gallies riding at anchor in a port belonging to Syphax, who was then at peace with the Carthaginians and Romans. Scipio arrived at that time, with two gallies, which might have been attacked and sunk by the Carthaginians before they could enter the port: a brisk wind rising carried them in, before the Carthaginians could weigh anchor; but out of respect to the king's authority they durst not attack the Romans in his harbour.

**IX**. But to return to the subject, which is, to decide how far the power of lawfully destroying an enemy, and all that belong to him, extends. An extent of which we may form some conception from the very circumstance, that even women and children are frequently subject to the calamities and disasters of war. There is no occasion to allege in this place, as an example, the conduct of the Hebrews, who slew the women and children of the Heshbonites, and who were commanded to execute vengeance upon the Canaanites, and upon all, who were involved in the same guilt Those examples, where God MANIFESTLY interposes his commands, are not to be drawn into a precedent for authorising actions of the SAME kind on DIFFERENT occasions. For the supreme and disposing power of God can never properly be compared with that, which men are allowed to exercise over each other. The Psalmist's expression of the Babylonian children being dashed against the stones is a much stronger proof of the custom commonly prevailing among nations, in the use of victory, to which the language of Homer bears a close resemblance, where the poet says, that "in the cruel rage of war, even the bodies of infant-children were dashed against the ground." Thucydides relates, that when Mycalessus was captured by the Thracians, they put all, even women and children to the sword. Arrian relates the same of the Macedonians, when they took the city of Thebes. And Gerimanicus Caesar, according to the account of Tacitus, laid waste whole cantons of the Marsians, a people of Germany, with fire and sword, to which the historian adds, "without sparing either age or sex." The Jewish women and children too were exposed by Titus, to be torn to pieces by wild beasts at a public spectacle. Yet neither of those generals were thought deficient in humanity, so much had custom reconciled the minds of men to this barbarous usage. So that the massacre of the aged, like that of Priam by Pyrrhus, is no way surprising.

**X**. The right of putting prisoners of war to death, was so generally received a maxim, that the Roman Satirist has founded an adage upon it, and said, 'that when you can sell a prisoner for a slave, it would be absurd to kill him." Words which imply the full power of doing so, if the captor thought proper. The commentators indeed assign the act of saving, as the derivation of the Latin word, servus, a slave. Thus Thucydides speaks of the prisoners taken at Epidamnus, and killed by the Corcyraeans, and Hannibal is reported to have massacred five thousand prisoners at once. Nor was this power limited by the law of nations to any particular time, though it was controuled by greater restrictions in some places, than in others.

**XI**. Besides many examples occur of suppliants, being killed. Both ancient poets and historians relate such actions, as ordinary practices, authorised by the laws of war. Augustin commends the Goths for sparing suppliants, who had fled to churches for refuge, and adds by way of comment, that "they deemed it unlawful to avail themselves of the power, which had usually been allowed by the laws of war. I

Nor did those who offered to surrender always experience the lenity and mercy, which they sought thereby. Tacitus relates, that when the city of Uspes was invested, the besieged sent a deputation with offers of an immediate surrender, and of no less than ten thousand slaves, on condition that the free-born should remain unhurt. The terms were rejected — A proof that such a rejection was thought conformable to the rights of war.

**XII**. But even after an unconditional surrender, we find that those, who had capitulated were sometimes put to the sword. In this manner the princes of Pometia were treated by the Romans, the Samnites by Sylla, the Numidians and Vercingetorix by Caesar. It was almost a standing practice with the Romans to crown their triumphs with the death of an enemy's generals, whether made prisoners actually in the field, or by capitulation. Cicero notices this custom in his -fifth speech against Verres. Livy may be consulted on this point in many parts of his history, particularly in the twenty-eighth book: and Tacitus also in the 12th book of his Annals. The latter writer, in the first book of his HISTORY, relates that Galba ordered every tenth man of those, whom he had, upon their earnest supplication, admitted to surrender, to be beheaded: and Caecina, after the capitulation of Aventicum, punished Julius Alpinus, one of the leading men, with death, as a chief promoter of the war, leaving the rest to the mercy or cruelty of Vitellius.

**XIII**. Historians sometimes account for this right of putting enemies to death, especially prisoners, or suppliants, either on the score of retaliation, or for obstinate resistance. These may sometimes be the real, but cannot be the JUSTIFIABLE motives of such proceedings. For the law of retaliation, strictly and properly so called, must be directly enforced upon the person of the delinquent himself. Whereas, in war, what is called retaliation frequently redounds to the ruin of those, who are no way implicated in the blame. The general consequences of war are thus described by Diodorus Siculus, "they could not be ignorant, *says he*, having learnt from experience, that all being involved in the common fortune of war, they are liable on both sides in defeat, to suffer the same calamities, which they themselves would have inflicted upon the conquered party."

But as the Neapolitans reply to Belisarius, in Procopius, no one can he thought deserving of punishment for a resolute adherence to the side on which he is engaged, especially when actuated by natural and just motives in his choice of that side. So far from incurring guilt by such a resolution, it is on the other hand more criminal for any one to desert his post: and so it was judged by the military laws of ancient Rome. Livy says, it was a capital offence, for which no fear of danger could be pleaded as an excuse. So that in the rigid application of this right, OWING TO ITS IMPORTANCE every one is left to use his own discretion, and there may be times and circumstances, in which the law of nations will justify its full exertion.

**XIV**. The same right was exercised upon hostages also, not only upon those who had bound themselves, as it were, by convention, but even upon those, who had been delivered up by others. Two hundred and fifty hostages were once massacred by the Thessalians, and the Volsci Aurunci to the amount of three hundred by the Romans. It is to be observed that children were sometimes given, as hostages, which we find was done by the Parthians, and by Simon, who was one of the Maccabees. And in the times of Porsena it was usual to deliver women, as hostages: a practice, which, as Tacitus informs us, was followed by the Germans.

**XV**. As the law of nations permits many things, in the manner above explained, which are not permitted by the law of nature, so it prohibits some things which the law of nature allows. Thus spies, if discovered and taken, are usually treated with the utmost severity. Yet there is no doubt, but the law of nations allows any one to send spies, as Moses did to the land of promise, of whom Joshua was one.

Persons of that description may sometimes be LAWFULLY employed by those, who are engaged in an EVIDENTLY just war. Others too, who have not such evident proofs of the justice of their cause, may plead the rights of war as a vindication for employing such persons.

But if any are to be found, who disdain to avail themselves of such a privilege, or opportunity, no argument either FOR, or AGAINST the LAWFULNESS of employing spies can be drawn from their conduct, which proceeds rather from a nobleness of mind, and a confidence in open strength, than from any decided opinion upon the subject.

## CHAPTER 5: ON THE RIGHT TO LAY WASTE AN ENEMY'S COUNTRY, AND CARRY OFF HIS EFFECTS.

*An enemy's property may be wasted and plundered — Things deemed sacred, how far exempted — Stratagem, how far permitted.*

**I**. CICERO, in the third book of his offices, has said that there is nothing repugnant to the LAW OF NATURE in spoiling the effects of an enemy, whom by the same law we are authorized to kill. Wherefore it is not surprising that the same things should be allowed by the LAW OF NATIONS. Polybius, for this reason, in the fifth book of his history, maintains, that the laws of war authorise the destruction of an enemy's forts, harbours, and fleets, the seizure of his men, or carrying off the produce of his country, and every thing of that description And we find from Livy that there are certain rights of war, by which an enemy must expect to suffer the calamities, which he is allowed to inflict, such as the burning of corn, the destruction of houses, and the plunder of men and cattle. Almost every page of history abounds in examples of entire cities being destroyed, walls levelled to the ground, and even whole countries wasted by fire and sword. Even in cases of surrender, towns have sometimes been destroyed, while the inhabitants were spared — an example of which is given by Tacitus, in the taking of Artaxata by the Romans; the inhabitants opened their gates and were spared, but the town was devoted to the flames.

**II**. Nor does the law of nations, in itself, considered apart from other duties, which will be mentioned hereafter, make any exemption in favour of things deemed sacred. For when places are taken by an enemy, all things without exception, whether sacred or not, must fall a sacrifice. For which it is assigned as a reason, that things which are called sacred, are not actually excepted from all human uses, but are a kind of public property, called sacred indeed from the general purposes, to which they are more immediately devoted. And as a proof of this, it is usual, when one nation surrenders to another state or sovereign, to surrender, along with other rights, every thing of a sacred kind, as appears by the form cited from Livy in a former part of this treatise.

And therefore Ulpian says, that the public have a property in sacred things. Conformably to which Tacitus says, that "in the Italian towns all the temples, the images of the Gods, and every thing connected with religion belonged of right to the Roman people." For this reason a nation, as the Lawyers, Paulus and Venuleius openly maintain, may, under a change of circumstances, convert to secular uses things, that have before been consecrated: and an overruling necessity may justify the hand, which has formerly consecrated the object in employing it as one of the resources and instruments of war. A thing which Pericles once did under a pledge of making restitution: Mago did the same in Spain, and the Romans in the Mithridatic war. We read of the same actions done by Sylla, Pompey, Caesar, and others. Plutarch in his life of Tiberius Gracchus says that nothing is so sacred and inviolable, as divine offerings: yet no one can hinder these from being removed or applied to other purposes at the pleasure of the state. Thus Livy mentions the ornaments of the temples, which Marcellus brought from Syracuse to Rome, as acquisitions made by the right of war.

**III**. What has been said of sacred things and edifices applies also to another kind of solemn fabrics, and those are sepulchral structures, which may be considered not merely as repositories of the dead, but as monuments belonging to the living, whether families or states. For this reason Pomponius has said, that these, like all other sacred places, when taken by an enemy may lose their inviolability, and Paulus is of the same opinion, observing that we are not restrained by any religious scruple from using the sepulchres of an enemy: for the stones, taken from thence, may be applied to any other purpose. But this right does not authorise wanton insult, offered to the ashes of the dead. For that would be a violation of the solemn rights of burial, which, as it was shewn in a preceding part of this work, were introduced and established by the law of nations.

**IV**. Here it may be briefly observed, that, according the law of nations any thing, belonging to an enemy, may be taken not only by open force, but by stratagem, provided it be unaccompanied with treachery.

## CHAPTER 6: ON THE ACQUISITION OF TERRITORY AND PROPERTY BY RIGHT OF CONQUEST.

*Law of nature with respect to the acquisition of things captured in war — Law of nations on the same subject — In what cases the law of nations confirms the capture of things moveable — Lands acquired by conquest — Lawful prize cannot be made of things not belonging to an enemy — Goods found on board an enemy's ships — Law of nations authorises the making prize of what an enemy has taken from others in war — Sovereigns may acquire possession and dominion through those employed by them — Acts of hostility divided into public and private — Territory may be acquired by a sovereign or people — Private and public captures explained — Discretionary power of generals in this respect — Prizes belong either to the treasury, or to those, who take them — Places sometimes given up to be plundered by the soldiery — Different methods of dividing spoils — Peculation, a portion of the spoils sometimes given to allies, who have supported the war — Sometimes given up to subjects — This illustrated by examples — Utility of the above practices — Whether things taken without the territory of either of the belligerent powers can be acquired by the rights of war — In what manner this right peculiarly applies to solemn wars.*

**I**. BESIDES the impunity allowed to men for certain actions, which have been mentioned before, there are other consequences and effects, peculiar to the law of nations, attending solemn and formal war. The law of nature indeed authorises our making such acquisitions in a just war, as may be deemed an equivalent for a debt, which cannot otherwise be obtained, or as may inflict a loss upon the aggressor, provided it be within the bounds of reasonable punishment. According to this right, as we find in the fourteenth chapter of Genesis, Abraham devoted to God a tenth part of the spoils, which he had taken from the five kings: and the inspired writer in the seventh chapter of his Epistle to the Hebrews gives the same interpretation of this passage. In the same manner the Greeks too, the Carthaginians, and the Romans devoted a tenth portion of the spoils of war to their deities. Jacob, in making a particular bequest to Joseph above his brethren, says, "I have given to thee one portion above thy brethren, which I took out of the hand of the Amorite with my sword, and with my bow." In this place, the expression, I TOOK, is used according to the prophetic style, where an event, that will for certain take place, is spoken of in the past time, and an action is here attributed to Jacob, which some of his descendants were to perform, supposing the progenitor and his children to be the same person.

Nor is it upon conjecture alone that such a right is founded, but the divine law giver himself pronounces sentence against a city that has rejected the offers of peace, and afterwards been taken by storm, that he gives all her spoils to the conqueror.

**II**. But according to the law of nations, not only the person, who makes war upon just grounds; but any one whatever, engaged in regular and formal war, becomes absolute proprietor of every thing which he takes from the enemy: so that all nations respect his title, and the title of all, who derive through him their claim to such possessions. Which, as to all foreign relations, constitutes the true idea of dominion. For, as Cyrus, in Xenophon observes, when the city of an enemy is taken, every thing that is taken therein becomes a lawful prize to the conquerors; and Plato, in his treatise on laws asserts the same. Cicero in his speech against Rullus says that Mitylene belonged to the Roman people by the laws of war, and the right of conquest; and, in the first book of his offices, he observes, that some things become the private property of those, who take possession of them, when unoccupied, or of those, who make a conquest of them in war. Theophilus, in his Greek institutes, calls the one the natural mode of acquisition, and Aristotle denominates the other the natural way of acquisition by the sword, without regarding any other reason, but the bare fact, from which the right arises. Thus Nerva, the son, as Paulus the lawyer relates, said that property arose from natural possession, some traces of which still remain respecting wild animals taken either upon the sea, or upon the land, or birds flying in the air. It is seen also in things taken in war, all which immediately become the property of the first captors. Now things are considered as taken from an enemy, when taken from his subjects.

Thus Dercyllides argues, in Xenophon, that as Pharnabazus was an enemy to the Lacedaemonians, every thing belonging to Mania, who was his subject, might be seized by the laws of war.

**III**. But in this question upon the rights of war nations have decided, that a person is understood to have made a capture, when he detains a thing in such a manner, that the owner has abandoned all probable hopes of recovering it, or, as Pomponius, speaking on the same subject, says, when a thing has escaped beyond pursuit. This takes place with respect to moveable things in such a manner, that they are said to be taken, when they are carried within the territories of the enemy, or places belonging to him. For a thing is lost in the same manner as it is recovered by postliminium. It is said to be recovered whenever It returns within the territories of its owner's sovereign, that is, into places, of which he is master. Paulus indeed has expressly said, that a power or state has lost a subject, when he has gone, or been carried out of the territories of that power: and Pomponius defines a prisoner of war to be an enemy, whom the troops of some other belligerent power have taken and carried into one of their own places; for be. fore he is carried into those places, he continues still a subject of the enemy.

The law of nations, in these respects, treated persons and things in the same manner. From whence it is easy to understand, what is meant, when in another place it is said that things taken from an enemy immediately be. come the lawful prize of the captors, but only upon the condition of those things continuing in their possession for a reasonable and certain time. Consequently it is plain, that ships and other things taken at sea cannot be considered as really the property of the captors, till they have been carried into some of their ports, or to some place where their whole fleet is stationed. For in that case all hope of recovery seems to have vanished. By a late regulation among the European powers, it has been made an established maxim of the law of nations, that captures shall be deemed good and lawful, which have continued in the enemy's possession for the space of twenty four hours.

**IV**. Lands are not understood to become a lawful possession and absolute conquest from the moment they are invaded. For although it is true, that an army takes immediate and violent possession of the country which it has invaded, yet that can only be considered as a temporary possession, unaccompanied with any of the rights and consequences alluded to in this work, till it has been ratified and secured by some durable means, by cession, or treaty. For this reason, the land without the gates of Rome, where Hannibal encamped, was so far from being judged entirely lost, that it was sold for the same price that it would have been sold for before that period.

Now land will be considered as completely conquered, when it is inclosed or secured by permanent fortifications, so that no other state or sovereign can have free access to it, without first making themselves masters of those fortifications. On this account Flaccus, the Sicilian, assigns no improbable conjecture for the origin of the word territory, because the enemy is DETERRED from entering it. At least there is as much probability in this conjecture, as in that of Varro, who derives it from the word terendo, treading the soil. Frontinus deduces it from terra, the earth, and Pomponius from the TERROR Of judicial authority exercised in each country. Xenophon however in his book on tributes, seems to accord with the first of these opinions: for he says, that in time of war the possession of a country is kept by walls, strong holds, and barriers.

**V**. It is a clear point too, that for any thing to become a prize or conquest by the right of war, it must belong to an enemy. For things, within an enemy's territory, for instance, in any of his towns or garrisons, cannot be acquired as property by the laws of war, if the owners of those things are neither subjects nor confederates of the enemy. It is observed in one of the speeches of Aeschines, that Philip, though at war with the Amphipolitans, could not lawfully take possession of Amphipolis, as a conquest, it being a city, which belonged to the Athenians. For as the enemy is likely to derive no assistance in the war, from things which neither belong to himself, nor to a confederate, no just reason can be assigned for taking them, and the right of making things change their owners by force is of too odious a nature to admit of any extension.

**VI**. The observation usually made, that all things on board an enemy's ships are to be deemed an enemy's goods, ought not to be received as a STANDING and ACKNOWLEDGED rule of the law of nations, but only as a maxim, indicating the strong presumption that both goods and vessel belong to the same owner, unless clear proof to the contrary can be brought. The States General of Holland made such a decision in the year 1338, at a time when the war with the Hanse-towns raged with the greatest violence, and the decision consequently passed into a law.

**VII**. According to the law of nations it is undoubtedly true, that things taken from an enemy which had been captured by him cannot be claimed by those, to whom they belonged before they were in the enemy's possession, and who had lost them in war. Because the law of nations assigned them to the enemy by the first capture, and then to the person, who took them from him by the second.

Upon this principle among others, Jephthah defends himself against the Ammonites, because by the laws of war they had lost the land, which they claimed, in the same manner, as another part had been transferred from the Moabites to the Amorites, and from the Amorites to the Hebrews. Thus David too claims and divides as his own, what he himself had taken from the Amalekites, and the Amalekites, before him, from the Philistines.

Titus Largius, as we are informed by Dionysius of Halicarnassus, when the Volscians laid claim to some possessions, which they had formerly held, delivered it as his opinion in the Roman Senate, that "the Romans were the fair and just owners of what they had gained by the right of conquest, nor ought they to be so weak as to abandon the fruits of their valour. For not only the people of that day, but their posterity also had a right to a share of those possessions: so that to abandon them would be treating themselves like enemies."

**VIII**. and **IX**. One great point, which the law of nations designed to establish, was that the effects or pos. sessions of one enemy should be considered by another, as things having no owner.

Things, belonging to no one, became the property of those, who find or take them, both of those, who, like sovereign powers, employ others in such service, and of those, who take them with their own hands.

Thus not only slaves, or the immediate members of a man's household, but all, who engage themselves, any way, in the service of others, may be said to acquire for their employers all the property, which they take or gain, even in those things, which apparently lie in common to all men, such as pearls, fish, or fowl.

Modestinus has justly said, "that whatever is naturally gained, like a possession, we may acquire through the means of any one we chuse to employ," and, upon the same principle, Paulus observes, that "in every acquisition, the exertion of mind and body must concur; the former purely our own, and the latter, either our own, or that of another. In the same manner possession may be taken for us by an attorney, guardian, or trustee, provided they do it on our account and in our name." The reason of which is, because one man may naturally be the voluntary instrument of another, with the consent of that other. So that the distinction made between persons in a servile and free condition, as to the acquisition of property, is a distinction only of the civil law, and applicable to its rules of transferring, acquiring, and confirming, property. And yet the emperor Severus afterwards applied these rules to the natural acquisition of things, not only from motives of utility, but, as he avowed himself, from motives of equity and justice. So that, apart from all authority of the civil law, it is an established maxim that what any one can do for himself, he can do through means of another, and doing such acts by another is the same as doing them himself.

**X**. A distinction must be made between actions in war, that are really of a PUBLIC NATURE, and the acts Of INDIVIDUALS occasioned by public war: by the latter, individuals acquire an absolute and direct property, in the things, which they take, and by the former, the state makes those acquisitions. Upon this principle of the law of nations Scipio treated with Masinissa, stating that as it was under the auspices of the Roman people, that Syphax was conquered and taken prisoner, himself, his wife, his kingdom, his territory, his towns, and subjects inhabiting those towns, in short, every thing belonging to him became a lawful prize to the Roman people. In the same manner, Antiochus the Great maintained that Coelo-Syria belonged to Seleucus, and not to Ptolemy, because Seleucus had been the principal in the war, to which Ptolemy had contributed his assistance. In the fifth book of Polybius, there is an account of the matter.

**XI**. Things immoveable are generally taken by some public act, such as marching an army into the country, or placing garrisons there. So that, as Pomponius has said, "lands taken from the enemy become the property of the state, and form no part of the booty belonging to the individual captors. I Thus among the Hebrews and Lacedaemonians, lands that were made a conquest, were divided by lot. The Romans too either retained conquered lands to let them out for rent, sometimes leaving a small portion to the ancient possessor, or divided them among colonists, whom they sent out, or made them tributary; innumerable instances of which we meet with in their histories, their laws, and treaties on the admeasurements of lands.

**XII**. But things moveable, whether inanimate, or living, are taken either as connected or unconnected with the public service. When unconnected with the public service, they become the property of the individual captors.*

*[**Editor's note**: But such captures cannot be made without authority from the sovereign.]

Reference may here be made to the remark of Celsus, that "enemy's goods found among us do not belong to the state, but to the prior occupant." By which are meant things found among us at the breaking out of a war. For the same was observed of persons, when, under the same circumstances, they were considered as goods taken.

On this subject there is a remarkable passage in Tryphoninus. "Those persons, says he, who have gone into a foreign country in time of peace, upon the sudden breaking out of war, are made slaves by those, among whom it is their misfortune to be found, being considered as enemies."

**XIII**. What has been said upon the law of nations, allowing individuals to acquire property by taking it from an enemy, must be understood as meaning the law of nations, prior to the regulations of civil laws upon that point. For the capture of an enemy's goods which at first appear to resemble things in common, which any one may seize, is now, like that of wild birds or beasts, subject to limitation by the laws of every state, being in some cases assigned to the sovereign, and in others, belonging to the captors. It may in some countries, indeed, be introduced as a rule of law for the whole of an enemy's goods found there to be confiscated.

**XIV**. The case is very different respecting what any one takes in actual engagements. For there every individual bears the character of his country, acting in her stead, and supporting her rights. Through the exertions of those individuals, the state acquires both property and dominion, with a power, according to the principles of civilized countries, of conferring them on whom she pleases.

This is not a practice of modern date, but one prevailing among the most free and independent nations of remote antiquity. The poets, and historians of those days, describe the hero, after the heat, the burden, and dangers of the day, carrying his spoils to the common stock, to be divided by the General among the army, after retaining his proper share to himself.

[**Translator's note:** The translation proceeds from the XV. to the XXIII. Section of the original, the intermediate Sections being only a confirmation of the preceding arguments by examples from ancient history.]

**XXIII**. It is observed by legal authorities to be a custom, which has silently gained ground, for either allies or subjects, who engage in war, without pay, and at their own risque and expence, to be rewarded with the captures that they make.

The reason, why allies have such a privilege, is evident. Because one ally is naturally bound to another to repair the losses, which he has sustained by entering into a mutual agreement to support a common cause. Besides it seldom happens, that services are given without some consideration in return.

Quintilian, applying the same reasoning to another case, alleges that it is but just for orators and advocates, who devote their whole time and talents to the business of others, to be requited for their services: as thereby they preclude themselves from acquiring gain in any other way.

It is most likely therefore that some advantage gained from the enemy is always expected, as a compensation for the loss and risque incurred, unless there is evidence to the contrary from some antecedent treaty, in which there is an express stipulation for gratuitous assistance and services.

**XXIV**. Such claim to a share of the spoils is not equally evident, where SUBJECTS ONLY are concerned. For the state has a RIGHT TO THEIR SERVICES. Still where ALL are not engaged in arms, but only SOME, those, who give up their time to the calling of soldiers, and expose their lives to its hazards, have a right to be rewarded and supported by the body politic: and as a compensation for this loss of time, and this personal danger, it is but reasonable they should have a share of the spoils.

With respect to allies there is an example in the Roman treaty, in which the Latins are admitted to an equal share of the spoil, in those wars, which were carried on under the auspices of the Roman people.

Thus in the war, which the Aetolians carried on with the assistance of the Romans, the lands and cities were ceded to the Aetolians, and the prisoners and moveable effects were given to the Romans. After the defeat of king Ptolemy, Demetrius gave part of the spoils to the Athenians. Ambrose, in speaking of the expedition of Abraham, shews the equity of this practice. He asserts that it was but just for those, who had assisted him as partners in the danger, to share in the prizes, which were their due reward.

As to what were the privileges of subjects in these respects, we have a proof in the conduct of the Hebrews, among whom it was usual for half of the spoils to be given to those, who were engaged in battle. In the same manner the soldiers of Alexander were allowed to appropriate to themselves whatever they took from individuals, except that it was usual for a considerable portion to be set apart for the king. So that it was made a subject of accusation against those at Arbela, who were said to have entered into a conspiracy for securing to themselves every thing that was taken, without contributing a due proportion of it to the treasury.

But individuals were not allowed in the same manner to appropriate to themselves the public property of an enemy, that is, such as belonged to the state. Thus when the Macedonians made themselves masters of the camp of Darius at the river Piramus, and every thing was given up to plunder, they spared the royal pavilion, in conformity to an ancient custom, "according to which, as Curtius observes, it was always reserved as the properest place, in which the victorious prince could be received."

There was a custom somewhat like this among the Hebrews who always placed the crown of the vanquished king upon the head of the conqueror, and assigned to him every thing that was taken, belonging to the royal house. hold, We read of the same conduct in Charles the great, who, upon conquering the Hungarians, gave up the private property as plunder to the soldiers, reserving for the royal -use all the public treasures.

Some things indeed are too inconsiderable to be made public property. It is a generally received maxim for such things to belong to the individual captors.

This was the practice in the ancient times of the Roman republic. A privilege not unlike this is sometimes given to seamen, who serve for pay. It is what the French call spoils, or pillage, including all wearing apparel, and all gold and silver under the value of ten crowns.

On this point different customs prevail in different countries. In Spain sometimes a fifth, and sometimes a third was allowed to the soldiers, and at others half was reserved for the crown. On some occasions, a seventh or tenth part was allowed to the general, and the rest belonged to the captors, except ships of war, which belong entirely to the crown. Sometimes a division was made in proportion to the hazard and expence: which was the case among the Italians, where the third part of the prize was assigned to the owner of the victorious vessel, another third to those who had merchandise on board, and the remaining third to the combatants.

In some cases it happens that private adventurers are not allowed the whole of their captures, a certain portion of which must go to the state or to those, who have received a grant of such prizes from the state. Thus in Spain, if in time of war ships are fitted out by private persons, one part of the captures, which they make belongs to the crown, and another to the Lord High Admiral. So likewise in France, and Holland, the tenth part of a prize belonged to the Admiral, a fifth also being previously deducted for the use of the state. But by land it is customary upon the taking of towns, and in battles, for every one to keep the prizes which he takes. But in excursions, every thing taken becomes the common stock of all engaged, being afterwards divided amongst them according to their respective ranks.

**XXV**. As a consequence deducible from the above positions, it may be observed, that if a people not engaged in war be made mediators in a doubtful matter respecting things captured in war, the cause must be adjudged in favour of him, who has on his side the laws and customs of the country, which he has espoused. But if no such right can be proved, the prize must be adjudged to the state, rather than to the individual captor. — The maxim indeed of Quintilian can never be admitted, that the laws of war can never be enforced in matters, that may be decided by judicial authority; and that, on the other hand, whatever has been gained by arms can be maintained by force of arms alone.

**XXVI**. It was observed in a former part of this chapter, that things, NOT BELONGING to an enemy, cannot be taken, although found with him. For this is neither consonant to natural justice, nor introduced by the law of nations. But if in those things the enemy had any right connected with possession, such as the right of pledge, retention or service, that would not obstruct the power of the captors.

It is a disputed point, both as to persons and things, whether they can be lawfully taken in the territory of a power at war with neither of the belligerents. In regard ONLY to the law of nations, as far as it allows us to kill an enemy wherever he is found, the PLACE has nothing to do with the question. But considering the rights of the sovereign, to whom that territory belongs, he undoubtedly has a right to forbid the seizure of persons, or the capture of things within his own dominions: and may demand satisfaction for the violation of that right. In the same manner, though beasts, that are wild by nature, become the property of those, who take them, still an owner may forbid any one to commit a trespass upon his lands in order to take them.

# CHAPTER 7: ON THE RIGHT OVER PRISONERS OF WAR.

*By the law of nations, slavery the result of being taken in solemn war — The same condition extends to the descendants of those taken — The power over them — Even incorporeal things may be gained by the rights of war — Reason of this — This right not prevalent to the same extent among Christian powers of the present day — The substitute used in place of this right.*

**I**. BY THE law of nature, in its primaeval state; apart from human institutions and customs, no men can be slaves: and it is in this sense that legal writers maintain the opinion that slavery is repugnant to nature. Yet in a former part of this treatise, it was shewn that there is nothing repugnant to natural justice, in deriving the origin of servitude from human actions, whether founded upon compact or crime.

But the law of nations now under consideration is of wider extent both in its authority over persons, and its effects. For, as to persons, not only those, who surrender their rights, or engage themselves to servitude, are considered in the light of slaves, but all, who are taken prisoners in public and solemn war, come under the same description from the time that they are carried into the places, of which the enemy is master.

Nor is the commission of crime requisite to reduce them to this condition, but the fate of all is alike, who are unfortunately taken within the territories of an enemy, upon the breaking out of war.

**II**. and **III**. In ancient times, while slavery was permitted to exist, the offspring, born during captivity or servitude, continued in the same condition as the parents. The consequences of such rules were of wide extent; there was no cruelty, which masters might not inflict upon their slaves; — there was no service, the performance of which they might not compel; — the power even of life and death was in their hands. However the Roman laws at length set bounds to such wanton power, at least to the exercise of it within the Roman territories.

Every thing too, found upon the prisoner's person, became a lawful prize to the captor. For as Justinian observes, one who was entirely in the power of another could have no property of his own.

**IV**. and **V**. Incorporeal rights, gained by the enemy, along with the person so captured, cannot be considered in the light of primary and original acquisitions. And there are some rights so purely personal in their nature, that they cannot be lost even by captivity, nor the duties attached thereto ever be relinquished. Of such a nature was the paternal right among the Romans. For rights of this kind cannot exist but immediately with the person to whom they originally belonged.

All these rights to prizes, which were introduced by the law of nations, were intended as an inducement to captors to refrain from the cruel rigour of putting prisoners to death; as they might hope to derive some advantage from sparing and saving them. From hence Pomponius deduces the origin of the word, SERVUS, or SLAVE, being one, who might have been put to death, but from motives of interest or humanity had been saved.

**VI**. (being the IX. of the original.) It has long been a maxim, universally received among the powers of Christendom, that prisoners of war cannot be made slaves, so as to be sold, or compelled to the hardships and labour attached to slavery. And they have with good reason embraced the latter principle. As it would be inconsistent with every precept of the law of charity, for men to refuse abondoning a cruel right, unless they might be allowed to substitute another, of great, though somewhat inferior rigour, in its place.

And this, as Gregoras informs us, became a traditionary principle among all who professed one common religion; nor was it confined to those, who lived under the authority of the

Roman empire, but prevailed among the Thesalians the Illyrians, the Triballians, and Bulgarians. Though such an abolition of slavery, and mitigation of captivity may be considered as of trivial import, yet they were effects produced by the introduction of the Christian religion, especially upon recollection that Socrates tried, but without effect, to prevail upon the Greeks to forbear making slaves of each other.

In this respect the Mahometans act towards each other in the same manner as Christians do. Though it is still the practice among Christian powers to detain prisoners of war, till their ransom be paid, the amount of which depends upon the will of the Conqueror, unless it has been settled by express treaty. The right of detaining such prisoners has sometimes been allowed to the individuals, who took them, except where the prisoners were personages of extraordinary rank, who were always considered as prisoners of war to the state.

## CHAPTER 8: ON EMPIRE OVER THE CONQUERED.

*Civil and sovereign jurisdiction acquired by conquest — Effects of such acquisition — Absolute power or mixed power gained by conquest — Incorporeal rights acquired in the same manner — Thessalian bond considered.*

**I**. IF INDIVIDUALS can reduce each other to subjection, it is not surprising that states can do the same, and by this means acquire a civil, absolute, or mixed, dominion. So that, in the language of Tertullian, victory has often been the foundation of dominion, and it often happens, as Quintilian remarks, that the boundaries of states and kingdoms, of nations and cities, can only be settled by the laws of war.

Quintus Curtius relates of Alexander, that he said, it was for conquerors to dictate laws, which the conquered were bound to receive. This has always been a general opinion and rule, thus Ariovistus, in Caesar, laid it down as an indubitable right of war, for the conqueror to impose whatever terms he pleased upon the conquered, nor did he suppose the Roman people would allow any one to interpose with them in the discretionary use of this right.

By conquest, a prince succeeds to all the rights of the conquered sovereign or state; and if it be a common. wealth, he acquires all the rights and privileges, which the people possessed. He gains the same right, which the state had before, to alienate the possessions, or to transmit them if he chuses to his descendants, by which means they will become a patrimonial territory.

**II**. The right of conquest may go even beyond this. A state may hereby lose its political existence, so far as to form an appendage to another power, which was the case with the Roman provinces: or if a king engaged in war against a state, at his own expence, has reduced it to complete subjection, his authority over it becomes an absolute, rather than a limited sovereignty. It can no longer be called an independent state, but, by the right of conquest, forms an integral part of the prince's immediate dominions. Xenophon in drawing the character of Agesilaus, commends him for requiring no other services and obedience of the cities he had conquered, than what is usually paid by subjects to their lawful sovereigns.

**III**. From hence it will be easy to understand what is meant by a mixed government, composed partly of civil, and partly of absolute power; — it is a government, where subjection is united with some degree of personal liberty.

We sometimes read of nations, that have been so far subdued, as to be deprived of the use of all warlike arms, being allowed to retain no instruments of iron, but the implements of husbandry; and of others, that have been compelled to change their national customs and language.

**IV**. States as well as individuals may lose their property by the laws of war: and even a voluntary surrender is in reality nothing more than giving up what might have been taken by force. For as Livy says, where all things submit to the power of arms, the conqueror may impose whatever terms, and exact whatever fines he pleases. Thus the Roman people by the victories of Pompey acquired all the territories, which Mithridates had gained by conquest.

The incorporeal rights too, belonging to one state, may pass to another by the rights of conquest. Upon the taking of Alba, the Romans retained all the rights belonging to that city. From hence it follows, that the Thessalians were released from the obligation of paying a sum of money, which they owed to the Thebans; Alexander, upon the taking of Thebes, having, as a conqueror, forgiven the debt. Nor is the argument used by Quintlian in favour of the Thebans, at all convincing: he maintains that nothing but what is of a tangible nature can pass by right of conquest, a class of things to which incorporeal rights can never be reduced: and that there is a material difference between inheritance and victory, the former of which may convey incorporeal rights, but the latter can give nothing except things of a solid and visible substance.

But on the other hand it may be justly said, that whoever is master of the persons, is master also of all the rights and things, which are vested in those persons, who are in that case considered as having nothing of their own. Indeed if any one should leave to a conquered people their rights, as a state, still there are some things belonging to that state, which he might appropriate to himself. For it is in his own power to determine, to what extent his generosity, or the exertion of his right shall go. Caesar imitated the conduct of Alexander, in forgiving the Dyrrachians a debt, which they owed to some one of the opposite party. But the kind of war, in which Caesar was engaged does not fall within the rules of the law of nations.

## CHAPTER 9: OF THE RIGHT OF POSTLIMINIUM.

*Origin of the term, postliminium — Where it takes effect — Certain things recoverable thereby — In what cases the right of postlimininm prevails in peace, as well as war — What rights are recoverable, and what rights not recoverable — When a people is not entitled to the right of postliminium — Extent of civil law in these cases — Deserters — Ransomed prisoners — Subjects — Lands recovered by right of postlimininm — Distinction formerly observed with respect to movable things — Modern practice.*

**I.** THE professors of law in former ages have given no more satisfactory account of the rights of postliminium, than they have done of those, respecting things taken from the enemy. The subject has been more accurately handled by the ancient Romans, but often still with a considerable degree of confusion, so that a reader cannot easily distinguish, what part they assign to the province of the law of nations, and what part to the civil law of Rome.

Amidst a great variety of opinions, upon the meaning of the word, postliminium, that of Scaevola seems the most natural, who derives it from the word post, signifying a return after captivity, and limen the boundary or entrance of the house, or from limes, a public boundary. Thus the ancients called exile or banishment, eliminium, that is, sending any one out of the boundaries of the country.

**II.** Postliminium therefore, according to its original signification, means the right, accruing to any one in consequence of his return home from captivity. Pomponius defines the right of postliminium to take place the moment any one enters a town or garrison, of which his sovereign is master; but according to Paulus he must have entered within the territories of his own country before he can be entitled to that right.

Upon this principle nations have, in general, gone so far, as to allow the right of postliminium to take place, where any person, or indeed any thing, coming within the privileges of postliminium, have arrived within the territory of a friendly or allied power.

By the term friends, or allies, used in this place, are not simply meant, those who are at peace with another power, but those who are engaged in the same war, and in a common cause with that power. So that all, who have come into the territories of such powers, are protected under the pledge of public faith. For it makes no difference with respect to persons or things, whether they are in the territories of those powers, or in their own.

In the territory of a friendly power, who is not engaged in the same cause with either of two belligerent parties, prisoners of war do not change their condition, unless it has been agreed to the contrary by express treaty; as in the second treaty between the Romans and Carthaginians, it was stipulated that if any prisoners, taken by the Carthaginians from powers friendly to the Romans, should come into ports subject to the Roman people, their liberty might be claimed: and that powers friendly to the Carthaginians should enjoy the same privilege. For this reason, the Roman prisoners taken in the second Punic war, when sent into Greece, had not the right of postliminium there, the Greeks being entirely neutral, consequently they could not be released, till they were ransomed.

**III**. According to the language of the ancient Romans, even free men might be restored by the right of postliminium.

Gallus Ælius, in the first book of his explanation of law-terms, defines a person restored to his original situation by the right of postliminium, to be one, who had gone from his own country, in a free condition, to another, and returned to his own in consequence of such right. By the right of postliminium a slave also who has fallen into the hands of an enemy, upon his release from thence, returns to the service of his former master.

As to the law of postliminium, horses, mules, and ships are considered in the same light as slaves. And whatever advantage this law gives any one in recovering persons or things from an enemy, the enemy in his turn has equal advantage from the same law.

But modern lawyers have made a distinction between two kinds of postliminium, by one of which, persons returned to their former condition, and by the other, things are recovered.

**IV**. The right of postliminium may extend to those, who are seized and detained in an enemy's country upon the breaking out of war. For though during the continuance of that war, there may be reason for detaining them, in order to weaken the enemy's strength, yet, upon the conclusion of a peace, no such motive and pretence can be devised for their release being refused or delayed. It is a settled point therefore that upon peace being made, prisoners of the above description always obtain their liberty, their claim to it being universally acknowledged.

With respect to other kinds of prisoners, every one used what he wished to be thought his right, except where fixed rules were prescribed by treaty. And for the same reason, neither slaves, nor things taken in war are restored upon a peace, except express stipulations be made to that purpose. A conqueror too, in general, wishes to have it believed that he had a right to make such acquisition; and indeed the departure from such a rule might give rise to wars without end.

**V**. and **VI**. A prisoner of war, upon his release, and return to his own country, is entitled to all his privileges THERE, and indeed to everything either corporeal, or incorporeal, which he might have before possessed in a NEUTRAL STATE, at the time of his captivity. For if such a state, in order to preserve her neutrality, considered his captivity as a matter of right on the part of the enemy, so also, in order to shew her impartiality, she cannot lawfully abridge his right to any thing he may reclaim upon his release. The controul therefore, which the person, to whom the prisoner belonged by the right of war, had over his effects, was not absolutely unconditional: for he might lose it, even against his will, whenever the prisoner came again under the protection, or within the territories, of his own sovereign. Along with the prisoner therefore he would lose everything, which was considered as an appendage to his person.

In cases where effects taken in war have been alienated, a question arises, whether the law of nations confirms the title, and secures the possession of the person, who has derived or purchased them from him, who was master of them by the rights of war, by having the prisoner in his custody at the time of alienation, or whether such things are recoverable; supposing the things to be in a neutral territory.

A distinction seems proper to be made between things recoverable by postliminium, and things excepted from that right: so that every alienation of the former must be qualified and conditional, but that of the latter may be absolute. By things alienated may be understood even those, of which a gift has been made, or to which the owner has relinquished every claim.

**VII**. Upon any one's returning to his former condition by the law of postliminium, all his rights are restored as fully, as if he had never been in the hands and power of the enemy.

**VIII**. The case of those however, who have been conquered by the arms of an enemy, and have surrendered themselves, forms an exception to this rule; because engagements of that kind must be valid, and honourably adhered to according to the law of postliminium. So that during the time of a truce, the right of postliminium cannot be claimed.

But where a surrender has been made without any express or positive convention the right of postliminium exists in all its force.

**IX**. What has been said of individuals applies to nations: so that a free people, who have been subjugated, upon being delivered from the yoke of the enemy by the power of their allies, will recover their former condition.

But if the whole population that constituted a state has been dispersed, the people can no longer be considered as the same: nor does the law of nations in such a case enforce the right of postliminium for the restoration of all effects formerly belonging to that people. For as the identity of a ship, or any other material object, can only be ascertained by the permanent union of its original parts: so a nation can no longer be regarded as the same, when every peculiar characteristic belonging to it is effaced.

The state of Saguntum therefore was no longer judged to be the same, when it was restored to its ancient possessors, at the expiration of eight years: nor could Thebes any longer be deemed the original city, as its inhabit. ants, had been sold- by Alexander for slaves. From hence it is evident, that the Thebans could not, by the right of postliminium, recover the sum of money, which the Thessalians had owed them: and that for two reasons: because, in the first place, they were a new people; and, secondly, because Alexander at the time that he was absolute master of the city had a right, if he thought proper, to relinquish the claim to that debt, which he had actually done. Besides, a debt is not in the number of things recoverable by the right of postliminium.

The rules, respecting a state, are not much unlike those laid down by the ancient Roman law, which made marriage a dissoluble tic, so that it could not be restored by the right of postliminium: but a new consent, and a new contract were necessary.

**X**. By the Roman civil law deserters were excluded from the right of postliminium.

**XI**. and **XII**. It is a point of much importance to the subject, and it was before declared in the affirmative, that nations, which have been under a foreign yoke, recover their former condition, even though their deliverance has not been effected by their former sovereign, but by some ally. It is a settled rule, where there is no express treaty to the contrary. At the same time it is but reasonable that such ally be indemnified for the expences incurred in accomplishing that deliverance.

**XIII**. Among things within the right of postliminium, lands in particular attract our attention. For, as Pomponius observes, upon the expulsion of an enemy lands naturally revert to their former masters. And in this sense expulsion is understood to take place from the time that his free and open access to a territory is entirely cut off.

Thus the Lacedaemonians, after taking Aegina from the Athenians, restored it to its ancient owners. Justinian and other emperors restored to the heirs of the ancient possessors of the lands, which had been recovered from the Goths and Vandals, still reserving against those owners all prescriptive rights, which the Roman laws had introduced.

The privileges belonging to lands attach to every right also connected with the soil. For religious or consecrated places, that had been taken by an enemy, when recovered returned, as Pomponius has said, to their former condition.

Upon the same principle it was provided by a law in Spain, that provinces, and all other hereditary jurisdictions, particularly supreme jurisdictions, should return to the original possessors by the right of postliminium; and those of an inferior kind, if reclaimed within the space of four years. Except that citadels lost by war always belonged to the crown, in whatever manner they were recovered.

**XIV**. On the contrary a general opinion prevails, that moveable property, which constitutes part of a lawful prize, is not recoverable by the right of postliminium. So that things acquired by purchase, wherever they are found, continue the property of the purchaser. Nor has the original owner a right to claim them, when found in a neutral state, or even carried into his own territory.

Things useful in war, as we find, were formerly an exception to this rule: an exception, which seems to have been favoured by the law of nations in order to induce men the more readily to provide them, in the hopes of recovering them, if lost. And this indulgence was the more easily granted, as most nations, at that period, in all their customs, seem to have had an eye to a state of warfare. — Among the things, coming under this description, ships of war, and merchant-ships are reckoned, but neither gallies, nor pleasure-boats: mules also are enumerated; but only such as are used to carry baggage: horses and mares too; but only such as are broken in to obey the bridle. And these are things, the bequest of which the Roman law confirmed, and which might come into the division of an inheritance.

Arms and cloathing indeed are useful in war, but still they were not recoverable by the right of postliminium; because the laws were by no means inclined to favour those, who lost either in war: and such a loss was deemed a disgrace, as we find from many parts of history. And in this respect, a distinction was made between a soldier's arms and his horse: because the latter might easily break loose, and fall into an enemy's hands without any fault of his rider. This distinction in moveable things seems to have prevailed in the western parts of Europe, under the Goths, even as far down as to the times of Boetius. For in explaining the Topics of Cicero, he speaks of this right, as a general custom of his day.

**XV**. But in later times, if not before, this distinction seems to have been abolished. For all intelligent writers speak of moveable effects as not recoverable by the right of postliminium, and it has evidently been decided so, in many places, with respect to ships.

**XVI**. The right of postliminium is quite unnecessary, before the things taken have been carried into some place of which the enemy is master, although they may be in his possession: for they have not yet changed their owner, by the law of nations. And, according to the opinions of Ulpian and Javolenus, the law of postliminium is no less superfluous, where goods have been taken by robbers and pirates, because the law of nations does not allow THEIR possession of the goods to convey any change, or right of property to THEM.

Upon this ground, the Athenians wished to consider Philip, as RESTORING, and not GIVING them Halonesus, of which they had been robbed by pirates, from whom he had taken it again. For things taken by pirates may be reclaimed, wherever they are found; except that NATURAL JUSTICE requires that the person, who has gained them out of their hands, at his own expence, should be indemnified, in proportion to what the owner himself would willingly have spent for their recovery.

**XVII**. But a different maxim may be established by the CIVIL LAW. Thus by the law of Spain, ships taken from pirates become the lawful prize of the captors: which may seem a hardship upon the original owners; but in some cases individual interest must be sacrificed to the public good: especially where the danger and difficulty of retaking the ships is so great. But such a law will 'not prevent foreigners from asserting their claims.

**XVIII**. It was rather a surprising maxim in the Roman law, which established the right of postliminium, not only between hostile powers, but between all foreign states, and, in some cases, between those, who were members of the Roman empire. But this was only a vestige of the rude and pastoral ages, before society was perfectly formed. So that even between nations, who were not engaged in public war with each other, a kind of licence resembling that of war prevailed.

In order to prevent such a licence from proceeding to all the calamities and slaughter of war, the laws of captivity were introduced: and, as a consequence of this, postliminium took place, which might be considered as a great step towards the formation of equal treaties, from the rules of which pirates and robbers were excluded, and which indeed they themselves despised.

**XIX**. In our times, the right of making prisoners, except in war, has been abolished not only among Christian states, but even among the greater part of Mahometans, those bands of society, which nature designed to establish amongst men, being in some measure restored.

But the ancient law of nations seems still in force against any rude or barbarous people, who, without any declaration or cause of war, consider all mankind as enemies. A decision has lately been made in the principal chamber of the parliament of Paris, declaring all effects belonging to the subjects of France, and taken by the Algerines, a people always engaged in predatory and maritime warfare with all other countries, if retaken, to belong to the captors.- At the same time it was decided, that, in the present day, ships are not reckoned among things recoverable by the right of postliminium.

[**Translator's note:** The tenth Chapter chiefly containing remarks that have been interspersed in other parts of the work, is omitted here.]

## CHAPTER 11: THE RIGHT OF KILLING ENEMIES, IN JUST WAR, TO BE TEMPERED WITH MODERATION AND HUMANITY

*In what cases strict justice allows the destruction of an enemy — Distinction between misfortune and guilt — Between principals and accessories in war — Distinction between unwarrantable and excusable grounds of promoting war — Sometimes right and laudable to forbear punishing an inveterate enemy — Every possible precaution requisite to spare the innocent — Especially children, women, and the aged, except they have committed atrocious acts — Clergymen, men of letters, husbandmen, merchants, prisoners — Conditional surrender not to be rejected — Unconditional surrender — Exceptions to the above rules, some of them considered, and refuted — Delinquents when numerous to be spared — Hostages to be spared — Unnecessary effusion of blood to be avoided.*

**I**. AND **II**. CICERO, in the first book of his offices, has finely observed, that "some duties are to be observed even towards those, from whom you have received an injury. For even vengeance and punishment have their due bounds." And at the same time he extols those ancient periods in the Roman government, when the events of war were mild, and marked with no unnecessary cruelty. The explanations given in the first chapter of this book will point out the cases, where the destruction of an enemy is one of the rights of lawful war, according to the principles of strict and internal justice, and where it is not so. For the death of an enemy may proceed either from an accidental calamity, or from the fixed purpose of his destruction.

No one can be justly killed by design, except by way of legal punishment, or to defend our lives, and preserve our property, when it cannot be effected without his destruction. For although in sacrificing the life of man to the preservation of perishable possessions, there may be nothing repugnant to strict justice, it is by no means consonant to the law of charity.

But to justify a punishment of that kind, the person put to death must have committed a crime, and such a crime too, as every equitable judge would deem worthy of death. Points, which it is unnecessary to discuss any further, as they have been so fully explained in the chapter on punishments.

**III**. In speaking of the clamities of war, as a punishment, it is proper to make a distinction between misfortune and injury. For a people may sometimes be engaged in war against their will, where they cannot be justly charged with entertaining hostile intentions.

Upon this subject, Velleius Paterculus observes that "to blame the Athenians for revolting, at the time they were besieged by Sylla, betrays a total ignorance of history. For the Athenians always continued so steady in their attachment to the Romans, that their fidelity became a proverbial expression. Yet their situation at that time excused their conduct, overpowered by the arms of Mithridates, they were obliged to submit to a foe within, while they had to sustain a siege from their friends without."

**IV**. and **V**. Between complete injuries and pure misfortunes there may be sometimes a middle kind of actions, partaking of the nature of both, which can neither be said to be done with known and willful intention, nor yet excused under colour of ignorance and want of inclination. Acts of pure misfortune neither merit punishment, nor oblige the party to make reparation for the loss occasioned. Hence many parts of history supply us with distinctions that are made between those who are the authors of a war, and principals in it, and those who are obliged to follow others, as accessories in the same.

**VI**. But respecting the authors of war, a distinction is to be made also, as to the motives and causes of war: some of which though not actually just, wear an appearance of justice, that may impose upon the well meaning. The writer to Herennius lays it down as the most equitable vindication of injury, where the party committing it, has neither been actuated by revenge, nor cruelty; but by the dictates of duty and an upright zeal.

Cicero, in the first book of his offices, advises the sparing of those, who have committed no acts of atrocity and cruelty in war, and that wars, undertaken to maintain national honour, should be conducted upon principles of moderation. And, in one of his letters, adverting to the war between Pompey and Caesar, he describes the struggle between those two illustrious men, as involved in so much obscurity of motives and causes, that many were perplexed in deciding which side to embrace. In his speech too for Marcellus, he remarks that such uncertainty might be attended with error, but could never be charged with guilt.

**VII**. Such forbearance in war is not only a tribute to justice, it is a tribute to humanity, it is a tribute to moderation, it is a tribute to greatness of soul. It was in this moderation, says Sallust, the foundation of Roman greatness was laid. Tacitus describes his countrymen as a people no less remarkable for their courage in the field, than for their humanity to the vanquished and suppliant.

On this subject, there is a brilliant passage in the fourth book to Herennius, where it is said, "It was an admirable resolution of our ancestors, never to deprive a captive prince of his life. For it would be truly a violation of common justice to abuse, by wanton cruelty and rigour, the power over those, whom fortune has put into our hands, by reducing them from the high condition, in which she had placed them before; their former enmity is forgotten. Because it is the characteristic of bravery to esteem opponents as enemies, while contending for victory, and to treat them as men, when conquered, in order to soften the calamities of war, and improve the terms and relations of peace. But it may be asked, if the enemy now treated with this indulgence would have shewn the same lenity himself. To which a reply may be made, that he is not an object of imitation in what he WOULD have done, so much as in what he OUGHT to have done."

**VIII**. Though there may be circumstances, in which absolute justice will not condemn the sacrifice of lives in war, yet humanity will require that the greatest precaution should be used against involving the innocent in danger, except in cases of extreme urgency and utility.

**IX**. After establishing these general principles, it will not be difficult to decide upon particular cases. Seneca says, that "in the calamities of war children are exempted and spared, on the score of their age, and women from respect to their sex." In the wars of the Hebrews, even after the offers of peace have been rejected, God commands the women and children to be spared.

Thus when the Ninevites were threatened with utter destruction, on account of their grievous crimes, a mitigation of the sentence was allowed, in compassion to the many thousands, who were of an age incapable of making a distinction between right and wrong.

If God, from whose supreme gift the life of man proceeds, and on whose supreme disposal it depends, prescribes to himself a rule like this, it is surely incumbent upon men, who have no commission, but for the welfare and preservation of the lives of men, to act by the same rule. Thus age and sex are equally spared, except where the latter have departed from this privilege by taking arms, or performing the part of men.

**X**. The same rule may be laid down too with respect to males, whose modes of life are entirely remote from the use of arms. And in the first class of this description may be placed the ministers of religion, who, among all nations, from times of the most remote antiquity have been exempted from bearing arms. Thus, as may be seen in sacred history, the Philistines, being enemies of the Jews, forbore doing harm to the company of prophets, that was at Gaba: and David fled with Samuel to another place, which the presence of a prophetic company protected from all molestation and injury.

Plutarch relates of the Cretans, that when all order among them was entirely broken by their civil broils, they abstained from offering violence to any member of the priesthood, or to those employed in the sacred rites belonging to the dead. From hence the Greeks came to denote a GENERAL MASSACRE by the proverbial expression of NO ONE BEING LEFT TO CARRY FIRE TO THE ALTAR.

Equally privileged with the holy priesthood are those, who devote their lives to the pursuit of letters, and other studies beneficial to mankind.

**XI**. Diodorus bestows an encomium upon the Indians, who, in all their wars with each other, forbore destroying or even hurting those employed in husbandry, as being the common benefactors of all. Plutarch relates the same of the ancient Corinthians and Megarensians, and Cyrus sent a message to the king of Assyria to inform him that he was willing to avoid molesting all who were employed in tilling the ground.

**XII**. To the above catalogue of those exempted from sharing in the calamities of war, may be added merchants, not only those residing for a time in the enemy's country, but even his natural-born, and regular subjects: artisans too, and all others are included; whose subsistence depends upon cultivating the arts of peace.

**XIII**. and **XIV**. More civilized manners having abolished the barbarous practice of putting prisoners to death, for the same reason, the surrender of those, who stipulate for the preservation of their lives either in battle, or in a siege, is not to be rejected.

The Romans, when investing towns, always accepted offers of capitulation, if made before the battering ram had touched the walls. Caesar gave notice to the Atuatici, that he would save their city, if they surrendered, before the battering ram was brought up. And in modern times it is the usual practice, before shells are thrown, or mines sprung, to summon places to surrender, which are thought unable to hold out-and where places are stronger, such summons is generally sent, before the storming is made.

**XV**. and **XVI**. Against these principles of natural law and equity an objection is sometimes derived from the necessity of retaliation, or striking terror, in cases of obstinate resistance. But such an objection is by no means just. For after a place has surrendered, and there is no danger to be apprehended from the prisoners, there is nothing to justify the further effusion of blood.-Such rigour was sometimes practised, where there were any enormous acts of injustice, or any violation of faith; it was practised also upon deserters, if taken.

Sometimes, where very important advantages may attend striking a terror, by preventing the same crimes in future from being committed, it may be proper to exercise the right of rigour in its full extent. But an obstinate resistance, which can be considered as nothing but the faithful discharge of a trust, can never come within the description of such delinquencies, as justify extreme rigour.

**XVII**. Where delinquencies indeed are such as deserve death, but the number of offenders is very great, it is usual, from motives of mercy, to depart in some degree from the right of enforcing the whole power of the law: the authority for so doing is founded on the example of God himself., who commanded such offers of peace to be made to the Canaanites, and their neighbours, the most wicked of any people upon the face of the earth, as might spare their lives upon the condition of their becoming tributaries.

**XVIII**. From the opinions advanced and maintained above, it will not be difficult to gather the principles of the law of nature respecting hostages.

At the time, when it was a general opinion that every one had the same right over his life, as over his property, and that right, either by express or implied consent was transferred from individuals to the state, it is not surprising that we should read of hostages, though harmless and innocent as individuals, being punished for the offences of the state: and, in this case, the consent of the state to such a regulation implies that of individuals, who have originally resigned their own will to that of the public; in whom, after such resignation, it indubitably vested.

But when the day-spring rose upon the world, men, obtaining clearer views of the extent of their power, found that God, in giving man dominion over the whole earth, reserved to himself the supreme disposal of his life, so that man cannot resign to anyone the right over his own life or that of another.

**XIX**. By way of conclusion to this subject it may be observed, that all actions no way conducive to obtain a contested right, or to bring the war to a termination, but calculated merely to display the strength of either side are totally repugnant to the duties of a Christian and to the principles of humanity. So that it behoves Christian princes to prohibit all unnecessary effusion of blood, as they must render an account of their sovereign commission to him, by whose authority, and in whose stead, they bear the sword.

## CHAPTER 12: ON MODERATION IN DESPOILING AN ENEMY'S COUNTRY.

*Lawfulness of despoiling an enemy's country — Forbearance of using this right, where things may be useful to ourselves, and out of an enemy's power — Forbearance in the hopes of speedy conquest, or where things are not immediately necessary to support an enemy, and aid him in maintaining the war — Buildings for the purposes of religion not to be wantonly destroyed — Advantages of this moderation.*

**I**. ONE of the three following cases is requisite to justify any one in destroying what BELONGS to another: there must be either such a necessity, as at the original institution of property might be supposed to form an exception, as if for instance any one should throw the sword of another into a river, to prevent a madman from using it to his destruction: still according to the true principles maintained in a former part of this work he will be bound to repair the loss: or there must be some debt, arising from the non-performance of an engagement, where the waste committed is considered as a satisfaction for that debt: or there must have been some aggressions, for which such destruction is only an adequate punishment.

Now, driving off some of our cattle, or burning a few of our houses, can never be pleaded as a sufficient and justifiable motive for laying waste the whole of an enemy's kingdom. Polybius saw this in its proper light, observing, that vengeance in war should not be carried to its extreme, nor extend any further than was necessary to make an aggressor atone justly for his offence. And it is upon these motives, and within these limits alone, that punishment can be inflicted. But except where prompted to it by motives of great utility, it is folly, and worse than folly, wantonly to hurt another.

But upon duly and impartially weighing the matter, such acts are oftener regarded in an odious light, than considered as the dictates of prudent and necessary counsels. For the most urgent and justifiable motives are seldom of long continuance, and are often succeeded by weightier motives of a more humane description.

**II**. It may be possible, under some circumstances, to detain what belongs to an enemy, so as to prevent his deriving advantage from it, in which case it would be an unnecessary and wanton act to destroy it. And to such circumstances the divine law has an eye, in ordering wild trees to be made use of for the construction of works in a siege, while fruit-trees, and every thing necessary for the support of man, ought, if possible, to be spared.

**III**. Where there is an expectation also of speedy victory and conquest, prudence will dictate to a general or commander of any kind the necessity of forbearing from all acts of destruction, by authorising and committing which he would only be injuring those possessions, that are likely to come into the hands of his own state or sovereign. Thus, as we are informed by Plutarch, when Philip had overrun Thessaly, destroying and plundering the whole country, Flaminius ordered his troops to march in a regular manner, as through a ceded country which had become their own.

**IV**. In the next place, it is unnecessary to destroy an enemy's country, when he has other sources, from which he can draw his supplies, as for instance, the sea or any adjoining territory. Archidamus, in Thucydides, attempting to dissuade the Lacedaemonians from a war with the Athenians, asks them, what object they propose to themselves by such a war? he asks them if they suppose that Attica can easily be laid waste owing to the advantage, which their troops have in superiority and numbers? but, says he, they have other dominions to furnish them with supplies, and they can avail themselves also of maritime importations. So that under such circumstances, it is best to leave agriculture unmolested, even on the frontiers of each side: a practice lately followed in the wars of the low countries, where contributions were paid to both parties, in return for such protection.

**V**. There are some things of such a nature, as to contribute, no way, to the support and prolongation of war: things which reason itself requires to be spared even during the heat and continuance of war. Polybius calls it brutal rage and madness to destroy things, the destruction of which does not in the least tend to impair an enemy's strength, nor to increase that of the destroyer: Such are Porticos, Temples, statues, and all other elegant works and monuments of art. Cicero commends Marcellus for sparing the public and private edifices of Syracuse, as if he had come with his army to protect THEM rather than to take the place by storm.

**VI**. As this rule of moderation is observed towards other ornamental works of art, for the reasons before stated, there is still greater reason, why it should be obeyed in respect to things devoted to the purposes of religion. For although such things, or edifices, being the property of the state may, according to the law of nations, be with impunity demolished, yet as they contribute nothing to aggravate the calamities, or retard the successes of war, it is a mark of reverence to divine things to spare them, and all that is connected therewith: and more especially should this rule be adhered to among nations, worshipping the same God according to the same fundamental laws, although differing from each other by slight shades of variation in their rights and opinions. Thucydides says that it was a law among the Greeks of his time, in all their invasions of each other's territories, to forbear touching the edifices of religion:

and Livy likewise observes that, upon the destruction of Alba by the Romans, the temples of the Gods were spared.

**VII**. What has been said of the sacred edifices of religion applies also to monuments raised in honour of the dead, unnecessarily to disturb whose ashes in their repose bespeaks a total disregard to the laws and ties of our common humanity.

**VIII**. Although it does not fall within the province of this treatise to inquire into the utility of war in all its various branches, but only to regulate its practices by confining them within due and lawful bounds; yet it will not be improper to observe that rules and practices derive much of their merit from the utility, with which they are attended. So that one great quality, to recommend the moderation above alluded to, will be found in its preventing the enemy from being driven to those resources, which men never fail, at last, of finding in despair. It is a just remark made by some Theologians, that all CHRISTIAN princes and rulers, who wish to be found SUCH in the sight of God as well as that of men, will deem it a duty to interpose their authority to prevent or to suppress all UNNECESSARY violence in the taking of towns: for acts of rigour can never be carried to an extreme without involving great numbers of the innocent in ruin. And practices of that kind, besides being no way conducive to the termination of war, are totally repugnant to every principle of Christianity and justice.

## CHAPTER 13: ON MODERATION IN MAKING CAPTURES IN WAR.

*Effects belonging to the subjects of an enemy, and taken detained as a pledge or debt — Not to be taken by way of punishment for another's offence — The debt or obligation, arising from a state of war, illustrated by examples — Forbearance in the exercise of such a right from principles of humanity.*

**I**. THE capture of an enemy's goods, even in JUST WAR, is not, in ALL CASES, perfectly justifiable, nor is the captor always exempt from the ties of restitution. For strictly speaking, according to the rules of pure justice, it is not lawful to seize or detain goods except to the exact amount of the debt which the enemy has incurred. Indeed goods may be detained beyond that, as a necessary pledge of security, but still upon the condition of being restored, as soon as the danger has ceased: RESTORED EITHER LITERALLY, OR BY SOME PROPER COMPENSATION BEING MADE.

Here then is a right of capture, which confers no right of property or acquisition. But when any thing may become due to us, either from a penalty or the non-performance of an engagement, in both cases a right to an enemy's goods, if they can be taken, is acquired. By the latter kind of debt not only the effects of the debtor himself, but those, belonging to his subjects, may according to the principles introduced by the law of nations be taken as a security.

This right of the law of nations is very different from that established in impunity alone, or depending upon the external force of judicial authority. For as by our private consent the person with whom we contract acquires not only an external and legal right over our property, but an internal right, proceeding from conscience, so he acquires the same right by a kind of common consent, which virtually comprehends the consent of individuals, in which sense the law is called the common compact or covenant of the state.

And in transactions of this kind it is most likely that nations approving of such a rule, introduced a law, which might not only prevent greater evils, but also enable every one to attain his own right.

**II**. But in the other kind of debt arising from penalty, or punishment, it does not appear, that nations consented to the establishment of any such right over the effects of subjects. For binding the property of one man for the offence of another is a kind of odious act, and therefore ought not to be extended farther than the law appears to have actually decreed. Nor is the advantage derived from the latter, by any means equal to that attending the former kind of debt. For what is due to us from damage, or the non-performance of a treaty may be considered as a part of our effects, but it is not so with the obligation to punishment, which is purely of a personal nature, therefore no loss is incurred by relinquishing this right.

Nor is the argument in the least weakened by what was said before respecting the Athenian law. For there it was maintained that subjects were not bound to suffer, because the state was amenable to punishment, but in order to compel the state to do what she ought to do, in bringing the guilty to punishment: a debt arising from duty, and relating to obligations of the former kind, rather than to those of the latter. For there is a difference between being obliged to punish another and being one's self amenable to punishment: tho' the latter may frequently arise from the neglect of doing the former, but still there is the same distinction between them, as between cause and effect.

The goods of subjects can only be taken by way of reprisal in return for other goods taken by the enemy; but they can never be taken as a punishment for the neglect of bringing offenders to justice. The delinquents themselves, in the number of whom may be reckoned those, who have neglected to discharge their duty in this respect, must answer for such offences.

**III**. The goods of subjects may be taken, and a property acquired therein, not only in order to obtain payment of the ORIGINAL debt, which occasioned the war, but of OTHER debts also, to which the same war may have given birth. And in this sense the words of those are to be taken, who maintain, that captures in war are not a perfect compensation for the principal debt, but only used as a means to enforce satisfaction for the damages sustained from aggressions. Thus the Romans, in their dispute with Antiochus, as related by Livy, thought it but right for that king to make reparation for all the expenses incurred in the war, which he had occasioned. Indeed any terms, that may be justly imposed upon the conquered may justly be enforced by war.

**IV**. The right of seizing the goods of the innocent subject of an enemy seems to have been introduced, in order to compel the original aggressor, or debtor to grant redress for the injury he had done: and although his falling on the innocent may be no way repugnant to what is legally right, it is in some measure a departure from the principles of humanity. On the other hand, history, especially the Roman history, abounds in examples of humanity, where lands have been restored to a conquered enemy, upon condition of their belonging to the STATE, and becoming subject to the payment of a tribute.

[**Translator's note:** The translation proceeds from the XIII. to the XV. Chapter of the original.]

## CHAPTER 15: ON MODERATION IN ACQUIRING DOMINION.

*How far internal justice permits us to acquire dominion — Moderation, in the use of this right over the conquered, laudable — Incorporating them with the conquerors — Allowing them to retain their dominions — Placing garrisons therein — Imposing tributes or other burdens — Utility of such moderation — Change in the form of a conquered government — The conquered permitted to retain some part of their former liberties — Especially in matters of religion — Clemency to be shewn.*

**I**. THAT equity and moderation towards individuals, which are so highly extolled, are still more deserving of admiration, when exercised towards nations and kingdoms; where injustice would be attended with more signal calamities, and moderation with more beneficial effects.

In just war the right of dominion over a people, and the sovereign power, which that people possess, may be acquired as well as any other right. But the claims to such a right ought by no means to be prosecuted beyond indemnity for aggression, and security against future evils.

But this motive, so necessary to be observed, especially in all treaties of peace, as well as in the use of victory, is often confounded with others. In other points a sovereign prince or state may relinquish a claim from a principle of moderation, but where the future security of their subjects is concerned, it is an act of cruelty rather than of moderation to relax too far in favour of a conquered enemy.

**II**. Aristotle has, more than once, said, that war is undertaken for the sake of peace, and toil endured in order to obtain rest. And in the same manner, Cicero has observed, that men go to war, that they may live in peace without molestation and injury. War too, as we are instructed by the teachers of true religion, may be made, to remove every thing that interrupts, and stands in the way of peace.

In the primitive ages, as we find from history, wars in general were made to preserve territories rather than to extend them. And any deviation from this rule was thought unlawful: thus the prophet Amos reproves the Ammonites for their love of making conquests.

**III**. The prudent moderation of the ancient Romans approaches nearly to this model of primitive innocence. For although they made conquests, they mitigated the fate of the conquered by incorporating them with themselves.

**IV**. Another mark of moderation in the use of victory is leaving to conquered kings, or nations the dominions, which they LAWFULLY held before.

Polybius highly extols the merit and wisdom of Antigonus, who, having Sparta in his power, allowed the inhabitants to retain their national polity and freedom.

**V**. Sometimes indeed a conqueror, though allowing a subjugated people to retain their dominion and sovereignty, must provide for his own security, by placing garrisons in their country.

**VI**. Contributions too are frequently imposed and levied, not so much by way of indemnity for expences incurred, as for a future security between the conqueror, and the conquered country. Upon the same principle, as was before observed, in explaining the nature of unequal treaties, conditions may be imposed also requiring a conquered power to deliver up a certain number of her ships and forts, and to reduce her troops to a limited number.

**VII**. But leaving to conquered powers a part or the whole of their dominions is not only sometimes an act of justice and humanity, but an act of sound policy also. Among other of Numa's institutions, his manner of celebrating the rites of TERMINUS, the DEITY OF BOUNDARIES, is much commended; for be prohibited the use of blood in those ceremonies, as an intimation that nothing was more conducive to the peace and harmony of the world, than for every nation to confine herself within her proper bounds.

In conformity to which maxim Florus observes, that it is more easy to make conquests than to keep' them. To which rule Plato, in his third book of Laws, adapts the proverbial expression of Hesiod, that HALF IS BETTER THAN THE WHOLE.

**VIII**. The Lacedaemonians and the Athenians anciently claimed no farther dominion over conquered cities and states, than purely wishing them to adopt forms of government like their own, the Lacedaemonians living under an aristocratic, and the Athenians under a democratic system. But whether such changes were conducive to a conqueror's security, it is not to our present purpose to examine.

**IX**. If it is not perfectly safe to forbear exercising ANY dominion over a conquered enemy, the matter may be so regulated as to leave him some portion of his former sovereignty and power. Thus among the Jews the sceptre remained with the Sanhedrim, even after Archelaus was deprived of his kingdom; and Alexander in many cases allowed Darius to remain a sovereign over others, while he required of him submission to himself.

**X**. Even though a conquered power was deprived of all sovereignty, she might be allowed to retain some of her laws, privileges, and magistracies of inferior importance. Thus, Pliny, in his letters, informs us, that in the proconsular province of Bithynia, the city of Apamaea was allowed to regulate the form of her government at her own pleasure, and, in other places, the Bithynians were permitted to retain their own magistrates, and their own senate.

**XI**. This indulgence ought to be shewn to every people, especially in their attachment to the religion of their forefathers, of which they should never be deprived but with their own consent and conviction. An indulgence, which Agrippa in his address to Caius, as cited by Philo in the account of his embassy, approves of, as highly grateful to the conquered people, and by no means prejudicial to the conqueror. At the same time a conqueror will take care that erroneous opinions do not prevail to the prejudice and overthrow of true religion, as was done by Constantine upon his crushing the party of Licinius, and afterwards by the Franks and other kings.

## CHAPTER 16: ON MODERATION WITH RESPECT TO THINGS EXCLUDED FROM THE RIGHT OF POSTLIMINIUM BY THE LAW OF NATIONS.

*Internal justice requires the restitution of things taken from others by an enemy in unjust war — Deductions made — Subjects and countries, if unjustly seized by an enemy, to be restored to their original sovereign — The time, when the obligation to restore them expires, defined — What is to be done in doubtful cases.*

**I**. How far things taken in just war become the property of the captors has been explained before. From which a deduction must be made of things recoverable by the right postliminium, those being no captures at all.

But things, taken in unjust war, are to be restored, not only by those, who have taken them, but by others also into whose hands they may have by any means fallen. For, as the Roman lawyers say, no one can convey to another a greater right than he himself possesses. The original captor had no just title to any property therein, neither can the person, deriving his title through him, establish any better claim A SECOND or THIRD possessor may have acquired a property therein, which the law presumes he has a right to, till the contrary be shewn, and for which an action may be maintained. Yet it is a right of which he cannot honestly avail himself against the real owner, from whom it was unjustly taken.

**II**. and **III**. Therefore such things are to be restored to those, from whom they were taken, which we find in ancient times was often done. Livy in relating the defeat of the Volscians and Aequi by a Roman Consul, says that the booty was exposed in a public place, for the space of three days, that every one, coming to recognise what belonged to him, might take it away.

But if any one has become possessed of such a thing by purchase, it may be asked, if he can charge the person from whom it was originally taken, with the price which he has paid for it? According to the principles before laid down, he certainly may charge as much to the person losing it, as the repossession of a thing, which he despaired of ever recovering, is worth.

The history of Abraham seems applicable to this subject, when he returned from his victory over the five kings. Being a man of noble and exalted piety, he would appropriate nothing to himself, but considering the things retaken, as his own right, in recompence for his labour and danger, he devoted a tenth part to God, after deducting the necessary expences, and divided a certain portion among his companions.

**IV**. AS THINGS are to be restored to their original owners, SO SUBJECTS are to be restored to their former lawful sovereigns.

**V**. The period also, when the obligation to restitution expires, is often a subject of inquiry. But this is a question, when arising between subjects of the same kingdom, which must be settled by the municipal laws of that country: but when the contending parties are the subjects of foreign powers, the matter can only be decided upon a conjecture of the time sufficient to constitute a presumed dereliction of property.

**VI**. But where the right of war is doubtful, it will be safest to follow the conduct of Aratus of Sicyon, in advising the new possessors in some measure to prefer taking a sum of money in lieu of the possession, and recommending the same maxim to the original owners, to prefer a sum of money, if they could obtain it, equivalent to the recovery of their right.

## CHAPTER 17: RESPECTING THOSE WHO ARE NEUTRAL IN WAR.

*Nothing to be taken belonging to neutrals, but under circumstances of extreme necessity, and with an intention to pay the full price of it — Conduct of neutral powers towards belligerents.*

**I** . IT MAY appear superfluous to speak of neutral powers, against whom no rights of war can exist. But as war, under the plea of necessity, occasions many aggressions to be committed against them, especially when bordering upon the seat of its operations, it may be necessary briefly to repeat a former assertion, that nothing short of extreme exigency can give one power a right over what belongs to another no way involved in the war. The case too is equally clear that no emergency can justify any one in taking and applying to his own use what the owner stands in equal need of himself. But even where the emergency can be plainly proved, nothing can justify us in taking or applying the property of another to our use,, beyond the IMMEDIATE DEMANDS OF THAT emergency. Where the CUSTODY of a thing, by securing it, is sufficient for the purpose, the USE and CONSUMPTION of it is absolutely unlawful. If the USE of it is necessary, it must not be ABUSED: and if the entire ABUSE of it be requisite, the full value should be paid.

**II** . Again, according to what was said in a preceding part of this book, it is the duty of those, who profess neutrality in a war to do nothing towards increasing the strength of a party maintaining an unjust cause, nor to impede the measures of a power engaged in a just and righteous cause. But in doubtful cases, they ought to shew themselves impartial to both sides, and to give no succour to besieged places, but should allow the troops of each to march through the country, and to purchase forage, and other supplies. The Corcyraeans, in Thucydides, say that if the Athenians intend to remain neuter, they ought either to prohibit the Corinthians from enlisting men in the territory of Attica, or to give THEM the same privilege. The Romans objected to the conduct of Philip king of Macedon, charging him with a double violation of treaties, both by injuring the allies of the Roman people, and assisting the enemy with supplies of men and money.

[**Translator's note:** The translation proceeds from the xviith to the xixth chapter of the original.]

## CHAPTER 19: ON GOOD FAITH BETWEEN ENEMIES.

*Good faith due to enemies of every description — Due even to pirates, and others of the same kind, in all treaties with them — A promise given to them, binding, when not extorted by fear — Oaths to be inviolably observed — The law of nations does not allow fear to be alleged as an exception to the above rules — Good faith to be observed even to a treacherous enemy — This obligation ceases, where one of the parties violates his engagements — Or refuses a just compensation — Even where the obligation arose from a different contract — From loss occasioned — Or from a penalty — Application of these principles to war.*

**I**. IT WAS before said that the number and extent of actions, lawful in war, may be considered either upon their own intrinsic merits, or as rising out of some antecedent engagement. The former point having before been fully explained, this is the proper place for discussing the latter, which comprehends the good faith of enemies towards each other.

Cicero, in his fifth book on the bounds of good and evil, has well observed that every one must approve and commend a disposition to adhere faithfully to our engagements not only from disinterested motives, but in some cases even in opposition to our own interest. And Augustine says that it is right to maintain the pledge of faith given to an enemy, for under the character of enemies men do not lose their right to the fulfilment of a promise, a right which every one possessed of reason is capable of. It is the power of reason and speech from which the obligation of promises springs. Nor is it to be supposed that, because it is lawful to deceive an enemy on some occasions, the same rule will authorise a violation of faith in engagements. For the obligation to speak the truth arises from causes antecedent in their existence to any state of warfare, and they are causes which a state of warfare may render it necessary to change or abridge. But a promise confers a new right of itself. A distinction which did not escape the notice of Aristotle, who, in speaking of truth, says that he does not consider truth and sincerity in engagements, with relation to justice or injustice, but as belonging to another class of virtues.

**II**. As to engagements with pirates, we may observe, that Pompey in a great measure concluded the disputes with them by treaty, sparing their lives, and allowing them places to reside in, on condition of their abandoning their former way of life. The law of nations indeed has not established the same mode of communication with them, as among regular enemies in just and lawful war: but still the very circumstance of their being MEN, entitles them to those privileges which are sanctioned by the law of nature, among which the observance of engagements is one.

**III**. Let us consider if a more specious argument than Cicero's may not be devised on this subject. In the first place it may be stated that atrocious malefactors, forming no part of a state, may be punished by any one whatever, according to the law of nature. For those, who may be punished with death, may upon the same principle be deprived of their property and all their rights. And among rights may be enumerated the right of requiring a fulfilment of promises and engagements: the guilty may therefore be deprived of this right by way of penalty. In reply to which it may be said, this will certainly be the case, if the person is treated with, but not as a malefactor: for the very act of treating with him shews that he is not considered any longer in that light, but as one entitled to all the rights of treaty, the criminal part of his character not being taken into the account, all penalties on that score being, as it were remitted. For every act of treaty must be interpreted so as to avoid absurdity.

**IV**. An objection to treating with pirates upon principles of good faith is deduced from their calling, which is to extort terms by fear. Now where a promise has been extorted., the promisor is released from his engagement, as having unjustly sustained a damage, by an act repugnant to the nature of human liberty, and to the nature of human action, which ought to be free.

This, it must be admitted, may sometimes happen, but does not apply to all promises made to pirates. For to make the person, to whom a promise has been given, liable to release the engagement, the promiser himself must have been forced to give the promise under impressions of unjust fear. So that if any one has promised a ransom in order to redeem a friend from captivity, he will be bound by his promise. For in this case there was no impression of fear, as he came voluntarily to make the contract.

**V**. A promise too made through the compulsion of fear will be binding, where it has been ratified by the solemn sanction of an oath: for in that case it is not only one man making an engagement to a fellow creature, but binding himself to God by the most solemn appeal: against' which neither fear nor any other motive can form an exception. Yet the heir of a promiser is not bound by any such obligation: because inheritances pass according to the rules of human intercourse established at the original institution of property: but the divine right to the fulfilment of oaths, as such, is not included in these. From the above arguments a conclusion may be deduced, that if any one violates a pledge given to such an enemy either upon oath or without oath, he will not on that account be liable to punishment among other nations, because from the general horror which piracy excites, nations have thought proper to pass over without notice the violation of rules of faith towards them.

[**Translator's note:** Sections VI, VII, VIII, IX and X of the original are omitted in the translation.]

XI. Solemn war, signifying such as is proclaimed and begun on both sides by authority of the sovereign or state, among its many other legal rights, includes also that of giving validity to every promise, which may be conducive to its termination, so that if either party, through an ill-grounded fear of further calamities, has, even against his will, made promises unfavourable, or acceded to terms disadvantageous to himself, such an engagement will be binding. For the law of nations allows belligerent powers to alarm each other, if possible, into submission upon the most unequal terms, in the same manner, as it gives a sanction to many things not strictly equitable according to natural and municipal law. For if such a practice had not been established, wars, which are so frequent, could never have been brought to a conclusion, an object so much for the interest of mankind.

These are the rights of war which Cicero says ought to be inviolably preserved with an enemy: for an enemy not only retains his natural rights in war, but certain other rights originating in the consent of nations. Yet it does not follow from hence that any one, who has extorted such a promise in unjust war, can, consistently with piety and the duties of a good man, retain what he has so received, nor can he compel another to stand to such engagements, whether upon oath, or not. For the natural and internal injustice of such a promise always remains the same, nor can the injustice be removed or altered, till it has received a new and free concurrence from the party, by whom it was given.

**XII**. The only impressions of fear, that can be lawfully inspired in regular war, are those which are approved of by the law of nations. Thus no one can avail himself of a promise, extorted from an ambassador under impressions of fear excited by the seizing of his person.

**XIII**. and **XIV**. There are two cases, in which a person may not perform his engagement or promise, without being guilty of treachery: and those are, where the conditions have not been fulfilled, or some compensation has been made. For in one and the same treaty all the clauses seem connected with each other, as a kind of condition expressing the intention of one party to fulfil his engagement, if the other shall do the same. Therefore Tullus, in replying to the Albans invokes destruction upon the head of that people who first rejected the just claims of ambassadors demanding restitution, wishing that all the calamities of war might fall upon them. For, says Ulpian, he shall no longer be held as a confederate, who has renounced a treaty, owing to some condition, on which it was made, not being fulfilled. For which reason, wherever it is intended otherwise, it is usually stated in express terms, that the violation of any particular clause shall not annul the whole treaty.

**XV**. The origin of compensation was explained in the second book of this treatise,* where it was said to be the power and right of receiving an equivalent, for some thing belonging to us, which is in the hands of another, or any thing due to us, which we cannot otherwise obtain: and much more then have we a right on the same account to detain any thing which is ALREADY IN OUR POWER, whether it be of a corporeal or an incorporeal kind. So that we are not obliged to perform a promise, if it be no more than equivalent to a thing of ours which the other party detains. Seneca, in his sixth book ON BENEFITS, says that a creditor often becomes under an obligation to his debtor, if he takes more than an equivalent for his debt. For though it may be granted that he has lent money, yet if by such a loan he has obtained the possession of lands, which he never bought, he changes situations with his debtor, and becomes a debtor in his turn.

**XVI**. It will be the same, if one of the contracting parties owes as much, or more, from some other engagement: and the debt cannot otherwise be obtained, than by taking advantage of the present contract, though it has no connection with the former debt. But in a LEGAL point of view, all actions are perfectly distinct, nor can their forms, their grounds, or their substance be confounded; but certain cases are confined to certain laws, to which it is necessary invariably to adhere: one law cannot be mixed with another, but every one in the prosecution of a right must tread upon invariable and beaten ground. But the law of nations does not regard such distinctions, it allows us to transgress them where there is no other means of obtaining our right.

**XVII.** and **XVIII.** The same may be said too, where the party exacting a promise, has not contracted any debt by engagement, but has done an injury to the promiser. And whatever is due by way of punishment may be balanced against a promise.

**XIX.** If while a law-suit is depending, the parties enter into an agreement of any kind, either to pay the costs, or to make good other damages, they cannot avail themselves both of this agreement, and claim a further compensation for the original matter in dispute. In the same manner, if during the continuance of a war the belligerents negotiate for a conclusion of the original dispute, they are supposed thereby to settle every cause of hostility, nor can they any further avail themselves of the rights of war, so as to enjoy both the advantages of them, and of negotiation, at the same time. For if this were the case, no treaties could ever be enforced with certainty.

It may be asked, of what nature are the things for which a promise of compensation should be given? In answer to which it may be observed, that such a promise or engagement may be made in lieu of some other obligation incurred during the course of a war: as for instance, where the breach of a truce has been committed, the rights of an ambassador violated, or any other action done, repugnant to the principles established by the law of nations among belligerent powers.

Still it must be observed that the parties, in making compensation, should abstain with the utmost caution from infringing upon the rights of a third person, especially where this can be done without abandoning the principles of the law of nations, which makes the effects of subjects answerable for the debts of the state. Besides it is the mark of a dignified mind to adhere to engagements even after receiving an injury. On which account the Indian sage Jarchas commended that king, who on sustaining an injury from a neighbouring and confederate power, said he should not think himself released from his sworn engagements, which were solemn acts, that no injustice on the part of another could repeal.

Almost all questions relating to pledges of faith given by one belligerent power to another, may be solved upon the principles before laid down, in explaining the nature and force of promises in general; of oaths, treaties, and conventions, and also in explaining the rights of the obligations of kings, and the method of interpreting doubtful points. But in order to remove every doubt and difficulty, perhaps a brief discussion of the most usual and practical topics of negotiation will not be deemed tedious.

## CHAPTER 20: ON THE PUBLIC FAITH, BY WHICH WAR IS CONCLUDED; COMPRISING TREATIES OF PEACE, AND THE NATURE OF ARBITRATION, SURRENDER HOSTAGES, PLEDGES.

*In monarchies the power of making peace a royal prerogative — In aristocracies and democracies, this right belongs to a greater number of persons — In what manner the public dominions or any part of them may be alienated — How far a peace concluded by the king binds the state, or his successors — Property of individuals ceded for the benefit of the state at the time of making peace — Indemnity to those individuals — Losses sustained in war — No distinction between things acquired according to the law of nations and the civil law — Transactions of the sovereign with foreign nations deemed valid from motives of public utility — General rule of interpreting the terms of peace — In doubtful cases the former state of things supposed to be continued by a treaty of peace — Things restored to the state they were in before the war — Independent states, voluntarily joining one of the belligerent powers cannot claim indemnity of the other — General amnesty — Private debts subsisting before the war not included therein — Restoration of captures — Rules respecting such restorations — Dubious points to be interpreted to the prejudice of the party dictating the terms — Distinction between new causes of war, and the breach of a peace — Rupture by any act contrary to the terms of peace in general — Infraction of a treaty by allies or subjects — Violation of a particular treaty — Heads of treaties — Penalties annexed — Unavoidable impediments to the fulfilment of a treaty — Peace continued at the option of the injured party — Relations of amity — How far receiving subjects and exiles may be considered as a breach thereof — Victory — War concluded by arbitration — Arbitrators bound by rules of strict justice — Absolute, and conditional surrender — Hostages can be detained for no other than the express cause for which they were given — Released by the death of the party for whom they were given — Obligation of pledges — Right of redeeming them lost.*

**I**. Good faith, either expressed or implied, must be the foundation of every treaty between hostile powers. And again the faith that is expressed is either of a public or a private nature, and the pledges given either by the sovereign, or inferior authorities in states constitute the public faith. It is, by such pledges given on the part of the sovereign power alone, that peace can be concluded, or the rights of war enforced. In the termination of every war, either the principal, or accessory causes are to be considered. Treaties are in general regarded as the principal instrument, by which wars are ended, and the mediation, or decision of a third person or power is deemed a secondary or accessory means.

**II**. The person, who has authority to begin a war, is the only one to whom the right of making peace can properly belong, according to the general maxim, that every one is the best judge in the management of his own affairs. From hence it follows, that public war can be made by the sovereign power alone on each side: a right which in every kingly government is very justly vested in the crown.

**III**. and **IV**. In popular or aristocratic forms of government, the right of making war, or concluding peace, is generally lodged in some public council or body, where a majority of voices may form treaties, conventions, or resolutions, which will be binding upon the dissentient part of such council. And all who are bound by a peace, whether approving it or not are entitled to its benefits.

**V**. In examining those objects, which form the most material part of treaties, we may observe, that kingdoms are not so much a patrimony, which may be alienated at pleasure, as a trust, placed in the hands of the sovereign for the benefit of his people. Indeed kings themselves are aware of this, even before the crown descends upon their heads, and they receive it upon condition of adhering to such sacred obligations.

Nor can such alienations ever be made, so as to be attended with consequences like those of private contracts, or to render the goods and effects of subjects answerable for such engagements. For if that were the case, the fundamental laws of the kingdom, prohibiting such alienations, would be of no effect.

To render the alienation of the whole public dominion valid, the consent of the constituted authorities of the state is requisite. And indeed to confirm the transfer of any particular portion, the consent of the whole body as well as of that particular member will be necessary: for otherwise such alienation would be like the violent separation of a limb from the natural body.

A whole people may in a case of extreme necessity transfer themselves to the dominion of another, a right which undoubtedly was reserved at the original formation of society.

Neither is there any thing to prevent a king from alienating his patrimonial and private possessions. Yet there may be parts of the royal dominion, which the sovereign cannot alienate from the crown, especially, if he has received it upon condition of making no personal appropriation of any thing belonging thereto.

There are two ways in which the possessions of the crown may become the patrimony of the king, either as separable or inseparable parts of the kingdom. In the latter case they can only be transferred with the kingdom itself, but in the former, they may be alienated by themselves. And where the crown is not patrimonial and hereditary, the restrictions upon the sovereign in this respect are much greater.

**VI**. A nation and a king's successors are bound by his engagements, in proportion to the power, which he derives from the constitution, of making such engagements. For though this power may not be absolutely unlimited, yet it ought not to be clogged with unnecessary restrictions. It should be such as may enable him to exercise his discretion and judgment on proper occasions for the benefit of his people.

The case will be different, where a king's power over his subjects is like that of a master over his household, more than of a sovereign over his state, as where he has entirely subjugated a people, or where his controul over their property is absolute. Thus Pharaoh purchased all the land in Egypt, and others have admitted strangers into their territories allowing them to hold lands upon such conditions. For here, there is another right in addition to that of a sovereign, and it is a right, which sovereignty alone without conquest could never have conferred.

**VII**. The right of sovereigns to dispose of the effects of individuals, in order to make peace, is often a disputed point, nor can they exercise this right over the property of subjects in any other manner than as sovereigns.

The property of subjects is so far under the eminent controul of the state, that the state or the sovereign who represents it, can use that property, or destroy it, or alienate it, NOT ONLY IN CASES OF EXTREME NECESSITY, which sometimes allow individuals the liberty of infringing upon the property of others, but on all OCCASIONS, where the public good is concerned, to which the original framers of society intended that private interests should give way. But when that is the case, it is to be observed, the state is bound to repair the losses of individuals, at the public expence, in aid of which the sufferers have contributed their due proportion. Nor will the state, though unable to repair the losses for the present, be finally released from the debt, but whenever she possesses the means of repairing the damages, the dormant claim and obligation will be revived.

**VIII**. There must be some hesitation in admitting the opinion of Ferdinand Vasquez, who maintains that the state is not bound to repair the losses, which are occasioned to individuals in the course of war, as those are accidents permitted by the rights of war.

For those rights regard the relation of foreign states and enemies to each other, but bear no reference to the disputes of subjects among themselves, who, being united in the same cause, ought to share the common losses, which happen to them in supporting the privileges of their society. It is a rule likewise established by the civil law, that no action can be brought against the state for the losses sustained in war, as every one is thereby induced to defend his own property with more earnestness and spirit.

**IX**. Some make a distinction between the property which subjects are entitled to from the law of nations and that which they possess by the authority of the civil law, allowing the king a more extensive controul over the latter, even to the power of taking it without cause or compensation, which is not the case with property of the former kind. But this is an improper distinction. For whatever may be the origin of property, it is always attended with peculiar effects according to the law of nature: so that it cannot be taken away for any other reasons than those inherent in the nature of property itself, or derived from some act of the owners.

**X**. The prohibition respecting the property of individuals being given up, except for some public advantage, is a matter resting entirely between a sovereign and his subjects, and a compensation for losses is an affair between the state and individuals. But in all transactions between a king and foreigners, the act of the king is sufficient to give them NATIONAL validity, not only out of respect to his personal dignity, but according to the law of nations, which renders the effects of subjects responsible for the acts of the sovereign.

**XI**. In interpreting treaties of peace, favourable circumstances are always to be taken in their utmost latitude, and unfavourable circumstances to be limited as strictly as possible.

Regarding purely the law of nature, the most favourable construction is that, whereby every one is restored to his own property and possessions. Therefore where the articles of a treaty are ambiguous, the construction should go so far, as to grant the party, who has evidently justice on his side, the object for which he went to war, and likewise indemnity for the losses which he has sustained.

But it is not allowable that either party should gain more than an indemnity, or demand any thing by way of punishment, which is of an odious nature.

As in making peace, it scarcely ever happens that either party will acknowledge the injustice of his cause, or of his claims, such a construction must be given, as will equalize the pretensions of each side, which may be accomplished, either by restoring the disputed possessions to their former situation, or by leaving them in the state, to which the war has reduced them.

**XII**. Of these two methods, in a doubtful case, the latter is preferred, as being the more easily adjusted, and occasioning no further change. From hence the -right of postliminium belongs to such prisoners, as are expressly included in the treaty. Neither are deserters to be given up, unless it be so agreed. For by the laws of war any power is allowed to receive deserters, and even to enlist them in his own army.

By such agreement other things remain in the hands of the possessors, by which is not meant a civil, but a natural possession: for in war BARE POSSESSION is sufficient, nor is any other kind looked for. And lands are said to be so possessed, when inclosed or defended by fortifications, for a temporary occupation by an encampment is not regarded in this case. Hence Demosthenes in his speech for Ctesiphon, says that Philip was anxious to make himself master of all the places he could seize, as he knew that upon the conclusion of a peace, he should retain them.

Incorporeal rights cannot be held but by the occupation of the things with which they are connected; as for instance, the services of lands, or through means of the persons, to whom they belong: but the holders of such rights lose them, when an enemy has become master of the country.

**XIII**. In that other mode of treaty, whereby possession, that has been disturbed in the course of a war, is restored, it is proper to observe that the last possession, immediately before the war began, is that, which is always meant, so that the individuals then unjustly ejected, may have recourse to law, either to obtain possession by a provisional decree, or to make good their claim.

**XIV**. If an independent people VOLUNTARILY and SPONTANEOUSLY place themselves under the controul and protection of one of the belligerent powers, such a people cannot be included among those entitled to restitution, which only belongs to those who have suffered losses by violence, through fear, or any lawful stratagem of war. Thus when peace was made among the Grecian states, the Thebans retained Plataea, observing that they neither owed their possession of it to violence, nor treachery, but to the free surrender of those, to whom it belonged.

**XV**. Unless there is an express stipulation to the contrary, it is understood that, in all treaties of peace, there is an implied assent that no actions are to be brought for losses occasioned by the accidental calamities of war, either to states or individuals. For those are natural consequences of a state of hostilities: and it is supposed that in doubtful cases, no belligerent would consent to be convicted of injustice.

**XVI**. The debts, owing to individuals, at the beginning of a war, are not to be thought thereby discharged. For they are not things acquired by the laws of war: for war only prevents the claim to them from being prosecuted, but by no means releases the obligation. So that when the impediment of war is removed, such debts retain their original force. For though it ought not to be presumed that any one should easily be deprived of a right subsisting before the war, yet this is to be understood of the rights arising out of the foundation of property, whereby a community and equality of goods was abolished. For states and governments, says Cicero, were originally and principally designed to preserve to every one the possession of his own property.

**XVII**. The right to claim lands or goods of any kind, by way of PUNISHMENT, is not of equal force with the above rules. For in transactions and treaties of that kind between kings and sovereign states, all claims of that kind seem and indeed ought to be relinquished, otherwise peace would be no peace, if the old and original causes of the war were allowed to remain and be revived. And the most latent and remote causes are supposed to be included in the most GENERAL TERMS, in treaties of peace, whereby they are sunk in oblivion.

**XVIII**. The rights of individuals to penalties are not supposed to be abandoned, resting entirely upon different grounds: because they may be decided by legal tribunals without appealing to the sword. Yet as our rights of this sort are not of the same kind with those of absolute property, and as penalties have always something odious in their nature, any faint verbal conjecture will be thought a sufficient presumption of their being remitted.

**XIX**. The objection made against taking away any rights, that existed before the war, applies chiefly to the rights Of INDIVIDUALS. For where the words of a treaty supply any probable conjecture, it is most natural to suppose that KINGS and NATIONS have more readily relinquished certain rights, especially in matters, where those rights are not clearly and fully ascertained. So that, giving the most favourable construction to their conduct, they are supposed to have been animated with the noble desire of rooting up and destroying all the seeds of war.

**XX**. All captures, made after a treaty is finished, must evidently be restored. For the treaty puts an end to all the rights of war.

**XXI**. But in treaties relating to the restoration of things taken in war, a more extensive interpretation must be given, where the advantages are mutual than where they incline only to one side.

In the next place all the parts of a treaty relating to persons are to be interpreted more favourably than those relating to things: and among those relating to things, priority is given to lands before moveable effects, and also among these, such as are in the hands of the state are held in more consideration than the possessions of individuals. And again, among things in the possession of individuals, those are more favoured which are held under a beneficial title, than those which are loaded with incumbrances, as things held by money payments, or by dower.

**XXII**. The person, to whom any thing is ceded by a treaty of peace, is entitled to the produce and fruits of it, from the time of such cession, and not farther back: a point maintained by Augustus Caesar in opposition to Sextus Pompey, who, upon Peloponnesus being ceded to him, claimed also the tributes and revenues, that were due for former years.

**XXIII**. The names of countries are to be taken according to the usage of the present time, not so much according to the popular acceptation, as to that of men of science, by whom those subjects are generally treated of.

**XXIV**. These rules also are of frequent use, whenever there is a reference to an antecedent, or to an ancient treaty. For in that case the qualities and conditions of the latter treaty are considered as a repetition of those expressed in the former. -And the person contracting is to be considered as having really performed his part of the engagement, which he certainly would have done, had he not been prevented by the party with whom he is engaged in dispute.

**XXV**. What some allege in excuse for a short delay in the execution of a treaty is not to be admitted as true, except some unforeseen necessity has occasioned the impediment. For though some of the canon-laws may favour such a plea, that is not surprising, considering they are framed solely with the view of promoting charity among Christians. But in this question relating to the interpretation of treaties, it is not so much our business to lay down what is best and properest for every one to do, nor even to state what religion and piety require, as to consider what every one may be compelled by legal authority to do.

**XXVI**. In doubtful matters it is usual for an interpretation to be given more prejudicial to the party who has dictated the terms, than to the other, because in general he is the more powerful: in the same manner, in explaining the terms of a bargain, a construction is generally given against the seller: as he may blame himself for not having spoken more clearly, and openly. Whereas the other, comprehending the terms in more meanings than one, might fairly select that most favourable to himself.

**XXVII**. It is a matter of frequent dispute what constitutes the breach of a peace. For it is not the same thing to break a peace, as to furnish new grounds and causes of war. There is a great difference between these things, both as to the penalty incurred by the aggressor, and as to the aggrieved party being, in other respects, released from his engagements.

There are three ways, in which a peace may be broken, — either by doing something contrary to the very essence Of ALL peace, — or something in violation of the EXPRESS terms of a PARTICULAR peace, — or something contrary to the EFFECTS, which are intended to arise from every peace.

**XXVIII**. A thing is done contrary to the very essence of all peace, when hostile aggressions are committed without any new grounds of war. But where any specious pretext can be assigned for taking arms, it is better it should be supposed purely an act of injustice, than an act of injustice accompanied with perfidy. It is hardly necessary to quote the words of Thueydides, who says, "it is not the party, who repels force by arms, but the power who first makes the attack, that violates a peace."

Having laid down these rules, it remains to be considered, who are the AGGRESSORS, and who are the AGGRIEVED PERSONS, in the breaking of a peace.

**XXIX**. There are some, who think that a peace is broken, when even those, who have been allies do any of these things. Nor indeed can it be denied, that such an agreement MAY be made, for one ally to become liable to punishment for the actions of another, and for a peace to be deemed ratified and permanent only upon conditions, partly arbitrary, and partly casual.

But it is hardly credible, unless there is the clearest evidence of it, that peace is ever concluded upon such terms. For it is contrary to all rule, and repugnant to the common wishes of those, who make peace. Therefore those, who have committed hostile aggressions, without the assistance of others, will be deemed breakers of the peace, against whom alone the injured party will have a right to take arms.

**XXX**. If subjects have committed any act of hostility without authority and commission from the state, it will form a proper subject of inquiry, whether the state can be judged responsible for the acts of individuals: to constitute which responsibility, it is evident that a knowledge of the fact, power to punish it, and having neglected to do so, are requisite.

A formal notice given to the sovereign of the offending subjects is supposed to amount to a knowledge of the fact, and it is presumed that every sovereign is able to controul and punish his own subjects, unless there be some defect in his authority: and a lapse of time, beyond what is usually taken for the punishment of civil offences in every country, may be construed into willful neglect. And such neglect amounts to a sanction of the offence.

**XXXI**. It is likewise frequently made a subject of inquiry, whether a state is answerable for the conduct of any of her people, who do not take arms by her authority, but serve in the armies of some other power engaged in war. The Cerites, in Livy, clear themselves upon this principle, that it was not by their authority their people bore arms. And it is a well-founded opinion that no such permission ought to be deemed as given, unless it appear from probable reasons that it was intended it should be granted: a thing sometimes done, according to the example of the ancient Aetolians, who thought they had a right to deprive every plunderer of his spoils. A custom the force of which Polybius expresses in the following words, "when other powers, friends and allies of the Aetolians, are at war with each other, the Aetolians may nevertheless serve in the armies on either side, destroying and spoiling their respective countries."

**XXXII**. Again, a peace ought to be deemed broken, not only by any act of violence done to the body politic itself, but to any of the subjects, without new grounds of war. For peace is made with a view to the security of every individual subject: as the state in making peace acts for the whole, and for all its parts.

Indeed even if new grounds of war should arise, every one may, during the continuance of peace, defend himself and his property. For it is a natural right to repel force by force: a right which it cannot easily be supposed that those, who are upon a footing of equality have ever renounced.

But to practise revenge, or use violence in recovering things taken away will not be lawful, except where justice is denied. justice may admit of some delay: but the other method demands prompt execution, and therefore should not be undertaken but in extreme emergency. But if the subjects of any country persist in a course of uniform crime, and aggression, repugnant to all natural and civil law, in defiance of the authority of their own government, so that the hand of justice cannot reach them, it will be lawful for any one to deprive them of their spoils, and to exercise upon them the same rigour, as if they were delivered up to punishment. But to attack other innocent persons on that account is a direct violation of peace.

**XXXIII**. Any act of violence also offered to allies, constitutes a breach of the peace, but they must be such allies as are comprehended in the treaty.

The same rule holds good, even if the allies themselves have not made the treaty, but others have done so on their behalf: since it is evident that those allies regarded the peace as ratified and valid. For they are looked upon as enemies, till it is certain they have consented to the ratification.

Other allies, or connections, who are neither subjects nor named in the treaty of peace, form a distinct class, to whom any violence done cannot be construed into an act of breaking the peace. Yet it does not follow that war may not be undertaken on such an account, but then it will be a war resting entirely upon new grounds.

**XXXIV**. A peace is broken by doing any thing contrary to the express terms of it; and by this is likewise meant the non-performance of engagements.

**XXXV**. Nor can we admit of any distinction between articles of greater or minor importance.

For ALL the articles of a treaty are of sufficient magnitude to require observance, though Christian charity may overlook the breach of them upon due acknowledgement. But to provide greater security for the continuance of a peace, proper clauses will be annexed to the minor articles, stating that any thing done against them shall not be deemed an infraction of the treaty: or that mediation shall be adopted in preference to having recourse to arms,

**XXXVI**. This seems to have been plainly done in treaties, where any special penalty was annexed. A treaty indeed may be made upon terms allowing the injured party his option either of enacting the penalty, or receding from his engagement: but the nature of the business rather requires the method of mediation. It is evident and proved from the authority of history, that one of the parties, who has not fulfilled his engagement, owing to the neglect of the other to do so, is by no means guilty of breaking the peace: as his obligation was only conditional.

**XXXVII**. If there is any unavoidable necessity to prevent one party from fulfilling his engagement, as for instance, if a thing has been destroyed, or carried off, by which the restoration of it has become impossible, a peace shall not thereby be deemed broken, the continuance of it not depending upon CASUAL conditions. But the other party may have his option, either to prefer waiting, if there is any reason to hope that the engagement may be fulfilled at some future period, or to receive an equivalent, or to be released, on his side from some corresponding article of the treaty.

**XXXVIII**. It is honourable, and laudable to maintain a peace, even after it has been violated by the other party: as Scipio did, after the many treacherous acts of the Carthaginians. For no one can release himself from an obligation by acting contrary to his engagements, And though it may be further said that the peace is broken by such an act, yet the breach ought to be taken in favour of the innocent party, if he thinks proper to avail himself of it.

**XXXIX**. Lastly, a peace is broken by the violation of any special and express clause in the treaty.

**XL**. In the same manner, those powers, who commit unfriendly acts, are guilty of breaking that peace, which was made solely upon condition of amicable relations being preserved. For what, in other cases, the duties of friendship alone would require, must here be performed by the law of treaty.

And it is to treaties of this kind that many points may be referred, which are discussed by legal writers, relating to injuries done without force of arms, and to the offences of insults. According to this principle, Tully has observed, that any offence committed after a reconciliation is not to be imputed to neglect, but to willful violation, not to imprudence, but to treachery.

But here it is necessary, if possible, to exclude from the account every charge of an odious kind. So that an injury done to a relation or subject of the person, with whom a treaty of peace has been made, is not to be deemed the same, as one done to himself, unless there are evident proofs that, through them, an attack upon him was intended. And an invasion of another's rights is often to be ascribed to new motives of rapacity, rather than to those of treachery.

Atrocious menaces, without any new grounds of offence, are repugnant to all terms of amity. Any one may assume this threatening posture, by erecting new fortifications in his territory, as a means of annoyance rather than offence, by raising an unusual number of forces: when it is evident that these preparations can be designed against no one, but the power with whom he has concluded peace.

**XLI**. Nor is it contrary to the relations of amity to receive individual subjects, who wish to remove from the dominions of one power to those of another. For that is not only a principle of natural liberty, but favourable to the general intercourse of mankind. On the same grounds a refuge given to exiles may be justified. But it is not lawful to receive whole towns, or great bodies, forming an integral part of the state. Nor is it more allowable to receive those, who are bound to the service of their own state by oath or other engagement.

[**Translator's note:** Sections XLII, XLIII, XLIV, & XLV, of the original, relating to decisions by lot and single combat, are omitted in the translation.]

**XLVI**. There are two kinds of arbitration, the one of such a nature that it must be obeyed whether the decision be just or unjust, which, Proculus says, is observed when, after a compromise, recourse is had to arbitration.

The other kind of arbitration is where a matter ought to be left to the decision of a person, in whose integrity confidence may be placed, of which Celsus has given us an example in his answer, where he says, I though a freedman has sworn, that he will do all the services, which his patron may adjudge, the will of the patron ought not to be ratified, unless his determination be just."

This interpretation of an oath, though comformable to the Roman laws, is by no means consistent with the simplicity of language considered by itself. For the justice of the case remains the same, in whatever way an arbiter is chosen, whether it be to reconcile contending parties, a character, in which we find the Athenians acting between the Rhodians and Demetrius, or to make an absolute decree.

Although the civil law may decide upon the conduct of such arbiters to whom a compromise is referred, so as to allow of an appeal from their decrees, or of complaints against their injustice, this can never take place between kings and nations. For here there is no superior power, that can either rivet or relax the bonds of an engagement, The decree therefore of such arbiters must be final and without appeal.

**XLVII**. With respect to the office of an arbiter or mediator, it is proper to inquire, whether the person has been appointed in the character of a judge, or with powers more extensive and discretionary than legal powers. Aristotle says that "an equitable and moderate man will have recourse to arbitration rather than to strict law, ADDING AS A REASON, because an arbitrator may consider the equity of the case, whereas a judge is bound by the letter of the law. Therefore arbitration was introduced to give equity its due weight."

Equity does not signify in this place, as it does else. where, that part of justice, which gives a strict interpretation of the general expressions of the law, according to the intention of the law-giver. For that is left to the judge. But it includes every thing, which it is more proper to do than to omit, even beyond what is required by the express rules of justice. -Such kind of arbitration being common among individuals and subjects of the same empire, it is recommended by St. Paul as a practice peculiarly proper for Christians. Yet in doubtful cases it ought not to be presumed that such extensive powers are granted. For where there is any obscurity it abridges this latitude of decision: and especially in contested matters, between independent sovereigns, who, having no common judge, are supposed to bind the mediators, and arbitrators, whom they chuse, by the strictest rules of law.

**XLVIII**. It is to be observed that arbitrators chosen by nations or sovereign princes may decide upon the matter in dispute, but not confer a possession, which is a matter that can only be decided by established rules of civil law, for by the law of nations the right of possession follows the right of property. Therefore while a cause is pending, no innovation ought to be made, both to prevent partiality and prejudice, and because, after possession has been given, recovery is difficult. Livy in his account of some disputed points between the people of Carthage and Masinissa, says, "the Ambassadors did not change the right of possession."

**XLIX**. There is another kind of arbitration, which takes place, when any one makes an absolute surrender of himself and all his rights to an enemy or foreign power. But still a distinction ought to be made, even here, between the bounds of right and wrong, limiting the submission of the vanquished, on the one hand, and the authority of the conqueror, on the other, to a certain degree.

For there are particular duties, which ought to be observed in the exercise Of EVERY right. Taking the right of the conqueror in its literal meaning and full extent, it is true that he is entitled to impose ANY terms upon the conquered, who is now placed, by the external laws of war, in a situation to be deprived of every thing, even personal liberty or life, much more then, of all his property, either of a public or private kind.

**L**. The first object of a conqueror should be to avoid committing any act of injustice, or using any rigour, except the demerits and atrocity of the enemy require it; to take nothing but by way of lawful punishment. Observing these bounds, as far as security allows, it is always laudable to incline to moderation and clemency. Sometimes even circumstances may require such a line of conduct; and the best conclusion of any war is that, which reconciles all contending claims by a fair adjustment, and a general amnesty. The moderation and clemency to which the vanquished appeal, are by no means an abolition but only a mitigation of the conqueror's absolute right.

**LI**. There are conditional surrenders, reserving to the individuals, certain personal privileges, and remains of their property, and to the state, certain parts of its constitution.

**LII**. Hostages and pledges may be considered as an appendage to treaties. And some of those hostages are a voluntary surrender, and others given by authority of the state as a security. For the sovereign has the same power over the persons and actions of his subjects, as over their property. But the state or its ruler will be bound to recompense individuals or their relatives for any inconveniences they may sustain.

**LII**. Though the law of nations may in its literal rigour allow of putting hostages to death, it can never conscientiously be enforced, but where they have committed crimes deserving of capital punishment. Neither can they be made slaves. Indeed the law of nations permits them to leave their property to their heirs, although by the Roman law provision was made for confiscating it to the state.

**LIV**. If it should be asked whether hostages may lawfully make their escape: it may be answered in the negative, especially if, at first, or afterwards, they have pledged their faith to remain, upon condition of being prisoners at large. But it does not appear that states so much intended to impose a hardship upon their subjects by forbidding their escape, as to give the enemy security for the performance of their engagements.

**LV**. The obligation of hostages is of an odious nature, as being unfriendly to personal liberty, and arising from the act of another. Therefore a strict interpretation must be given to such engagements, so that hostages delivered on one account cannot be detained on any other, nor for any contract, where hostages are not required. But if in another case there has been any violation of good faith, or any debt contracted, hostages may be detained, not as hostages, but in the capacity of subjects, whom the law of nations makes liable to be seized and detained for the acts of their sovereigns. To guard against which, provision may be made by additional clauses for the restoration of hostages, whenever the engagement for which they were delivered has been fulfilled.

**LVI**. Whoever has been delivered as a hostage for other prisoners, or for the redemption of other hostages, will naturally be released upon the death of those persons. For by death the right of the pledge is extinguished in the same manner as by the ransom of a prisoner. And therefore, according to Ulpian, as a PERSONAL debt is confined to him, who has contracted it, so one person, being substituted for another, cannot be detained any longer than while the obligation of that other continues.

**LVII**. The decision, whether hostages can be detained upon the death of the sovereign, by whom they were delivered, must depend upon the nature of the engagements, which he has made. If they are PERSONAL, they continue in force only during his natural life, but if they are what are called REAL or more PERMANENT treaties, they pass with all their consequences to his successors. For ACCESSORY articles cannot authorise any deviation from the GENERAL rule of interpreting the fundamental and principal points of a treaty, but the accessory articles themselves ought rather to be explained in conformity to those general rules.

**LVIII**. A cursory observation may be made, that hostages are sometimes considered, not as appendages, but as forming the principal part of an engagement, where any one is bound not for himself, but for another, and, in case of non-performance, being obliged to pay damages, his hostages or sureties are answerable in his stead. There is not only some thing of harshness, but even injustice in the opinion that hostages may be bound for the conduct of another even without their own consent.

**LIX**. Pledges have some characteristics in common with hostages, and some peculiar to themselves. It is a common characteristic of both to be detained for something else that is due, except where public faith is given, and provision made to the contrary. Pledges may be detained with greater latitude than hostages; which is one of their peculiar characteristics, there being less of odium in the former case than in the latter: THINGS being of a nature more proper for detention than PERSONS.

**LX**. No time can bar the redemption of a pledge, whenever the engagement for which it was given is fulfilled. For it is never to be presumed that engagements proceed from new causes, when old and known causes can be assigned. If a debtor therefore has forborne to redeem a pledge, we may still suppose that he has not abandoned his original engagement, unless there be clear proof to the contrary: as if, for instance, though desirous of redeeming it, he has been prevented, or suffered a space of time to elapse unnoticed, that would be requisite to imply his consent.

## CHAPTER 21: ON FAITH DURING THE CONTINUANCE OF WAR, ON TRUCES, SAFE-CONDUCTS, AND THE REDEMPTION OF PRISONERS.

*Truces of an intermediate denomination between peace and war — Origin of the word — New declaration of war not necessary after a truce — Time from whence a truce and all its correspondent obligations and privileges commence — A retreat may be made, or fortifications repaired during a truce — Distinction respecting the occupying of places — The case of a person prevented from making his retreat, and taken in the enemy's territories at the expiration of a truce, considered — Express terms and consequences of a truce — Breach of a truce by one party justifies a renewal of war by the other — Penalty annexed — Truce broken by the acts of individuals — Rights belonging to safe-conducts without a truce — Persons in a military capacity how far allowed the benefit of a safe-conduct — Privileges of goods arising from thence — Attendants of the person protected by a safe-conduct — Safe-conduct does not expire upon the death of the grantor — Safe-conduct given to continue during the pleasure of the grantor — Protection thereof extending beyond his own territory — Redemption of prisoners favoured, and not to be prohibited by law.*

**I.** and **II.** IN THE midst of war there are certain points generally conceded by the belligerent powers to each other, which Tacitus and Virgil call the intercourse of war, and which comprehend truces, safe-conducts, and the redemption of prisoners. Truces are conventions, by which, even during the continuance of war, hostilities on each side cease for a time. DURING THE CONTINUANCE OF WAR; for, as Cicero says, in his eighth Philippic, between peace and war there is no medium. By war is meant a state of affairs, which may exist even while its operations are not continued. Therefore, as Gellius has said, a peace and a truce are not the same, for the war still continues, though fighting may cease. So that any agreement, deemed valid in the time of war, will be valid also during a truce, unless it evidently appears that it is not the state of affairs, which is considered, but the commission of particular acts of hostility. On the other hand, any thing, agreed to, to be done, when peace shall be made, cannot take place in consequence of a truce. There is no uniform and invariable period fixed for the continuance of a truce, it may be made for any time, even for twenty, or thirty years, of which there are many instances in ancient history. A truce, though a repose from war, does not amount to a peace, therefore historians are correct in saying that a peace has often been refused, when a truce has been granted.

**III.** After a truce a new declaration of war is not necessary. For upon the removal of a temporary impediment, the state of warfare revives in full force, which has only been lulled asleep, but not extinguished. Yet we read in Livy, that it was the opinion of the heralds' college, that after the expiration of a truce war ought to be declared. But the ancient Romans only meant to shew by those superfluous precautions, how much they loved peace, and upon what just grounds they were dragged into war.

**IV.** The time, generally assigned for the continuance of a truce, is either some uninterrupted period, of a HUNDRED DAYS, for instance, or a space limited by some artificial boundary of time, as the Calends of March. In the former case, the calculation is to be made according to the natural motion of time: whereas all civil computations depend upon the laws and customs of each country. In the other case it is generally made a matter of doubt, whether in naming any particular day, month or year, for the expiration of a truce, that particular day, month, or year, are comprehended in the term of the truce, or excluded from it.

In natural things there are two kinds of boundaries, one of which forms an inseparable part of the things themselves, as the skin does of the body, and the other only adjoins them, as a river adjoins the land, which it bounds or washes. In either of these ways voluntary boundaries may be appointed. But it seems more natural for a boundary to be taken as a part of the thing itself. Aristotle defines the extremity of anything to be its boundary: a meaning to which general custom conforms: - thus if any one has said that a thing is to be done before the day of his death, the day on which he actually dies is to be taken into the account as forming part of the term. Spurinna had apprised Caesar of his danger, which could not extend beyond the Ides of March. Being accosted, respecting the matter, on the very day, he said, the Ides of March are come, but not passed. Such an interpretation is the more proper where the prolongation of time is of a favourable nature, as it is in truces, which are calculated to suspend the effusion of human blood.

The day, FROM which any measure of time is said to begin, cannot be taken into the account; because the word, FROM, used on that occasion, implies separation and not conjunction.

**V**. It is to be observed that truces, and engagements of that kind immediately bind the contracting parties themselves from the very moment they are concluded. But the subjects on either side are only bound from the time that those engagements have received the form of a law, for which public notice and the regular promulgation are necessary. Upon this being done they immediately derive their authority to bind the subjects. But if notice thereof has only been given in one place, the observance of them cannot be enforced through the whole dominions of the respective sovereigns at one moment, but sufficient time must be allowed for the due promulgation of them to be made in every part. Therefore if in the meantime the subjects on either side have committed an infraction of the truce, they shall be exempt from punishment, but the contracting parties themselves shall be obliged to repair the damages.

**VI**. The very definition of a truce implies what actions are lawful, and what are unlawful during the continuance of it. All acts of hostility are unlawful either against the persons or goods of an enemy. For every act of violence during a truce is contrary to the law of nations. Even things belonging to an enemy, which by any accident have fallen into our hands, although they had been ours before, must be restored. Because they had become theirs by that external right according to which such things are adjudged. And this is what Paulus the lawyer says, that during the time of a truce the law of postliminium cannot exist, because to constitute the law of postliminium there must be the previous right of making captures in war, which ceases upon the making of a truce.

Either party may go to or return from, any particular place, but without any warlike apparatus or force, that may prove a means of annoyance, or be attended with any danger. This is observed by Servius on that passage of Virgil, where the poet says, "the Latins mingled with their foes with impunity," where he relates also that upon a truce being made between Porsenna and the Romans during a siege, when the games of the circus were celebrating, the generals of the enemy entered the city, contented in the lists, and were many of them crowned as conquerors.

**VII**. To withdraw farther into the country with an army, which we find from Livy that Philip did, is no way contrary to the intention and principles of a truce: neither is it any breach of it to repair the walls of a place, or to raise new forces, unless it has been prohibited by special agreement.

**VIII**. To corrupt an enemy's garrisons, in order to seize upon the places which he holds, is undoubtedly a breach of the spirit and letter of any truce. For no such advantage can justly be gained but by the laws of war. The same rule is to be laid down respecting the revolt of subjects to an enemy. In the fourth book of Thueydides, Brasidas received the city of Menda, that revolted from the Athenians to the Lacedaemonians during a truce, and excused his conduct upon the plea of the Athenians having done the same.

Either of the belligerent powers may take possession of places that have been deserted: if they have been REALLY deserted by the former owner with the intention never to occupy them again, but not merely because they have been left unguarded, either BEFORE, or AFTER, the making of a truce. For the former owner's right of dominion therein still remaining renders another's possession of them unjust. Which is a complete refutation of the cavil of Belisarius against the Goths, who seized upon some places during a truce, under pretext of their being left without garrisons.

**IX**. It is made a subject of inquiry, whether any one being prevented by an unforeseen accident from making his retreat, and being taken within the enemy's territories, at the expiration of a truce, has a right to return. Considering the external law of nations, he is undoubtedly upon the same footing as one, who, having gone into a foreign country, must, upon the sudden breaking out of war, be detained there as an enemy till the return of peace. Nor is there any thing contrary to strict justice in this; as the goods and persons of enemies are bound for the debt of the state, and may be seized for payment. Nor has such a one more reason to complain than innumerable other innocent persons, on whose heads the calamities of war have fallen. Nor is there occasion to refer to the case, which Cicero has alleged, in his second book ON INVENTION, of a ship of war driven by the violence of the wind into a port, where by law it was liable to confiscation. For in the former case the unforeseen accident must do away all idea of punishment, and in the latter, the right of confiscation must be suspended for a time. Yet there can be no doubt but there is more of generosity and kindness in releasing such a person than in insisting upon the right of detaining him.

**X**. The express nature of a convention renders some things unlawful during a truce, as for instance, if it is granted only in order to bury the dead, neither party will have a right to depart from those conditions. Thus if a siege is suspended by a truce, and nothing more than such a suspension is thereby granted; the besieged cannot lawfully avail himself of it, to convey fresh supplies of troops and stores into the place. For such conventions ought not to prove beneficial to one party, to the prejudice of the other, who grants them. Sometimes it is stipulated that no one shall be allowed to pass to and fro. Sometimes the prohibition extends to persons and not to goods. In which case, if any one, in protecting his goods, hurts an enemy, the act will not constitute a breach of the truce. For as it is lawful that either party should defend his property, an accidental circumstance cannot be deemed an infringement of that personal security, which was the principal object provided for by the truce.

**XI**. If the faith of a truce is broken by one of the parties, the other who is thereby injured, will undoubtedly have a right to renew hostilities without any formal declaration. For every article in a treaty contains an implied condition of mutual observance. Indeed we may find in history instances of those, who have adhered to a truce-till its expiration, notwithstanding a breach on the other side. But on the other hand there are numerous instances of hostilities commenced against those, who have broken their conventions: a variation, which proves that it is at the option of the injured party to use or not to use his right of renewing war upon the breach of a truce.

**XII**. It is evident that, if the stipulated penalty is demanded of the aggressor, and paid by him, the other party can no longer maintain his right of renewing the war. For the payment of the penalty restores every thing to its original footing. And on the other hand, a renewal of hostilities implies an intention of the injured party to abandon the penalty, since he has had his option.

**XIII**. A truce is not broken by the acts of individuals, unless they are sanctioned by the authority of the sovereign, which is generally supposed to be given, where the delinquents are neither punished nor delivered up, nor restitution is made of goods taken away.

**XIV**. The rights belonging to a safe-conduct are a privilege distinct from the nature of a truce, and our interpretation of them must be guided by the rules laid down respecting privileges.

Such a privilege, to be perfect, must be neither injurious to a third person, nor prejudicial to the giver. There. fore in explaining the terms, in which it is couched, a greater latitude of interpretation may be allowed, especially where the party suing for it receives no benefit, but rather confers one, and still more so where the advantage, accruing to the individual from thence, redounds also to the public benefit of the state.

Therefore the literal interpretation, which the words may bear, ought to be rejected, unless otherwise some absurdity would follow, or there is every reason to suppose that such a literal interpretation is most conformable to the will and intention of the parties concerned. In the same manner, on the other hand, a greater latitude of interpretation may be allowed, in order to avoid the same apprehended absurdity, or to comply more fully with the most urgent and forcible conjectures respecting the will of the contracting parties.

**XV**. Hence we may infer that a safe-conduct, granted to SOLDIERS, includes not only those of an INTERMEDIATE RANK, but the HIGHEST COMMANDERS. For that is a signification strictly and properly authorised by the words themselves, although they MAY be taken in a more LIMITED meaning. So the term clergymen includes those of episcopal as well as those of inferior rank, and by those serving on board a fleet, we mean not only sailors, but all persons found there, who have taken the military oath.

**XVI**. Where a free passage is granted, liberty to return is evidently implied, not from the literal force of the expressions themselves, but to avoid the absurdity which would follow the grant of a privilege, that could never be made use of. And by the liberty of coming and going is meant a safe passage till the person arrives in a place of perfect security. From hence the good faith of Alexander was impeached, who ordered those to be murdered on the way, whom he had allowed to depart.

Any one may be allowed to go away without being allowed to return. But no power can properly refuse admitting any one, to whom he has granted leave to come, and on the other hand, his admission implies such a leave to have been given. GOING AWAY and RETURNING are indeed very different, nor can any construction of language give them the same meaning. If there be any mistake, although it may confer no right, it exempts the party from all penalties. — A person permitted to come shall only come ONCE, but not a SECOND TIME, unless the additional mention of some time may supply room to think otherwise.

**XVII**. A son shares the fate of his father, and a wife of her husband no farther than as to the right of residing, for men reside with their families, but in general undertake public missions without them. Yet one or two servants, though not expressly named, are generally understood to be included in a safe-conduct, especially where it would be improper for the person to go without such attendants. For every necessary consequence is understood to go along with any privilege that is given.

**XVIII**. In the same manner no other effects are included in a safe-conduct, but such as are usually taken on a journey.

**XIX**. The name of attendants, expressed in a safe-conduct, granted to any one, will not allow him to extend the protection of it to men of atrocious and criminal characters, such as pirates, robbers, and deserters. And the COUNTRY Of the attendants being named shews that the protection cannot extend to those of another nation.

**XX**. The privileges of a safe-conduct do not, in doubtful cases, expire upon the demise of the sovereign who granted it, according to what was said in a former part of this treatise on the nature of favours granted by kings and sovereign princes.

**XXI**. It has often been a disputed point, what is meant by the expression used in a safe-conduct, that it shall continue during the PLEASURE OF THE GRANTOR. But there seems most reason and truth in the opinion of those, who maintain that the privilege shall continue, till the grantor make some new declaration of his will to the contrary. Because, in doubtful cases, a favour is presumed to continue, till the right, which it conveys, is accomplished. But not so, where all possibility of WILL in the grantor has ceased, which happens by his death. For upon the death of the person all presumption of his WILL continuing must cease: as an accident vanishes when the substance is destroyed.

**XXII**. The privilege of a safe-conduct protects the person, to whom it is given, even beyond the territories of the grantor: because it is given as a protection against the rights of war, which are not confined to his territory.

**XXIII**. The redemption of prisoners is much favoured, particularly among Christian states, to whom the divine law peculiarly recommends it as a kind of mercy. Lactantius calls the redemption of prisoners a great and splendid office of justice.

## CHAPTER 22: ON THE FAITH ON THOSE INVESTED WITH SUBORDINATE POWERS IN WAR.

*Commanders — Extent of their engagements in binding the sovereign — Exceeding their commission — The opposite party bound by such engagements — Power of commanders in war, or of magistrates with respect to those under their authority — Generals cannot make peace, but may conclude a truce — Extent of their authority in granting protection to persons and property — Such engagements to be strictly interpreted — Interpretation of capitulations accepted by generals — Precautions necessary till the pleasure of the sovereign be known — Promise to surrender a town.*

**I**. ULPIAN reckons the agreements, entered into between the generals of opposite armies during the course of a war, among public conventions. So that after explaining the nature of the faith pledged by sovereign powers to each other, it will be proper to make a short inquiry into the nature of engagements made by subordinate authorities; whether those authorities bear a near approach to supreme power, as commanders in chief, or are removed to a greater distance from it. Caesar makes the following distinction between them, observing that the offices of commander and deputy are very different; the latter being obliged to act according to prescribed rules, and the former having unqualified discretion in matters of the highest importance.

**II**. The engagements of those invested with such subordinate powers are to be considered in a double point of view, whether they are binding upon the sovereign, or on y upon themselves. The former of these points has been already settled in a former part of this treatise, where it was shewn that a person is bound by the measures of an agent, whom he has appointed to act in his name, whether his intentions have been expressly named, or are only to be gathered from the nature of the employment. For whoever gives another a commission, gives him along with it every thing in his power that is necessary to the execution of it. So that there are two ways, in which persons acting with subordinate powers may bind their principals by their conduct, and that is, by doing what is probably thought to be contained in their commission, or apart from that, by acting according to special instructions, generally known, at least to those, with whom they treat.

**III**. There are other modes too, in which a sovereign may be bound by the previous act of his minister; but not in such a manner as to suppose the obligation owes its EXISTENCE to that action, which only gives occasion to its fulfilment. And there are two ways, in which this may happen, either by the consent of the sovereign, or by the very nature of the thing itself. His consent appears by his ratification of the act, either expressed or implied, and that is, where a sovereign has known and suffered a thing to be done, which can be accounted for upon no other motive but that of approval and consent.

The very nature and obligation of all contracts imply that one party is not to gain advantage by the loss of another. Or if advantage is expected from a contract, the contract must be fulfilled or the advantage abandoned. And in this sense, and no other, the proverbial expression, that whatever is beneficial is valid, is to be understood.

On the other hand a charge of injustice may fairly be brought against those, who condemn an engagement, yet retain the advantages, which they could not have had without it.

**IV**. It is necessary to repeat an observation made before, that a sovereign, who has given a commission to another, is bound by the conduct of that person, even though he may have acted contrary to his secret instructions, provided he has not gone beyond the limits of his ostensible, and public commission.

This was a principle of equity, which the Roman Praetor observed in actions brought against employers for the conduct of their agents or factors. An employer could not be made answerable for any act or measure of his factor, but such as was immediately connected with the business, in which he employed him. Nor could HE be considered as an appointed agent, with WHOM the public were apprized, by due notice, to make no contract — If such notice was given, without having come to the knowledge of the contracting parties, the employer was bound by the conduct of the agent. If any one chuses to make a contract on certain conditions, or through the intervention of a third person, it is right and necessary for that person to observe the particular conditions on which he is employed.

From hence it follows that kings and nations are more or less bound by the conventions of their commanders in proportion as their laws, conditions, and customs, are more or less known. If the meaning of their intentions is not evident, conjecture may supply the place of evidence, as it is natural to suppose that any one employed would be invested with full powers sufficient to execute his commission.

A person acting in a subordinate capacity, if he has exceeded the powers of his commission will be bound to make reparation, if he cannot fulfil his engagement, unless he is prevented from doing so by some well known law.

But if he has been guilty of treachery also, in pretending to greater powers than he really possessed, he will be bound to repair the injury, which he has WILFULLY done, and to suffer punishment corresponding with his offence. For the first of these offences, his property is answerable, and on failure of that, his personal liberty: and in the latter case, his person or property, or both must be answerable according to the magnitude of the crime.

**V**. As a sovereign or his minister is always bound by every contract, it is certain the other party will also be bound by the engagement: nor can it be deemed imperfect. For in this respect there is a comparative equality between sovereign and subordinate powers.

**VI**. It is necessary to consider too what are the powers of subordinate authorities over those beneath them. Nor is there any doubt that a general may bind the army, and a magistrate, the inhabitants of a place by those actions, which are usually done by commanders, or magistrates, otherwise their consent would be necessary.

On the other hand, in engagements purely beneficial, the advantage shall be on the side of the inferior: for that is a condition comprehended in the very nature of power. Where there is any burdensome condition annexed it shall not extend beyond the usual limits in which authority is exercised; or if it does, it shall be at the option of the inferior to accept or refuse that condition.

**VII**. As to the causes and consequences of a war, it is not within the province of a general to decide them. For concluding and conducting a war are very different things, and rest upon distinct kinds of authority.

**VIII**. and **IX**. As to granting truces, it is a power which belongs not only to commanders in chief, but also to inferior commanders. And they may grant them for themselves, and the forces immediately under their command, to places which they are besieging or blockading: but they do not thereby bind other parts of the army. Generals have no right to cede nations, dominions, or any kind of conquests made in war. They may relinquish any thing of which a complete conquest has not been made: for towns frequently surrender on condition of the inhabitants being spared, and allowed to retain their liberty and property: cases, in which there is no time for consulting the will and pleasure of the sovereign. In the same manner, and upon the same principle this right is allowed to subordinate commanders, if it falls within the nature of their commission.

**X**. As commanders, in all such engagements, are acting in the name of others, their resolutions must not be interpreted so strictly as to bind their sovereigns to greater obligations than they intended to incur, nor at the same time to prove prejudicial to the commanders themselves for having done their duty.

**XI**. An absolute surrender implies that the party so capitulating submits to the pleasure and discretion of the conqueror.

**XII**. In ancient conventions a precaution was usually added, that they would be ratified, if approved of by the Roman people. So that if no ratification ensued, the general was bound no further than to be answerable for any advantage that might have accrued to himself.

**XIII**. Commanders having promised to surrender a town, may dismiss the garrison.

[**Translator's note:** The XXIII Chapter of the Original, on Private Faith in War, is omitted in the translation.]

## CHAPTER 24: ON TACIT FAITH.

*Tacit faith — Example of in desiring to be taken under the protection of a king or nation — Implied in the demand or grant of a conference — Allowable for the party seeking it to promote his own interest thereby provided he uses no treachery — Meaning of mute signs allowed by custom.*

**I**. BOTH public, private, and mixed, conventions admit of tacit consent, which is allowed by custom. For in whatever manner consent is indicated and accepted it has the power of conveying a right. And, as it has been frequently observed in the course of this treatise, there are other signs of consent besides words and letters: some of them indeed naturally rising out of the action itself.

**II**. An example of such tacit agreement may be found in the case of a person coming from an enemy, or foreign country, and surrendering himself to the good faith of another king or people. For such a one tacitly binds himself to do nothing injurious or treacherous to that state, where he seeks protection, a point which is beyond all doubt.

**III**. In the same manner, a person who grants or requests a conference, gives a tacit promise, that he will do nothing prejudicial to the parties, who attend it. Livy pronounces an injury done to an enemy, under the pretext of holding a conference, a violation of the law of nations.

**IV**. But such a tacit promise, to take no advantage of a parley or conference, is not to be carried farther than what has been said. Provided all injury and injustice are avoided, it is reckoned a lawful stratagem, for any one to avail himself of a parley in order to draw off the enemy's attention from his military projects, and to promote his own. The device, by which Asdrubal extricated his army from the Ausetanian forests, was of this kind, and by the same means Scipio Africanus, the elder, gained a perfect knowledge of Syphax's camp. Both these circumstances are related by Livy.

**V**. There are certain mute signs, deriving all their force and meaning from custom; such as the fillets, and branches of olive formerly used: among the Macedonians pikes erected, and among the Romans shields placed upon the head, were signs of a suppliant surrender obliging the party to lay down his arms. In the present day a white flag is a sign of suing for a parley. Therefore all these methods have the force of express declarations.

# CHAPTER 25: CONCLUSION

*Admonitions to the observance of good faith — Peace always to be kept in view in the midst of war — Peace beneficial to the conquered — To the conqueror — And to be chosen in cases where the issue is doubtful — To be religiously observed — Prayer — Conclusion of the work.*

**I.** HERE seems to be the proper place to bring this work to a conclusion, without in the least presuming that every thing has been said, which might be said on the subject: but sufficient has been produced to lay a foundation, on which another, if he pleases, may raise a more noble and extensive edifice, an addition and improvement that will provoke no jealousy, but rather be entitled to thanks.

Before entirely dismissing the subject, it may be necessary to observe, that, as in laying down the true motives and causes, that alone will justify war, every possible precaution at the same time was taken to state the reasons for which it should be avoided; so now a few admonitions will not be deemed superfluous, in order to point out the means of preserving good faith in war, and maintaining peace, after war is brought to a termination, and among other reasons for preserving good faith the desire of keeping alive the hope of peace, even in the midst of war, is not the least important. For good faith, in the language of Cicero, is not only the principal hold by which all governments are bound together, but is the key-stone by which the larger society of nations is united. Destroy this, says Aristotle, and you destroy the intercourse of mankind.

In every other branch of justice there is something of obscurity, but the bond of faith is clear in itself, and is used indeed to do away the obscurity of all transactions. The observance of this is a matter of conscience with all lawful kings and sovereign princes, and is the basis of that reputation by which the honour and dignity of their crowns are maintained with foreign nations.

**II.** In the very heat of war the greatest security and expectation of divine support must be in the unabated desire, and invariable prospect of peace, as the only end for which hostilities can be lawfully begun. So that in the prosecution of war we must never carry the rage of it so far, as to unlearn the nature and dispositions of men.

**III.** These and these alone would be sufficient motives for the termination of war, and the cultivation of peace. But apart from all considerations of humanity, the INTERESTS of mankind would inevitably lead us to the same point. In the first place it is dangerous to prolong a contest with a more powerful enemy. In such a case some sacrifices should be made for the sake of peace, as in a storm goods are sometimes thrown overboard to prevent a greater calamity, and to save the vessel and the crew.

**IV.** Even for the stronger party, when flushed with victory, peace is a safer expedient, than the most extensive successes. For there is the boldness of despair to be apprehended from a vanquished enemy, dangerous as the bite of a ferocious animal in the pangs of death.

**V.** If indeed both parties are upon an equal footing, it is the opinion of Caesar, that it is the most favourable moment for making peace, when each party has confidence in itself.

**VI.** On whatever terms peace is made, it must be absolutely kept. From the sacredness of the faith pledged in the engagement, and every thing must be cautiously avoided, not only savouring of treachery, but that may tend to awaken and inflame animosity. For what Cicero has said of private friendships may with equal propriety be applied to public engagements of this kind, which are all to be religiously and faithfully observed, especially where war and enmity have ended in peace and reconciliation.

**VII.** And may God, to whom alone it belongs to dispose the affections and desires of sovereign princes and kings, inscribe these principles upon their hearts and minds, that they may always remember that the noblest office, in which man can be engaged, is the government of men, who are the principal objects of the divine care.

www.ingramcontent.com/pod-product-compliance
Lightning Source LLC
Chambersburg PA
CBHW080539240926
51846CB00005BA/944
*9783988686497*